Sexing the Mind

SEXING THE MIND

Nineteenth-Century Fictions of Hysteria

Evelyne Ender

Cornell University Press   *Ithaca and London*

First published 1995 by Cornell University Press.

Printed in the United States of America

⊚ The paper in this book meets the minimum requirements of the American National Standard for Information Sciences—Permanence of Paper for Printed Library Materials, ANSI Z39.48–1984.

Library of Congress Cataloging-in-Publication Data

Ender, Evelyne, 1955-
  Sexing the mind : nineteenth century fictions of hysteria /
Evelyne Ender.
    p. cm.
  Includes bibliographical references and index.
  ISBN 0-8014-2826-2 (alk. paper). — ISBN 0-8014-8083-3 (pbk. : alk. paper)
  1. James, Henry, 1843-1916—Knowledge—Psychology. 2. Sand, George, 1804-
1876—Knowledge—Psychology. 3. Fiction—19th century—History and
criticism. 4. Hysteria in literature. 5. Sex (Psychology) in
literature. 6. Psychoanalysis and literature. 7. Literature, Comparative—American
and French. 8. Literature, Comparative—French and American. Women in literature.
I. Title.
PS2127.P8E53 1995
813'.409353—dc20   95-11137

For Taline

Contents

Preface   ix

Introduction   1

ONE
Nineteenth-Century Hysteria: The Medical Context   25

TWO
Henry James and George Sand:
Scenes of Passion, Scenes of Hysteria   67

THREE
The Bostonians: Representing the "Sentiment of Sex"   99

FOUR
Engendering the Mind: James, Freud, and George Sand   135

FIVE
Reading Sexual Difference: The Case of George Sand   187

SIX
"Girls and Their Blind Visions":
George Eliot, Hysteria, and History   229

"Always Secrets of the Alcove":
A Postscript   273

Bibliography   289

Index   301

Preface

"Un livre est un ami," wrote Michel de Montaigne a long time ago. In my experience, this still seems true: over these few years this book has acquired something like a friendly presence and substance. It has also demanded the care, the consideration, the love that we associate with friendship. It has kept me company, moreover, not because mine is a lonely life, but because so many voices and ideas that were shared with friends or colleagues have been woven into it. "How is your book?" they would ask, as if inquiring about a person's state of health or mind. "Where are you with your book?" my daughter, to whom this is dedicated, would say. This book is also a friend because woven into its texture is the babbling and later the chattering voice of my son, Vahé, who grew up with it.

But it also has this special meaning and presence in my life because, as a book about literature and about my encounters with writing and reading minds (Sand, Eliot, Woolf, Flaubert, James, and Freud as well as some significant contemporary critical voices), it has achieved a unique feat that only the bond of reading can effect for us: "it has freed me from many things, in particular from the solitude in which every reading woman finds herself when she tries to comprehend in some measure what is happening to her." This last sentence and the notion of the "bond of reading" are not of my own invention: these are the words of Michèle Le Doeuff, in *Hipparchia's Choice*, and of Shoshana Felman, in *What Does a Woman Want?* It seems right that I should first acknowledge the inspiration that they have brought to this project. Because of their books, I shared their thoughts even before I knew them, and I recognize now the intellectual debt I owe to each. It is because of their example, as philosophers and critics, that in this book I took the risk that I did—that I wrote as I did. As Virginia Woolf wrote: "The risk must be run; the mark made."

My deepest gratitude—and this is not mere rhetoric—goes to my two teachers at the University of Geneva. Without George Steiner I would never have started this project, for which he has never since failed to provide me with ideas, further challenges, and intellectual instruments. He will recognize how often in this book I have tried to answer him, as if, sitting one on each side of a table in his Geneva office or Cambridge home, we were caught once more in our lively conversations—as in an agon upon which our destinies depended. Gregory T. Polletta has provided me, throughout these years, with his invaluable insights and criticisms. To him I owe my education in fiction—fiction as a "form of experience." This book is my apprentice work—the result of his teaching, his guidance, and his support.

To Janet Beizer I owe a special debt: in giving me her generous confidence, she determined the fate of this text; this book now also exists as the record of a unique intellectual friendship. Peter Brooks will recognize as well, I trust, the place he holds in this text: his knowledge in a field that we share and his wonderful willingness to discuss a number of crucial critical questions have been a decisive influence.

This book carries as well the mark of several precious conversations with Jean Starobinski, Tony Tanner, Denis Hollier, and Peter de Bolla. Among my contemporaries, I would like to single out Edward Bizub, Yves Citton, Juan Rigoli, and Barbara Will who, as they shared some of my critical passions, helped me at some crucial stages of my work. My thanks also go to my colleagues in the English Department at the University of Geneva, particularly André Kaenel and Marc Redfield, but also John Blair, Wlad Godzich, and Richard Waswo. Michel Jeanneret, who has long been following my progress in the Faculty of Letters, has given me his generous and constant support and offered insightful critical comments in the earlier stages of this work. I thank as well Andrea Othon-Goin for her patient and tactful help as a research assistant and typist, and Kathryn Gohl for her admirable diligence and tact as a copyeditor. To Anthony Mortimer, the best of stylists, I have a special debt: he began long ago to teach me how to write an English prose that would not sound too French and ended up reading, pencil in hand, my entire manuscript.

xi

Preface

I am deeply grateful to my editor, Bernhard Kendler, for his unrelenting patience and for his wonderful willingness to carry on a transatlantic dialogue, as well as for his choice of readers. Martha Noel Evans, Ned Lukacher, Lynda Zwinger, and Marcia Ian have each, with their different and sometimes diverging comments, helped me give shape and clarity to this work. They should find, I hope, in this finished product a response if not some reward for their thoughtful and provocative criticisms and encouragement.

Part of the research and writing was made possible by a grant given by the Fonds National de la Recherche Scientifique. A very fruitful summer spent at the School of Criticism and Theory at Dartmouth College, under the direction of Geoffrey Hartman, also made a decisive difference to my project. It reinforced the critical, theoretical, but also friendly ties with the American academic scene. That first prolonged stay in Hanover, N.H., set the pattern for regular exchanges with the United States; it led as well to a richly fulfilling stay at Yale University. As a result, this book hovers between two linguistic territories: it first took shape in French and was then rewritten in English, and, unless I have noted otherwise, all translations are my own. Materially as well as spiritually, the book is the product of many transatlantic exchanges. It is thus not only destined for my friends and colleagues in the English-speaking world; but, writing and rewriting it, I also had in mind my friends and students in Geneva.

E. E.

Geneva

Introduction

Flaubert at the Beach: The Literary Perspective

I have spent a full hour looking at bathing ladies. What a picture! What a hideous picture! In the old days, people would bathe here without distinctions between the sexes. But now, there are divisions, posts, nets made to prevent, an inspector in uniform (what an atrocious and lugubrious thing, the grotesque!). So yesterday, from the place where I was standing, with my specs on my nose and in the full sun, I gazed for a long time at the women bathing. Humankind must have become quite imbecile to lose so completely any notion of elegance. There is nothing more distasteful than the bags that encase the ladies' bodies and those hair bands made of oilcloth. What airs! What a gait! And the feet! Red, skinny, hardened with bunions, deformed by their footgear, as long as shuttles and as wide as beetles. And in the middle of all that, some brats in bad humor, whining and crying. At a distance, grandmothers with their knitting and "gentlemen" with their gold-circled spectacles, reading the newspaper and, from time to time in between the lines, looking approvingly at the immensity. This made me dream all evening of running away from Europe to settle in the Sandwich Isles or in the forests of Brazil. There, at least, the beaches are not spoilt by ill-shaped feet and such fetid individualities.

The day before yesterday, in a forest near Touques, at a charming spot near a fountain, I found some cigar butts together with crumbs of pâté. There had been a party! I had written of this in *Novembre* eleven years ago! There it was pure imagination; the other day it was experience. All that we invent is true, you can be sure of that. Poetry is as precise as geometry. Induction is worth deduction, and, when you reach a certain point you never get it wrong, concerning the soul. Right now, my poor Emma Bovary is suffering and weeping in twenty villages of France.

(*Correspondance* III, 290–91)

Thus Gustave Flaubert wrote to Louise Colet in August 1853, showing his distaste for the "distinction between the sexes" that so struck him when, peering through his glasses, he noticed that there was now a line, a demarcation, and a surveillance to ensure that the sexes remained separated. Forty years later, Henry James wrote in *The Bostonians* about the same thing, calling it the "sentiment of sex," while in the same year, Sigmund Freud argued in a letter to his fiancée that the difference between men and women is the most important among them.[1] Divisions, posts, nets; women on one side and men on the other: my own critical gaze has been drawn repeatedly to the textual scenes that recounted such an engendering. This book aims at demonstrating from the perspective of literature, but through the observant and suspicious gaze of a historian and pseudoanalyst, the significance and some of the consequences for the individual subject of the "enormous system of oppositions" that turns around the fact of sexual difference.[2] Gender, I argue, is a literary construct as much as a political, social, or economic one, and we can elicit its workings and its logic from the literary or critical discourses of Sand, Flaubert, Eliot, James, or early Freud better than anywhere else. A questioning about sexual difference, a desire to maintain its truth-value, or a subversive intent that on the contrary wants to deny its significance inform, together or separately, with the force of an obsession the representations and the writing, the thoughts and the desires of their texts.

This work traces the role of gender and the force it exerts in the descriptive, narrative, and theoretical projects focusing on the subject's "interiority" which unite these authors.[3] In their texts, the "enigmatic

1. For a detailed discussion, see the last section of Chapter 3.

2. "It would be necessary to reconsider all the boundaries between consciousness and the unconscious, as between man and animal and an enormous system of oppositions," writes Jacques Derrida in his essay "How to Avoid Speaking: Denials" (18). My own inquiry focuses on the figure of hysteria, as the privileged site of a division between consciousness and the unconscious, knowledge and ignorance, and also masculinity and femininity. I thus want to elicit from the complex and enormous system of oppositions articulated around hysteria a definition of gender as part of a history of subjectivity.

3. For a contemporary discussion of interiority, see the chapter "Disembodying the Female Voice" (146–51 in particular) in Kaja Silverman's book *The Acoustic Mirror: The Female Voice in Psychoanalysis and Cinema* as well as the section titled "From Interiority to Gender Performatives" (134–41) in Judith Butler's *Gender Trouble: Feminism and the Subversion of Identity*. Nancy Armstrong's discussion in *Desire and Domestic Fiction: A Political History of the Novel* (particularly in her introduction) of the relation between

truth of sexual difference" gets rewritten as a drama of desire, power, and knowledge articulated around scenes of engendering.[4] In our experiences as women or as men, gender is also the product of such scenes, but they vanish into the quotidian of our existence. And if the performance necessarily leaves its mark, it is usually meant to be so ordinary and natural that it grows into us and it can hardly be retrieved. But the literary texts I have chosen to study exhibit their scenes of engendering in a spectacular, hysterical fashion; they draw attention to the fact that gender is the product of such a theater. In this way, they reveal what is the secret of gender—that it is fiction, that it depends on such scenes to come into existence. Thus, if the literary utterance is my prime object, it is not for art's sake, but because it reverberates with meanings that are of inevitable historical and political significance.

Like Flaubert then, I believe in the relation between literature and experience, between the fictions conceived in the imagination and our private, subjective histories. The scenes of hysteria and the gender fables that have repeatedly drawn my critical gaze eventually constitute historical documents, but not before they have been understood and rethought critically as literary artifacts, as representation and writing.[5] The works on hysteria by nineteenth-century French doctors and the texts by George Sand, Gustave Flaubert, George Eliot, and Henry James that make up the material of this work are thus the object of a substantive and formal, narratological enquiry which aims at eliciting, from such examples, the relations between literature, gender, and the history of their internalization as consciousness.[6]

---

gender and the emergence of a psychological model of subjectivity—which emphasizes the significance of writing—provides another important introduction to the question of interiority.

4. Shoshana Felman begins *What Does a Woman Want? Reading and Sexual Difference*, with the following statement: "This is a book on love, desire, prejudice, confusion, 'many varieties of error,' insofar as they are all determined by the enigmatic truth of sexual difference" (2). Like her, I believe that sexual difference is the principle and origin that sustains and determines what in the case of this study could be termed the errancies of language that constitute literature.

5. "Gender fable" is a term that, to my knowledge, was first used by Armstrong and that Butler defines in the following fashion: "Gender fables establish and circulate the misnomer of natural facts" (*Gender Trouble*, xiii).

6. In that sense my method owes much to phenomenology as defined by Octave Mannoni in "Je sais bien mais quand même." He writes: "It is a matter of presenting examples, but without relying on a chronological order or applying principles, but in such a way that these cases, so to speak, begin to interpret one another" (*Clefs pour l'Imaginaire ou l'Autre Scène*, 33). The difficulties or risks inherent in this inductive process cannot be overlooked: the essential concepts that sustain this project (such as gender, consciousness,

It is then through an act of imagination, an act of reading, that I too have encountered the Emma Bovarys who haunt the dense woods of nineteenth-century fiction or, sometimes even now, the walks of life. Like Flaubert, then, and I am even prepared for a moment to endorse his vocabulary, I have been drawn by something concerning their souls. My critical gaze, like his, first dwelt on the spectacle of gender and then shifted to a more inward scene: that of Freud's early explorations—in his *Studies on Hysteria* and *Fragment of a Case of Hysteria*—of the "hidden recesses of the soul"; of George Sand's dealings, fictional and autobiographical, with a "state of the soul that searches itself"; George Eliot's literary investments in the "consciousness of a girl"; and James's critical obsessions with Sand's "mind expanding with longing and desire."[7] If, however, I did not abide by Flaubert's conviction that poetry can be as precise as geometry—that the literary performance responds to analysis and theorization—this volume would look like just another nineteenth-century novel or critical text, with me, the romancing critic, eavesdropping on a long line of weeping, suffering Bovarys.

Emma Bovary, as is well known, represents a case of hysteria.[8] She has become the emblem and the muse for a critical project that dwells extensively on the representations of hysterical women. What defines her condition is a form of dissociation, which Flaubert renders most palpably in his literary representation: she exists as the outward bodily inscription of an inner state, which neither the outer voice of the narrative (the omniscient narrator) nor its inner voice (the protagonist's stream of consciousness) can retrieve. Hysteria defines here an existential predicament which Flaubert's heroine embodies with the force of an icon: she seems to me symptomatic of a time that was held in awe in front of woman's hystericized body, and saw in that body the demise of her mind. In this figure, existence is reconceived in the feminine mode as hysterical suffering—to be is to suffer, in the body's pains and secret ecstasies, the slings and arrows of fortune. But the hysteric subject in literature merely answers the nineteenth-century doctors' learned maxim, *pati natae*—born to suffer. Even the vacuity of mind that we recognize in Emma (the "fog in her head") has its counterpart in the contemporary

---

sexual identity) could only be developed incrementally in their various "phenomenological" apparitions. Therefore this introduction, at best, provides some working definitions of these notions, but their full meaning unfolds across the different chapters of this book.

7. For a discussion of Freud and the "hidden recesses of the mind," see Chapter 4; for Sand see Chapters 2 as well as 5, for Eliot Chapter 6, and for James Chapters 2 and 4.

8. Charles Baudelaire was the first to argue this notion in his review of the book in 1857 ("*Madame Bovary* par Gustave Flaubert," in *L'art romantique*).

medical textbooks, where hysteria is but the paroxysmic form taken by woman's inability to deal with impressions and to articulate them as thought.[9]

This book begins then with an examination of nineteenth-century medical representations of hysteria and its counterpart, modesty, and moves in the second chapter to a detailed discussion of Henry James's critical texts on George Sand. The third chapter focuses on the theme and the representation of hysteria in James's *Bostonians*, in an attempt to decipher the discursive principles that promote the more discrete forms taken by the "law of gender." It appears indeed that the nineteenth-century obsession with a gender-marked subjectivity, which can be documented in medical and literary discourses alike, has found in the figure of the *Hysterika* (the hysterical *woman*—the term is gender-marked in German) its crucial point of articulation. Meanwhile, a desire to express the value of gender shapes James's literary criticism and theory in the same way as it informs the scientific descriptions of the *médecine morale.*

The fourth chapter constitutes the turning point of this work: using Flaubert's famous tag "Mme Bovary c'est moi" as a point of departure, it examines the experience of gender from a literary and epistemological point of view. The emphasis falls this time on the relation between the writer and his subject and between the analyst and the hysterical woman. A detailed analysis of James's criticism concerning his conception of the literary subject paired with a reexamination of Freud's analytical model in the case history of *Dora*, enables me to raise the question of gendered subjectivities and to present a critique of the male imaginative and epistemological appropriation of the female subject.

The last two chapters determine another shift of focus, this time toward women's literary expression of hysteria. My discussion of George Sand's *Valentine* and *Histoire de ma vie* (in Chapter 5) and of George Eliot's *Daniel Deronda* (Chapter 6) aims at examining the articulation of knowledge, femininity, and hysteria from a woman's perspective and as a thematic and stylistic feature of writing. But Eliot's literary questioning has determined the last turn of my argument and shaped my own critical reflections in a decisive fashion. As she writes the story of Gwendolen Harleth, Eliot explores the fate of the female subject and

9. " 'Ah, yes!' returned Félicité. 'You're like old Guérin's daughter. . . . It seems she'd got a sort of a fog in her head, the doctors couldn't do a thing with her, and no more could the *curé*" (Gustave Flaubert, *Madame Bovary*, 122).

raises, to a hysterical pitch, the question of a feminine consciousness. This question has become my own: for if, as I argue throughout this work, the figure of the *Hysterika* addresses us with its demand "read me" and thus represents, from an allegorical perspective, the question of the subject and of gender, it seems fit that my response to this demand, as a reader of Eliot's hysteria, should lead me no further than to articulate her question—the question that her hysterical writing raises. This work ends then with the following interrogation: Can literature or does literature offer the evidence of a new consciousness in the making, of a consciousness that is now, with Sand, Flaubert, Eliot, and James, a gender-inflected consciousness?

Henry James and Female Pathos: The Critical Perspective

"The universe forcing itself with a slow, inexorable pressure into a narrow, complacent, and yet after all extremely sensitive mind, and making it ache in the process," says one of the voices in Henry James's "Conversation" on *Daniel Deronda* (*Essays on Literature*, 990), a novel that also tells a story of hysteria. The critic seems to have singled out in Eliot's text the theme that most appeals to his own sense of narrative: a woman's aching mind. But he has caught as well, with unerring perspicacity, what is really wrong with Gwendolen Harleth—that for which her bodily symptoms (her hysteria) are merely a figure. The story Eliot tells in her novel is of the demise of a woman's mind and its translation into the melodrama of hysteria. Because the story is told in an exemplary fashion, it has given a decisive inflexion to my critical text and determined my conclusion.

But in this introduction I turn to the writer whose critical and theoretical insights and blindnesses have opened the way for this inquiry. This project owes more to him than just the inspiration that his own acute imaginative perception of feminine figures could have conveyed.[10] Henry James holds in it the function of the "archcritic" who directed my attention to the significance of the scenes of engendering that became, in turn, the object of my own reflections. In a book that is centrally concerned with the pedagogy of gender and its transmission from male master to female pupil, this extradiegetic pattern should not be overlooked. It appears repeatedly in my dealings with other "masters of

10. "Finally, who can forget the facility with which James-as-narrator or speaking subject establishes imaginary alignments with feminine characters—Fleda Vetch, the governess in *The Turn of the Screw*, Isabel Archer, or Maisie, to name but a few" (Kaja Silverman, "Too Early/Too Late: Subjectivity and the Primal Scene in Henry James," 177).

reading": Freud, most prominently, but also Pierre Reboul, Lionel Tril-ling, Tony Tanner, Neil Hertz, and, closer to home, George Steiner and my teachers of the "Geneva School," tutelary figures whom I face with my insistent questioning about the meaning of gender.[11] It seems fitting, then, that I provide my readers, here at the outset, with the last but exemplary lesson on gender and hysteria that I learned from Henry James.

In Milly Theale of *The Wings of the Dove*, James has provided us with an unforgettable representation of an aching female mind, but a mind that is also very significantly the product of bodily symptoms. Indeed, the heroine is identified by the author as a "throbbing consciousness," in a catachresis that speaks vividly of a way of being held in the confines of some somatic and immanent experience and yet defined by its aware-ness and its ability to register impressions and dwell on them as thoughts. For the critic Peter Brooks, the heroine is "the active, doomed and silenced centre of the novel" ("Introduction," xxi). Active because she has a mind, doomed because she is afflicted with a fatal illness, and silenced for reasons I shall explain in a moment, Milly Theale is a late avatar of the hysteric. Working closely as he does on the relation be-tween body and mind and playing up moreover the silence (or should we say the gap or the abyss) that separates them, James seems in this novel to have given a metaphysical or philosophical turn to the hysteric's predicament. Afflicted with an unnamed physical pathology and with a mind that relentlessly yet secretly tries to make sense of her existence, this young woman is singled out as a subject who comes closer than any other to the secrets of an inward-turned, mental or "moral" existence.

What determines the value of Milly Theale is certainly not the mere fact of her illness, for which the text offers scarce evidence (James does not dwell on the symptoms, although we know that "there is something to speak of the matter with her"), but rather the overall existential con-dition that it represents, as well as its philosophical implications.[12] This

---

11. "At the end of the line, who pays? and why? Questions of gender enter here: when these dramas turn violent, women are frequently the victims of choice—are they bound to be?" writes Neil Hertz (*The End of the Line*, 223). Not only do my interpretations rep-resent various attempts to meet the overriding question of why women frequently pay, which hysteria inevitably raises. But in their repeated, obsessive stagings of the question of gender, these interpretations end up doing violence to the text, or, to use Hertz's for-mulation, they constitute "actings-out of historical experience" (223). The literary history of hysteria that is sketched out in this study corresponds then to a certain history of gender, which leads me to envisage the violence done to the subject in the name of gender.

12. James uses this phrase in his *Autobiography* to convey the diagnosis of "the great

condition is diagnosed in a formulation which, cryptic and idiosyncrat-ically Jamesian as it may seem, sheds unparalled wisdom on the hyster-ic's predicament: "It was perhaps superficially more striking that one could live if one would; but it was more appealing, insinuating, irresis-tible, in short, that one would live if one could" (*Wings of the Dove*, 181).

"Would" speaks of desire and "could" speaks of possibility, implying the presence of some external principle or law, and James plays with the two modal verbs in an attempt to define two different situations. On the one hand, he shows us the voluntarist attitude, built on hard-earned realism, which believes in the subject's ability to transcend the initial existential *données*, whose example is Kate Croy, with her hand-to-mouth existence—there, "one could live if one would." On the other hand, we have the predicament represented in Milly Theale, who is en-dowed with a life that is the object of a wager between a desire and an external force. The frail flame of that life depends on her ability to face, or rather to endure, what fate holds in store for her. She embodies, in a sublime and pathetic way, an existence defined not as action, but as resilience, as the resilience of a mind in the face of adversity. She then is the sacrificial victim of a metaphysical battle that opposes desire and the law.

For the philosophic mind, and such is James's here, this is inevitably a more "appealing, insinuating, irresistible" proposition, because it de-fines a universal human condition. And yet in James's *Wings of the Dove*, as in all the texts I present in this study, this proposition—which cor-responds to the hysteric's fate—is applied exclusively to the represen-tation of the female subject. In addition, the imperative that determines in an overriding fashion any subjective existence is, without exception, that of gender. My readings reveal indeed the repeated articulation, around the hysteric, of an urge to define and maintain the value and meaning of sexual difference by setting down the "law of gender"—a law rendered manifest in the various injunctions, prescriptions, and dis-cursive structures destined to ensure that "woman be a woman."

This "could," which afflicts the hysteric subjects of the texts that I examine with the force of a law, is the form taken by a cultural imper-ative that, in the nineteenth-century bourgeois world, tended to model

---

surgeon" whom he had consulted about his obscure hurt: "the inconvenience of my state had to reckon with the strange fact of there being nothing to speak of the matter with me" (417). For a detailed discussion, see Chapter 3.

subjectivity in terms of a grammar of the sexes. Indeed, the conditions of possibility for a female existence were the object of a relentless scrutiny and of a process of policing that gives flesh and substance to James's modal verb "could." Its principle is the discursive articulation and the maintenance of proper gender distinctions—what James, in his discussion of George Sand, called the "sense of differences." Hysterical women suffer from gender, but they do not know it and they cannot say it. Here again, Milly Theale constitutes a prime example of the depths of unspokenness that characterizes their predicament: her silence marks her unfathomable acquiescence with her female condition, while her muffled shrieks express its horror.

The sick and sublime Milly Theale, entrusted to the hands of a competent and understanding physician, is indeed a version of the *Hysterika*, afflicted as she is with a mysterious illness whose symptoms mark a spiritual or mental condition. The meaning of the illness depends, meanwhile, in a crucial fashion on the physician's unusual insight and depth of perception: the doctor of the *médecine morale* (such as Dr. Briquet or Dr. Brachet, whose work I examine in Chapter 1), the gifted physician (Sand's Monsieur Faure in *Valentine* or James's Sir Luke), or the psychoanalyst (such as Freud) will testify, over or against the bodily symptoms, to the spiritual, mental, or psychical nature of the woman's illness. But this means that if we pay close attention to the process of representation, we will see that *her* mind is consistently framed within *his* conceptions: she owes her subjective definition to his appropriation. "Mme Bovary c'est moi," says Flaubert, but we must face the full implications of this statement, as we need to acknowledge that the mental, psychic space is the object of an epistemological wager whose spoils are inevitably gender-marked.

James's epistolary conversation with his brother about the death of his cousin Minny Temple provides a vivid illustration of such a wager. For behind the image of Milly Theale we find another representation of a suffering femininity, in the figure of James's ailing cousin framed in his autobiographical writings. On learning in March 1870 that his beloved cousin had died, the author is moved to write a long letter to William, in which he remembers her as the ideal woman and the figure of his dreams (*Selected Letters*, 76–81). It has often been argued that the "real" Minny Temple was the model for the "literary" Milly Theale, although, in light of Minny's function in James's autobiography, such an opposition between real and fictional can hardly be sustained. For her portrayal reveals above all, in stark features, the forces and desires that underlie the representation of a female subject whom James's writing has converted into an object of aesthetic contemplation and sentimental adoration.

She has also become a feminine counterpart for a writer in search of masculinity. "Her image will preside in my intellect, in fact, as a sort of measure and standard of brightness and repose," James writes, having said earlier, "the more I think of her the more perfectly satisfied I am to have her translated from this changing realm of fact to the steady realm of thought. There she may bloom into a beauty more radiant than our dull eyes will avail to contemplate." Embalmed in his thoughts and the object of an unabashed idealization, the dead Minny Temple of James's letter has become his muse. More troubling even are James's introductory words: "She was at any rate the helpless victim and toy of her own intelligence—so that there is positive relief in thinking of her being removed from her own heroic treatment and placed in kinder hands." The religiosity and idealization of James's language can barely hide the strange perversion whereby the negation of her "feminine" intelligence (which, if we believe the author, predestined her somehow to an early death) allows for a conversion that makes of her a "presiding image in his intellect."[13]

When, in the preface to *The Portrait of a Lady*, the writer meditates on the creation of a heroine, Isabel Archer, whom he has endowed with the "high attributes of a Subject," he resorts to the model provided by George Eliot's narrator in *Daniel Deronda*: "in these frail vessels is borne onward through the ages the treasure of human affection" (*Literary Criticism*, 1077).[14] It seems then that the impulse that sustains the act of imagination and determines the representation of the female subject derives from "human affection," love, or *philia*. James's letter on the death of this cousin could naturally be considered a moving tribute to his affection for a woman who herself "belong[ed] to the deep domestic moral affectional realm" (in a wording that corresponds neatly to the nineteenth-century vision of the ideal woman). And yet we are not far from the strange rituals of Stransom lighting candles for his dead in *The Altar of the Dead*. Indeed, the idealization of the dead woman, in the

13. In a similar vein, James says about his sister: "the extraordinary intensity of her will and personality really would have made the equal, the reciprocal life of a 'well' person—in the usual world—almost impossible to her—so that her disastrous, her tragic health was in a manner the only solution for her of the practical problem of life" (To Mr. and Mrs. William James, May 1874, in *Selected Letters*, 275).

14. As it turns out, James misquotes; instead of "delicate," he wrote "frail."

name of deep affection, sheds (particularly when put next to the later story) a strange light on the relation between the writer and his female muse. The textual and literary relationship between the author and his beloved subject acquires disturbing necrophilic overtones.[15] But this loving conversion of a woman into a figure of the mind (or should we say "for his mind"?) shows above all the artist's preference for her figurative as against her literal value. We could even say that the idea of woman enables him to put his own intelligence to work, although this formulation ends up overlooking the disturbing emotional charge and latent violence of this writerly strategy.[16]

But this is precisely where the concept of hysteria, as a pathological disturbance of representation tied to the notion of gender, shows its heuristic value. The stakes of such a relation between, on the one hand, the ailing, idealized figure of a woman and, on the other, her sympathetic but deeply troubled "analyst" fall naturally into a pattern of gender definitions and conflicts. In this cognitive but also inevitably passionate involvement with femininity (for the pursuit of knowledge follows the way of love), the male literary and analytical mind is inevitably called upon to question its masculinity. "She never knew how sick and disordered a creature I was and I always felt that she knew me at my worst. I always looked forward with a certain eagerness to the day when I should have regained my natural lead, and one friendship on my part at least might become more active and masculine (*Selected Letters*, 77)." Thus the grief-stricken James ends up confessing in this letter his deep concern about his own ability to "be a man." But as he takes this strange, unexpected turn, expressing deep anxieties about his sexual identity, the writer appears to fall into a pattern of hysteria, of the kind that was familiar to Baudelaire and Flaubert alike: "Hysteria! . . . that mystery . . . which is expressed in the case of women by the sensation of an ascending and asphyxiating lump . . . and which translates itself in

15. In an essay on poetics, "The Philosophy of Composition," Edgar Allan Poe wrote, in a similar spirit (but, I imagine, without the irony or overtones that from my perspective would mark such a statement): "The death, then, of a beautiful woman is, unquestionably, the most poetical topic in the world—and equally is it beyond doubt that the lips best suited for such topic are those of a bereaved lover" (19).

16. This formulation is discussed in the preface to *The Portrait of a Lady*: "Challenge any such problem with any intelligence, and you immediately see how full it is of substance; the wonder being, all the while, as we look at the world, how absolutely, how inordinately, the Isabel Archers, and even much smaller fry, insist on mattering" (Henry James, *Literary Criticism: French Writers, Other European Writers, the Prefaces to the New York Edition*, 1077).

the case of excitable men into powerlessness and a liability to excesses of all kind (quoting Baudelaire on *Madame Bovary*, in *L'art romantique*, 649).

Indeed, if for my cases of hysteria I have resorted to the writings of Henry James and, in a second stage, Sigmund Freud, it is not because of the singularity of these authors; nor is it to elicit some peculiar Jamesian or Freudian idiosyncracy. It is because they present some of the most elaborate and challenging instances of the relation between the phenomenon of hysteria and the question of gender. They speak, as I shall argue, in the spirit of the age, of an age deeply concerned with definitions of femininity. In this process, meanwhile, they bring gender into the picture and drama of the mind.

Freud Taking a False Step: A Historical Perspective

"The helpless victim and toy of her own intelligence," the phrase describing James's beloved cousin, could have been a fit epigraph to Chapter 5 of this book, devoted to George Sand's "mental hysteria."[17] But it could as well be applied, in a more specific sense, to Dora, whose hysterical symptoms bespeak, according to her analyst, her intelligence concerning a certain kind of knowledge. "For where there is no knowledge of sexual processes even in the unconscious, no hysterical symptom will arise; and where hysteria is found," Freud claims, "there can no longer be any question of 'innocence of mind'" (*SE* VII, 49). The complex articulation of knowledge, femininity, and hysteria which is analyzed in the later part of this book from the perspective of the woman's literary expression, using George Sand and George Eliot as examples, should first be situated in its historical context. This is why I present, by way of an introduction, a particularly revealing instance of prejudice against woman's intelligence. The prejudice takes the general form of an inability to make the distinction, in the case of the female mind, between the acquisition of knowledge and erotic fulfilment.

This conflation is so deeply engrained in nineteenth-century discourses about women's knowledge that it shows up, most unexpectedly, in the telltale confusion that comes under Freud's pen in his analysis of Dora's second dream. Taking a false step, he no longer distinguishes between reading and loving (*lesen* and *lieben*): the overriding force of equating woman's knowledge with sexual license leads him to spontaneously associate Dora's desire for knowledge with erotic ambitions. This con-

17. I borrow this phrase from the nineteenth-century physician Pierre Briquet.

fusion speaks tellingly of the persistent valorization of woman's "innocence of mind," which relied on a long pedagogical tradition intent on surveilling and protecting the virgin minds of young women from the corrupting influence of bookish knowledge.[18]

Freud's "false step" occurs in his interpretation of the following dream-thought: "she went calmly to her room, and began reading a big book that lay on her writing table."[19] In the adjective "calmly" he finds confirmation for "the dream's power of fulfilling wishes," for the "big book" must deal with a forbidden subject, about which children read "in fear and trembling," while their parents are "in the way when reading of this kind is going on." Having resorted to this piece of wordly wisdom, the analyst goes back to the girl and her dead father, and adds: "Dora's father was dead, and the others had already gone to the cemetery. She might calmly read whatever she chose," a statement which he repeats with a significant difference at the end of the paragraph: "If her father was dead she could read and love as she pleased." This modulation from the original phrase "lesen, was ihr beliebte" (read "whatever she liked") to the revealing *lesen* and *lieben* (read and love) shows then that in the author's mind, and under the father's law, reading and loving are somehow the same thing. With the death of the father, the daughter can now choose to read or to love as she pleases; wishing him dead, the hysteric expresses her yearning for erotic and intellectual freedom. But while the violence against the father represented in the dream is an indictment of his coercive power, it gives as well the measure of the repression felt by Freud's patient.

This is why the analyst's slip of the pen must also be interpreted: in the first place, it reveals Freud's unconscious endorsement of a patriarchal plot where fathers and their substitutes exert control over their daughters' bodies and minds. As a result, the two partners of this analytical "conversation" find themselves locked in the same structure: Dora in her dream, Freud in his interpretation, she in rebellion, but he in his acquiescence meet with the law of gender as it is applied to woman's knowledge. There the female subject's search for knowledge and erotic

18. My own interpretations, in Chapter 5, of a number of episodes in George Sand's autobiography explore some of the psychical and intellectual consequences, for the female mind, of this cultural enforcement of ignorance in the name of modesty.

19. Here I borrow the metaphor (*Fehltritt*) that enabled Freud to disentangle Dora's symptom of a hysterical pregnancy—an appropriate figure, I believe, since my concern is to criticize Freud's symmetrical fantasy of patriarchal domination. My discussion bears on the paragraph where Freud gives his interpretation of Dora's reading (*Fragment of a Case of Hysteria,* SE VII, 100).

desire is met with the command that, as a "nubile girl," she must remain intellectually ignorant and sexually pure.[20] But since loving and reading are merged, the converse applies as well: she must remain ignorant in sexual matters and keep her purity of mind. The assumption is then that in the case of women, the knowledge that pertains, directly or indirectly, to the sexed body will leave its imprint on the soma. This is how hysteria is reconceived in terms of knowledge: as the paroxysmic form taken by a guilty secret, revealed by bodily symptoms or exposed in the more spectacular scenes of hysteria.

In this context, let us look at Freud's familiar words concerning the hysteric's loss of innocence, which appear in his well-known discussion on the language of analysis ("j'appelle un chat un chat" [*SE* VII, 48–49]) in *Fragment of a Case of Hysteria*: "There is never any danger of corrupting an inexperienced girl. For where there is no knowledge of sexual processes even in the unconscious, no hysterical symptom will arise; and where hysteria is found there can no longer be any question of 'innocence of mind' in the sense in which parents and educators use the phrase" (*SE* VII, 45). From this perspective, the hysteric can be defined as she who, caught between showing and not showing that she knows, has irremediably lost her *Gedankenunschuld* (literally, the innocence of her thoughts). The aim of the analysis is then not so much to cure her of her emotions and passions than to assess the extent of her "guilty" knowledge. Probing relentlessly into the moral and intellectual state of the hysteric's mind, Freud ends up showing that hysteria marks a knowledge that does not know itself. In the words of the philosopher Maurice Merleau-Ponty: "dans l'hystérie et dans le refoulement, nous pouvons ignorer quelque chose tout en le sachant" (In cases of hysteria or repression, one can be ignorant of a certain thing and yet all the while know it [189]).

If hysterical symptoms can be defined as the bodily translation of a knowledge present in the mind, the secret of hysteria is not of the order of the body but corresponds to a mental representation: it is indeed, in the often-quoted definition by Jean Laplanche and Jean-Bernard Pontalis, "a malady through representation."[21] It could be argued then that hysteria signals a failure of thought or of consciousness—or even that it provides, in its symbolic bodily manifestations, the negative of a consciousness. However, for the nineteenth century and for the early Freud

20. As we shall see in this book, the theories (and fantasies) of nineteenth-century hysteria often turn around a woman who is literally, or figuratively, on the eve of marriage.

21. Jean Laplanche and Jean-Bernard Pontalis present this definition of hysteria in *Vocabulaire de la psychanalyse* (178), in reference to the model elaborated by Pierre Janet.

(as his false step shows, it seems impossible to conceive of woman's mind outside of a moral frame), hysteria is the counterpart to conscience—a moral response to an immoral situation. Its stigmas testify to a virtuous and often admirable denial of a sexual awareness marked with an interdiction. As the erasure from the mind and the visible (and usually painful) projection on the body of her modesty, hysteria saves the woman. Indeed, since it designates woman's conscience or, to quote James, confirms her affiliation to "the deep domestic moral affectional realm," the illness has become a mark of election: it afflicts the best of women, namely, those singled out by their high susceptibility to what the nineteenth-century French doctors called, in a revealing phrase, the *affections morales*.

This example highlights, meanwhile, an important feature of the representations I examine in this work—the relationship between hysteria and the various forms of censorship that are applied to the sexual domain. The censorhip can hardly ever be ascribed solely to the social interdiction (such as assumes, for instance, that girls or unmarried women should not be exposed to certain kinds of representations). Nor can it be attributed exclusively to some inner reticence that prevents the hysterical subject from experiencing, acknowledging, or expressing the pleasures or passions that pertain to the sexed body. My critical readings show that the hysterical responses to the woman's text (exemplified in Freud's analytical encounter with Dora and James's criticism of George Sand) correspond to scenarios of engendering which are promoted in the name of morality and civilization, but which are also sustained by private fantasies and anxieties. The stage on which hysteria is played out is thus necessarily double: it faces one way toward a cultural imperative, and in the other toward the most intimate obsessions concerning femininity and masculinity. My interpretation of the Sandian scene of hysteria confirms, meanwhile, that the veil of modesty, which falls between the woman's inquisitive gaze and the sexed body, is often not of her own making: it has been woven by those (and they can be men or women, as this book shows) whose power is sustained by her ignorance.

From a historical perspective, Freud builds his defense against the accusations he might pollute the hysteric's mind by using the same stance as does Jean-Jacques Rousseau. "You can leave her in my good hands since anyway she is already fallen" is Rousseau's argument in his first preface to *La Nouvelle Héloïse*, where he tries to defend the value of a literary project centered on the depiction of erotic passion. There is no risk of corrupting her, he claims, for the mere fact of her taking up such a book proves that "the worst has already happened"—"le mal était fait d'avance": "A chaste girl has never read any novels. . . . And she who, in spite of this title,[22] will dare to read a single page is a lost girl, but she cannot ascribe her fall to this book, the evil was committed before. Since she began, let her continue to read, there is nothing left for her to lose" (vi). What better evidence for the persistence of moral and pedagogical strictures concerning the female mind than these converging strategies, which associate the analyst with the eighteenth-century writer? But this rapprochement shows also an interesting structural analogy between the scene of analysis and that of reading. Through their ability to conjure up mental representations normally forbidden to women, the scenes of fiction, like the analyst's discourse, are liable to instigate a dangerous process of corruption; the vicarious passions of literature and the transferential stage of analysis threaten to trouble the purity of mind that defines true womanhood.[23]

While woman constitutes the central value in the epistemological quest for a gendered subjectivity, it looks as if, blindfolded and unable to speak, she might be fatally excluded from such a pursuit. Within such a structure, the figure of the hysterical woman comes into prominence precisely because she is neither in nor out of ignorance. Guilty in that "she knows," but innocent since that knowledge remains a secret to herself, the hysteric embodies the contradictions and paradoxes of a sexual ideology that wants, in the name of her supposed modesty, to deny woman access to the scenes of passion. However, a close examination of the figurations of hysteria in Sand's *Valentine* and Eliot's *Daniel Deronda* shows that something can be learned, on the subject of woman's mind, from her active implication as a writer in the scenes of her hysteria.

The Philosopher Reflecting on a Riddle: The Theoretical Perspective

The image that sustains this inquiry is that of an encounter, sometimes passionate or antagonistic and, more rarely, empathetic and reflective, between the figure of the hysteric and her reader, observer, analyst. In the nineteenth century such an encounter constituted the significant site for a discussion of the mind and for its engendering; it also provided a stage for a questioning about sexual identity and consciousness, "that

---

22. The complete title is *Julie ou la Nouvelle Héloïse: Lettres de deux amants.*

23. For a discussion of this subject from a general historical perspective, see "Drawing the Veil," the second part of Chapter 1, where I define the notions of *pudeur* and *pudicité*.

thing," in Derrida's words, "that, more and more, one avoids discussing as if one knew what it is and as if its riddle were solved" ("How to Avoid Speaking," 17). The distinguishing mark of the model of consciousness provided by Derrida in this essay is its reliance on negativity: consciousness is defined by the ability *not* to say, *not* to show. It is then present as a secret, whose "uncontrolled manifestations," writes Derrida, "are direct or symbolic, somatic or figurative" (18). My own emphasis on the various forms of negation constitutive of hysteria has naturally lead me to adopt the Derridean model, and I have examined in a number of nineteenth-century texts "the direct or symbolic, somatic or figurative" manifestations of the secret of consciousness. But with a difference, however: focusing on hysteria, which dwells on the boundaries between the sexes, I have added the dimension of gender to Derrida's questioning of the secret and given a feminist inflection to his philosophic presuppositions. It is on this difference that I want to dwell for a moment in an attempt to define what might be the relevance of this study for our contemporary interests in questions of gender and of feminist theory.

"Here one would be tempted to designate, if not to define consciousness as that place in which is retained the singular power not to *say* what one knows, to keep a secret in the form of representation" (17), writes the philosopher. Chapter 6 of this book, which takes the form of a close reading of *Daniel Deronda* from the perspective sketched out by the narrator when s/he speaks of the "consciousness of a girl," offers a tentative counterpart to Derrida's cautious (but "gender-free"—there is no mention of sexual difference in his essay) speculations about what defines consciousness.

The hysteric's response to the (patriarchal) law of gender takes a form expressed most aptly in Lynda Zwinger's words: "I tell and don't tell you that I know and don't know what I can't and can tell" (122). In its textualized form, hysteria plays, moreover, with another kind of duplicity: it finds, in its figures and intensities, a language that reveals the presence of something that is unpresentable. But this formulation, which ascribes a kind of willful agency to literary language, is of course inappropriate: textual hysteria results truly from the "uncontrolled manifestations" that we owe to the figurative force of writing itself. In other words, from under the frames of representation, writing gives way, spontaneously, to the "oblique, faltering" utterance of hysteria.[24] The secret

---

24. Lacan formulates it as "une initiative détournée, balbutiante et ligotée d'une crise qui excède le spectacle" (the indirect, faltering, fettered initiative of a crisis that exceeds the spectacle) (*Le séminaire VII: L'éthique de la psychanalyse*, 64).

becomes manifest in the displacements and unusual intensities produced in the process of writing. The rhetorical force of literature speaks then of a consciousness that cannot allow itself to speak, or, to use Luce Irigaray's words, they are the sign that "something [has] been repressed from speech and [is] spoken in-between in 'hieroglyphic symptoms' " (174).

The figure of the hysteric, as my discussions of *Fragment of a Case of Hysteria* and *Daniel Deronda* show, is instrumental then in a game of secrets around questions of knowledge, of the mind, of consciousness. The object of repeated questionings, because there always seems to be more to her than meets the eye,[25] the figure represents in an emblematic fashion the ability "to keep a secret in the form of a representation" which precisely, according to Derrida, defines or at the least designates consciousness (17). Her symptoms single her out as the keeper of a secret which, for as long as "she" maintains her hold over the minds of the observers, analysts and readers, acts as a reminder of what Freud called "das verborgenste Seelische" or the philosopher calls "consciousness."[26] Thus my readings of the hysteric do not as matter of fact take the direction of a psychoanalytical interpretation intent on deciphering the marks of an unconscious. My concern is to keep in focus the repeated gestures of negation or repressive injunctions that, for a certain period in history, came to bear on the minds of women. Hysteria thus enables me to ultimately address, from a historical perspective, the question of a gender-inflected consciousness.

"Some would say, perhaps imprudently, that only man is capable of speaking, because only he can *not* show what he could show" ("How to Avoid Speaking," 17) writes Derrida, still on the subject of the secret and of consciousness. His formulation takes us back to the Jamesian emphasis on "would" and "could" concerning Milly Theale's existential predicament. Recall that in his representation of an ailing female subject, James revealed the gap that separates a desire from the conditions of its realization, the possibilities given for its fulfilment. My inquiry into these various textual representations of hysteria shows, meanwhile, that the

25. The peal of questions at the beginning of *Daniel Deronda* ("Was she beautiful or not? and what was the secret of form or expression") exemplifies this in a memorable fashion.

26. The term appears in *Fragment of a Case of Hysteria* (Dora) (*SE* VII, 78): "the task of making conscious the most hidden recesses of the soul is one which it is quite possible to accomplish," Freud claims. Whereas the Strachey edition translate *das Seelische* as "the mind," I follow the original more closely in this case and use the nineteenth-century term "the soul."

proposition "one would . . . if one could" defines the impossibility of language or of verbal symbolization characteristic of this condition. But this inquiry reveals as well that this impossibility cannot be ascribed solely to the hysterical subject's psychology, but that it begins with her inscription within a pedagogical tradition that relentlessly denies to women the ability to move from impressions and sensations into the realm of thought and language. The figures of hysteria act as a vivid reminder of the fact that, for certain categories of subjects, consciousness remains secret, not because of a choice but as an imposed condition.[27]

But to speak in the neuter or the universal mode may be to overlook the historical evidence suggesting that consciousness works differently for women. When applied to a (hysterical) female subject, the philosopher's proposition must be marked with a different emphasis. The hysteric's scream or the utterance that is silenced in her throat demands a different formulation: she is incapable of speaking, because she would show what she *can not* show. For indeed, if there is always a logical, theoretical possibility that she might reveal her secret (for it exists as representation and can thus be translated into various "languages"), what my delving into the texts of hysteria has made insistently present is the weight of moral stricture and of pedagogical, writerly injunction that opposes the constitution of woman's consciousness. The violence and the hysteria that surround "a mind expanding with longing and desire" (as James describes George Sand) show well enough what happens when a woman begins to reveal her secrets. To envisage consciousness in its negative form, as an active or willful silencing of "what is expressible in words" (Derrida) or as a form of "positive nonacting" (which is the analyst's privilege according to Lacan) is one thing.[28] But to experience as a pathological condition, namely as hysteria, the cul-

27. The exile from language, from culture, from knowledge seems to be a determining factor in hysteria (on this subject, see François Roustang's suggestive remarks in *Un destin si funeste*). But recent historical development shows that gender no longer prevails as a predominant factor. New medical evidence indicates that hysteria, which in its narrower nosological sense had been on the wane for a number of decades, has been diagnosed in recent years (and often in spectacular manifestations of conversion or grand mal) in Western European countries among patients who have been cut away from their culturally distant home countries (such as exiles, refugees, and foreign emigrants) and who are deprived of a language in which to express their mental and emotional deprivation.

28. Lacan's text on transference ends, resoundingly, with the following statement: "I believe, however, that transference always has this same meaning of indicating the moments where the analyst goes astray, and equally takes his or her bearings, this same value of calling us back to the order of our role—that of positive nonacting [i.e., *un non-agir positif*] with a view to the orthodramatization of the subjectivity of the patient" ("Intervention on Transference," 103).

tural and historical strictures on woman's reading, thinking, knowing, is another. And it is precisely that other aspect which is here my concern, as I have undertaken to "save" or to "free" the hysteric, through acts of reading, from this nonknowledge, from a secret that is in her case a form of nonconsciousness, of *méconnaissance*, which she owes to the internalization of the cultural interdiction.[29]

Hysteria is thus redefined within this literary and historical project as a textual phenomenon and as a form of discourse situated at the intersection of body and mind but turned inward, toward some unspoken, unpresentable desire and knowledge. It is characterized by a denial, which, I argue, originates in the subject's internalization of the prohibition on reading, knowing, or thinking about the sexed body. This interdiction has had momentous consequences for the history of women's minds: the epistemophilic drive begins as sexual curiosity; to repress it is to cast a shadow over the whole structure of mental life (as my inquiry into Sand's autobiography shows). Moreover, as a founding gesture that defines the difference between men and women with regard to knowledge, woman's exclusion from the knowledge of sex sustains a whole edifice of exclusion which prohibits women's curiosity in other domains.

This project responds to the negation of woman's mind with an act of reading and interpretation. And the hysteric, as I demonstrate in my discussion of the case history of Dora, calls precisely for such a reading. While her body is the surface of an "inside" and, like a vessel, conveys or displays the traces of a secret history, it is also an object that offers itself for interpretation. In the very process, as she issues this invitation to the reader, the hysteric becomes a subject in the intersubjective scenario that she tries to bring about. Charting in detail some of these encounters between the hysteric and her observer-analyst-reader, my work shows, however, the limits or failures of such a plot: the conversation or the encounter summons up again, fatefully, the same mechanisms of engendering and seems to obey a compulsive need to maintain the distinction between the sexes. Thus, while the hysterical scenario represents a questioning of gender ("Where am I that is supposed to be

29. The question of speaking as a woman or speaking for a woman bears no resolution as Shoshana Felman and Gayatri Spivak have taught us. But an analytical frame, provided it be "dialogic" or truly intersubjective, makes it possible to envisage a model of transmission and interpretation that, I believe, can allow us to speak for another. This project could then be defined as a female genealogy of writing and reading whose inheritance is this awareness or problematization of gender, which the hysteric and her "analyst" promote in the exchange or transference that occurs in the guise of reading.

a woman?" the hysteric's body seems to be asking), it can merely trigger, on the part of the interpreter, the symmetrical question (If this is what woman can be, how am I to be a man?). Thus, with each feeding the other's hysteria, this intersubjective scene displays increasingly complex and intense rituals of engendering as if to ensure that the difference between men and women be restaged or played out again. Gender is thus represented at the very core of that *Seelensleben* (life of the soul) that is the object of the quest, the ultimate enigma of the scene of hysteria.

Meanwhile, the war of the sexes that is waged around the hysteric's "soul" inevitably raises questions of property and appropriation. When the secret is wrested from her and carried to the front of the stage in the form of a representation, whose consciousness do we uncover? His? Hers? Some transsubjective or intersubjective knowledge that yet bears the mark of the gendered scene that brought it to light? None of my texts raises these kinds of question, which belong to our more recent understanding of subjectivity and give to representation its political dimensions. They are studied by contemporary philosophers, notably Stanley Cavell, whose work on hysteria in psychoanalysis and film leads him to assert that "by the beginning of the twentieth century the fact of the existence of the mind had become believable primarily in its feminine (one may say) passive aspect" (352). On the other hand, the scenarios of passion and knowledge that are enacted in and around the nineteenth-century scenes of hysteria speak obsessively of sexual difference, not as a fact, of course, but as an idea, principle, or theory. Gender is then the logical foundation around which the discourse of the subject can be deployed and defines the secret from which consciousness necessarily originates.

But to go the way of such a deconstructive "drift" is to be trapped in a grammar that overlooks the consequences of the desire or need for sexual difference which emerges so clearly from the different scenarios of hysteria that I examine. And it is to overlook also the foundational nature of these repeated gestures of engendering: these gestures, I claim, have gradually left a sediment, a history of internalized gender norms.[30] This literary investigation into hysteria has indeed led me to envisage again and again what are some of the existential, cultural, and historical

---

30. "Consider that a sedimentation of gender norms produces the peculiar phenomenon of a 'natural sex' or a 'real woman' or any number of prevalent and compelling social fictions, and that this is a sedimentation that over time has produced a set of corporeal styles," writes Butler (*Gender Trouble*, 140). While her work has helped me clarify, in a decisive fashion, the implications of my own literary research (begun several years before her book came out), my own project emphasizes a sedimentation that over time has produced as set of *mental* styles.

consequences of the guilt enforced on woman's intelligence in the name of her exclusion from sexual knowledge. It has shown as well how much is lost, by way of a mutual understanding between men and women, with the enforcement of the law of gender. For gender can only be maintained through a certain expenditure of power: the prescriptions that emerge from the nineteenth-century doctors' studies of hysteria, the hysterical violence that characterizes James's repeated attempts to frame Sand's language of passion within the conventions of sexual identity, Freud's insistent projection of himself in the hysteric's body—all testify to the presence of a regulatory force that produces gender.

A close examination of the literary, medical, and early psychoanalytical discourses on hysteria makes it possible to highlight the pervasive place held by regulations of gender within the more encompassing nineteenth-century project of a psychological description of subjectivity. The various gender fables I interpret in the course of this study, and which constitute its major points of articulation, all have one obvious subject matter—the state of the soul or mind of woman.[31] They also enable me to highlight how reading and writing intervene in the process of gendering, for it is ultimately from this dialectic of reading and writing that the picture of a gender-marked consciousness emerges. This is why a thematic approach to hysteria must necessarily be combined with a narratological and rhetorical analysis: gender, as the meaning imposed upon sexual difference and as the translation into the mental domain of a bodily fact, must necessarily be understood as a textual effect.

Thus, to study the texts and the textuality of hysteria is to be brought back to an inner stage, where the spectacular performance of hysteria represents a call for attention and an invitation to read, to decipher the workings of the mind. The subjectivity that she represents cannot be confined to a body held in the thralls of its passional enactments. On

31. The two terms "soul" and "mind" are of course not interchangeable in spite of what might be indicated in Strachey's choice of translating *das Seelische* as mind as against the more literal meaning of "soul" in the expression *das verborgenste Seelische*. During the period covered by my book, stretching from the 1830s of Sand's early writings to the works of Freud and James at the end of the nineteenth century, the two terms slide from one signification to the other. Shaping that movement, an epistemological shift concerning interiority seems to be taking place. "Soul" would then correspond to the earlier denomination and configuration, whereas "mind" (increasingly present in James's texts on Sand for instance) fits our more modern understanding of a psychic economy. Given the fact that in this volume I have emphasized questions of knowledge, "mind" imposed itself in most cases as the better choice, but historical accuracy requires that I register the presence of these two competing terms. I am well aware, meanwhile, that I am touching upon an immensely complex problem in history of ideas and philosophy, which lies however beyond the scope of this literary and theoretical inquiry.

the contrary, the hysteric's body is merely the visible form given to the secrets of a consciousness. The riddle represented in her symptoms goes back to a consciousness inflected by gender. Or, to use a different formulation, the key to her hysteria is the thought, the idea of gender. This book attempts to turn away from the celebration of hysteria as some ineffable body language or sublime *jouissance*; it tries to go beyond the aporia of a deconstructive approach (where the question that the hysteric addresses to gender initiates merely a replay of the logic of gender). While the unexplained semiotic uncertainties and intensities that characterize the interplay of representation, writing, and hysteria are thus met with an act of reading and criticism, the symptoms displayed by the nineteenth-century hysterics gradually acquire a symbolic value. They mark the place held by gender in the recent history of consciousness and enable us to document some of the more private and subjective consequences of the gradual emergence of gender in the modern era.[32]

The hindsight our contemporary views have given us enables us, I believe, to become the archeologists of the gendered subject. The *Nacht-räglichkeit* or belatedness that inevitably afflicts such a project is not that of nostalgia, however. It proceeds from a desire, a reader's desire, to know why the inscriptions of desire, knowledge, and gender that were held in the secret chambers of Sand, Flaubert, Eliot, James, and Freud have had such a lasting hold on our imaginations. Inspired by the wide-ranging implications of Flaubert's famous pronouncement, "Mme Bovary c'est moi, d'après moi," this critical project has ultimately led me to explore the textual enigma of femininity expressed in the hieroglyphs of hysteria. An interrogation about writing has thus made me endorse the stance of a reader and follow, unwittingly, a critical impulse and imperative that Virginia Woolf identified in one of her novels: "She imagined how in the chambers of the mind and heart of [this] woman . . . were stood, like the treasures in the tombs of kings, tablets bearing sacred inscriptions, which if one could spell them out would teach one everything, but they would never be offered openly, never made public. What art was there, known to love or cunning, by which one pressed through into those secret chambers?"[33] This book reflects, then, an education into reading.

32. For an overall discussion of a "history of increasing sexualization," see "Does a Sex Have a History" in Denise Riley's *"Am I That Name?" Feminism and the Category of "Women" in History.*

33. This passage describes Lily Briscoe's encounter with Mrs. Ramsay in Virginia Woolf's *To the Lighthouse* (50). For a theoretical perspective on similar scenes (in James, Sand, and Freud), see the second part of Chapter 4, beginning with "Between Women."

CHAPTER ONE

Nineteenth-Century Hysteria:
The Medical Context

Hysteria! Why wouldn't this mystery become the matter and the substance of a literary work, this mystery that the Academy of medicine has not yet solved, and which is expressed in the case of women by the sensation of an ascending and asphyxiating lump (I am only talking about the main symptom) and which translates itself in the case of excitable men into powerlessness and a capacity for excesses of all kinds.

—Baudelaire, *L'art romantique*

In May 1874 Gustave Flaubert wrote to his friend George Sand: "I am going to get rid of my congestion on the top of a mountain in Switzerland, following the advice of Doctor Hardy, who calls me 'a hysterical woman,' a profound statement, I find" (*Correspondance,* 467).[1] In the postscript of his next letter, signed "Cruchard," he added a tentative definition of his self-inflicted nickname: "More Cruchard than ever. I feel decrepit, flabby, worn out, sheik, deliquescent, in short, calm and moderate, which is the ultimate of decadence." In obedience to his doctor's prescription, he had just spent "twenty days on the Righi in order to breathe a little, to become sober, and to get rid of his neuropathy" (469). But Switzerland meant deep boredom: "Since you know Switzerland, no need to tell you more. And you would probably despise me too much if I told you that I am bored to death there" (475). A prolonged stay in a Magic Mountain village could indeed not have been the best remedy for this kind of hysterical behavior.

The letters of George Sand and Gustave Flaubert show that his hysteria took at times a more specific form, closer to the medical definitions. It is not only a disease of the imagination (such as his Emma Bovary experiences): the term describes as well his own ailing body. In a letter of 1867, Flaubert draws the list of his physical symptoms: "I feel pal-

---

1. The translations of the Flaubert-Sand letters are my own, but were emended whenever I felt Aimée Mackenzie or Francis Steegmuller provided better versions.

pitations in the heart for nothing—easy to understand, by the way, in an old hysteric like myself. For I maintain that men are hysterical just like women, and I am one of them. When I wrote *Salammbô* I had read 'the best authorities' on that subject and I have recognized all my symptoms: the *globus hystericus* and the harrowing pain at the back of the head. This is the outcome of our nice occupation: we torment ourselves body and soul" (*Corresponance*, 118). The fuller clinical picture would comprise as well certain hallucinations (described in a letter to Taine) and his seizures, which at the time were ascribed to his epilepsy, but might just as easily have been the paroxysmic expression of hysteria.

Flaubert's hysteria could be understood in its historical context as just another case in the epidemic of an illness so prevalent in his day that, according to Dr. Pierre Briquet (a contemporary of Flaubert), "one woman out of four as well as a sizable number of men seem to be affected by it."[2] It might also find a partial explanation in the writer's interest in medical textbooks. Flaubert, the son of a doctor, had read Bichat's *Anatomie générale* and his *Recherches physiologiques sur la vie et la mort*, Cabanis's *Rapport du physique et du moral*, Daremberg's *Histoire de la médecine* (and his *La médecine, histoires et doctrines*), and Garnier's *Traité des facultés de l'âme*. He also claimed to have studied "the best authors on hysteria," such as Jean-Louis Brachet (*Traité de l'hystérie*) and Pierre Briquet (*Traité clinique et thérapeutique de l'hystérie*). Given such abundant medical knowledge, one might risk the hypothesis that this case of hysteria may have been the outcome of readerly empathy—one which, under the writer's pen, produced descriptions and figurations that take on the appearance of the real, of a real case. Flaubert's hysteria thus belongs to literature, as an instance of the transformation of medical representations into literary production, as is attested by his letters to Sand on the subject.

The textbooks he had read drew on a variety of domains and discourses, and may well have encouraged the rich imaginative qualities that characterize his evocations of the illness. A nineteenth-century medical treatise typically would have combined, under the heading of hysteria, hard physical sciences (such as anatomy and physiology), clinical observations, speculations about the mind as well as philosophical and moral discussions, and mythical or literary examples. Matching the doctor's conception, the writer's hysteria expresses his aesthetic, moral, and

---

2. The figure, taken from Briquet's extensive study, is cited in Pierre Larousse's *Grand dictionnaire universel du XIXème siècle*.

psychological concerns. Flaubert's disquisitions on hysteria involve, moreover, a discussion of sexual difference, of that which at the time was called *le sexe*.[3] For if, according to Naomi Schor, "their correspondence constitutes an exemplary attempt at carving out an intersubjective arena where sexual identity is shifting, mobile, severed from anatomy, unhampered by social norms" (*George Sand and Idealism*, 199), their exchanges on the theme of hysteria are the scene of an implicit, and sometimes explicit, questioning on the subject of the difference between the sexes. Thus Flaubert presents himself sometimes as *un vieil hystérique*, sometimes as *une femme hystérique*, and his insistence on being one or the other makes it clear that the subjective content of the illness must inevitably be gender-marked. In other words, the writer shows that although hysteria exists in both women (usually) and men (sometimes), its gender can never be a matter of indifference; hysteria seems, in effect, to have become the testing ground for sexual identities. The fullest enumeration of his symptoms opens the way for some thoughts on his powers of identification and on the sex changes they entail. While rereading *Consuelo* and *La comtesse de Rudolstadt* he felt " 'amoureuse' de Liverani,"[4] and he concludes musingly that "this is because I have the two sexes maybe" (118).[5]

But this exchange of letters on hysteria takes a markedly more serious turn when George Sand, in her answer to Flaubert, expresses her ideas about sexual difference (*le sexe*). She responds to "Cruchard," in an unsigned letter:

3. *Le sexe* is what distinguishes men from women (from the Latin word *secare*, "to cut, to divide"). But this epistolary conversation between Flaubert and Sand shows that the older sense of the term, which emphasizes the mere fact of difference, was gradually giving way to the modern concept of sexuality. The *Grand Robert* proposes 1889 as the year *sexe* was first used to mean "l'ensemble des questions sexuelles (v. *sexualité, érotisme*)," while the more traditional *Littré* does not mention the newer sense of the word.

4. The quotation marks emphasize the irregularity of the feminine grammatical gender as applied to the male subject. The translation of these nineteenth-century French authors reveals indeed the emergence of a notion of gender that is no longer merely grammatical; it testifies to a growing awareness of the complex cultural meanings associated with sexual difference. Gender is not merely a fact of language, but a question of subjective definition.

5. In French, this passage reads, "j'ai les deux sexes." This formulation, in terms of "having a sex" rather than "being of one or the other sex," now seems awkward. The linguistic shift, however, registers a major change of sensibility, namely, the emergence of a gendered consciousness or being. Working on a parallel line of enquiry, Riley concludes her discussion of the place assigned to woman in the nineteenth-century elaboration of spirituality with the revealing statement: "As the neutral domains of the soul had contracted, so it had become possible to *be* a sex" (*"Am I That Name?"* 43).

But what is it then to be hysterical? I have perhaps been that also. Maybe I am hysterical, but I don't know anything about it, since I never probed into this thing—I heard about it but did not study it. Is it not a kind of unease or anguish, caused by the desire of an impossible something or other? In that case, we are all affected by this strange illness, that is when we are endowed with some imagination; and why would such an illness have a sex?

And there is more, for the people who are strong in anatomy: *there is only one sex*. A man and a woman. This is so much the same thing that it is hard to understand why societies have fed on a heap of subtle distinctions and reasonings on this subject. I have observed my son's childhood and development and the same in my daughter. My son was like myself, namely, much more of a woman than my daughter, who was a failed man. (*Correspondance,* 121)

What George Sand reveals here in substance is a conception of masculine and feminine as a difference within: the man and the woman, two declensions within the paradigm "one sex." While many of her contemporaries, such as the specialists in hysteria whose theories are discussed later in this chapter, were working hard at establishing a naturalized sexual identity, Sand expresses here her opposition to a model that ascribes a foundational value to the difference between the sexes. "There is only one sex" is underlined in Sand's text: in its dismissal of a binary logic (one or the other sex), this statement would have had, in her day, the force of an oxymoron, and it is only within the modern notion of sexuality that it can really make sense. While acknowledging the existence of sexual difference, she highlights in her examples the versatility of its manifestations, which are detached from the anatomy, as if she had in mind some notions akin to our contemporary sexual positions, or to the French describing the assumption of sexual difference: "sexuation". She also acknowledges the effects of a belief in this difference—"the heap of subtle distinctions and reasonings"—and she concludes her discussion with an instance of what, to our modern critical gaze, might look like images of gendered subjectivities which would call for the words "feminine" and "masculine."

In her discussion of this passage, Naomi Schor argues that Sand's statement relies on a conventional model of androgyny; I suggest more optimistically that what the writer advances here, in a typically coy fashion, is the idea of gender.[6] Considering Sand's own disclaimer ("I don't

6. Naomi Schor describes this passage as "a curious combination of the radical and the conventional," but emphasizes in her interpretation what she deems the conventional aspects of Sand's conception, exemplified in her "sexism" and even "heterosexism" as well as in her single-sex model "of the order of the androgyne" (*George Sand and Idealism,*

know anything about this") it might of course be exaggerated to ascribe to her the elements of a theory of gender. After all, she developed her thoughts on the question almost casually, à propos of hysteria, and certainly made no claims for her scientific knowledge: since she had not studied the question, she could only speak from experience, as a mother. But if Sand is not a theoretician, let it be granted at least that here she writes about her awareness of gender.

In this conversation on hysteria she gets the better of Flaubert. Whereas he appears to flounder playfully in the murky limbo of his personal malaise, she provides a definition of the illness that approximates, in an uncanny fashion, what the philosopher Monique David-Ménard later writes on the question in 1986. Her notion that hysteria is the expression of a suffering bound up with the transgressions of the imagination or desire—hysteria as the pathological expression of the impossible—sketches the path to the philosopher's claim that hysteria is bound up with the failure of the symbolic, and is a construct of desire and thought around some impossible *jouissance*.[7] Whereas Flaubert's medical inclinations encourage him to play up the physical, bodily dimensions of the disease, Sand conceives of it as a phenomenon of the mind. When he insists on ascribing a sexual definition to the illness, she turns it into a universal human condition that touches those who have imagination.

My own inquiry into nineteenth-century medical texts on hysteria has led me to chart the rugged territory of a domain made up of science and imagination, where hysteria has become the figurehead for "the subtle distinctions and reasonings" that societies have fed upon the subject of sex. My inquiry traces as well the inscription of hysteria's symptoms and etiology on the sexualized body, and from there into the mind, as part of a gendered identity. I thus show that, pace Sand, the disease has a sex, not given by nature of course, but produced by discursive formations infused with various mythologies concerning the female body and mind. But I might as well say at the outset that George Sand, and not Flaubert, has given the inspiration to this project: it was begun under the aegis of a feminist suspicion that an epidemic of hysteria of a kind that included no less than one woman out of four might teach more about the prejudice of male science than about hysteria or femininity,

196). My own parti pris goes the other way; however, in the last section of Chapter 5, I analyze Sand's intellectual timidity and her "hysterical" resistance to thinking.

7. Monique David-Ménard defines this construct in "How the Mystery of Conversion is Constructed," pages 47–63 of *Hysteria from Freud to Lacan: Body and Language in Psychoanalysis*.

and would tell us more about minds than about bodies. The final section of this chapter thus shows how the "mental hysteria" (a term I owe to Jean-Jacques Virey) ascribed to nineteenth-century women is in effect the telltale sign of a regime of gender discrimination, where women function as the blank pages of men's texts, and where, moreover, sexual identity exists only as a parody or masquerade. While she plays, hysterically, at being a woman, he can reassure himself that he is a man.

Styles of the Flesh

Polymorphous, whimsical, elusive—this is how hysteria appears to the nineteenth-century doctor. Dr. Briquet, for instance, with his acknowledged taste for "the study of positivist science," began his detailed book on the subject by expressing strong reservations, for "hysteria is the very model of the unstable, the irregular, the fantastic, the unexpected . . . it is governed by no law, no rule . . . and no serious theory" (*Traité clinique et thérapeutique de l'hystérie*, iii), and yet he ended up publishing a treatise of more than seven hundred pages on the subject. The quest for the meaning of hysteria requires indeed the skills and dedication of a devoted reader: as a sign reinvented by every patient, it can only respond to the most persistent and detailed inquiry. To pierce its secrets would mean achieving distinction, and like so many of his colleagues Briquet seemed drawn by the very difficulty of the pursuit: the studies on hysteria seemed to proliferate in the nineteenth century at the same rate as the illness itself, like an epidemic.[8]

The first concern is to establish, with the help of anatomy or physiology, the organic origins of the illness. But because its manifestations are so various and complex, and the treatment so hazardous, a broader etiological approach is also necessary. Its enigmatic and sometimes spectacular aspects speak to the imagination and encourage an aesthetic approach, which is vividly present in descriptions that dwell at length on the bodily symptoms. But the body of the nineteenth-century hysteric is also the site of social and ethical regulations and of a power struggle whose violence is unmistakeable. "Nothing is more punitive than to give a disease a meaning—that meaning being invariably a moralistic one.

---

8. This suggests, of course, that the illness results from a certain cultural and ideological configuration, which is what contemporary epidemiological approaches show as well: "The too frequent confusion . . . of typically socialized feminine behaviour with the diagnosis of hysteria must be kept in mind in any discussion of the epidemiology of the hysterical personality" (Mardi J. Horowitz, *Hysterical Personality*, 153).

Any important disease whose causality is murky, and for which treatment is ineffectual, tends to be awash in significance," writes Susan Sontag in her study of tuberculosis (58). The truth of her remark has found painful confirmation in our AIDS-haunted time. The texts on hysteria reveal a similar connivence between, on the one hand, the desire to know and understand the disease and, on the other, the urge to impose a whole array of moral norms. This preliminary inquiry into nineteenth-century medical representations of hysteria aims therefore at highlighting the complex mesh of discourses of knowledge, desire, and power that coalesce in the image of the hysteric. It focuses simultaneously on the emergence of a new topography of the disease, which reveals, in its remapping of the body-mind divide, an increasingly complex image of femininity.

The works of Voisin, Virey, Brachet, and Briquet, which span the years 1826 to 1859, all reject the older anatomical theories that tended to ascribe hysteria to the disorders of the uterus or to the whole genital system. For these doctors the origin of hysteria lies in some inherent predisposition: the hysteric is more easily affected by certain existential or social predicaments because endowed with a surplus of some quality such as passion (for Voisin), sensibility (Virey), nervous excitability (Brachet), or impressionability (Briquet). However, except for Voisin, these doctors persist in their conviction that the illness must be related to some anatomical or physiological dysfunctioning. The older model of the disease connected the symptoms to a specific part of the body marked by some excessive or pathological process. The new doctors too believe that hysteria originates in the body, but not in one part only; the totality of the female body, in its substance and its behavior, now participates in the illness.[9] Knife in hand, they therefore delve into its very fiber in order to detect the traces of an innate susceptibility to hysteria.

In *Traité de l'hystérie* Brachet, for example, celebrates with zest and in almost poetic terms the radical difference that characterizes the anatomized female body. The undisguised aim of this poetry of the shapes, tissues, organs, and physiological systems is to render legible, in the signs of nature, that is, in the organic body, an image of woman founded on the complex elaboration of a radical difference between the sexes. Extrapolating, systematizing, the doctor invents the features of a femininity

9. Hysteria enables us to document a historical process that has been described by the philosopher Denise Riley: "The whole meaning of 'woman' had been transformed once the concept of the female person as thoroughly sexed through all her regions of being had become entrenched" (*"Am I That Name?"* 43).

that is no longer only ascribed to the reproductive sphere: women's bod-ies are inherently, in their smallest details, marked by significant distinc-tions.

Brachet's chapter titled "Etudes du physique et du moral de la femme" provides a good example. Having summarized most of the received opin-ions on the illness, the physician opposes to them his own scientific com-petence: long used to the amphitheater, he knows how to "perceive those nuances which distinguish women" (63). For indeed, "It is not only through the uterus that woman is what she is; she is such in her whole constitution. From head to foot, outside and inside, whatever part of the body you examine, you will find that she is everywhere the same. Everywhere will you find that her tissues and her organs differ from the same tissues and organs in a man" (63). But one need not be an anat-omist, since the difference is perfectly clear on the surface:

What a difference already in outward appearance, between this elegant and pretty figure and that tall and vigorously built body; between these graceful and round lines and those bones and muscles harshly revealed! What a difference between these soft and delicate features, and those protuberances, rough and vigorous, and those profound depressions. Doesn't her delicate and bright complexion distinguish her from man's complexion? Doesn't her hair always distinguish her from man's hair? Isn't her hair and the floss that shades some parts of her body much more delicate and softer? Don't we find significant differences between the sweet and sentimental expression of her physiognomy and the rude, martial, and sometimes harsh or majestic appearance of man? Every part of her body shows the same differences. Every part reflects the woman in her. Brow, nose, eyes, mouth, ears, chin, cheek, everything has its singularity, everything takes the imprint of her sex. (63–64)

Brachet approaches his anatomical inquiry into woman with the imag-ination of a poet; in his hand, the surgeon's knife that uncovers the organs, the tissues, the fibers, turns easily into the writer's pen. The descriptions of the female body are redolent with epithets evoking her delicacy, her softness, or refinement. Such "complicity between aesthetics and medicine" produces indeed what Judith Butler, in her study of gen-der, calls "styles of the flesh" (139).[10]

10. For a discussion of the complicity between aesthetics and medicine, see Barbara Johnson, "Is Female to Male as Ground Is to Figure?" as well as Michèle Le Doeuff, "Les chiasmes de Pierre Roussel." On the question of the stylization of the body, Butler writes: "if the body is not a 'being,' but a variable boundary, a surface whose permeability is politically regulated, a signifying practice within a cultural field of gender hierarchy and compulsory heterosexuality, then what language is left. . . . I suggest that gendered bodies

While they try to establish the characteristic features of the female body, the medical descriptions intersect with contemporary literary representations. Some pages of Brachet's treatise seem to have been lifted out of Balzac's *La peau de chagrin* or *Le lys dans la vallée*.[11] This is a common feature of our doctors' works. Not only does their language mime that of literary descriptions, but they often borrow their prime clinical examples from fiction or mythology. These hysterical women go by the names Cleopatra, Lucretia, Phèdre, or Clarissa. Fictional creatures and cases drawn from the doctor's practice belong to one single descriptive project; they are part of a "generalized continuum which collectively produces the category 'woman'" (Solomon-Godeau, 236). That it should be possible to relate these texts on hysteria to Abigail Solomon-Godeau's study of erotic photography reveals to what extent Brachet and his colleagues drew on the conventions of nineteenth-century representation.[12] If woman as a unified concept exists, as she insistently does in these texts on hysteria, it is as a uniform, unified type. Thus Brachet can write: "Women seem to have been thrown into one common mould: among them one comes across a much more restricted variety of constitutions than among men. The exceptions are a mistake of nature" (64). Not surprisingly then, the doctor's search for the significant differences constitutive of "woman" both relies on and produces an amazing number of clichés. Scientific observation, from surface to depth into the inmost recesses of her anatomy, (re)produces the nineteenth-century topoi of what constitutes femininity. The treatise on hysteria looks increasingly like an *étude de moeurs*, a manual of hygiene or a treatise on morality. Science gives way to myth.

This close and spontaneous association of body and mind, a body that is intimately scanned by the anatomist's gaze and a mind scrutinized for its *affections morales*, is related to the emergence of a psychological discourse on the subject.[13] But more importantly, as Judith Butler sug-

---

are so many 'styles of the flesh.' These styles are never fully self-styled, for styles have a history, and those histories condition and limit the possibilities" (*Gender Trouble*, 139).

11. This represents, as Anthony Mortimer has reminded me, a case of reciprocal influences, and the reverse applies as well: Balzac was fascinated by medicine and often used medical metaphors in his own fiction.

12. See Abigail Solomon-Godeau's *Photography at the Dock: Essays on Photographic History, Institution, and Practices*, in particular, "Reconsidering Erotic Photography: Notes for a Project of Historical Salvage," which belongs to the section of the book titled "Photography and Sexual Difference."

13. The term *moral* in the context of nineteenth-century psychiatry can be devoid of ethical connotations. It refers merely to "what belongs to the soul, in opposition to what belongs to the physical aspect" (*Littré*); it is synonymous with *mental, physique* (*Trésors*

gests, this "psychological core" appears to be linked to the notions of "the ineffable interiority of [the subject's] sex and its true identity" (136). Given the systematic and repetitive nature of the doctors' descriptions, a brief overview will suffice. Voisin, who confines himself to a few general observations on anatomy, attributes to the female character the very same features of delicacy, softness, and grace that Brachet saw in the woman's body. Likewise Briquet, who tends to emphasize the moral aspect of the illness, resorts to a vocabulary that can be ascribed indifferently to external, physical traits and moral, psychological aspects. However, the descriptions of anatomy and physiology are increasingly related to an emerging psychological sphere, while the etiology of the disease is ascribed to some inner, mental causes. When Virey and Brachet insist on examining hysteria from a scientific perspective, they nevertheless end up reproducing, in the languages of anatomy and physiology, what are in fact its "moral" features. Whereas Voisin, who seems more interested in the "spiritual intimacy" of woman, speaks the language of sensibility and of Rousseau: "While my predecessors have been impressed by the striking qualities of woman, they have not given enough consideration to her sensibility, the natural violence of her feelings and of her inclinations, the predicaments of her social position . . . ; in one word, they have not read deeply enough into her heart; they have not unveiled its secrets, seen its agitations and torments, and, because of their ignorance of this *inner moral situation*, they have looked elsewhere for the causes of these nervous illnesses," (131, emphasis mine). Thirty years later, Pierre Briquet grapples with the etiology of hysteria by probing relentlessly into woman's "inner moral situation" and asking for the stories of her unhappiness. By 1859 the "female malady" is indeed firmly anchored in the psychological sphere.[14]

Meanwhile, in the remaining observations on the physiology of woman, the drift toward speculation has become very apparent. Not that physiology produces knowledge about sexual difference; on the contrary, the fantasies born from a collective imagination of femininity sustain the errancies of the physiological inquiry. Brachet, for example, affirms, but cannot demonstrate, that the female nervous system is more impressionable so that the delicate nervous fiber of a woman "receives an influence that is quicker, more active and delicate, but also less strong

---

de la langue française). In the medical context, the term owes its popularity to Pierre Cabanis's study *Rapports du physique et du moral de l'homme* published in 1808. This *médecine morale* is discussed more fully, through a literary example, in Chapter 5.

14. I borrowed this phrase from Elaine Showalter's groundbreaking study, *The Female Malady: Women, Madness, and English Culture, 1830–1980.*

and deep" (*Traité de l'hystérie*, 66). The idea is soon made into a principle so that he can adduce an impressive congeries of arguments: woman's impressionability is the source of her lymphatic temper, of a noticeable difference in her excretory functions, it makes her reach her full development earlier and have "rounder, softer and more delicate curves" (67). "Everybody knows," writes Brachet, "how easily the tears flow in a woman, how her perspiration and her cutaneous secretions come easily and abundantly, how quick her digestion is, because of the ready formation of gastric juice and of the more immediate secretion of her spleen. How finally the secreted urines seem to press and accumulate in her bladder to be evacuated more readily" (67). On the strength of such "observations," situated in a nebulous zone between physiology and the theory of emotions, Brachet comes to his decisive point: "you will see how both sensibility and mobility are different in the woman from what they are in the man. . . . Since we are so to speak immersed in an atmosphere of incitations of all kinds, the effect in woman is that her cerebral *appareil sensitif* is constantly active, that it continually receives strong impressions, that its life, in short, is only made of sensations, it is a real life of sensations" (68).[15] And he concludes, having asserted that this is why "painting and especially music have such a powerful sway over her," that "in man the intelligence comes first, and the impression second" (72), whereas "sensibility constitutes the whole of woman" (75).

"What is the state of a nervous system that is capable of such burning sensibility?" Virey asked in 1834 in the middle of his treatise, *De la femme sous ses rapports physiologique, moral et littéraire*, which deals abundantly with hysteria. This question still haunted Brachet in 1847; he tackled it at the end of his chapter "Etudes du physique et du moral de la femme." If one admits that women have a natural predisposition toward hysteria, he asks, why are they not all hysterical? Medical science is not yet able to answer such a question (which, he claims, is of "une haute physiologie pathologique") with a demonstration. But the conviction remains that, inscribed in the physiological processes, there must be a difference (*une modification*) that can account for this natural, almost spontaneous evolution from femininity into pathology. What such reasoning makes apparent, of course, is that while women are characterized

15. Or should one say "her life" rather than "its life"? The grammatical ambiguities of Brachet's prose make it impossible to distinguish if the phenomenon characterizes woman as a whole, or only a physiological process. The scientific description may be no more than a decoy destined to confirm the received opinion that "woman" equals "sensations."

by a modification, they can only figure as an exception or an accident in a system whose norm is the masculine. According to Brachet, "We shall then admit as a demonstrated fact that woman presents a special physiological modification of her nervous system, and especially of her cerebral nervous system; that she owes to this modification the differences that she presents in the exercise of this function, in her intelligence and in her character. We can then conclude that her greater predisposition toward hysteria is due to this modification, whereas hypochondria would typically be a man's lot" (*Traité de l'hystérie*, 96–97). In fact, the physiological cause of hysteria and of femininity (for so neat is their alignment that one can be substituted for the other) remains obscure and ungraspable. But against such uncertainties Brachet offers a single, resounding statement, "l'hystérie, c'est la femme," which succeeds in addressing the medical question (it is women—and not men usually—who are hysterical) as well as the sexual ideology (women are, by nature, hysterical). Mapped onto sexual difference, mental illnesses can be symmetrically divided: Brachet's treatise on hysteria finds its counterpart in his study on hypochondria, a masculine complaint.

In 1859 Briquet took up the same challenge and concluded with similarly ambiguous results, as a closer examination of his arguments shows. The following pronouncement relies on a problematic confusion between nature, represented by "l'encéphale de la femme," and culture, in the guise of a "destinée providentielle": "It is well established that there exists in the brain a portion that is destined to the affective passions; now, because of the social destination that has been assigned to her, in woman this portion is endowed with a quicker sensibility than that of man. From the liveliness of this sensibility derives a mode of reaction which is also particular to woman and which, whenever an impression on that portion of the brain has been either too strong or too painful, manifests itself in reactions which are also peculiar to her" (395). From the impersonal phrase "it is well established" (similar to Brachet's earlier formulation "everybody knows"), down to the slippery logical alignment, every rhetorical move of such a paragraph points to the confusions of the argument. In the guise of etiology, the science of hysteria can often do no better than confirm its own assumptions and prejudices.

Yet the seven hundred pages of Pierre Briquet's *Traité clinique et thérapeutique de l'hystérie* surely represent a monument of a positivist science. As a physician working in the Hôpital de la Charité, he and his assistants compiled statistics on 430 cases. He emphasizes in his treatise the etiology of the illness, which is skillfully organized along the main categories of *causes prédisposantes* and *causes déterminantes*, and, unlike his predecessors, Briquet kept his work free from literary contamination. He seemed to have read every traditional source on the subject, from Hippocrates to Galen, and was also well acquainted with the theories of his contemporaries. Confirmation for his hypotheses was sought among his partners, the urban family doctors: he was indeed determined to avoid the pitfalls of a traditional scholarly approach and to rely on observation and experience. But his magnum opus demonstrates little beyond the fact that the hysteric suffers from her propensity or her predisposition toward suffering. Since hysteria results from the coincidence between a developed sensibility and some particular circumstance or situation destined to affect it, and since women are by nature more sensitive (Briquet likes to use the word *impressionable*), then hysteria is necessarily connected to the female condition:

In order to fulfill the great and noble mission devolved upon her, it was indispensable that [woman] be endowed with a great susceptibility to affective impressions [*impressions affectives*], that she be able somehow to feel everything in herself, and unfortunately, here as in everything else, the good can also produce evil, hysteria thus comes from this great susceptibility to affections. Let us imagine a man endowed with the faculty of being affected in the same way as a woman, he would become hysterical and consequently unfit for his predestined role, namely, that of protection and of strength. Hysteria in a man means the overthrow of the laws constitutive of our society. (101)

The opinion of our four doctors can be summarized as follows: Hysteria: *cause prédisposante* = femininity, *cause déterminante* = excess of emotion. "La femme est faite pour sentir et sentir c'est presque l'hystérie" (woman's destiny is to feel, but to feel is almost hysteria, 50), writes Briquet, and not surprisingly, he finds that one out of four women is affected by the disease. At this point, nineteenth-century hysteria looks very much like a parody of femininity. The cases of hysteria detected in men are very rare (one out of a hundred, Brachet claims [*Traité de l'hystérie*, 492]), and they are invariably ascribed to a process of feminization due to a faulty education or a defective constitution; it is such a short step from femininity to hysteria that in a man the illness can only be an aberration or else the sign of degeneracy. Thus Brachet writes: "This is why the man who is feminized by some constitutive predisposition, whether innate or acquired, by his education, by some prolonged or special illness, by a languid and overtly sentimental life, by excessive sensual pleasures, and so on, this is why, I say, this man who seems to have eyes, feet and hands only *ad honores* will be liable to experience

hysteria" (98).[16] Indeed, the nineteenth-century study of hysteria participates in a conceptualization of a radical difference between the sexes,
seemingly grounded in anatomical and physiological knowledge but in
fact based on moral and cultural assumptions. This difference must be
present from birth: Brachet denounces Rousseau's conviction that "in
childhood there was no sex" (*Traité de l'hystérie*, 65). Although education or surroundings may exert some influence, the determining factor
of hysteria consists in being female. When the whole of the woman's
body bespeaks her propensity toward the illness, the discourse on hysteria all too easily enters into a circular logic, which plays off hysteria
against femininity. Woman "is" her anatomy and her physiology, and
beyond the aberrations, corruptions, and pathology that threaten her
undoing, she remains herself, that is, as nature made her. "La femme
reste femme" (76), writes Brachet, and "in spite of their efforts and
their energetic style, one finds confirmation of the woman in Mme Rol-
land, Mme Deffant, in Mme Staël [*sic*], and even in this George Sand
who appears to be ashamed of the sex that she should have honored"
(73).

Such a belief defines the scope and the intent of the *médecine morale*
that was professed by Voisin, Virey, Brachet, and Briquet: "true medicine in the case of women always consists in reinstating the order of
nature" (*De la femme*, 74) writes Virey. Once he has described the illness
and explored its causes, the doctor must find the necessary remedies to
bring woman back to herself ("rendre la femme à elle-même"), to her
own sphere and to her natural state or condition ("à son naturel").
Brachet presents in his concluding remarks what looks like a radical
prophylactic: "one needs then, from very early on, to instruct the young
girl to be what she is, and to be it fully: this is the only way to prepare
for her a life of calm and to ensure that she will be happy" (*Traité de
l'hystérie*," 497).

"Does being female constitute a 'natural fact' or a cultural performance, or is 'naturalness' constituted through discursively constrained performative acts that produce the body through and within the categories
of sex?" asks Judith Butler in the first pages of *Gender Trouble* (x). The
preceding pages, with their emphasis on the systems of knowledge that
defined or produced the nineteenth-century hysteric, appear to provide
an indirect answer to this question.

---

16. Brachet used the phrase "avoir l'hystérie," as one would say "avoir la gale" or
"avoir la fièvre." This suggests that while women *are* hysterical, men catch hysteria like a
foreign body or infection.

An Inextricable Maze

"Who will sound these impenetrable abysses, who will pursue the secret windings of this inextricable maze made of whims, dissimulation and fickle will, where a quick, exalted sensibility plays and, more mobile than the air, is not always certain of its own determinations? When man is so ignorant of his own heart, how could woman know herself better? and what woman has ever confessed all her secrets?" (170). This resounding question, which prefaces the chapter of Voisin's book titled "De la femme morale," can only be rhetorical. The answer is implicit: who but a man endowed with the penetrating, perspicuous mind that characterizes the practitioner of the *médecine morale*. The reverberations of such a statement are still felt in Freud's infamous introductory words to his lecture on femininity,[17] which Luce Irigaray rephrases, shrewdly: "It would be a question for you, men, of talking amongst yourselves, as men, about woman, who cannot be interested in a discourse concerning the enigma, the logogriph, which she represents for you. The mystery that woman *is* will then constitute the *aim*, the *object* and *the stakes* of a male discourse, of a debate among men, which she would not question, which would not concern her. And, ultimately, why would she want to know about it?" (9). If woman indeed does not know herself, her mystery draws, inexhaustibly, the doctor's science and curiosity. Thus Brachet echoes, in his treatise on hysteria: "woman is an inexhaustible topic and one that is maybe impenetrable, both from a moral and from a physical perspective" (62). However, what distinguishes the nineteenth-century form of this scientific presumption with its gendered structuration, where "she" is the object to which "he" applies his lens (which still resounds in the Freud of the 1930s), is the openness with which the claims are stated. The inquiry into the feminine is explicitly presented in light of a project that is both scientific and moralistic, descriptive and prescriptive. Later versions skillfully evade the ideological and cultural presuppositions that inform their similar undertakings. When the nineteenth-century physician explores the mysteries of wom-

---

17. "Throughout history people have knocked their heads against the riddle of the nature of femininity. . . . Nor will *you* have escaped worrying over this problem—those of you who are men, to those of you who are women this will not apply—you are yourselves the problem" (Freud, *New Introductory Lectures ou Psycho-Analysis, SE* XXII, 114). In her critical reading of this passage, Felman writes, "His question: 'What is femininity?' in reality asks: 'What is femininity—*for men?*' " (*What Does a Woman Want?* 43). My own close reading of nineteenth-century descriptions of hysteria confirms the truth of this axiom, and the gist of Felman's discussion titled "The Riddle of Femininity" (41–43) provides an illuminating subtext to my own commentary.

an's hysteria, he presents himself in the guise of the moralist, intent on indicting, in the paroxysmic form of femininity that the illness expresses, the weaknesses that lurk dangerously in every female. Voisin considered himself a historian of humankind, and Brachet made high claims for himself as a practitioner. Both faced the mysterious depths of the female subject with a moralist's eye. Yet this *médecine morale*, while normative and dogmatic in its intent, involves methods that open up new fields of investigation that are best described as psychological. This critical inquiry can shift therefore from the delineations of hysteria in a constructed body to trace a psychological model that emerges as the doctor probes the imagined depths of woman's mind.

As it became a disease of the cerebral parts or the nervous system, hysteria acquired mental and spiritual characteristics, and entered the field of language. The new *médecine morale* encouraged verbal encounters between the doctor and the patient; our physicians often projected themselves in the role of interlocutors predestined to answer the patient's verbalized complaint. They strongly recommended that the physician listen to his patient: the story of her complaint would offer evidence for the particular *affections morales* or the general *impressionabilité* that lay at the source of the illness. But this exploration into the contradictory and troubling aspects of the feminine soul required some caution: it should not disturb the established picture of femininity. Her complaint needed, for instance, to be validated by the visual observation of her symptoms. Whatever the discoveries, they must be interpreted in light of one central conception, which held that woman is a creature of purity and suffering. The symptoms of hysteria could then be adduced to confirm the validity of this construct.

But hysteria has always had a bad name, so this task was not simple. This explains the doctors' recourse to a dissociated structure, where the negative pole is held by woman's susceptibility to strong passions and the positive by the ideal of purity and chastity that she also embodies. The illness thus shows the struggle of the proper lady against the monster and eventually becomes a compromise formation: woman is essentially pure but is subjected to emotions that appeal to her senses; hysteria reveals the violence done to her mind by her emotions. It testifies to the acuity with which her pure mind experiences and registers the strong or disturbing emotions which result from her innate impressionability. "What a mysterious being! She is an angel, she is a tiger!" Brachet exclaims (*Traité de l'hystérie*, 83), and, he adds, she may show such passion, violence, or even cruelty that she is "revolting in her obscenities" (82). The violent and grotesque images that describe the hysteric's symptoms are but the underside of the anatomist's lyrical language. This is how Virey describes a seizure of epileptic hysteria: "During the hideous paroxysms of the illness, the sick creature rolls on the floor, while the eye rolls in its orbit: she shrieks, or rather she howls, she produces a foamy saliva, and struggles with such violence that several men can hardly contain her. In the midst of these horrible scenes, the belly is tense, noisy, as if the genital organ were expressing loudly its contractions and its aches: there are frequent eructations, and after a considerable time sometimes, the patient seems to emerge as if from some deep somnambulistic sleep" (*De la femme*, 103). Brachet does not fail to notice that, as a display of femininity, this kind of scene is singularly lacking in poetry: "Nothing depoeticizes woman more than those furors which estrange her from herself" (83). For Virey, on the other hand, it seems that the hysterical body, so expressive and so alive, holds a secret attraction, which is conveyed in a poetic prose filled with alliterations: "un démon secret s'agite, pour ainsi dire, dans les entrailles, et titille des ovaires gonflés d'une liqueur luxuriante" (a secret demon stirs, so to speak, in her entrails and titillates her ovaries, which are swollen with a rich liquor, [*De la femme*, 91]). Such a passage, almost untranslatable in its figurative and phonetic evocations, inevitably suggests that some inexpressible pleasure can be found in the contemplation and imaginative re-creation of the hysteric's bodily display. It conjures up, in the guise of medical description, the scene of a seduction. For the pursuit of hysteria owes as much to intellectual ambition as it does to a veiled desire inevitably present in these encounters where the two sexes meet: the lady hysteric, the male doctor.

But this is only a passing stage. Such illicit pleasures are gradually relinquished in favor of the sober lines of a descriptive prose which prevents such lyrical flights: Brachet and Briquet confront the symptoms of hysteria with the help of dry, methodical clinical charts. They are convinced that a more rigorous and learned analysis of the symptoms should enhance the understanding of an illness that, despite the more common and old-fashioned assumptions, is not due to sensuality, but owes everything to woman's sensibility and virtue. The claims of Brachet and Briquet for a serious, positivistic science lead them to privilege the image of an angelic woman against that of a *femina sensualis* depraved by her sensual passions. Brachet recommends at the end of his treatise that doctors avoid using the word "hysteria" in front of their patients, for "it seems to indicate either a disreputable cause or else depraved tastes, they must not utter the word and should use instead such expressions as nervous illness, vapors, etc." (513). Briquet, who has striven throughout his work to show that hysteria cannot be connected to the genital parts, expresses relief when it turns out that his patients let him into "secrets that are not shameful" (633). Whereas Larousse's first edition of *Grand dictionnaire universel* (1865–76) still linked hysteria and lust ("un appétit vénérien excessif"), the supplement published twenty years later, whose new authorities were Brachet and Briquet, divested the illness of its erotic connotations.

Woman's general propensity toward hysteria was ascribed, it will be recalled, to the very substance of her body, while the source of the illness was located in some nobler part of her organization, such as the nervous system or the brain. The seeming confusion between these two theories gets subsumed under an image of the body that is no longer sensual, but has become a moralized and psychologized entity. Hysteria offers indeed a way of reconciling these superficial contradictions: the hysteric bears in the flesh a transcription of her spiritual qualities, and her symptoms are the visible trace of the affects that are in excess of what she, the woman (or should one say "it," her pure mind?), can contain, process, or suppress. The kinds of semiological analyses that might detect in her symptoms the marks of sensual depravation are sedulously avoided in favor of sublimating visions that emphasize the features of sexual difference without referring to the sexed body. It then becomes possible to argue that hysteria results from a profound sensibility (Voisin, 101, 131), an extreme delicacy of feelings and nerves that are very impressionable (Briquet, 48, 101), or the predominance of feelings over ideas (Virey, *De la femme*, 175). The disease must be taken as the mark of this "affective superiority" that characterizes woman (Brachet, *Traité de l'hystérie*, 74); it is in fact the very token of her moral sense, of a "painful struggle between the inclinations of nature and the rigorous duties prescribed by morality and religion" (Voisin, 36).

As I have suggested, the desire to exculpate woman from her sexuality in this fashion is most apparent in Brachet and Briquet. Virey's theories, on the other hand, which are less hampered by the need to moralize woman and emphasize her sexual passion and her inclinations toward erotic fantasies, would fit quite smoothly in the picture of hysteria that Freud first drew in *Studies on Hysteria*.

Woman is perhaps even more than man under the sway of this erotic delirium. In her case, an inner system of extremely sensitive organs, especially during the menstrual period, a thin and slender muscular system that gives more power to the nervous system, a stricter law of modesty which, by repressing desire, only increases it, a more unpredictable imagination, a more tender heart, senses that are more delicate and hence more irritable, everything conspires to provoke, in woman, a state of exaltation that she is unable to master. . . . This is why in mental asylums there are more cases of madness due to love in women than in men. While the symptoms of hysteria disturb the health of so many women, how many other mental hysterias, that remain secret, unknown, ferment in their tender souls, provoke those violent whims, those temporary enthusiasms, those passing exaltations that others just as fugitive have replaced, caught in this never-ending fickleness. (Virey, *De la femme*, 340–41)

Virey's visions of a "mental hysteria" inhabited by sensual images preceded Brachet and Briquet by a whole generation, but the need to moralize appears to have prevailed over the earlier attempts at constituting a more complex psychological frame for the disease, one that included, for instance, notions that would later be called "sexuality" or "repression." Briquet can thus congratulate himself on finding that the modern hysteric is not swayed by the passions of Racine's Phèdre, but on the contrary must be distinguished by her virtue: "I finally recognized that hysteria was not that shameful illness whose mere name acts as a reminder . . . of the line of our great tragic poet: 'C'est Vénus tout entière à sa proie attachée,' but that is was due instead to the existence, in woman, of the most noble and admirable feelings, which she alone is capable of experiencing" (Briquet, v, quoting from Racine's *Phèdre*). The sway held by the erotic in the overall conception of hysteria can no doubt be measured by intensity of the rhetorician's defensive move, but it is in the various aspects of a prescriptive discourse articulated around hysteria that it can be highlighted more fully.

Let Woman Remain a Woman

The doctors' prescriptions can be read for the conceptions of the illness which they reveal, but they also offer precious indications concerning the "regulatory practices of gender formation and division" (Butler, 16) in the nineteenth century. A survey of the various forms of treatment and prophylactic advice adds new elements to the "categorical fictions" (32) that are adduced in the construction of a female subject. No doubt the landscape will begin to look all too familiar, but the growing boredom the reader may experience seems unavoidable. It is only by tracing the manifold logical and rhetorical moves that characterize the representations of hysteria and by recognizing the regular intervention or interference of ideological conceptions in the phenomenal and experiential approaches that one can assess the full scope of the nineteenth-century construction of gender. The emblematic figure of the *Hysterika* needs to be firmly inscribed in our minds as a point of reference; the sheer cumulative weight of evidence drawn from these medical treatises can indeed give to the models of femininity depths and shadings that will be helpful throughout this study.

The hazardous nature of the various suggested treatments betrays, meanwhile, how tenuous the hold of these theories on the phenomenon itself has remained. Since specific remedies too often had a contrary effect, the physicians tended to rely on the safer prescription of nonspecific medication: they favored anodynes and sedatives, which were to prevent or else assuage the strongest manifestations of the illness, such as hysterical seizure. For the less acute symptoms they offered mainly prophylactic advice and recommended a regular lifestyle. The hysteric was to be kept busy, preferably with manual work: it was well known that books, especially novels, or too much theater-going, or overall idleness could be fatal to the hysterical temper. Indolence was proscribed; some form of exercise, such as walks or travel, were highly recommended, the latter especially in the case of "thwarted affections." Marriage or childbearing could sometimes have miraculous effects, but did not guarantee the cure, and the prescription of these two particular remedies was on the decline.

Briquet, and he is not alone, suggests calming the hysteric through the power of the gaze ("par la force du regard"): "I have sometimes," he writes, "managed to modify convulsions *en fascinant les malades* [literally, "casting a spell over them by a look"], that is, by appealing to the methods used in magnetism, but this has only produced temporary relief, and besides not all patients can equally be influenced by such a practice" (707–8). This ocular remedy seems justified within an allopathic conception of prescription: the physician's suggestive and powerful gaze would be the natural counterpart to an illness that is defined by its opposite. The hysteric's gaze is typically blank, or unfocused, or then obsessively fixed on one object; she is often described as rolling her eyes in a wild fashion. This roving, unmastered gaze (when it is not totally absent, as when she is in some deep somnambulic sleep or experiences a seizure) typifies then her unconsciousness.[18] But not all the remedies

18. On the nineteenth-century doctor's gaze, see Juan Rigoli's excellent discussion in "Lectures aliénistes, lectures aliénées (le déchiffrement de la folie dans la psychiatrie française de la première moitié du XIXème siècle)," in particular 140, 142–43. For a discussion of the "phallic gaze" see Luce Irigaray, *Speculum*, 53–54.

The lack of consciousness (figured as the absence of the gaze) is a characteristic trait of

enlisted for the treatment of hysteria are as innocuous as a magnetic or hypnotic gaze: faradization is, for instance, still the choice treatment in cases of aphonia, and an abundance of ice-cold water under various forms is used to get rid of the illness.[19]

Nonetheless, because it is so difficult to cure hysteria, the doctors' efforts naturally went toward finding a prophylactic. It is here that the law of nature—"the woman remains a woman"—must be turned into an injunction, "woman must remain a woman." The doctor's prescriptive language cannot, however, avoid the familiar paths of circularity, clichés, and repetition. How can one ensure that a woman remains a woman, if not by conforming the woman to the constructions of a "natural femininity." The observation of a fact (but, what is a fact?) gives way to the invention or fabrication of a fiction, or else, the fiction preceding the pursuit of knowledge, the edifice of science is built on the shaky foundation of an all-encompassing, radical sexual difference. What remains true is that femininity and hysteria are the object of a joint, self-enhancing construction of femininity, whose main features are indicated below.

The first of these fictions is particularly insidious, since it associates the illness with the fatality or predicament of the female condition. While the Bible obviously lends authority to the association of woman with suffering, confirmation is also found in the lore of antiquity.[20] Brachet quotes Seneca's *pati natae* in his claim that hysteria represents no more than the natural outcome of femininity, given that woman is predestined to suffer. The reasoning appears to be the following. Woman being the weaker sex, she is quintessentially "une malade"—"femina omnen bis patitur morbum," writes Virey (*De la femme*, 85) quoting Van Helmont.

---

hysteria and epitomizes the nineteenth-century vision of femininity discussed in this book. Woman is described by Nietzsche in *The Will to Power* as "a closing of one's eyes to oneself" (quoted by Mary Ann Doane, "Veiling over Desire," 122). The question of the gaze is discussed more specifically in Chapters 5 and 6, using the examples of George Sand's Valentine and George Eliot's Gwendolen Harleth.

19. Faradization, according to *Webster's Third New International Dictionary*, is the "application of a faradic current of electricity (as for therapeutic purposes)." According to Freud's report, this treatment seems to have been used among others in the various attempts to cure "Dora" of her aphonia: "The diagnosis that this was once more a nervous complaint had been established long since; but the various methods of treatment which are usual, including hydrotherapy and the local application of electricity, had produced no results" (*SE* VII, 22). A remedy commonly recommended for aphonia was drinking a mixture of cold water and crushed ice; perhaps this is the hydrotherapy mentioned by Freud.

20. "Unto the woman he said, I will greatly multiply thy sorrow and thy conception; in sorrow thou shalt bring forth children" (Gen. 3:16).

It is well known, moreover, that she is destined to suffer by a providential decree: if her true destination is procreation, her life will naturally be dominated by the sufferings of menstruation and childbearing, which in turn justify her being more subjected to the laws of society, of opinion and conventions. It is then doubly natural that woman, who is made to suffer, should become that enigmatic object of pity, namely, a hysteric: "Our forerunners were deprived of the lights of psychology, it is possible too that they have not observed with sufficient attention: otherwise, far from considering that woman is essentially born for happiness, they would have seen in her a creature not exactly predestined to all kinds of misfortune, but nevertheless worthy of inspiring, in so many respects and in a large number of circumstances, the strongest interest and the most affectionate pity" (Voisin, 132–33). Voisin's vague and confused description testifies to one certain fact, namely, his desire to recognize in the female condition the markings of some innate suffering. Elsewhere it is woman's higher susceptibility to the *affections morales* that gets enlisted: she is endowed with a particular tenderness and sensibility, so that "all the wretched belong to her: devoted to the oppressed and the weak, she shares their affections, she endorses their sufferings, she will walk to the scaffold with the victim; and contented with such sacrifices, she asks for no sweeter reward than to be loved" (Virey, *De la femme*, 171). At the same time she is more susceptible to bodily pain, not only because procreation is her fate, but because everything in her constitution makes her liable suffer, as Briquet attempts to demonstrate in vivid terms:

If from the moral sphere one moves to the physical, one sees that a woman is extremely impressionable in all the parts of her body: the smallest disturbance will give her a migraine, light that is too bright hurts her eye, the sight of a disgusting object makes her shiver; smells that are too strong make her faint, foods that are too spicy makes her sick, strong drinks burn her throat and her stomach. Touch her roughly, and her skin will be bruised and she will feel pain, if the air is charged with emanations or electricity she will suffocate, she can hardly stand heat or cold. Women are so prone to sensations that you will hardly ever find one who will not, on some strong emotion, experience oppression in the epigastrium, a feeling of suffocation and stifling, constriction in the throat, discomfort and agitation in her limbs, tears and sobs. (48)

Thus, in the female body, sensations are immediately converted into symptoms, and hysteria is but an intensification of the experience of femininity. If woman is sensitive in the extreme and if hysteria is a form of extreme sensitivity, then hysteria is being a woman. It is a haunting thought that a sizable number of cases of hysteria may well have been diagnosed on no better evidence than that which is epitomized by such a syllogism.

Once it has been understood that hysteria is attuned to the woman's "providential" bodily afflictions, and she deserves above all understanding and sympathy, it becomes easier to offer prophylactic advice meant to alleviate the burden and the dangers inherent in her condition. She must first be kept away from excessive stimulations: violent passions, too much excitement, or unseasonable emotions must be avoided at all costs. A regulated life (*une vie réglée*) is a favorite expression. Part of that rule involves the sedulous avoidance of any form of activity that might tax her mind since her body naturally deserves the utmost attention: "one must avoid leading her astray in the deep study of the sciences, in the dark maze of metaphysics or among the dusty shelves of erudition" writes Brachet as a warning (*Traité de l'hystérie*, 502). Indeed, if woman is herself a labyrinth destined for his conquests, the unraveling of its paths and the exploration of its depths must remain the doctor's privilege.

The woman's predestined need for privacy and intimacy offers further justifications for these injunctions. Indeed, in that great chain of a feminine being that can be deciphered in the nineteenth-century discourse on hysteria there are few discrepancies, and overdetermination is the rule. Thus woman's different anatomy is also invoked to explain the necessity for such an inward turn: just as "nature has drawn to her inside her most secret organs" (Virey, *De la femme*, 69), she is necessarily a secret being, destined to the more intimate pleasures of the home and hearth. And Virey explains further: "Since everything in man must aspire to open and to extend outward since the warmth and the vigor of his sex imposes on him this law of expansion on a physical and on a moral level, everything in woman must concur somehow toward the closing, the gathering of her affections, her thoughts, her actions around one focal point,[21] which is that of reproduction and the raising of a family. This truth is not owned by our institutions, nature proclaims it" (181). Indeed the conventional wisdom of Thomas Gray's "many a flower is born to blush unseen" is also part of French medical thought, where it seems to conjure up not only images of secrecy, intimacy, and interiority but also the need for surveillance. Woman, the same doctor writes, is

---

21. The word for "focus" and "hearth" is the same in French; the pun is evocative, but untranslatable.

"a fresh-blown flower that is afraid of opening to the burning midday sun," destined to resist relentlessly "the obsession of the outside" (Virey, 69). While Brachet echoes:

Private instruction is necessary to women, whose existence, like that of a violet, must enfold modestly in obscurity. . . . In spite of the most active surveillance, young girls educate each other in those things about which they should long have remained in ignorance. These vivid imaginations, so keen on impressions, so curiously eager for any forbidden things . . . will not miss any opportunity to learn about love [*des choses de l'amour*]. . . . This is how chastity, innocence, moral virginity are lost, moral virginity this sweet flower, this delicious fragrance without which physical virginity will leave us later with only the body of a woman. (*Traité de l'hystérie*, 508–9).[22]

The concern expressed here speaks unambiguously of an enterprise of definition of the female subject, that under the guise of medical advice reveals a general cultural anxiety concerning not only women's bodies, but the state of their minds. The privilege of knowing, and especially of knowing about the sexual, the erotic, and, one assumes, about the facts of sexual difference, must remain within the male province. As for the other sex, it must be protected, body and soul or rather body and mind, from the contamination of outside knowledge. Hysteria is a disease related to the affections and the sensations, and to woman's general sensibility, and in order to ward off an always threatening propensity to respond too strongly to affects, a ban is put on imagination, impression, curiosity. No illicit conversations, no reading that might stimulate the imagination or could leave strong impressions other than religious or moral, or that might encourage a (natural) curiosity. The remedies destined to ward off hysteria are the same as those that are invoked when it comes to keeping her virtue untainted: nothing like a happy ignorance!

22. I quote the passage in full as an example of Brachet's literary vein; it could be related as well to my discussion "Between Women" in Chapter 4: "In spite of the most active surveillance, girls will teach each other certain things which they should never know. Those lively imaginations, so eager for impressions and so curious about anything forbidden, and the more excited for being brought together, will not miss a single opportunity to learn about love [*les choses de l'amour*]. If one of them knows something and has lifted a corner of the mysterious veil, she becomes the others' governess. Their secret little chats, their caresses, which seem so naive, those virginal delicacies [*friandises*] and their pussy-like play [*chateries*] that Balzac talks about, rouse and develop their senses too early. This almost always leads the girls to be acquainted with some illicit pleasures which are the beginning of depravation. This is how they lose their chastity and innocence, and also their moral virginity, this sweet flower, this delicious fragrance, in the absence of which physical virginity will give you merely the body of a woman"(*Traité de l'hystérie*, 509).

The threat may come from outside: Brachet dwells complacently on the dangers of female friendships. Servants, governesses, and bad company generally are also under accusation (*Traité de l'hystérie*, 509). But the danger seems to be lurking inside as well: the notion of a female sensibility is synonymous with imagination, and "the sufferings of hysteria" are but the offsprings of a "delirious imagination" (Virey, *De la femme*, 82). Such a conception lies behind the overall condemnation of books, and the doxa can be summarized as follows: the immoderate consumption of novels is the secret cause of those disorders of the imagination that lead to hysteria. In the name of realism Voisin condemns "the reading of those books that exalt a certain kind of passions, feed the mind with illusion and ideas that contradict the real state of society" (137). Virey fears that the young woman might confuse her desires with the fiction of novels—while he himself feels free to invoke the shade of Richardson: "It is most urgent to eliminate anything that might irritate this sensibility and encourage its extravagant whims. At such a time, novels, even those that are of the purest morality, give fuel to her burning passions; the heart is indeed still so naive! . . . Happy this new Clarissa if she can avoid the wiles of an enterprising Lovelace" (82). Taking Mme de Staël as his authority, Brachet attempts to set down the rule for woman's education in such a way that the dangers of science (physical and metaphysical) and of the novel may be simultaneously avoided. She must be neither totally ignorant nor a bluestocking, else "nervous illnesses will just begin to pour down on her" (505). Everything must conspire to bring her back to "nature's aim," which lies in the expression of her true femininity; under the guise of prophylactic advice on hysteria Brachet sketches out a pedagogical project specifically designed to ensure woman's subservience to "her duties:"

You must give the young girl an education, do not feed her with shameful ignorance which later would be her shame. Rousseau was wrong in neglecting her too much. But be sure to enclose this education within fair boundaries so that she will always be brought back to nature's goal. Tell her often, in Mme de Staël's words, that *her first destination is less the exercise of her intellectual faculties than the accomplishment of her duties.* Do not allow her any other reading than that of useful and interesting works. Woe to the young girl who devours novels before she has known the world! Her excited imagination deceives her and leads her astray, and she creates a world that will cause her many disappointements. Besides, as Mme de Staël also says, the theater and novels leave no room in the mind for historical facts nor do they leave room in the heart for the wretched. (505)

The emphasis falls indeed on what turns out to be the first axiom for the nineteenth-century pedagogical project for women: the denial of the intellect and the substitution of an external imperative, called "duty." The edification of conscience as against the development of consciousness. All the elements in the construction of femininity that can be traced around hysteria conspire to promote one major division in the grammar of the sexes, where "she" is defined as affect, passion, emotion and "he" is endowed with the prerogatives of knowledge, mind, and reason. The kinds of maxims Brachet delivers here are indeed sustained by the confident though unspoken assumption that the phenomenon of hysteria must be tackled within the traditional frame of woman's passion and man's reason. And if hysteria means an excess of passion's irrational powers, it must necessarily be opposed by the force of the doctor's superior male reason. Such a plot seems familiar enough.

Our treatises on hysteria, however, also reveal another, less obvious story which shows that it would be a mistake to rely on this simple opposition. For in truth the hysteric does have a mind, and moreover she is, according to our doctors, endowed with a set of qualities and abilities that might enable her to avoid hysteria, even when her "whole nature" makes her prone to incur its ravages. It is her innate or acquired modesty (*la pudeur*) which gives woman the ability to keep at bay the excesses that her feminine nature is liable to incur. Armed with her modesty, she holds promises other than the mere passivity of a victim under the sway of her female condition. For the nineteenth-century doctor, modesty represents then the natural antidote to hysteria; it intervenes, as a restraining force, when her nature threatens to exceed its bounds and begins to acquire pathological traits. As such it provides an interesting counterpart to the text of woman's passion, emotions, and affects that we have deciphered so far, for as it defines her ability to protect herself from or to resist the invasion of a forbidden sexual knowledge or experience, it becomes in effect the repository of a discourse about sexuality. Although modesty is recognizable above all in its behavioral or physical manifestations, it is defined, unlike hysteria, mainly as a feature of the mind. A closer examination of modesty will thus enable us to focus on the scenarios of engendering articulated around the question of (sexual) knowledge.

Drawing the Veil

Under the rubric *pudeur*, Larousse's *Grand dictionnaire universel du XIXème siècle* gives the etymology of the word, derived from the Sanskrit *pad* meaning "fear, what makes one flee," and offers as a first definition "sentiment of fear or timidity that one experiences with things that are contrary to decency." *Pudeur* is thus the name given to a subjective reaction characterized by a physical response (flight) and a mental impression (fear) that arise in the presence of indecency—those unnamed "things" of the sex and the body.[23] It resembles hysteria in that it too involves simultaneously a corporeal process and a mental, moral, or psychological reaction. Through a bodily sign which eludes language, it registers, like hysteria, some inner experience pertaining to the mental sphere. But unlike the hysteria of our nineteenth-century doctors, which was increasingly detached from the sexual body, *pudor* is explicitly connected to the sexual domain and is about the subject's insertion and intervention in the field of sexual representations. It signals the subject's withdrawal or desired exemption from the scene of passion or seduction; in other words, what it expresses is the fear or repression of sexuality.

Pudor is a feminine virtue: it is the instrument of the regulation of desire, which has been providentially entrusted to women. It was of crucial importance in the nineteenth century, following a trend which, Ian Watt argues, was defined in the preceding century: "the eighteenth century witnessed a tremendous narrowing of the ethical scale, a definition of virtue in primarily sexual terms" (57). In the nineteenth century, pudor had become an inherently feminine behavior—somewhat

23. This term has no exact equivalent in English. Both "modesty" and "shame" have strong other connotations which *pudeur* does not include: the former carries the general sense of moderation or, more specifically, freedom from vanity, whereas the latter evokes a consciousness of guilt, error, or misdemeanor that is situated in the wider context of social, intersubjective relations (one can be ashamed for somebody else, but *pudeur* can only be a personal emotion). This is why I have, in most cases, translated the French term into English as "pudor"; the decision to use the obsolete English term may be the cause of some stylistic awkwardness, but it enables me to be more precise in my definition of *pudeur* and the allied term *pudicité*.

The ambiguity of the English terminology is discussed by Ruth Yeazell in *Fictions of Modesty: Women and Courtship in the English Novel*. She quotes Havelock Ellis's comment in "The Evolution of Modesty" on the distinction that French makes between *modestie* and *pudeur*, but expresses her belief that the terminological question is more complex, because of the changes that necessarily occur in an *histoire du sentiment* (240, n. 10). In her discussion of Roussel, Michèle Le Doeuff writes: "Ce terme de la pudeur nous ramène à la question du sexe," and she emphasizes in a note that this eighteenth-century physician uses the term in a very modern and precise sense, namely, in a specifically sexual context ("Chiasmes de Pierre Roussel," 194–95). I discovered these two studies too late in my work to be influenced by them, but the convergence between my own inquiry and theirs should not go unnoticed: it testifies to some mysterious pattern in the history of ideas which has set the American critic, the French philosopher, and the Swiss author on similar tracks.

paradoxically, however, since the model of a femininity swayed by sensations and incapable of rational or mental control leaves women hardly any space for taking action or initiative. But in fact, the medical descriptions define it in such a way as to deprive it of what might be its conscious, controlled aspects: it is presented as a reaction, like an innate and thus unconscious response to a negative stimulus. It works then as a negation, which takes the form of a bodily gesture or attitude, and is directed against an external event or some inner experience defined by its sexual nature; it represents the simultaneous acknowledgment and denial of the sexual body. As a logical counterpart to hysteria and, for our doctors, a recognized antidote, pudor enables us to supplement with new aspects the figure of *femina psychologica* which we traced in the medical dicussions on hysteria.

With hysteria's counterpart, there arises the question of woman's relation to passion and to knowledge, and also that of her subjective stance as a creature capable of action and reaction. The developments and modifications of the notion of *pudeur* that can be traced in the work of our four doctors (and are also recorded in the changing dictionary definitions) show how the abstract, often allegorized virtue is turned into a mental feature that defines woman's ability to protect herself from the dangerous internal or external impressions that might provoke hysterical symptoms. Pudor is perceived as a mode of action and corresponds to a more or less self-willed subjective stance, when hysteria seems to hold woman passively in the sway of her general feminine impressionability. It involves the notions of negation, denial, or erasure, while in the case of hysteria, the emphasis falls on the display of symptoms and turns the body into a spectacle. And yet the silencing entailed by pudor must somehow be understood as representing woman's knowledge and action, while the hysteria, in spite of its seemingly active manifestations, is, as we saw repeatedly, the sign of her passive submission to the ills of her condition and to the doctor's science. This chiasmic structure, characteristic of the relation between hysteria and pudor, defines the relation between sex and the mind as it was conceived in the nineteenth-century models of femininity. But beyond its documentary and historical value, it determines the structure of this theoretical inquiry into questions of consciousness and gender.

Pudeur figures prominently in the texts on hysteria by Voisin, Virey, and Brachet. As a moral virtue and, increasingly, as a psychological trait, it represents a defense or weapon which, because it protects women against their passions, naturally makes them less prone to hysteria. In

Briquet's treatise, on the other hand, *pudeur* determines woman's difficulty or resistance in articulating her passions, affections, and sufferings; it no longer acts as a prophylactic but is, on the contrary, one of the possible causes of the illness. This theory, which looks forward to the early psychoanalytical models, is the object, in Chapter 5, of a more detailed discussion related to the writings of George Sand. But here I sketch out briefly the evolving model of pudor as a way of tracing further the process of interiorization that we saw at work in hysteria.

The changing definitions of the term overlap with the evolution of hysteria: it becomes, increasingly, a psychological and subjective feature characteristic of femininity, whereas before it was above all a "social virtue" providentially ascribed to women. For Voisin and Virey, at the beginning of the century, it is the manifestation of a natural law that determines woman's civilizing, restraining influence by demanding that she veil her charms and hide her erotic feelings. As a gift of providence, it bridles the passions and allows for the propagation of the species to occur with the necessary discrimination and without debasement (Virey, *De la femme*, 68–69). It is an instrument of social regulation, which creates its own system of values: the careful management and hoarding of her charms renders woman more desirable and also prevents sexual excesses.[24] Moreover, and here Virey borrows Rousseau's argument, pudor, as it puts obstacles in the way of desire, is bound to refine and ennoble the passions. Within this first conception, though it is defined as woman's prerogative, it participates in a general system of sexual regulation. With Brachet, however, it becomes a constitutive trait of femininity—a sentiment or emotion that is particular to the female subject who only knows privacy, intimacy, and secrecy. The restraint that pudor involves will take her back to her inner self: let the world (meaning the other sex) deal with passions at first hand; she will be screened off from them by her ability to resist, by her *pudeur*.

The shift in the meaning of the term is shown as well in the fact that an older term is reintroduced—*la pudicité* (pudicity)—which harks back to the original sense. *La pudicité* designates an abstract virtue independent of its historical and individual manifestations, whereas *pudeur* now corresponds to a psychological trait rendered manifest through the subject's corresponding action or bodily reaction. Here is how the *Grand*

24. On this subject, see Butler's discussion of Mary Douglas's *Purity and Danger*: "the very contours of 'the body' are established through markings that seek to establish specific codes of cultural coherence. Any discourse that establishes the boundaries of the body serves the purpose of instating and naturalizing certain taboos regarding the appropriate limits, postures, and modes of exchange" (*Gender Trouble*, 131).

dictionnaire universel du XIXème siècle defines the older virtue: "The Romans only knew *la pudicité*; they had erected altars devoted to it and used to represent it on medals in the shape of a woman of stern demeanour, clad in her *stula*. Sometimes standing, or most often sitting, she would, with her right hand, draw a veil over her face and hold across her body, in her left hand, a spear." As an abstract virtue, pudicity can be allegorized in an image borrowed from antiquity. To give it the shape of a woman is to elicit recognition through its most common form, but pudicity does not as a matter of fact rely on the notion of a gendered *subjectivity*. A comparision with another illustration provided by the dictionary, but this time of *la pudeur*, is useful. The example is modern: it refers to a painting by Greuze which shows "*la Pudeur* holding back on her naked breast a drapery that seems to be slipping from her shoulders."[25] The capitalized term refers to an image by the eighteenth-century painter, often reproduced as an engraving, and it might seem to define another allegorical representation, where the woman is but a form given to the idea. But a glance at the painting, which finds confirmation in the critical discussions of this well-known picture, shows in fact a move beyond allegory, toward the representation of a female subject involved in an act that denotes her modesty: *la pudeur*, in Greuze's depiction, characterizes the gesture of a woman who, with the help of a characteristic prop, is caught in the act of protecting her nakedness from the gaze of an implicit spectator. We are now faced with a scene where the woman appears to perform for a (desiring?) viewer, and where the sense is blurred and ambiguous: the gesture of modesty begins to resemble that of seduction. In fact, such a representation is not much different from the striking iconographical example of the *Hysterika* that Freud provides in *Hysterical Phantasies and Their Relation to Bisexuality* and uses again in *Some General Remarks on Hysterical Attacks*: the figure of an unnamed woman is on display; she holds back with one hand the garment that the other hand attempts to pull away from her body.[26] The gesture expressing pudor is a major component of the one picture that, in each text, illustrates a case of hysteria. Furthermore, the representation renders visible a "symptomatic" attitude of protection or withdrawal which corresponds implicitly to the perception of a sexed body.[27]

25. The *catalogue raisonné* of Jean-Baptiste Greuze's work offers the following description of a painting titled *La Pudeur* which was later reproduced as an engraving by Paul Rajon: "Three-quarter portrait of a girl with bared shoulders; the hands are crossed on the breast" (*Oeuvre de J. B. Greuze*, 1908).

26. These two texts are discussed in Chapter 5.

27. In her book David-Ménard analyzes in an analogous fashion (as an "alliance be-

The phenomenon thus implies a turning away from or the negation of the field of sexual representations that links her, the actress, to him, the spectator of her bodily display.

The notion of *pudeur* has evolved in such a way as to conjure up the picture of a woman caught in the gesture of drawing a veil over her body. The veil (or its equivalent, the drapery or dress) fulfills an essential function: it separates, protects her from "it," the gaze that is charged with passion or sexual inquisitiveness; it prevents her from showing "it" to the other's gaze, the "it" referring this time to the passion experienced by the woman; it provides an obstacle, a dividing line between him and her.[28] A characteristic of our nineteenth-century medical texts is that they do not attempt to name or further define this unknown factor or quantity: "it" or the "thing" is vaguely encompassed in the notion of "passion," but the new definition of pudor, like that of hysteria, shies away from the more openly sexualized notions that characterized the earlier vision. Yet the veil that is meant to occult or to erase reveals also, quite ambiguously, what there is to hide or what must be canceled out. In their discussion of Greuze, the Goncourt brothers associate his representations of a *pudeur virginale* with an "angelic hypocrisy" and "a natural deceitfulness," and they detect in his use of drapery and veils "a mischievous coquetry" which they find "most irritating."[29]

Like hysteria then, nineteenth-century representations of pudor reveal a process of gendering: it is typically "she" who hides behind the veil while "he" figures on the side of the inquisitive, sexually charged gaze. Indeed, in the wake of the philosophical work by Derrida and by Irigaray on the veil, and of Mary Ann Doane's studies on representation, it would be tempting to desubstantialize and dehistoricize the veil of modesty, which, it turns out, was an important figure in the medical conceptualization of hysteria.[30] The veil would then be the visible mark of the process of partitioning and apportioning of sexual difference that

---

tween the organic and the erotogenic") a specific bodily manifestation of pudor—a case of blushing first studied by S. Feldmann (*Freud to Lacan*, 59–63).

28. "The imagination that dwells on the modest woman's clothing is—obviously—visual: even as it focuses on what she keeps unseen, the theory of 'Modest Concealments' appeals primarily to an eroticism of the eye," writes Yeazell (*Fictions of Modesty*, 47).

29. "Greuze was well able to paint at will pictures that were either moral or salacious," wrote Charles Normand in his 1892 study of Greuze (*Jean-Baptiste Greuze*, 70). The author of *Greuze et son temps*, Camille Mauclair, from whom I borrowed the quotes by the Goncourt brothers, comments similarly on the false ingenuity that characterizes Greuze's several pictures of young ladies draped in their chaste veils (267).

30. See Jacques Derrida, *Spurs: Nietzsche's Styles*; Irigaray, *Speculum*, 143–45; and Doane, "Veiling over Desire."

was elaborated in these nineteenth-century medical texts. What lies on each side of this veil are the fictions of a female sexual identity with their male counterparts. The veil hides and shows at the same time, and, as a provocation to the gaze, it holds a decisive function in the polarization of the sexual identity that can be traced in the figurations of hysteria. The close alliance of pudor and hysteria, with its suggestion that the veil determines a femininity that is either virtuous or pathological, leaves the doctor on the other, masculine side, with a desire to see what lies behind that screen. As both Luce Irigaray and Mary Ann Doane have shown in their feminist readings, this veil is the instrument of a metaphysics that tends to connect truth, and the pursuit of truth to the depth created by the veiling of woman. It becomes then the emblem of an epistemological process infused by sexual desire. In the words of Luce Irigaray: "mystery—*husteron?*—that will always modestly stand *behind any mirror* and that will repeatedly fuel the desire to see more and know more of it" (127).

It would be a mistake, however, to assume that in this process woman remains a passive victim, severed from knowledge and unaware. In Brachet's treatise on hysteria we find an exemplary passage on the theme of women's pudor, which deserves to be read like a gender fable. This vivid and memorable example was meant to provide, I believe, a fuller definition of woman's identity. But close examination of this tale casts a real uncertainty concerning women's role in this rehearsal of *pudeur.* (Were they the willing instruments of this scenario? Or were they its rebellious and mocking victims?) And beyond, such a neat story inevitably raises the suspicion that it was set up so as to suit the purpose of its teller. My own interpretation of this tale is meant to give the measure of my own skepticism about the examples and models of sexual identity provided by these nineteenth-century physicians. While nothing in this fable can account for the heroines' seeming or genuine compliance with the fictions of sexual identity that it promotes, the tale gives some indication of the kinds of forces that were brought to bear on women under the guise of a cure or a prophylactic against hysteria. But more important, it constitutes a further example of the process of gradual internalization of pudor which I have documented so far; in this story, the veil is indeed no longer an object, but a mental, moral, psychological value. It seems fitting, therefore, to preface Brachet's fable with Nietzsche's thoughts on pudor in *The Gay Science*:

On the subject of female pudor: —This is an absolutely astonishing and monstrous thing about the education of ladies [*vornehmen Frauen*]—there exists maybe no greater paradox. The whole world agrees in educating them in as much ignorance as possible on erotic subjects [*eroticis*] and in endowing their souls with deep shame concerning these things, as well as the most extreme intolerance and fear when somebody alludes to them. (II, 71)

A Gender Fable

Although we have said that sex belongs to any age [*le sexe est de tous les âges*], each period of life stamps it with its particular character, and it is always easy to distinguish through their play and their feelings a young girl from the nubile or from the married woman. Sex never lies; except that it may take on different features which it would doubtless be interesting to study, but which we only need to indicate. Thus, pudor, this sentiment which is nature's gift to the woman so as to double the price of her charms and which an intelligent woman [*une femme d'esprit*] would never want to relinquish. . . .

I delivered a lady: it was her tenth child, and her seven girls were alive: a boy was born. The second of her daughters, aged fifteen, and one of the prettiest creatures I have ever seen, approached eagerly when she heard the child's first cries. "Well," she exclaimed, "it's a boy."—"How did you recognize it?" I asked with a smile. This poor damsel answered nothing, but blushed down to the whites of her eyes, and withdrew hiding her face and giggling all the while. This was the modesty of innocence in its absolute naivety. Six months later I delivered a lady of her third child: the first two were girls. Her sister, still unmarried and aged twenty-two was present at the birth. "Well," exclaimed the young aunt, "it's a boy."—"How did you recognize it?" I asked as well. "I saw it was not a girl and thought it was a boy," she answered me, and did not show the least embarrassment. This was the modesty of an educated person, who showed the tact appropriate to her situation. Three or four years later, I delivered a lady of her second child: an aunt aged thirty-three and not married was present; she was overwhelmed with joy at the sight of a boy. I asked her the same question:—"how did you recognize it?." "Somebody told me," she answered smiling. These were the modesty and the tact of a person accustomed to the ways of the world. (Brachet, *Traité de l'hystérie*, 94–95)[31]

Read in its context, Brachet's exemplary story on the theme of *la pudeur* (which could be taken as a joke told at the expense of women) shows that the notion is by this time well anchored in a discursive frame involving the gaze, the sexed body, and a coercive force.[32] As it is no longer

31. The next paragraph begins in the most revealing fashion, with the image of an unveiling: "Voilà donc bien dévoilé pour nous la base du caractère de la femme: il repose sur sa sensibilité physique et morale" ("Here the basis of woman's character is unveiled to us: it consists in her physical and moral sensibility").

32. On "the act of joking and the predicament of sexual difference," see Felman's discussion in *What Does a Woman Want?* 92–99. "Like the act of theorizing, the act of joking is rhetorically addressed to *male accomplices*," she writes, and seems thereby to

inscribed in the woman's constitution (as a virtue or an instinct), pudor becomes an acquired virtue, which evolves over time and can have its own history. It is now the sign or the product of civility, manners, and social graces and belongs to woman's education into femininity. It defines as well a certain class of women: Nietzsche describes them as *vornehmende Frauen* (genteel, distinguished ladies) and Brachet calls them *femmes d'esprit*, but this kind of wit, one assumes, is only possible in the vicinity or in the midst of a salon. That pudor is no longer the original imprint of femininity but has become one of femininity's acquired traits is revealed in the contrast made with *pudicité*: "The blush that pudor provokes bears witness already to the knowledge or the suspicion of a misdemeanor [*une faute*] that can only be met by rebuke; *pudicité* however, incapable of failing, soars above any blame like an angel on earth," write the authors of the *Grand dictionnaire universel du XIXème siècle*. The divergence between *pudeur* and *pudicité* tells much about the duplicity with which woman's sexual knowledge has been conceptualized, and this duplicity informs this fable as well. If indeed, as the dictionary claims, *pudicité* is "the principal ornament of woman" and is what characterizes "the feature of a modest person" ("le caractère des personnes pudiques"), but as such assumes "a knowledge or suspicion of a misdemeanor," how can a woman regain her originary, pristine virtue? How will she lose the taint of sexual knowledge?

The difference between the two terms implies a temporal course whose order of precedence is not immediately apparent. Did she fall into knowledge, in some negative progress toward sexual awareness? Or on the contrary, does pudor precede *pudicité*, the latter representing the culmination of some moral ascent? Whatever the sequence there is one certainty, namely, that a knowledge of sexuality always represents a negative quantity in the case of women: it marks a corruption, a decline from femininity, which must be held in check. Or else it speaks of an original taint, which requires purification or exculpation. Although free from the most obvious moralizing aspects, Brachet's anecdote is concerned with such an enterprise of rectification.

In this process the physician uses two instruments: a critical, analytical gaze, which, as has been suggested, is always on the alert in the study of hysteria, and his moral and scientific authority which enable him to fullfill his prescriptive and pedagogical mission. Pudor is now firmly entrenched in the field of the gaze, as is rendered obvious in the new

provide an apt gloss for this gender fable, which is older than Irma's dream from Freud's *Interpretation of Dreams* which she analyzes.

dictionary definition: *pudeur*, "this feeling of an extreme delicacy which makes woman fear to show herself or blush under a look that is too free." This definition combines the woman's fear of exposure with her awareness of sexual desire. What this scenario of modesty makes very clear is that the "symptom" springs up under his gaze: he looks at her, who seems in him *un trop de liberté* that signifies some forbidden erotic content. Modesty, caught in the act, now denotes sexual embarrassment.

But in Brachet's fable it conveys sexual awareness simultaneously mastered by repression. "I did not see," says each of the women in her own way and each outdoing the other in her skills—signaling, meanwhile, what must not be seen for fear of shame. The last one does it beautifully indeed: acting, it seems, in concert with the physician. For in this instance pudor, translated into an exchange of words between doctor and "patient," takes the form of a masterfully controlled performance: she has found the words to match his questioning and, as a docile pupil, takes her cue from him. But here again Nietzsche affords a fit commentary: "The young women try very hard to appear superficial and thoughtless; the most artful among them put on a kind of impudence" (*Gay Science*, 71).

But the fable gains from being read also from a historical perspective. "Prior to communicating knowledge one will appeal to the intelligence," says a modern definition of maieutics. Since Brachet's story is about the delivery of knowledge under male supervision, the temptation to refer to Plato's pedagogical model in *Theaetetus* seems irresistible. Plato's story, which shows a male midwife delivering men of their ignorance, needs to be rewritten, however, with a reversal of the genders (underlined in the text): "Well, my art of midwifery is in most respects like theirs; but differs in that I attend *women* and not *men*, and I look after their souls when they are in labor, and not after their bodies; and the triumph of my art is in thoroughly examining whether the thought which the mind of the young *woman* brings forth is a false idol or a noble and true birth" (10–11). Ironic play may be the best response to Brachet's fable, where, acting like a midwife skilled in maieutics, the physician prides himself on eliciting the right answers from his women.

This is an instance of what Henry James would have called "women performing on the market-place" (the woman's bedroom has indeed been changed into a stage for the display of circus animals).[33] Yet in this instance the indecency is not related to naked bodies or immodest, drool-

33. Henry James writes: "The lovers are naked on the market-place and perform for

ing confessions, as James would have it. Brachet's treatise offers to the reader's complacent attention a general picture destined to identify the particular quality of the female *mind*, which is defined here by its social skills. But this kind of prattle at the bedside of the woman in confinement has, it turns out, historical antecedents. A satirical genre of the seventeenth century, known as the *caquets de l'accouchée*, typically tells the story, written by a man, of what women say to each other at the bedside of a woman in confinement. Well publicized, this "facetious discourse" was popular in its day. Brachet, however, is different from the eavesdropping and prattling male narrator of the *caquets* in that he makes the implicit claim that this story is an example of his science.[34] In other words, this story may recount a joke played on women, but it is not presented as such. Nor is it even perceived as an indecent intrusion, on the part of the physician, into the world of women and midwives.[35]

Let us now pursue the path of this science. The education of women, it seems, entails the acquisition of social customs and values. The progress that leads from the gigglish innocence of the naive girl to the tact of the worldly lady is that of civilization. But how much mental energy must be spent in forgetting, repressing what they know—for instance, that boys differ from girls in that . . . Or else how many tears, fits of anger, or embarrassed giggles before they are able to play their roles smilingly in what looks like the script of a novel of manners. The conduct book replaces the textbook, and becoming a proper lady means facing with increasing ease and detachment the encroachment of belief over evidence. What she sees is glossed over by what she has learned, for one does not teach young girls, one coaches them. "Be sure to enclose this education within fair boundaries so that the [the girl] will always be brought back to nature's goal." Brachet writes in his treatise (*Traité de l'hystérie*, 505). The veil of modesty stands between the woman and

the benefit of society" ("George Sand," in *Literary Criticism*, 744). This idea is developed in the next chapter.

34. Domna Stanton's brilliant presentation of the *Caquets de l'accouchée*, which I heard at Yale in 1989, first drew my attention to this literary genre (which she plans to discuss in a forthcoming book). I also owe some aspects of my description to Georges Mengrédien, who writes about this form that it is "one of the rare representatives of the realist literature of the beginning of the seventeenth century . . . which makes it possible to have access to the privacy of some *petites bourgeoises* of the time" (*La vie littéraire au XVIIème siècle*, 46–47).

35. On the controversy between midwives and doctors, Angus McLaren in "Medicine and Private Morality in France, 1800–1850" cites a revealing title: *L'indécence aux hommes d'accoucher les femmes* (P. Hecquet, 1708).

the phenonemal world so "that she may appear superficial and thoughtless," to repeat Nietzsche's words, and it is meant to keep her enshrouded in beliefs, when the experience of her senses and the observation of the world would make her mind alive. Brachet's fable on the modesty of women plays off the knowledge defined by authority against the evidence derived from experience. In its ultimate consequences it speaks of the demise of women's consciousness.

"One can be ignorant of a certain thing and yet all the while know it." From a philosophical point of view, the fable can be interpreted in the light of Merleau-Ponty's paradox, which defines hysteria and repression; it provides the key, meanwhile, to the philosophic sense of this tale (*Phénoménologie*, 189). Modesty functions in Brachet's fable as the instrument of repression, the name given to "the operation whereby the subject tries to push back and to maintain in the unconscious the representations (thoughts, images, memories) attached to a drive."[36] The drive is, in this instance, epistemophilic: it demands to know and it wants to see the other's sex in order to find evidence for the two genders and to answer the question "Where do babies come from?" These two enigmas represent crucial landmarks for the development of a subject whose intellect will map the world in ever widening circles starting from her body and that of her mother. The solution of these two riddles will enable the subject to define her identity, namely, to position herself on the horizontal axis of sexual difference and the vertical axis of origins and generation.[37] But the physicians's script has an overriding power: the fable tells about his desire to get confirmation on the question of castration. It provides him with the necessary reassurance concerning his masculinity.

Indeed, when read allegorically as a story that plays his knowledge against her modesty, the fable is destined to confirm his sense of sexual difference: only women would accept to play this game of castration, enter his plot, and forego reason. In short, this story represents one more instance of successful phallogocentrism and functions as a myth whose purpose is to confirm women's abilities to endorse their proper gender roles. Performing modestly and decorously as these ladies do, they re-

36. Here I quote Laplanche and Pontalis's definition of repression, in *Vocabulaire de la psychanalyse*, 392.

37. See Freud's discussion in *Three Essays on the Theory of Sexuality* (SE VII, 194–95). In his wake, André Green, writing on castration, adds that this complex "works as a structural principle . . . which compels the subject to position himself or herself as such in relation to the structure and to affirm the particularities of his or her sexual identity with regard to himself and to the other sex" (*Le complexe de castration*, 46).

confirm the particularities of their sexual identity with regard to the other sex: the boy child is the test case and the doctor the authority. The feminine identity is then merely the reflection of the other sex, it is staged around *it* (the phallus-boy) and held in its place by the physician's masterful, knowing gaze. "Of course," writes Irigaray in a way that clarifies—retrospectively—the stakes of the conversation between the physician and his women, "we cannot overlook the fact that the, hysterical, woman is particularly adept at submission, suggestion, fiction even, with regards to the other's discourse-desire. And what she brings to the analysis is not foreign to what one expects her to say there. . . . And if she did not say it, why would she be there anyway? On this stage organized, also, through/for her 'penis envy'? And what would the analyst understand in her desire that would not correspond to *his/her* envy?" (64–65).

That this feminine identity is the product of difference (in other words, of the assumption of castration) cannot prevent us, however, from reading the fictions that it sustains or produces. The fable constructs, as any of our texts on hysteria naturally would, sexual identity around the female sex ("the sex that never gives the lie to itself") and yet assumes on the part of the woman the denial of that through which the difference is signified. The young girl blushes and hides her face. "It isn't a girl" says the one who, marriageable, shows in this at least a knowledge of her own sex. The "somebody told me" represents the acme of femininity, of a knowledge that is dissociated from herself and that should rightly be called by the name of *pudicité*, as the absolute denial of the sexed body. Each stage of this growth into femininity and of this disowning of knowledge is matched by another articulation of body and language. The girl has no words for it but plays in her body the scenario of modesty. The grown-up woman recites her lesson impassively. The woman of the world does not blink but shows in her smile her connivence with her interlocutor. Intelligence has become here a form of shared dissimulation, of *Erheuchlung* to borrow once more Nietzsche's word.

And yet they must have seen it and known it, the little boy's sex. And didn't they, each in turn, burst into silent, mental laughter at the absurdity of the question: "How did you recognize it?" But the situation is so compelling, the scenario so recognizable, that repression is featured as a comedy of manners. Indeed, the staging of such a performance relies on their skill and compliance with the rules of the genre. If they had been devoid of this necessary intelligence concerning sex and their gender roles, their behavior could not have remained smoothly polite, they would have acted out, hysterically. And then, truly hysterical, they would have shown there, in their symptoms, how deeply ignorant they were of what they knew.

As the philosopher reminds us, hysteria is not merely, as Brachet and his colleagues would have it, the aberration of passion, but also of knowledge. The learning of ignorance and the sustaining of that denial tend to exact their price in the form of symptoms. Freud argues that there is a direct relation between the subject's ability to solve the question of sexual difference and his or her intellectual development, and he offers as a positive instance Leonardo da Vinci, and as a negative one, women: "Their upbringing forbids their concerning themselves intellectually with sexual problems though they nevertheless feel extremely curious about them, and frightens them by condemning such curiosity as unwomanly and a sign of a sinful disposition. In this way they are scared away from *any* form of thinking, and knowledge loses its value for them because they are subjected to a moral law that tends to inhibit sexual curiosity" ("*Civilized*" *Sexual Morality and Modern Nervous Illness, SE* IX, 198–99). "I think," he writes further, "that the undoubted intellectual inferiority of so many women can rather be traced back to the inhibition of thought necessitated by sexual suppression" (199). If sexual morality stands in the way of mental progress, then Brachet's lesson in modesty is about regression and about the enforcement of ignorance.

"Je sais bien mais quand même" (I do know it, but all the same); this statement, which for Octave Mannoni summarizes the fetishist's stance, provides another gloss for Brachet's fable—this time from a psychological perspective.[38] Fetishism is about belief, about the belief in the originary fact of castration, but accompanied by a doubt or a form of skepticism which demands that the subject repeatedly seek confirmation of the reality of castration. Read in light of this definition, Brachet's fable reveals the doctor's own involvement in a fetishist scenario: one may well hold the belief, as he does, that women are born women, and yet want to ensure that they prove their femininity. The doctor's maxim, *le sexe est de tous les âges*, expresses his belief in the foundational value (at least when women are concerned) of the distinction between male and female. And we know that Brachet argues repeatedly that this difference is radical and absolute, as well as visible in all the details of appearance and behavior; it is also manifest, he claims here, at every stage of a woman's life. But although pudor is an inherently female

---

38. For an extended discussion of this concept, see "Je sais bien mais quand même," in Mannoni, *Clefs*.

virtue, it must be put to the test. Brachet exhibits proudly the spoils of this pedagogical trick: all three women display their natural modesty, but in varying degrees of competence. "I do know it, but all the same": Brachet's fable is destined to provide the precious reassurance that the veil always remains where it belongs; it confirms the belief in the value of sexual difference; the veil of her ignorance is then *his* fetish. The fable therefore reveals a gendering of consciousness. The doctor of the *médecine morale* who puts himself on display in order to provide the reassuring fact that there is such a thing as castration repeats a male plot, which Luce Irigaray describes as "the process of a construction of consciousness where woman repeatedly figures as the site where repression is inscribed" (65). His science thus relies on a scene born from his fantasy and is destined to give him confirmation, among other things, of the amputation of her mind.

But the fable reveals simultaneously a fetishist attitude on the part of the women. Read literally, for what it shows, it offers the confirmation of women's redoubled compliance with the law of gender: not only do they pay tribute to the value of the phallus, but they give it credence in their blind, obedient performance. The heroines of Brachet's fable know that "it is a boy," even as they pretend not to know what it is that signifies his gender, and they show their belief in sexual difference, even while they overlook its existence. In other words, the denial of the signifier of anatomical difference does not blind them to the signified: they of course recognize the child's gender. It is indeed possible to believe in gender while remaining ignorant about the sexes, and this is another fetishist stance.[39] If, as the fable shows, the subjective, psychological sphere of femininity can only be acknowledged on the condition that she, the woman, close her eyes to the evidence of sexual difference, this does not prevent her from knowing about gender—about its manifestations in the order of the law and the symbolic. And one is naturally linked to the other: she who knows how to read the signifier of the masculine gender knows what it is to be a woman, and thus takes upon herself her feminine gender.

Brachet's fable acts as a reminder of the connivence between men and women that ensured the perpetuation of that one fetish, the phallus, as what is simultaneously perceived and denied. This, I claim, is ultimately

---

39. Mannoni discusses the relation between sex and gender from the perspective of language and of semiotics in "L'ellipse et la barre," in *Clefs*, 60–63. See also André Green's discussion, from a psychological and psychoanalytical point of view, of the fact that recognition of gender does not necessarily entail a knowledge of sexual difference (*Complexe de castration*, 36).

the crux of the fable: woman's modesty is here no more than a figure; it hides a process of engendering which can be shown to intersect with a differentiated definition of consciousness. While in telling this tale the physician promotes his own awareness of himself as a man, the women, who act in this masquerade like actresses in a play, are taught to ignore what they know about the difference between the sexes. If they are conscious in such a scene, that is, if they are not merely hysterical, then such a consciousness is defined by the erasure of sexual knowledge, which is replaced by an acknowledgment of their situation as gendered subjects. In this conclusion, I find myself echoing what is Simone de Beauvoir's conviction in *Pour une morale de l'ambiguïté*, namely, that oppression can penetrate so deep into subjectivity that consciousness itself can be no more than the effect of the oppressive situation.[40] To examine these nineteenth-century treatises on hysteria is to come to the awareness that the conviction of a totally sexualized identity, which founded the intellectual adventure of these several doctors, is one of the forms taken by the oppression that bears on women.

40. On this subject, see Sonia Kruks's illuminating discussion in "Genre et subjectivité: Simone de Beauvoir et le féminisme contemporain," 14.

CHAPTER TWO

Henry James and George Sand: Scenes of Passion, Scenes of Hysteria

> The mind seems not to have isolated and contracted itself in the regions of perception but to expand with longing and desire.
> —Henry James, "George Sand,"
> in *Literary Criticism*

"These are days in which one's modesty is, in every direction, much exposed, and one should be thankful for every veil that one can hastily snatch up or that a friendly hand precipitately muffles one withal" (*Selected Letters*, 291) writes James in a letter to Edmund Gosse, sketching out what appears to be a typically Jamesian move of withdrawal behind the facade of active discretion. James's practice as a writer often relies on a similar desire to erect screens. But screens not only hide; they also designate and put on display what is to be hidden, creating in the very process a transgressive desire. Moreover, such veilings and gestures of modesty inevitably refer to a perception of sexuality: "the rhetoric of sexuality," writes Shoshana Felman, "is the rhetoric of screens" ("Rereading Femininity," 29). The general theme of this chapter is a reflexion on a theory of representation that relies on screens and turns them into instruments of aesthetic, moral, but also sexual discrimination. Its object lies in the extensive body of critical texts that Henry James wrote on George Sand—she who, according to him, "lifted the veil from her personality with a tolerably unshrinking hand."[1] But my attention is directed in particular to the more troubled aspects of this critical relationship, evidenced in the "textual hysteria" that arises several times in

---

1. Henry James, "Letter from Paris," in "George Sand," in *Literary Criticism: French Writers, Other European Writers, and the Prefaces to the New York Edition*, 703. All subsequent references to James's essays on Sand are to this edition.

the course of James's encounters with the figure of the woman writer. George Sand is here not only the pen name of a "scribbling woman" who fascinated the nineteenth-century imagination; it is also that of the screen-woman—the figure who holds for James, the literary critic and theoretician, the place of the erotic, sexualized body. Reading James reading Sand is to be faced with a scene of knowledge that is also, in a powerful and sometimes disturbing fashion, the scene of sexuality. The hysterical scenarios that I discuss here must be taken as evidence of the complex association, in nineteenth-century representations of subjectivity, between aesthetic or moral stakes and questions of sexual identity or gender.

Before entering into the finer discriminations of the Jamesian text of hysteria, it might be useful to examine briefly the connections between representation, hysteria, and sexual identity in one of their more spectacular manifestations, namely, in the flurry of emotions that greeted the publication of *Madame Bovary*. The trial of the author, on grounds of the immorality (read "indecency") of the representation of the heroine, brings sharply into focus the conflict of interests between, on the one hand, a desire to see and to know "woman," and on the other, the need to see and know only those aspects of her that are deemed (re)presentable.[2] The law court becomes the stage of an implicit debate between the claims of the writer and the expectations of his readers on the question "What, of woman, can be said and shown?" While the obvious object of the legal contention is literary censorship, it achieves another purpose: it brings to the fore the question of sexual identity, since it stages in the arena of a public, collective debate, and around the figure of a woman, the question of where to draw the veil. The need to impose censorship on the representation of female passion overlaps in fact with an attempt to define sexual identity and to apply the pressure of the "law of gender" to Flaubert's writing. While arguing about the

2. Both the "irrepresentable" and the "unpresentable" or "unrepresentable" designate the absence of representation. In this book, however, the emphasis falls on the latter two terms, for this attempt to trace a history of the gendered subject in nineteenth-century writing reveals the weight of cultural and social interdiction that came to bear on the representation of woman's desire or "passion" (to use the nineteenth-century word, which is also the one used by James in relation to Sand). The emergence of this "unrepresentable" is related to gradual internalization, applied to women, of the censure on the sexual body, which was shown in my inquiry into *pudeur*. Only in the last chapter of this volume, with the apparition of the sublime in *Daniel Deronda*, does the concept of the irrepresentable (i.e., the radical absence of representation due to foreclosure, and not merely to repression) become a valid term.

representation of the heroine, the court of law sketches the contours of a sexual morality whose centerpiece is the notion of a proper femininity.[3]

Thus the accusation cites in extenso the scenes in Rouen where the adulterous Emma meets with her lover in "the warm room . . . destined to the intimacies of passion" ("Appendix," in *Madame Bovary*, 626–27). The scenes played in the alcove are deemed morally offensive, but they fascinate the readers, especially the tableau of Emma's *déshabillage*: "She snatched off her dress and tore at the thin laces of her corsets, which whistled down over her hips like a slithering adder." But also that other tableau, which shows Emma (naked?), folding her naked arms in a gesture of modesty and hiding her face in her hands. "There was nothing in the world so beautiful as her brown head and white skin against that crimson background," comments the narrator from the perspective of the aesthete. But for the tribunal, precedence must be given to the moral examination of the work, and aesthetic admiration is replaced by moral abhorrence: what gets praised as "une peinture admirable sous le rapport du talent" (a wonderful depiction from the point of view of talent) is judged as being "une peinture exécrable du point de vue de la morale" (an abominable work from the point of view of morality). While undeniably charged with erotic contents, Flaubert's novel is surely not pornographic. Yet the representation of a female passion, although sanctioned by a horrible death, makes the readers avert their gaze from its aesthetic rewards. The fiction of an "Emma" takes on, it seems, the carnality of a female body in its natural, threatening state: "Chez lui point de gaze, point de voiles, c'est la nature dans toute sa nudité, dans toute sa crudité!" (In his works, no gauze, no veils, what you have is nature fully naked and absolutely crude [627]). "Let there be veils": the prosecution's outcry, like that of James in his own time, shows to what extent nineteenth-century aesthetics is still embroiled with moral questions, especially when it comes to representing women.

It is around the famous, scandalous episode of the cab that the resistance seems to have concentrated, with a shrill insistance that verges on collective hysteria. Yet the scene exists merely as a thing of the imagination: it had immediately been censored and never appeared in the *Revue de Paris*. But, claims Sénard, Flaubert's lawyer, in his defense, "from this suppression, the whole trial arose" (646). Indeed, the *scène du fiacre* imagined, remembered, gossiped about draws all the attention,

---

3. For a firsthand account of this famous trial, see the appendix in the Pléiade edition of the novel (Flaubert, *Oeuvres I*). Throughout I have quoted Alan Russell's translation of *Madame Bovary*. The passages that I quote were all cited as evidence during the trial.

like a screen held up for a general, collective act of projection. But in its textual form too, the scene is conceived like a screen. The carriage has engulfed Emma and Leon in an impenetrable obscurity. What then dwells in it is merely a void, the blinds remain drawn, except for a brief moment when a hand shows, throwing out of the window some bits of torn paper. Literary censorship marks with a gap what has become unpresentable; this little anecdote about Flaubert's cab shows that when the veil falls it inevitably provokes, on the part of the reader, a kind of overinvestment of the imagination in a sexual scenario, which is a manifestation of hysteria. Had it not been endowed with an excessive susceptibility to passion, had it not been so impressionable, Flaubert's audience would never have put up such a resistance, it would not have demanded censorship.

The image of a cab, all blinds drawn, holding a man and a woman and traveling up and down the streets of Rouen, has given rise to speculations, too many speculations, asserts Sénard: "People have surmised lots of things which did not exist, as you saw when reading the text of this passage. But, by God, do you know what has been surmised? That in the canceled part there was probably something analogous to what you will have the goodness to read in one of the most marvelous novels sprung from the pen of an honorable member of the Académie Française, M. Mérimée" ("Appendix," in *Madame Bovary*, 645).[4]

As he advocates that the scene be freed from its taints of indecency, that the cab be emptied of its obsessively naked bodies, Sénard asks, in perfectly bad faith, for the impossible: that the audience close its eyes to a picture staged to encourage the curious, voyeuristic gaze. (What can the cab veil or hide if not the denuded body of female passion, Emma caught in the act with Léon?) This kind of denial would not be much different from that which Brachet obtained from his performing ladies of modesty: the readers would have to overlook or rather ignore what they know only too well, that the cab holds the revelations of a sexed body. There is, however, a significant difference: in Brachet's story the object of the blind gaze was the male sex; in the evidence presented

---

4. In Prosper Mérimée's tale "La double méprise," republished in 1853, the scene of seduction takes place in a cab and is recounted in some detail. The first stages of a *déshabillage*, some fragments of the lovers' conversation, and a description of a disorderliness suggesting the aftermath of some *ébats amoureux* are unmistakable signs of the seduction, but these are not censored. The very fact that Flaubert's text elides the scene altogether (he creates a frame that circumscribes a blank picture) transforms the cab into a "phantasy machine." The repression is then all the stronger for having to deal with the boundless, uncontrollable space of phantasy.

against Flaubert, that object is, conspicuously, the body of Emma in the thralls of passion. The blinds of the cab, those veils thrown over this movable and all too public *scène d'alcôve*, provoke a scene of hysteria of the kind that I sketch out more fully in tracing the narrative of Henry James's involvement as a critic and writer with the mythical George Sand.

Eight texts on George Sand, spread over a period of nearly fifty years (1868 to 1914), testify to Henry James's enduring fascination with the writer.[5] Indeed, James wrote as much on her as on Balzac or George Eliot. His most important critical texts on the author overlap in a significant fashion with his own "middle period," with such works as *The Spoils of Poynton*, *The Bostonians*, and his two books on women and sexual knowledge, *What Maisie Knew* and *The Awkward Age*. These are in fact the troubled years of James's career, years which Leon Edel describes as belonging to "some kind of psychological regression to earlier phases in his juvenile and adolescent being and helplessness" (*Selected Letters*, 283). They also correspond to the period of his life when James was experimenting with the theater. These texts then, written in 1897 and 1899, are remarkable for the fascination for sexual drama that they exhibit and for the peculiar psychological intensities that they reveal in a number of scenes of James's own making.[6] They have determined my own critical approach.

Implicit in this inquiry is the assumption that the critic's work bears, in this instance, very closely on questions related to his own identity as a male writer. My explicit interest lies, however, in uncovering in James's critical work the elements of a reflection on the representation of gender and the relationship between gender and writing.[7] When such a supremely self-conscious writer and theoretician of the novel encounters the mythical figure of the woman writer George Sand, the result is, I would claim, an unequaled set of reflexions on and representations of nineteenth-century models of gender. Although they are complex and

5. Actually there are nine pieces, if we include James's brief account of Hippolyte Taine's "Letter on George Sand," where the American critic cites abundantly from Taine's essay or merely paraphrases it.

6. "Making scenes" or rather "making a scene," James not only takes an aesthetic commitment to a certain mode of representation but also creates a drama where he projects his own powerful emotions.

7. Whereas Leland S. Person highlights the subjective dimension of such a problematic ("Coming to terms with what he called the riddle or mystery or question of Sand meant researching his own gender identity and the gender of his literary authority" ["Henry James, George Sand, and the Suspense of Masculinity," 518]), my own study emphasizes the theoretical dimensions of James's critical writings.

often difficult to the point of obscurity, James's critical texts also provide extraordinary insight into the literary figurations of sexual identity. Hysteria, meanwhile, is no longer the object of representation; it is, in the case of these texts, the figure, or rather the symptom, that lies behind the work of criticism and representation and determines the particular drifts and emphases of James's writing. The term is, therefore, used here not for its historical let alone clinical value, but as a heuristic model that produces a number of theoretical insights.

It would have been possible to envisage the texts that James wrote on Sand from a chronological perspective and to align them within a narrative of development, putting the emphasis, for instance, on the pedagogical aspects of their relation. Sand teaches him how to write about passion, something he could not have learned from his English and American forerunners. His different critical encounters with her could then be mapped onto the several stages of an unfolding literary vocation and aesthetic discovery. However, the complex and repetitive patterning of James's discussion of Sand, which is marked moreover with unusual intensities, calls for a different critical narrative, one informed by a psychoanalytical awareness. A reading of these texts along the lines of an aesthetic Bildungsroman could indeed not accommodate the recurrent, sometimes obsessive critical gestures of James's prose, whereas an analytical approach can: it relies on a different temporality and makes of desire the text's shaping force. Such an interpretation must not be understood, however, as offering primarily psychological insight into the writer's mind: if it enables us to catch glimpses of James's "subject position" (a term I prefer to Leland Person's "gender identity"), these are the by-products of a more general inquiry. James's progress across the Sandian territory makes it possible to witness not only the critical and theoretical axioms but also some of the psychological mechanisms and rhetorical maneuvers that determine a certain aesthetic consciousness, and its workings as representation. Thus I am not primarily interested in uncovering the author's private pains and ecstasies: to me they are significant as symptoms of the general workings of representation within a certain historical period. In other words, I take these encounters of the author-in-the-making with the woman writer to represent an effect of a wider discursive formation, which, in its attempts to "legislate" on the relation between life and art, ends up applying its force more pointedly to the relation between body and text, and more precisely even to the relation between sexuality and textuality. Of this discursive formation, the various scenes of passion and scenarios of hysteria that I decipher in these texts constitute the symptoms.

Henry James and George Sand

Seduction and Resistance

The first moment in this critical relation is placed under the sign of admiration and of James's secret desire to emulate George Sand. For her talent, in a field that he himself is attempting to conquer, namely, the representation of passion and psychological depths, is unquestionably beyond what has been achieved by the English novelists.[8] Written on the occasion of her death, in 1877, James's first extended essay on the woman writer pays tribute through the metaphors of warfare and conquest.

She may claim, that although she has the critics against her, the writers of her own class who represent virtuous love have not pushed her out of the field. She has the advantage that she has portrayed a *passion*, and those of the other group have the disadvantage that they have not. In English literature, which, we suppose, is more especially the region of virtuous love, we do not "go into" the matter, as the phrase is (we speak of course of English prose). We have agreed among our own confines that there is a certain point at which elucidation of it should stop short; that among the things which it is possible to say about it, the greater number had on the whole better not be said. (*Literary Criticism*, 724)

The French writer has thus conquered a new territory whose boundaries the "native" writers have rarely crossed. James's literary topography is not new, of course: whereas in the map of passion Britain figures on the side of virtue, purity, and reticence, the French, less modest, are firmly encamped on the side of the sensual and the erotic. If, for instance, the novels of George Eliot speak of eros, it is with such lack of fire, writes James, that "they seem to foreign readers, probably, like vast, cold, commodious, respectable rooms, through whose window-panes one sees a snow-covered landscape, and across whose acres of sober-hued carpet one looks in vain for a fireplace or a fire" (725).[9] George Sand, mean-

---

8. "It comes to me that her meeting with him in town must be *une scène de passion*— yes, I must give my readers that," writes James in his *Notebooks* when planning his work for *The Spoils of Poynton* (*Complete Notebooks*, 156). This chapter shows how the *scène de passion* constitutes the underlying narratological structure in James's writing, like a matrix destined to produce representations.

9. In this light, James's thoughts on Jane Austen, in a letter to George Pellew (the author of a dissertation on this writer), are particularly interesting: "In of course an infinitely less explicit way, Emma Woodhouse and Anne Elliot give us as great an impression of 'passion'—that celebrated quality—as the ladies of G. Sand and Balzac" (*Selected Letters*, 189). There are thus two half-expatriates, both of them women, in James's literary geography of passion: Jane Austen and George Eliot.

while, is singled out for her ability to represent passion: she "celebrated a single passion, the passion of love" (700).

While she represents passion, however, the writer "may be said to have pretty thoroughly explored the human soul" (700) and "thrown a great deal of light on the rest of our nature." In this, claims James, she remains superior to Balzac, who, as "an incomplete and partial witness" of the "passion of love" (700–701), had to remain content with a superficial form of realism. It turns out that James is not interested in passion for passion's sake: his admiration for the woman who rides "the high horse of 'passion' " (771) is inseparable from the recognition that Sand's writing of longing and desire speaks of "an extraordinary familiarity with the things of the mind, the play of character, the psychological mystery" (714). The different stages of James's eulogy reveal indeed his allegiance to a form of representation that includes sexual passion and acknowledges its shaping force. She, George Sand, knows about "the ardent forces of the heart" (724) and thus shows superior insight into the mysteries of the human soul.

"A great mind curious about all things, open to all things, nobly accessible to experience, asking only to live, expand, respond," the critic writes. His praise relies indeed, in a revealing fashion, on the notion of inclusion, but also on that of depth, of what the critic calls the "inward drama":

They speak above all for the author's great gift, her eye for the inward drama. Her hand is always on the fiddle-string, her ear is always at the heart. It was in the soul, in a word, that she saw the drama begin, and to the soul that, after whatever outward flourishes, she saw it confidently come back. She herself lived with all her perceptions and in all her chambers—not merely in the showroom of the shop. (753)

Here the choice of figures shows, better than any discursive explanation, where the appeal of Sand's work truly lies for James. The musical image is banal enough, and seems to be in fact a commonplace of Sandian criticism ever since Renan declared the writer to be (in an image on which James embroiders a few times) "the aeolian harp of our time" (705). The metaphor of the house is original, however, and suggests that the writer's expanded vision reveals to the spectators not only the most visible surfaces, but the depths of interiority—the chambers and not only the showroom. The house of representation that James sketches out in his admiration for Sand speaks tellingly of a conception of depth and of inwardness for which her writing has been singled out; it speaks of "things of the mind" and of "psychological mystery."[10]

But at the back of the house, at the threshold of certain "chambers," is also where James's resistance begins.[11] If the mystery has to do with passion, more precisely with sexual passion ("the passion of love"), then the appeal must necessarily be compounded with some form of inhibition or resistance. Such exposure might indeed lead to the collapse of civilization; this is how the writer justifies implicitly and, on a few occasions, explicitly his resistance to Sand's works. The newly expanded stage of representation holds in store such scenes as require that the veil be drawn over them. Thus, admiration soon gives way to a form of mingled appreciation which first shows as resistance but gives way to offensive strategies.

An important aspect of James's critical writings on Sand can be related to the elaboration of defenses against illicit revelations: he argues, in the name of decency and modesty, for the importance and value of the very screens whose removal he had earlier acknowledged and praised in Sand's writing. In his sometimes shrill indictment of the principle of "show all" and "say all," James is clearly changing sides.

The first move in this double stragegy of retreat and aggression takes the form of repudiation of Sand's earlier qualities as a realist. She has now become a romantic or even a romancer; James uses against her the image of a balloon: "to embark on one of her confessed fictions is to have . . . a little too much the feeling of going up in a balloon. We are borne by a fresh cool current and the car delightfully dangles; but as we peep over the sides we see things—as we usually know them—at a dreadful drop beneath" (754). This figure is part of the accumulated evidence on the score of her inveterate romanticism. She is thus described as a bird, nightingale, or lark: "the writer who best answers to Shelley's description of the skylark singing 'in profuse strains of unpremeditated art' " (712). She is a "great improviser," who writes effortlessly, easily, with no sign of work, "as a bird sings" (717), remaining true to her origins

---

10. Cf. "To feel as George Sand felt, however, one had to be, like George Sand, of the true male inwardness" (James, *Literary Criticism*, 748).

11. In his preface to *La femme de trente ans*, Pierre Barbéris, in his attempt to situate Balzac's work in its historical context, mentions that "in 1832–34, the conjugal bedroom of the king of France, with its double bed [lit à deux places] has become a symbol and a national monument" (45). The back chamber, the bedroom, the alcove are all endowed with symbolic meaning and appear repeatedly in this work in my discussion of passion and knowledge. For a fuller commentary, see my postscript.

as the granddaughter of a bird catcher (709). While in the first pages written on Sand James singles out "the confidence with which the imagination appeals to the faculty of utterance" (697), that spontaneity and ease of expression have now become a liability. She produces a prose that is alternately "limpid," "fluent," "liquid," and as "loose" and "fluid" as water. The writer's ease gets redefined as objectionable facility.

But most objectionable of all, it seems, is Sand's ability to move spontaneously, uninhibitedly from experience to expression. In the middle of her most troubled time with Musset, she can still "sit down to her perpetual manuscript" (703). "George Sand lived her remarkable life and drove her perpetual pen" (739); the near epigrammatic quality, with the parallelism given to "life" and "pen," turns such a statement into an accusation of the too immediate proximity between life and writing. She is, it seems, able to convert life (*her* life) into the all-encompassing text of her novels, letters, and autobiographical writings. And she appears to accomplish this without hard work or the misgivings of conscience. But what happens to art when it knows no restraints and is without the "mysterious fullness" that, in the words of James's brother William, we owe to Henry's scene making?[12] And where then is truth?

The next stage of James's critique is predictable enough; it goes toward showing that Sand had an uneasy, or rather a too comfortable relation with truth. What she lacks then is the "method of truth": "She was contemplative; but she was not, in the deepest sense, observant. She was a very high order of sentimentalist, but she was not a moralist" (733). And further: "Does any work of representation, of imitation, live long that is predominantly loose? It may live in spite of looseness; but that, we make out, is only because closeness has somewhere, where it has most mattered, played a part. It is hard to say of George Sand's productions, I think, that they show closeness anywhere; . . . the sense of fluidity is fundamentally fatal to the sense of particular truth. The thing presented by intention is never the stream of the artist's inspiration; it is the deposit of the stream" (759).

The framework that emerges from James's critical discourse is predictable enough: it corresponds to James's own often-expressed preference for form, as it is formulated, for instance, in his letter to Hugh Walpole, the apprentice writer: "Form alone *takes*, and holds and preserves, substance—saves it from the welter of helpless verbiage that we swim in as in a sea of tasteless tepid pudding, and that makes one ashamed of an art capable of such degradations" (*Selected Letters*, 400).

12. See "The Scenic Method" in the next chapter.

The danger lies indeed in the combination of fluidity and the kind of literary concoctions that are typically the specialty of ladies.[13] The writer's next objection is against the tea maker: "Some readers may charge her with a graver confusion still—the incapacity to distinguish between fiction and fact, the truth straight from the well and the truth curling in steam from the kettle and preparing the confortable tea" (*Literary Criticism*, 751). Form is preferable to her effusive sentimentality. Sand's writing is but a long stream of words, sprung from her imagination and inspiration, but truth is either pure like water from the well or shaped and carved like stone. Meanwhile, in its phrasing, the critic's indictment relies here again, insistently, on a representation of a sexual identity: after all, George Sand's signature, it should not be forgotten, belongs to a woman.

Turning the conventional assumptions about women and men into threatening weapons, James's critical moves are clearly sexist. The literary phenomenon is regularly and predictably brought back to its "sexual" determinations; the qualities and defects of George Sand's work are simply the product of their author—a woman after all. The critic's discourse slides all too easily from the general assertion, spoken by a "man of maxims," into an indictment founded on the writer's sex. Indeed, her faults as a writer are characteristic of women in general. See, for instance, her imagination: "It is indefatigable, inexhaustible; but it is restless, nervous, and capricious; it is, in short, the imagination of a woman" (699), or her faulty intellect: "George Sand invites reperusal less than any mind of equal eminence. Is this because after all she was a woman, and the laxity of the feminine intellect could not fail to claim its part in her?" (731). And James suggests that in her work there are to be found neither facts nor specificity nor truth. This can easily be accounted for: she is a woman, a Frenchwoman moreover, and a coquette, who knows how to veil the truth in the elegant garments of what must surely be pretended modesty: "There is something very liberal and universal in George Sand's genius, as well as very masculine; but our final impression of her always is that she is a woman and a Frenchwoman. Women, we are told, do not value the truth for its own sake, but only for some personal use they make of it. My present criticism involves an assent to this somewhat cynical dogma" (712). James's "Women, we are told," drowned in his elaborate argumentation, enables us to catch him in the

---

13. On the association of femininity with the economy of fluids, see Janet Beizer's impressive analysis in *Ventriloquized Bodies: The Narrative Uses of Hysteria in France, 1850–1900*.

act of wielding the blunt weapon of sexism. That he should resort to such obvious artillery is, if anything, the sign of the hold that the figure of George Sand exerts over him. That such a weapon has a tendency to backfire soon becomes obvious as the critic finds himself embroiled in the confusions that surround Sand's sexual identity. Her being a woman looks now like mere contingency, for doesn't she, to all intents and purposes, behave like a man? James broaches the topic of her masculinity in relation to her divorce: "[She] was too imperious a force, too powerful a machine, to make the limits of her activity coincide with those of wifely submissiveness" (716), and he concludes that her determination to address herself to life at first hand is "not what is usually called womanly, was not modest nor delicate" (717). "To live at first hand" is repeated twice, not only because, applied to George Sand's capacity for experience, it appears to threaten the critic's earlier confident assertions about what constitutes feminine (and masculine) behavior: typically women do not live but, from behind the screen of their modesty, they watch the others act and perform. James's astonishment can only spring from his unexplained sense of confusion and implication in this phenomenon: the stance of the observer, the attitude of renunciation, the vicarious participation in life and its pleasures are typically his, and," writes Richard Brodhead, "intimate and erotic passion has the customary status, in James as in Hawthorne, of a pleasure at second hand" (*The School of Hawthorne*, 188).[14] How can *she* manage to live at first hand when this is denied to *him*?

Since the enigma of woman only increases in density, while the critic's ability to read her from the perspective of her sexual identity declines accordingly, James's last defense is to abandon his pretensions to read Sand's works in order to turn to the safer ground of her existence. From the uncertain ground of aesthetic/sexist discussion, the critic moves to the strong convictions of moral discourse and proceeds, meanwhile, in his wily way: "It will help us to understand this extraordinary responsiveness of mind and fertility of imagination to remember that inspiration was often embodied in a concrete form; Madame Sand's 'incidents' were usually clever, eloquent, suggestive men" (*Literary Criticism*, 726).

14. In *Venice Desired* Tony Tanner speaks of "The stance and role of the observer figure—with all that it implies of refusal of participation and attendant sterilities" (165). Michael A. Cooper, in "Discipl(in)ing the Master," identifies the importance of writing as a form of vicarious (sexual) experience: "it was perhaps only when writing, when losing himself in the complex emotions and situations of his created characters, that he allowed guiltless ardor to wash freely over his psyche. By authoring a narrative, he could bind himself into a Girardian triangle across which his passion would then string itself"(75).

The shift is clearly perceptible: if in 1868 her writing could be said to "reflect all the convex vault of nature" (698), eleven years later it reflects her experiences with the other sex. In his 1897 article, on the occasion of the publication of *Elle et Lui*, a novel based on Sand's affair with Alfred de Musset, James asks musingly whether the whole "Sandian enterprise" cannot be reduced to the intellectual and especially financial exploitation of "a store of erotic reminiscences" (738). He had wondered in the earlier essay whether this woman, who showed the stamp of masculinity in her first acquaintance with life and for whom *"le style c'est l'homme . . .* is particularly true" (726), ought not be put in a completely different category.[15] If, to follow the thread of James's reasoning, "her inspiration was often embodied in a concrete form; Madame Sand's 'incidents' were usually clever, eloquent, suggestive men," then what is her writing if not the result of her ability to sell her charms albeit in a deferred mode? With respect to her remarkable life, it is only because she manages to contemplate it from a certain eminence, that this life is not given the name it deserves: "The disposition to cultivate an 'acquaintance with life at first hand' might pass for an elegant way of describing the attitude of many young women who are never far to seek, and who render no service to their own sex—whatever they may render to the other" (717). The final stab of James's pen is carefully wrapped in a tendentious rhetoric. It is, however, no more than the logical development of the critic's earlier inquiry into the writer's pedigree, where it turns out that the "apostle of the rights of love *quand même . . .* was more sensibly the result of a series of love affairs than most of us" (710). Seen from a moralist's eminence, Sand's work and life end up looking like an aberration and a scandal; why not call it then a case of literary prostitution?

The Story of a Passion

"The mind producing [such descriptions] seems not to have isolated and contracted itself in the regions of perception but to expand with

15. The joke about the man determining her style (*Literary Criticism*, 726) hints, of course, at Sand's sexual promiscuity. "This making acquaintance with life at first hand is, roughly speaking, the great thing that, as a woman, Madame Sand achieved; and she was predestined to achieve it. She was more masculine than any man she might have married; and what powerfully masculine person—even leaving genius apart—is content at five-and-twenty with submissiveness and renunciation?" (716), writes James in line with his later preoccupation with "living" (as exemplified in the famous scene between Little Bilham and Strether in *The Ambassadors*: "Live all you can; it's a mistake not to"). Are we meant to understand that living is masculine while renunciation would then be feminine?

longing and desire," writes James in his earliest article on Sand. The remark bears on her style, and accounts for his early attraction toward the woman writer; it also explains, I believe, his later, uneasy fascination. Indeed, in George Sand's style, namely, in her powers of expression and her ability to infuse her writing with passion, the writer found a model of expression and of representation that deserved to be put to the test. In a second stage of his critical relation with the writer, James is therefore increasingly drawn not to the work of the writer but to the various scenarios of passion, which seem to circulate, mythically, around the provocative, scandalous figure of the woman writer. The mental and imaginative contemplation of these scenes of passion, or rather, their materialization on the page, is never devoid of an erotic charge. It is there that a kind of compromise formation begins to take shape as a process of critical, but also emotive distanciation. But this is also where James's theory of representation, which is haunted by questions of gender and sexuality, takes its roots. This theory is concerned, centrally, with reticence and modesty. It proclaims the need to throw a veil over the revelations of some feminine mystery; it advocates a way of ensuring, through the proper partitioning and allocation of differences, that the proper distinctions of sexual difference be maintained.

As I hope to show, however, the scene of James's theorization is also that of his hysteria, as a site of resistance to the textual-sexual pleasures that her works seem to offer and, simultaneously, as the mark of the instability or impossibility of proper identification. The veil of theory that James attempts to place between himself and the too expressive, too intense pleasures that he discovers in her writing is the form taken by his modesty and resistance. But modesty, it will be remembered, can be both a defense against hysteria and one of its causes;[16] this explains the double-bind that characterizes James's situation in his encounters with George Sand. The scene of passion staged in Sand's writing calls for a similarly intense scene on James's side, but in the guise of a defensive move. But the writing that springs from such resistance ends up matching hysteria against passion. At such a point the difference between the observer/critic and the performer/writer collapses; James the critic and theoretician ends up representing his own displaced passion and thus inevitably his hysteria.

The process is double: while James's writerly performance meets the scene of passion with an analogous hysterical intensity, at the level of his critical narrative and theoretical system, he asserts, as forcefully as

16. See "Drawing the Veil" in the preceding chapter.

can be, the need for a difference. Maintaining or creating such a difference should justify his own identity as a "man writer." The hysterical scenarios that result from such a process, however, reveal precisely that it is impossible to maintain a single alignment and, for that matter, a proper sense of those differences. It should be remarked, meanwhile, that what appears to be James's irresistible need, in his textual encounters with Sand, to raise (to a hysterical pitch) the question of sexual difference does not determine his gender. This compulsion to discuss and to restage gender in his writing reveals, on the contrary, the precariousness of his sexual identity. His masculine stance is the result of a repression of the feminine: it is sustained by his violent rejection of the feminine traits he now identifies in Sand.

Crucial to James's theoretical construction is the recognition of what truly constitutes George Sand's predicament—her inability to make the proper distinctions:

She positively got off from paying—and in a cloud of fluency and dignity, benevolence, competence, intelligence. She sacrificed, it is true, a handful of minor coin—*suffered by failing wholly to grasp in her picture of life certain shades and certain delicacies.* . . . She doesn't know . . . her right hand from her left, the crooked from the straight and the clean from the unclean: it was a sense she lacked or a tact she had rubbed off. (751, emphasis mine)

While seemingly endorsing somebody else's ideas, James slyly manages to introduce a new instrument of assessment, which will enable him to diagnose her worst defects. This criterion, as is implicitly shown in his statement of the case, is that of moral discrimination. The change of registers emerges clearly: the evaluation is no longer founded on aesthetic grounds (what a style!) but on morality (what shamelessness!), and for the moralist, George Sand and her work are of course problematic. She does not make the difference between virtuous and vicious love, and "her sense of purity was certainly defective" (728)—and James concludes that "the author had morally no taste" (730). The two discourses, aesthetics and morality, are similarly blended in the following statement: "On one side an extraordinary familiarity with the things of the mind, the play of character, the psychological mystery, and a beautiful clearness and quietness, a beautiful instinct of justice in dealing with them; on the other side a startling absence of delicacy, of reticence, of the sense of certain spiritual sanctities and reservations" (714). Such a confusion enables James to erect, in the name of aesthetics, a theory of representation which is founded on moral distinctions. This is how the question

that resonates across the critical scene of James's relation to Sand—
"How could she live her remarkable life and drive her perpetual pen?"—
finds a seeming resolution. The key to the enigma must lie, James suggests, with Sand's immoral attitude toward life. While for so long Sand's
style (the ease of her expression; her ability to glide spontaneously, in-
nocuously from existence into writing) has teased James out of thought,
a shift in critical stance might lead him out of his predicament.

This is where James's critical writings on George Sand produce their
first gender fable, in an anecdote that obviously holds an enduring fascination for James since he recounts it twice over during the course of
twenty years. It can be summarized in the following fashion: In the early
morning following one of their love nights, Prosper Mérimée wakes up
to find George Sand "in a dressing-gown, on her knees before the domestic hearth, a candlestick beside her, and a red madras round her
head."[17] The woman is busy lighting a fire; she wants to get back to her
writing. Under James's pen, this short tale becomes a fable, whose substance, James suggests, offers "the very key to the enigma" of the woman
writer. Its general theme is obvious enough: it is the scandal of the
woman writer, yet another example of her inability to maintain the decencies, distinctions, or differences that the bedroom scene called for.
Stepping out of bed to sit down at her writer's desk, she converts the
bedroom into a study and proves thereby how totally immune she is to
this precious sense of (sexual) differences. In the process, James suggests,
she throws a shadow not only on her own femininity but also possibly
on Mérimée's virility.[18] In other words, the seamless continuity between
Sand's amorous life and her intellectual, writerly pursuit depends on her
defiance of his (Mérimée's) male vanity and *her* supposedly female susceptibility to passion. In his account of the scene James identifies visibly
with the male actor. What remains to be shown, however, is the complex
fate, from the point of view of James's theory of representation, of such
an identification.

The anecdote is given its most elaborate form in "She and He: Recent
Documents," published in *The Yellow Book* in 1897. This article was

17. The first account can be found in James's 1876 "Letter from Paris" (*Literary Criticism*, 703). But I discuss in detail the fuller version of the story and the ensuing commentary (739–43), which appeared in the *The Yellow Book* in 1897.

18. But could anything undermine a virility that, for James, seems so unquestionable?
In the continuation of his comment on Sand's "true male inwardness," he expresses his
faith in Mérimée in no ambiguous terms: "This, we surmise, was the case with most of
her lovers, and the truth that makes the idea of a *liaison* with Mérimée, who *was* [i.e.,
when Musset was not] of a consistent virility, sound almost like a union against nature"
(*Literary Criticism*, 748).

written on the occasion of the publication of Sand's letters to Musset in the *Revue de Paris*. A few weeks later, James comments somewhat cryptically in a letter to Morton Fullerton, "My contribution to that flurry of old *romantique* dust was as interesting to me as some of the sentiment it breathed couldn't fail to make it" (*Selected Letters*, 302). At the beginning of his essay on Sand he writes more tellingly but more impersonally: "the perusal of the letters . . . will have stirred in an odd fashion the ashes of an early ardour" (*Literary Criticism*, 736). These two statements reveal the extent of James's implication in the scene of passion between Sand and Musset which is the subject of their letters. The fable belongs then to the vicarious, secondhand experience (to use the author's own distinction) of another's passion. With James as a witness, the story of Mérimée and Sand, screened by another erotic entanglement (Musset and Sand), looks increasingly like a primal scene.[19] James is now involved in a textual scene of passion as in a fantasy that offers a setting to his own desire, but the scenario is so inchoate and confused that I can only hope to unfold gradually its "uncanny mutability."[20]

This layered scene of passion looks not only backward but forward, toward another, differently composed erotic triangle involving Sand, as a kind of presiding deity, and Henry James and Edith Wharton. "I know of no such link of true interchange as a community of interest in the dear old George" (*Letters* IV, 603), James writes, after one of their joint visits to Nohant, Sand's fabled home and the site of her own love affairs. One might speculate about the meaning of "true interchange," but unquestionably in this new configuration James no longer holds the role of the third man. James's terms suggest that the structure of the Sandian scene of passion might inspire a "first hand" experience. But we shall come back later to this particular reverberation of the story; for the time being, let it suffice that the fabled scene of passion, with George Sand firmly anchored at its center, instigates a system of screens which function like mirrors for James's authorial desire. But now for the morality that James gives to the story:

19. On this notion, see Silverman's article "Too Early/Too Late." While dealing primarily with James's fiction (mainly *The Ambassadors* and *The Awkward Age*), this article, which appeared when my own study of James's criticism was already completed, highlights in James's writing—but with more emphasis on theoretical and psychoanalytical material—narratological and subjective configurations which overlap with my own discoveries.

20. "Perhaps this uncanny mutability of self, desire and syntax is defended against by narrative, by the novel," writes Lynda Zwinger (*Daughters, Fathers, and the Novel: The Sentimental Romance of Heterosexuality*, 131). But literary criticism did not (for James at least) entail the kinds of generic constraints that characterize the novel; as a freer form, it can produce the most unstable and lurid of scenarios, as is the case here.

To the firm admirer of Madame Sand's prose the little sketch has a very different value, for it presents her in an attitude which is the very key to the enigma, the answer to most of the questions with which her character confronts us. She rose early because she was pressed to write, and she was pressed to write because she had the greatest instinct of expression ever conferred on a woman; a faculty that put a premium on all passion, on all pain, on all experience and all exposure, on the greatest variety of ties and the smallest reserve about them. (*Literary Criticism*, 740)

James's "literary quarrel," as he calls it (740), begins precisely here, with a reassertion of Sand's talents for expression. His disquisition on the case—his theory—reveals, however, the underside of such a praise, namely, a distaste for the exhibition of female passion, which functions like the secret cause or impulse behind the theorization.

The critic launches his elaboration of his theory of representation by stating at the outset that the question is rendered the more complex for involving two planes: "it takes place for each of us within as well as without" (740). The scene of passion exists as something represented, as an object held in view, but it belongs also to some inner staging where, no longer held at a distance by the gaze, it appears in the subjective form of a desire. In its internalized form, the revelation is thus the product of the spectator's desire to see and to know. No longer the thing represented, it is the embodiment of the force—one might almost be tempted to say the "drive"—of representation.

I have just retraced, in an abstract formulation, the set of questions that are presented in a two-voiced debate in James's critical prose. But the effort of abstraction is necessary if one wants to capture the full force and intent of James's text and to understand, moreover, the central question that he addresses to Sand's writing: "'What *is* then forsooth our business?' the genuine analyst may always ask" (740). This pointed question constitutes the very site of James's theorization and must be located at the conjunction of the outer and inner planes of representation. For—and James is at pains to show this in his critical debate—the two planes cannot be separated; the scene to be observed by the spectator exists also as the scene of his desire. This explains why the question of representation in James's theory can only be handled from the particular, personal position of the spectator and analyst, who is of course the writer. He will, in his own writerly stance, become the regulating principle of what of "life" is to be seen and what of "life" needs to be known. He will in his own consciousness (or should we say in his own conscience?) legislate on what kinds of representations can inhabit the space of his writing.

James's prose defines the stakes of the debate sharply enough. Thus, if the writer is indeed an analyst inquiring after the motivations and psychological determinations of a subject, wouldn't he naturally want to know everything? If not, how will he work with his knowledge? The question is then, writes James, to know "when to push in and when to back out." The figure is layered with evocations: the image of penetration speaks of an uncanny physicality, possibly the bodily representation of male desire. But it belongs to another field of evocations as well: it evokes the "house of representation" and is a resurgence of James's early discourse of admiration for Sand (not merely the showroom but the chambers). Indeed, James continues, "There is not a door you can lock here against the critic or the painter, not a cry you can raise or a long face you can pull at him, that are not quite arbitrary things" (741). This then is James in the persona of the defender of an aesthetics of free and complete unveiling, claiming that the pursuit of knowledge should remain free and uninhibited. In this vein, he concludes, the Sandian story becomes the best illustration that "the continuity of life [can have its] equivalent in the continuity of pursuit, the renewal of phenonema in the renewal of notation" (741). Following such an account, the imperative behind representation would be to say all, and its motor, the compulsion, to go for depths and further revelations.

In order to present the other side of the case and to indict Sand's inveterate romanticism of self-revelation, James enlists, in a somewhat contrived union, Emile Zola's complacent revelations about himself. In keeping with the unabashed curiosity and inventory that characterizes naturalism, Zola has allowed the publication of a physiological *enquête* where the critic finds even sharper testimony for the dangers of total revelation: "a marvellous catalogue or handbook of M. Zola's outward and inward parts, which leaves him not an inch, so to speak, to stand on. . . . For M. Zola . . . everything is for the public and no sacrifice worth thinking of when it is a question of presenting to the open mouth of that apparently gorged but still gaping monster the smallest spoonful of truth" (741). From such a perspective, the naturalist aesthetics appear to be merely a systematic and elaborate form of Sand's self-exhibition. Here too the model is necessarily double, involving this time the writer and his reader: both are united, it seems, in investing the work of representation with their prurient curiosity. An aesthetics of full notation is inevitably linked to a libidinal economy, which makes of the writer an exhibitionist and of his reader a voyeur. This is why the author advocates censorhip. It might be worth remembering at this point Freud's discussion of censorship in his *Introductory Lectures on Psycho-Analysis*; not only does he define the term but he recalls the images James himself used to express the notion: "Let us therefore compare the system of the unconscious to a large entrance hall. . . . Adjoining this entrance hall there is a second, narrower, room—a kind of drawing room—in which consciousness, too resides. But on the threshold between these two rooms a watchman performs his function: he examines the different mental impulses, acts as a censor, and will not admit them into the drawing-room if they displease him" (*SE* XVI, 295). There are some interesting differences: in James's scenario the figure crossing the threshold does so in the role of a spectator (and not as an actor); the division in James speaks, more suggestively, of a drawing room and a chamber (or bedroom?). And of course, while Freud faces the scene from the perspective of the unconscious, James stands on the other side and speaks of conscious choice and envisages the scene from the perspective of consciousness.[21] He promotes nevertheless in this text an entity or agency whose function is to distinguish and separate which among different possible representations can be made present and which cannot—this presumably in the name of a higher, more noble form of consciousness. The Jamesian analyst chooses then to face the other way, toward the civilized space of some Victorian family drawing room. The peroration of his theoretical excursus turns around the telling phrase "the triumphs of civilisation."

"Nothing often is less superficial than to ignore and overlook, or more constructive (for living and feeling at all) than to want impatiently to choose," James argues, and he concludes: "there are secrets for privacy and silence; . . . they may take their place among the triumphs of civilisation" (*Literary Criticism*, 742). The critic's theory of representation advocates then a gesture of modesty, involving screens and veils; it relies on the concept of taste, but also on some other, less easily definable value, "living and feeling," whose status is, however, undoubtedly moral. To say all entails a loss, but the existence of an unpresentable

---

21. Discussing doors and thresholds, Nicholas Royle develops the following associative thread in relation to *Wuthering Heights*: "a door is both the entrance and what closes up the entrance. To enter through a door is to cross the threshold. A threshold is 'the place or point of entering.' In its so-called figurative sense, the word also designates 'the limit of consciousness' " (*Telepathy and Literature: Essays on the Reading Mind*, 50). This commentary further illuminates James's use of the same figures, and the stakes appear to be the same; in my example too the question is one of "the limit of consciousness."

(what lies behind the veil as the effect of the denial of certain representations) guarantees the preservation of such values as a meaningful existence ("living"), sentiment and perception ("feeling"), and culture ("civilisation"). This model gives legitimacy to the distinction between truth and information which is here the founding stone of James's theory of representation. Truth is what ignores, overlooks, and operates on a system of selection which is ambiguously aesthetic as well as moral.

Here too James finds an uncanny echo in Freud's model of secondary repression. As is the case with dreams, representations in literature must fulfill their functions without insulting "the ethical, aesthetic and social point of view" (*Introductory Lectures on Psycho-Analysis*, SE XV, 142). This is for James where truth begins: with a presiding consciousness that selects among possible representations those that are acceptable to "ethical and aesthetic purposes." On the other side, together with Zola and Sand, lies information with its generalized "loquacity," its distasteful and threatening tendency toward the exhibition of the "all and everything." The drift of this discussion looks familiar enough, and it brings to mind a significant passage from a letter to Violet Paget (Vernon Lee), another woman writer. This is how James tries to discourage her from including the sexual dimension in the representation of her characters: "It will probably already have been repeated to you to satiety that you take the aesthetic business too seriously, too tragically, and above with too great an implication of sexual motives. . . . And then you have impregnated those people too much with the sexual, the basely erotic preoccupation; your hand has been violent, the touch of life is lighter" (*Selected Letters*, 206).

Thus, one might say, James's response to Sand's writing, his theoretical defense, is another manifestation of his characteristic prudery: "These are days in which one's modesty is, in every direction, much exposed, and one should be thankful for every veil." To focus, however, on the gesture of modesty would be to overlook the other stakes of James theory of representation. One cannot lose sight of the fact that James erects his theoretical construct in response to, or rather as a defense against, George Sand's writing of "longing and desire" and of passion (another case of the "implication of the sexual motives" with the "aesthetic business"). It should be noted too, in relation to the passage we have just examined, that the distinction between truth and information, as the decisive instrument of the evaluation of the work of representation, is aligned with, and hence sustained by, other systems of difference. Distinguishing sharply between the private and the public sphere, the difference between truth and information relies on an aesthetics of the veil (of the presentable and unpresentable) as against the confessional mode, with its endless chattering, and its untoward exhibitions. Our earlier inquiries into James's critical encounters have already shown that such alignments are inevitably part of a system of sexual differentiation. If indeed the theory of representation that Henry James builds around George Sand seems related to his desire for maintaining the differences between the sexes, it is essential to pursue our analysis of the dramaturgy of the scene of passion that haunts the critic's disquisitions on representation.

A Story of Hysteria

When faced with a scene of passion, James's habitual, or should we say, preferred, move is the retreat: backing out of the backchamber or bedrooom, which, because it speaks too much to one's passion and not enough to the intellect, is unworthy of presentation. This is the point of the forceful argument he addresses, in French, to Paul Bourget, on receipt of his latest novel, *Mensonges*:

It seems to me that the proceedings of love [*les procédés de l'amour*] constitute a very special part of our being, whose essential characteristic is that they lend themselves to *action*, and not to reflection. This element of action is everyone's own business, but as soon as reflection intervenes—as soon as one begins to intellectually flounder in it, as a novelist, as a painter, the thing becomes unhealthy and unpleasant. This is why an infinity of tact and taste is needed in order not to flounder—it is a question of application, a very practical question. . . . Never would it occur to me to want to know what happens in their bedroom, in their bed, between a man and a woman. (*Letters* III, 222)

Because this passage expresses James's position in a measured, explicit, and argumentative form, it provides a useful foil to the strange outburst which ends James's theoretical defense in his 1897 article. Indeed, James's theoretical discussion reaches its climax, or more appropriately, comes to a crisis around the vision of nakedness, or, as James puts it a few pages later, around this particular image: "the lovers are naked in the market place and perform for the benefit of society" (*Literary Criticism*, 744). Theory is here the response to what remains for him, as for the readers of *Madame Bovary*, the ultimate test: how to react to the public revelations of the bedroom. Censorship seems to be the most apt strategy: rather than "serv[ing] our esthetic results . . . hot and hot," the artist, who proclaims elsewhere that "art is icy," advocates "a restrictive instinct" (786). And yet our second gender fable, in the shape of the strange culmination of James's criticism on Sand, conveys nothing of the writer's icy detachment. It comes, so to speak, "hot and hot" and carries a disturbing charge of drama and violence:

When we meet on the broad highway the rueful denuded figure we need some presence of mind to decide whether to cut it dead or to lead it gently home, and meanwhile the fatal complication easily occurs. We have *seen*, in a flash of our own wit, and mystery has fled with a shriek. These encounters are indeed accidents which may at any time take place, and the general guarantee in a noisy world lies, I judge, not so much in any hope of averting them as in a regular organisation of the struggle. The reporter and the reported have duly and equally to understand that they carry their life in their hands. There are secrets for privacy and silence; let them only be cultivated on the part of the hunted creature with even half the method with which the love of sport—or call it the historic sense—is cultivated on the part of the investigator. They have been left too much to the natural, the instinctive man; but they will be twice as effective after it begins to be observed that they may take their place among the triumphs of civilisation. Then at last the game will be fair and the two forces face to face; it will be "pull devil, pull tailor," and the hardest pull will doubtless provide the happiest result. Then the cunning of the inquirer, envenomed with resistance, will exceed in subtlety and ferocity anything we to-day conceive, and the pale forewarned victim, with every track covered, every paper burnt and every letter unanswered, will, in the tower of art, the invulnerable granite, stand, without sally, the siege of all the years. (742–43)

In this instance, James's criticism is not analytical and argumentative, but seems to be infused with lurid representations and obscure scenarios. The lead is not given to the writer, but to the writing, which insistently, confusedly matches the Sandian scene of passion with another passionate scene—but one whose dramaturgy remains undecipherable and which seems to correspond to a fantasy. Discussing scenes in relation to fantasy, Jean Laplanche and Jean-Bernard Pontalis write suggestively that "the subject, although always present in the fantasy, may be so in a desubjectivized form, that is to say, in the very syntax of the sequence in question" ("Fantasy and the Origins of Sexuality," 26). In this episode, the power of the fantasy overrides the syntax, to such an extent that James's prose appears to be the theater of some barely legible text of desire and abjection. While the sentences are grammatical, in the usual sense of this word, and work in a seemingly discursive pattern, the text's rhetoric gestures to us, its readers, in an appeal to decipher its signification. James's style is here doubly hysterical, not only in the constant displacements of the pleasure scene into its reversal, or "aversion" to use the Jamesian term, but also because, while brought to such a pitch, it cannot maintain one single, let alone any proper identification.

The overall scenario of the passage calls repeatedly for uncertain or conflicting readings, such as can only be matched not by statements but by questions. What further defines this case of textual hysteria is the demand for our own vicarious participation, as readers, in the textual scene.[22] The confrontation with the undecidability of James's rhetoric cannot result in a stable, univocal commentary. Faced with such illegibility, the commentator can do no better than produce an uncertain paraphrase in the form of questions, but cannot take sides. Thus: the observer and/or reader (for who is this "we"?) meets in the street a pitiful denuded figure (a prostitute? an exhibitionist? a fallen man or woman?), who flees in horror ("mere platonic horror"?).[23] Or is it the observer or witness himself who flees? Or maybe what flees is the third term of the allegory—some kind of female (?) mystery. Whatever its exact nature or its definite appearance, the thing that is seen evokes a "fatal complication" (a term that sounds like a typically Jamesian obfuscation), which requires the organization of a struggle.[24] The sheer density and waywardness of the figuration render several representations of such a passage illegible,[25] but leave us nonetheless in no uncertainty concerning the affects that haunt such writing: a combination of desire, pleasure, and repulsion, finally marked by this "shriek." Such a scenario, while violent, is unquestionably infused with an erotic charge and haunted by conflicting identifications.

Act one (the vision) and act two (the organization of the struggle) of this psychomachia or phantasmagoria reveal a confusion of parts and of sexual roles. Is the denuded figure Zola? Sand and Musset? Or their double, Sand and Mérimée? Or is it maybe George Sand herself? The impossibility of distinguishing justifies a more abstract description: as the roles of these different figures merge into one another, the denuded

22. The reader's implication in the textual scene of hysteria is discussed more fully in my final chapter.

23. This is how, in a florid letter to Howard Sturgis, James talks about his attitude in the face of Edith Wharton's divorce: "I can neither *do* anything, write to her or be written to, about it—and ask myself why therefore cultivate, in the connection, a mere platonic horror—which permits me neither to hold her hand nor to kick his tail" (*Selected Letters*, 396). "Mere platonic horror" describes James's favorite attitude when the social or literary scene becomes too openly or violently sexual.

24. See "The Painter's Touch" in the following chapter.

25. "There is such a growing sense of violence here that one is indeed inclined to send for the police, if not to call up the army," writes Tanner (*Venice Desired*, 192).

figure, formerly exhibiting him/herself, turns imperceptibly yet eventually brutally into a figure of resistance. While becoming the prey of the inquirer, s/he undergoes such a metamorphosis as leaves him/her like an apparition in some gothic tableau, a "pale forewarned victim" finding refuge from the ruthless pursuit of its assailants in the tower of art. "Every track covered," "every paper burnt," "every letter unanswered"—that the last move of this textual crisis should take us back to the familiar terrain of the writer's own assertions, for instance, in his preface to *The Tempest* or *The Aspern Papers*, comes as no surprise. We know of James's resistance to "*intimissima* confidences" (*Selected Letters*, 287), and especially to those that pertain to the female body, as our earlier, more general discussion has shown.

But nowhere had we encountered such uncontrovertible evidence of a Medusa-like scenario as the reassertion of masculinity around the revelation of the female body.[26] "The tower of art, the invulnerable granite, stand[ing], without a sally, the siege of all the years"—the figures speak vividly an encounter with her nakedness that calls for the reassertion of a hardened virility. This reminds us that the denuded Sand remains, after all, in spite of so many tropings, what lures James into his critical pursuit. Meanwhile, one cannot forget that the last act of this phantasmagoria, with its insistent reassertion of a hardened resistant stance, proceeds from an identification with the "reported" or the "pale forewarned victim." Yet the first act was but a replay, in a hyperbolic mode of theory, of the original scene of passion, with the critic as a spectator of the illicit revelations of a she-writer. The subject of the utterance manages thus to be both "devil and tailor": subject and object of the gaze, inquirer and victim. The authorial stance also hovers undeterminedly between a feminine and a masculine identification. The last move, which could easily be interpreted as an overacting of a masculine position, should not blind us to the fact that the real threat to be avoided lies in the possibility of being engulfed totally in the mystery, that is, in the feminine. The consequences of such a collapse would be far-reaching: not only the end of knowledge, but also of subjectivity, and beyond, of sexual difference.

Thus, the morality of this second gender fable is the product of James's hysterical theorization: hysteria leads to the collapse of meaning and to the dissolution of the construct that the critic had relentlessly attempted to erect around George Sand, the woman writer. Trapped in a scene of

26. See Freud's brief essay on *Medusa's Head* as well as Neil Hertz's "Medusa's Head: Male Hysteria under Political Pressure" in *The End of the Line*.

passion of his own making, the critic writes his own undoing. Such a textual-hysterical scene can represent no identity, no gender, and no knowledge; it can only perform the fantasies that lie beyond the representation. This process, however, needs to be examined more carefully.

The Erotics of Writing

"Today narrative theory . . . seeks to understand the nature of the structuring and destructuring, even destructive, processes at work in textual and semiotic production," Teresa de Lauretis writes, and adds further: "the very work of narrativity is the engagement of the subject in certain positionalities of meaning and desire" (*Alice*, 105–6). In the wake of such a project, and under the influence of the work of Jean Laplanche and Jean-Bernard Pontalis on fantasy, Kaja Silverman suggests that we decipher in the scenarios of passion represented in film the " 'scene' of authorial desire," and she introduces the concept of a "fantasmatic": "The fantasmatic generates erotic tableaux or *combinatoires* in which the subject is arrestingly positioned—whose function is, in fact, precisely to display the subject in a given place" (*Acoustic Mirror*, 216).

If these theories of narrative help our understanding of James's theoretical style, and thus provide the theory for my previous attempt at interpreting him, they do not, however, answer all the questions that the passage raises. The representation of the scene of passion evokes in this instance not only the subject's insertion in the field of desire and of sexual identifications, it speaks also of knowledge. Yet desire and knowledge are so closely welded together in James's theoretical account that it might be more appropriate to envisage, on the one hand, "an erotic desire" and on the other "an epistemophilic desire," while granting that the distinction is merely heuristic. It is in light of these categories that James's writings on Sand need to be reexamined from the perspective of gender, sexuality, and writing.

The hysteria that characterizes James's theorization is thus part of a wavering between a system of pleasure and repulsion, on the one hand, and of a construction of knowledge on the other. His confrontation with the power of expression of the woman writer ("the greatest gift of expression ever conferred on a woman") turns insistently around the revelations of a female body inscribed in the "longing and desire" of Sand's writing. James's critical discourse in the pages we have just analyzed works indeed through the representation of scenes of passion, of denuding and unveiling, and it is the nude or the naked figure that traps the writer in the sexual economy of his own imaginary projections. But James's vicarious, voyeuristic participation in the erotics of the woman writer calls for a masculine resistance involving a violence that is the measure of his illicit desire. The theoretical framework, infused as it is with an erotic subtext, thus inevitably produces a scene of engendering. In this way James develops, in the guise of a theory of representation, an erotic or pornographic text that culminates in an attempt to assert his own difference as sexual difference.[27] George Sand's questionable, problematic identity (Is she a man or is she a woman? Can her behavior still be called feminine?) ends up challenging the critic's own sexual identity.[28] James's scene of hysterical *passio*, together with his subsequent "overacted" reaffirmation of a masculine stance, testifies to the power of a writer and a writing that carries its own troubling of gender categories over into the camp of the reporter, observer, inquirer.

The " 'scene' of authorial desire" cannot reside then in a stable construction; it challenges any attempts at defining a unified, consistent position for the subject. Such here is the hold of rhetoric over grammar that even the attempt to locate the subject in the very syntax or sequence of such a passage, to follow Laplanche and Pontalis's more radical suggestion, is defeated by the contradictory intensities that lacerate its texture. The "scenario of passion" has thus been brought to such a pitch of uncertain wavering, a wavering between subject positions and identifications, that it is truly hysterical. Indeed, James's one conviction, that to resist and to draw the veil represent "the triumphs of civilisation," seems to tower like a wreck, almost ready to topple, to be itself swal-

27. Surely the text is not pornographic in the narrow sense of the word, but as suggested by Solomon-Godeau's larger definition: "What permits the recognition of the erotic or the pornographic in any given historical moment would seem to reside in a mode of address, a syntax, a rhetoric of the image" (*Photography at the Dock*, 231).

In these texts about a woman writer, James's unusual propensity to create scenarios that display nakedness belongs to what one might call "a pornographic imagination." This pornographic streak is clearly related to a concern about sexual difference: "Among the concerns of a certain type of pornography," Annette Kuhn writes, "is a construction, an assertion of sexual difference. But if pornography participates in, reflects, conditions . . . Western discourses around sexuality and sexual difference, it is by no means the only category of representation to do so" (*The Power of the Image*, 23). What this examination of James's criticism ultimately shows is how criticism and theory can be enlisted to reflect and condition "Western discourses around sexuality and sexual difference."

28. On this point, see Butler's illuminating commentary, from a general philosophical perspective: "Inasmuch as 'identity' is assured through the stabilizing concepts of sex, gender, and sexuality, the very notion of 'the person' is called into question by the cultural emergence of those 'incoherent' or 'discontinuous' gendered beings who appear to be persons but who fail to conform to the gendered norms of cultural intelligibility by which persons are defined" (*Gender Trouble*, 17).

lowed by the surrounding welter of passions and emotions. If earlier on, theory could act as a defense against hysteria, theory now seems to lead up to hysteria. In his effort to imagine which representations must be fended off if the writer wants to remain in the icy fields of his art, the critic is drawn into the heat of the battle and loses all composure.

In her discussion of erotic photography, Abigail Solomon-Godeau evokes the pursuit of a knowledge of sexual difference that lies behind such representations. The erotic stagings of James's text obey the same principle: they too take the form of "the tantalizing display of what can be penetrated only in imagination," and furthermore, "in offering the forbidden sight to (masculine) scrutiny and investigation, [they] appear to produce knowledge," while "thwart[ing] the more profound question—the riddle (or threat) of femininity itself—which is neither answerable nor representable" (230). Indeed, when in his 1897 essay James claims that he has found the "very key to the enigma" of George Sand, it is true only in so far as he has known how to frame an erotic scene. He has chosen a perspective, created a tableau, and given the enigma the textual shape of a gender fable. The same holds true, but with diminished success, of the second episode or fable. Both scenes are the instruments, or rather the mental scenery, of his attempted theorization, but they do not provide the ultimate answer. The question remains. What is it that ultimately tantalizes and repels him in the woman writer? What is it that draws his gaze and yet makes him want to avert his face? Some mystery peculiar to the woman, "which is neither answerable nor representable." Hence the critic's endless, relentless questioning.

The hysteria triggered by James's attempts at theorizing representation around the Sandian revelations of the feminine is the sign of an impasse in knowledge, which is the by-product of his anxiety concerning his sexual identity but which goes back ultimately to the arbitrariness that defines the law of gender. As a motor, principle, and force, gender does not bear so much thinking. This is where, I believe, the lesson of these texts loses from being brought back to the individual dimensions of James's biography. If indeed the scenarios we have uncovered here show him, in the words of Leland Person, "researching his own gender identity and the gender of his literary authority" (518), they also have a transindividual and historical meaning. They confirm that the attempt to solve the riddle of the feminine inevitably ends with the confirmation of a masculine stance.[29]

29. In this James's critical narrative is merely a replay, but at the more abstract level of critical writing and theory, of the scenario that Shoshana Felman put into evidence in

These then are the complex lessons that James's texts can teach us on the theme of gender and representation in the nineteenth century. First, that truth and inwardness are a function of the veil that must necessarily be drawn between the spectator or observer, and the sexual body with its secret pleasures. Indeed the two cornerstones of the system of values which the critic produces in the course of his discussion of Sand, namely, that of inwardness and of the truth of the subject, cannot be created independent of the screens that define, according to James, the work of representation or the conditions of "representability." Second, that the scopophilic economy that characterizes such a system is a predictably gendered construction: the object of the spectacle is always feminine, while masculinity depends crucially, if one believes James's concluding move, on the stance of the observer. Furthermore, like the narrative and dramaturgy of censorhip we analyzed in the controversy around *Madame Bovary*, these texts show that the stakes of representation are ambiguously poised between the aesthetic discourse and the moral, while the discourse of morality is simply the defense offered in resistance to the revelations of the female body. Finally, they show too that the attempt to master sexual difference, in other words to ground the representations of subjectivity on the delineations and possible legislation of a "sexual identity," inevitably leads to an aporia. Any attempt to seize on what constitutes the difference ends up producing not the knowledge, but some hysterical enactment of the impossibility of distinguishing. Thus sexual identity appears to be an inherently deconstructive construct. On the other hand, what produces the fiction or the illusion of sexual difference is surely a system of representation where (masculine) knowledge or consciousness overrides (feminine) passion and maintains the separation between spectator and spectacle.

When, in 1914, James closes his textual encounters with George Sand, he redefines their differences: "Our own experiments, we commonly feel, are comparatively timid, just as we can scarce be said, in the homely phrase, to serve our esthetic results of them hot and hot; we are too

---

her interpretation of Balzac's *La fille aux yeux d'or*. There is an important difference, however, between the fictional text, "which opens up an ironic space which articulates the force of the question of femininity as the substitutive relationship between blind language and insightful pregnant silence" ("Rereading Femininity," 44), and the critic's text, which reveals a negation or silencing of the other's voice or desire that seems almost complete. James's preference for reading around the signature of George Sand the woman's biographical fate rather than the writer's texts puts the question of her femininity at an infinite remove. Another way of stating this difference might be to say that whereas in the fictional text sexual difference is already deconstructed, James's readings of Sand testify to his stubborn desire to uphold its value in the face of its constant drifts and dissolutions.

conscious of a restrictive instinct about the conditions we may, in like familiar language, let ourselves in for, there being always the question of what we should be able 'intellectually' to show for them" (*Literary Criticism*, 786–87). The "restrictive instinct" is what separates him from her, whose "mind . . . seems not to have isolated and contracted itself in the regions of perception, but to expand with longing and desire" (699). It is also a modulation on the theme of the observer, spectator of life, as he is finally represented in the guise of Lambert Strether in *The Ambassadors*, who learns too late about the price of such a renunciation and its "attendant sterilities" (Tanner, *Venice*, 165). Representation is most often for James the result of a move of "isolation and contraction" in the sphere of perception and reflection. The stance of the observer, the technique of the reflector—these are narratological strategies that enable him to frame off the scenes of passion so that the proper separations between experience and art can be maintained. To make scenes is to rely on "an ocular and imaginative possession" of the object of representation; it means displacing onto another scene what might otherwise implicate too narrowly the subject in the representation. One can thus detect, in other words, in this supremely gifted writer a resistance to writing itself.[30] James's scenic method offers him the foundation for his knowledge and the source of a secret, vicarious pleasure. But it is inevitably built on the renunciation of the certain pleasure of the text, pleasure of the language, of the kind that James witnessed in his encounters with George Sand's writing, and her "instinct of expression" (*Literary Criticism*, 740). There might have been a trace of envy as he expressed his admiration, very early on, for "the confidence with which the imagination appeals to the faculty of utterance" (697).

That James was aware of his loss can be seen in a context that touches directly and crucially on the story of his textual encounters with George Sand. In a letter written to Edith Wharton in March 1912, where he dwells at length on "our dear old George" (he had just read a copy of her letters marked with Wharton's underlinings), James lets his pen run loose. Playing with words, lacing his English prose with fragrant French

30. Garrett Stewart's reflections on the phonemic patterns and particularly on the "phonic drift" present in certain kinds of prose throw an interesting light on this question (in *Reading Voices: Literature and the Phonotext*). Stewart opposes the looser forms of writers who do not resist the pressures of the phonemic ("writing of this kind, both fluent and polyvalent, might serve to rescue the standards of prose discourse from the stranglehold of insistent cerebration, from the march rather than the flow of phrasing" [285]) to James's characteristic stylistic stance: "There are only rare moments in Henry James, for instance, when the sound shape of words is recruited for something like an overt rhetorical effect" (219).

expressions, dotting his page with exclamation marks, he weaves a double text: the rhetorical play staged around "dear old George" acts a screen for an erotic emotion that he wants to share with the other woman. "It will be a joy when we can next converse on these and cognate themes—I know of no such link of true interchange as a community of interest in dear old George"; with these words, he concludes his intimate talk about Sand.

But his own part in the conversation has already been performed—in the pages of his letter, with a style and a language so uninhibited as to present a surprising contrast with the usual circumlocutory, circumstantial Jamesian prose. This is more than just glibness (the typically Sandian quality); the prose seems to express above all some kind of sheer linguistic glee, an endless and self-sustaining play with language. In his introduction to the correspondence of James and Wharton, Lyall Powers analyzes with brio one instance of wordplay that acted as a shared joke between James and Wharton (the name of her car, Pagellino, is "redolent of illicit Venetian romance (or was to Edith and Henry)—a mixture of the exotic and the erotic and evocative of George Sand and Alfred de Musset"), and he comments on the love in/of language that pervaded James's relations with Wharton (13–14). Here indeed the writer seems to have left far behind his former "Platonic horror," the obvious motor of so many of his discussions of Sand. He ends up, however, envying the French and their providential language. For in that language so many more things can be expressed and thus begin to seem possible (language seems to lead to performance in this instance): "To have such a flow of remark on that subject, and everything connected with it, at her command helps somehow to make one feel that Providence laid up for the French such a store of remark, in advance and, as it were, should the worst befall, that their conduct and moeurs, coming after, had positively to justify and do honour to the whole collection of formulae, phrases and, as I say, why not simply do all the things there for them to inevitably say, why not simply do all the things that would give them a rapport and a sense?" (*Letters* IV, 603).

A language that is so close to action, the easy proximity between "imagination" and "utterance," and, beyond or before, their proximity with action: all of this takes us back to the enigma of George Sand. What teased James out of thought, it will be remembered, was her uncanny ability to move from the doing to the writing: "she lived her remarkable life, she drove her perpetual pen." The new solution to the riddle, which James sketches out here, is no longer moral ("she had no sense of distinctions, none of the sanctities and reservations"), it is literary. "It is a question of style, of one's relation to language," James seems to be saying now. It turns out, somewhat ironically, that the author had known this for a long time, ever since his 1897 essay where he states that Sand's style gave her "an unfair advantage in every connection" (*Literary Criticism*, 740).

The affirmation that an act of language and pleasure need not be mutually exclusive marks a crucial stage in James's critical awareness. It might explain, among other things, the pleasures of friendship that James experienced with this other woman writer, Edith Wharton. Compared to James's defensive and offensive strategies when faced on the page with George Sand, this episode, characterized as it is by a pleasure in language, a language that is pleasure, suggests that some kind of breakthrough has occurred in James's work. The hysterical intensities we witnessed in his apologies for representation now belong to the past. The general implications of such a change are provocative enough: they suggest that a true interchange between a man and a woman writer might have taken place much earlier, if only James had known when to abandon the sense of their differences in order to learn unimpededly from George Sand's great gift for expression.

CHAPTER THREE

The Bostonians:
Representing the "Sentiment of Sex"

Acts and gestures, articulated and enacted desires create the
illusion of an interior and organizing gender core, an illusion
discursively maintained for the purposes of the regulation of
sexuality within the obligatory frame of reproductive
heterosexuality. . . . The displacement of a political and discursive
origin of gender identity onto a psychological "core" precludes an
analysis of the political constitution of the gendered subject and
its fabricated notions about the ineffable interiority of its sex or of
its true identity.

—Judith Butler, *Gender Trouble*

In 1914, following publication of Wladimir Karénine's biography of
George Sand,[1] James took a last retrospective glance at Sand and, in the
guise of a historian and observer of contemporary culture, succeeded in
disengaging himself from the Sandian scene of passion and its troubling
intensities:

Madame Sand's abiding value will probably be in her having given her sex,
for its new evolution and transformation, the real standard and measure of
change. This evolution and this transformation are all round us unmistakable;
the change is in the air; women are turned more and more to looking at life
as men look at it and to getting from it what men get. In this direction their
aim has been as yet comparatively modest and their emulation low; the
challenge they have hitherto picked up is but the challenge of the "average"
male. The approximation of the extraordinary woman has been practically, in
other words, to the ordinary man. George Sand's service is that she planted
the flag much higher—her own approximation at least was to the
extraordinary. She reached him, she surpassed him, and she showed how, with
native dispositions, the thing could be done. So far as we have come these

1. Wladimir Karénine was a woman writing under a male pseudonym; her real name
was Varvara Dmitrievna Komarova.

records will live as the precious text-book of the business. (*Literary Criticism*, 775)

This excerpt reveals indeed a new critical mode, with James sketching out the changed territory of sexual definition, where Sand figures prominently as the reference. "The standard and measure of change," she exemplifies the possibility of endowing woman with an identity that reaches beyond the ordinary man, toward the "extraordinary." She has shifted the boundaries, James claims, of what a woman can do (and be) and thus has set up a challenge for the other sex. This represents a decisive change in critical attitude: the critic has relinquished his former conceptions of a subjectivity defined as sexual identity, that is, as a process of differentiation ultimately grounded in the body and related to the corresponding psychological traits. He now envisages, through the exemplary George Sand, forms of action or of "cultural production" which redefine, by "making history," the notions of femininity and, by their inevitable implication in the process, those of masculinity. In other words, abandoning the model of sexual identity, James now speaks of sexual difference in terms of representation or performance. To reformulate James's text in the vocabulary of gender may seem anachronistic, but an attentive reading of the introductory pages of his last essay shows that his conception of sexual difference can readily be translated into our contemporary critical discourse.

Commenting on the biography allows him to ground his appreciation not on the writer but on the woman and provides another way, for the bewildered critic, of taming or "domesticating" the troublesome figure of the woman writer. To position her squarely on the terrain of her life is to avoid further complications and potential hysteria. How indeed could James have remained immune from the generalized fascination with the myth of George Sand? The unnatural and unaccommodating aspect of that figure persists to the very end, presenting a constant obstacle to logical argumentation: on two consecutive pages, James speaks once of gender (in the context of historical shifts), then of sexual identity (relying on an essentialist vision). As a body that exhibits its desires and as a voice that proclaims its passions, the woman writer triggers forms of resistance and of blindness for which the critic is at once the most subtle and the most eloquent spokesman. This is how, for instance, she is ultimately defined as a man: the famous Sandian costume (trousers, boots, and coat) have become for James the symbol of her "true identity"; they show that she was "to all intents and purposes," a man. According to James, "The writer of these lines remembers how a distinguished and intimate friend of her later years, who was a very great admirer, said of her to him just after her death that her not having been born a man seemed, when one knew her, but an awkward accident: she had been to all intents and purposes so fine and frank a specimen of the sex" (780). This may be the last of James's contradictory turns, and it is only the most blatant; it shows him once more trapped in a system of gender differentiations. For while the figure cut by George Sand seems to trouble his notions of sexual identity, he seems nonetheless incapable of fully relinquishing this mode of thinking. This leads him to repeatedly rephrase the enigma of George Sand from the perspective of a sexual grammar, still running the risk of its illogicalities and deconstructive drifts. But in his obsession with sexual identity James is a voice speaking for a certain epistemology of the subject associated with particular conventions of representation. James's textual encounters with George Sand belong to a historical narrative that reaches far beyond some private drama between a male writer in the making and a woman writer of somewhat dubious reputation; they enable us to witness significant shifts, modulations, and innovations in the representation of what constitutes a subjectivity. This is the topic I pursue in this chapter, while matching the opposed and competing theories of sexual difference that James develops around Sand with a novel of James's that is similarly fraught with ambiguities and antagonistic conceptions, *The Bostonians*.

I then follow James's argument closely and, applying the critic's words on Sand to his own case, "squeez[e] for its last drop of testimony such an exceptional body of illustration as we here possess." These evocative terms constitute, it turns out, and after so many declarations suggesting that Sand's literary reputation deserves to be on the wane, James's strong recommendation that we read her: "This means accordingly, we submit, that those of us who at the present hour 'feel the change,' as the phrase is, in the computation of the feminine range, with the fullest sense of what it may portend, shirk at once our opportunity and our obligation in not squeezing for its last drop of testimony such an exceptional body of illustration as we here possess" (779). Thus the critic enjoins those interested in the "situation of women" or, to be more precise, in a historical shift in the definition of the feminine subject to scan her work.[2] Such is the scope of James's critical turnabout that he appears here in the posture of a feminist, eager to promote a reflection on "the com-

---

2. Or perhaps it is just her life? With the phrase "a body of illustration," James does not commit himself either way. Yet, as we shall see, the choice of reading the text or the woman cannot be a matter of indifference.

putation of the feminine range." The reversal is less surprising than may appear: in such a guise, feminism is but the obverse side of a critical currency whose metal is the sexual criterion. Whereas, traditionally, feminism envisages the actual and possible representations of "woman," sexism—such as we witnessed it in James's earlier mode—is about the assignation of women in the codes and conventions particular to a society or a culture. Both discourses turn around the woman, both are immediately concerned with questions of representation.

Meanwhile, in their span of about forty years, James's critical reflections on George Sand converge as one unified but complex statement related to her sexual identity: she is at once the scandal, the enigma, and the example of her sex. The woman writer has therefore been defined in the three discrepant modes of a sexist discourse, of a discourse of sexual identity, and eventually of a feminist discourse. In the first, she was represented as a permutation of contradictory roles: neither a man nor a woman, more man than woman, and if woman, a prostitute. In the second, she looms ominously as an enigma, and in the third she is the exemplary embodiment of the extended range given to the feminine. While each of the turns taken by James's critical discussion represents an attempt to develop his thinking and his knowledge about what appears to be her uncontrovertible difference, and while each produces its own kind of aporia, it is in James's last text that the questioning around (her) sexual difference shows most openly its epistemological and ideological stakes.

The first section of James's essay not only summarizes his final position on Sand but also highlights the main stakes of *The Bostonians*. The critic begins by affirming that Sand shows the full scope of her femininity precisely when, through "appropriations," she acts like a man and "deals with life exactly as if she had been a man" (779). He concludes, almost two pages later, by issuing a veiled warning against her "annex[ing] the male identity." For although this feat reveals her exceptional qualities, it also anticipates, James adds, what looms ominously in his time—the disappearance of sexual difference. Resuming his stance as a historian and sociologist, James thus attempts to situate George Sand's undertaking in light of "great world and race movements," stating that she has become the "image, the particular case" of "a revolution, or a shift of accent." In short, she is the precursor of a cultural revolution that might place women in a position of strength, and this at the very site where, since time immemorial, only men stood. Not, of course, that she has reclaimed power for herself in the political terrain; his present discourse makes it clear that her "representativity" lies in her work as a writer and in her extraordinary life, which are both related to "her immense imagination, the imagination of a man for range and abundance" (781).

Summarized in this fashion, the congeries of ideas that emerge from James's analysis appear paradoxical at the very least, but reading a section of his own prose shows how he manages, in a masterful fashion, to weave his way into and out of his feminist argument. The casuistry is remarkable, and so is, of course, the rhetoric which conjures up the tableau of some kind of apocalypsis. For Sand's ability to challenge the representations of sexual difference constitutes for James the ultimate threat to the edifice of values which is here, as before, his intellectual (and also psychological) home.

The force of George Sand's exhibition consorts, we contend, none the less perfectly with the logic of the consummation awaiting us, if a multitude of signs are to be trusted, in a more or less near future: that effective repudiation of the *distinctive*, as to function and opportunity, as to working and playing activity, for which the definite removal of immemorial disabilities is but another name. We are in presence already of a practical shrinkage of the distinctive, at the rapidest rate, and that it must shrink till nothing of it worth mentioning be left, what is this but a war-cry (presently itself also indeed as a plea for peace) with which our ears are familiar? (780)

James's last pronouncements on Sand coincide with the beginning of the First World War, and they are also contemporary with the feminist "plea for peace." But this crisis cannot be identified with the war: it takes place in the cultural and social spheres at large. For what "Sand's exhibition" challenges is the "distinctive," namely, the quality that makes at once for the singularity and the difference of the sexes. "Exhibition" belongs to James's earlier vocabulary (that of the woman making a spectacle of herself) and still signifies visibility, display, performance. However, the site of that exhibit has changed: no longer private, the spectacle of an unseemly Sand is envisaged as part of a collective cultural and social stage. In her, and all those who follow her standards, James now deciphers the undoing of the differences between man and woman and a blurring of the boundaries between the feminine and the masculine. To celebrate her feminism is then also to give the lie to a certain form of culture or civilization. Or is it not rather to abandon it altogether, since for James, civilization itself is founded on the sense of just such a difference? This time, far from being only the effect of a private, personal involvement in the scenes of Sand's making, James's anxiety results from his awareness, as a historian of gender, that her influence circumscribes and defines a period in the representation of subjectivity, of which she marks paradoxically both the advent and the decline.

From her early works in the 1830s to the last reverberations of her mythical stature in his critical work, she is the representative figure for an epistemology of the subject founded simultaneously on the notions of interiority and sexual identity. With her prose "filled with longing and desire," she teaches her reader how to represent passion and how thus to express a deeper and more encompasssing form of subjectivity, but in the very process of changing the norms of the representation of the subject, she also marks the dawn of a new era, of an era where the very notions of the feminine and masculine are so blurred as to fade one into the other. The ultimate lesson James draws from Sand is that of "the effective repudiation of the *distinctive*" and of "the practical shrinkage of the distinctive." This awareness, I believe, constitutes the beginning point of *The Bostonians*, the one novel where he is primarily concerned with "the decline of the sentiment of sex." Returning to his earlier novel should allows us to deepen our understanding of James's complex intellectual and psychological stance concerning questions of gender. Furthermore, an examination of the narratological and ideological underpinnings of his text can make us grasp the wider historical implications of the mode of representation which James promotes. But the primary object of the ensuing discussion, which focuses relentlessly on this single novel, is to elicit from this example a sharper understanding of what constitutes and determines the "illusion of an interior and organizing gender core" (Butler, 136). A literary text of this kind, which professes to be a work of realism and moreover claims to register the spirit of its time concerning the "sentiment of sex," offers a unique opportunity for analyzing what could be called the "gender effect" (using a coinage modeled on Roland Barthes's "l'effet de réel"). Having established James's investment in sexual identities and the corresponding gender anxiety in his last writing on George Sand, I examine the textual formation of a "gender core" from a triple perspective: as a set of linguistic and literary choices, as the projection and product of the writer's fantasies, and as the assumption of a prevailing ideology concerning sexual difference.

The Scenic Method

The Bostonians differs from most of James's other fiction in that it does not begin, in the usual fashion, with a "germ," that is, with a story overheard or told to him, which the author decides to enlarge. *The Note-books* reveals that the novel represents the writer's response to a con-temporary phenomenon and a historical situation.[3] James has adopted the stance of an observer of the American social scene: "our social con-ditions," "our social life," are formulations that reveal his allegiance to some native context, and the critic Quentin Anderson rightly echoes that the "novel seems to use as its point of departure a shared mass of social perceptions and judgements" (*American Henry James*, 48). But here, as for his last essay on Sand, James writes in the guise of a historian of gender, and his project shows the main concerns expressed in his critical texts on the French writer: the questions of woman, of sexual difference, and of feminism.

The novel is similarly fraught with an ambiguity of purpose and style. "Incomparably witty and absolutely serious" (*Great Tradition*, 138)—such are the terms of F. R. Leavis's praise responding to the general tonality of a text that combines the descriptive aspects of sociological study and social satire, and yet is infused with an elegiac sense of loss. The description in *Notebooks* highlights what are potentially contra-dictory elements: a formal, stylistic project concerned with achieving a "pictorial quality," a descriptive project (representing contemporary American society), and, in addition, a subjective vision inflected by a nostalgia for intimacy and for an enigmatic value called the "sentiment of sex." Given the challenge of such a complex and contradictory en-terprise, it comes as no surprise that James's 1886 novel should have been given a tepid reception and provoked a sense of failure in its au-thor.[4]

3. All subsequent references to the novel as well as to the notebook entry of April 1883 (a transcription of a letter sent to his publisher describing his project) correspond to the edition of the novel cited in the bibliography.

4. But *The Bostonians* was greeted warmly on its republication in the mid-forties and widely acclaimed as a piece of American realist writing. Lionel Trilling's brilliant (but biased) introduction succeeded in bringing this novel to the forefront of critical attention. It has known another, very recent, critical revival, so that during the time of my own work on it, Tony Tanner, Alfred Habegger, and, somewhat later, Claire Kahane each published critical pieces indispensable to the ongoing reflections on gender in James's writ-ing. Before any of these pieces became available, I had singled out *The Bostonians* for its significant representations of the private and collective hysteria attached to questions of sexual identity and its obvious links with James's writings on Sand. More important even, because of James's explicit and well-documented interest in questions of writing and rep-resentation, *The Bostonians* was meant to constitute a prime document for a critical ex-amination of the intersection between aesthetics and ideology which defines the nineteenth-century discourse of gender. This is why, in spite of the inevitable convergences I found between some of my "discoveries" and the ideas of Tanner ("*The Bostonians* and

The author himself seems to have been so little satisfied with his book that he eventually chose not to include it in his New York Edition: the book conceived as a work of depiction and representation, in the realist vein and in emulation of the French writers—Daudet, explicitly, but also, as always, Balzac, and possibly even the naturalist Zola—had failed.[5] Thus James writes to his brother, while the text is coming out in serialized form:

I am more conscious than any other of the redundancy of the book in the way of descriptive psychology, etc. . . . I have overdone it.

And adds later,

All the middle part is too diffuse and insistent—far too describing and explaining and expatiating. The whole thing is too long and dawdling. This came from the fact (partly) that I had the sense of knowing terribly little about the kind of life I had attempted to describe—and felt a constant pressure to make the picture substantial by thinking it out—pencilling and "shading." I was afraid of the reproach (having *seen* so little of the whole business treated of,) of being superficial and cheap.[6]

His analysis of the case is clear enough: lacking the knowledge of the reality that he wanted to represent, the writer feels compelled to fill the gaps, but ends up overdoing it. The novel, it turns out, is overwritten and marred by an excess of description and psychological analysis. Begun under the auspices of realist mastery, the narration takes on, because of this compensatory logic, some unusual intensities and a disturbing

---

the Human Voice"), Alfred Habegger (*Henry James and the "Woman Business"*), and Claire Kahane ("Hysteria, Feminism, and the Case of *The Bostonians*), this chapter remains.

This coincidence of interests seems significant from the perspective of a history of ideas or a literary history. Because it meets our contemporary concerns and anxieties about gender in a provocative fashion, *The Bostonians* has come again recently to the forefront of critical discourse. The text then "reads us." Tony Tanner, for instance, concludes his essay in a revealing fashion, in a note that implicitly acknowledges that today the critic must be held accountable for the text's sexual politics.

5. On the American influence on the novel, see Richard Brodhead, *The School of Hawthorne*, 150–53. On the subject of the European influence, Oscar Cargill writes: "In his first major effort in their direction, Henry James demonstrated that he had read the French naturalists to his advantage. His *environment of ideas* is as substantial as Zola's environment of things" (*The Novels of Henry James*, 137).

6. This was quoted in F. O. Matthiessen, *The James Family*, 319. All subsequent references to the correspondence between William James and his brother on *The Bostonians* as well as James's discussion of the scenic method are to this book.

violence. The tone is often shrill, the forms given to the representation are excessive and theatrical. This phenomenon was remarked upon, early on, by Leon Edel: "*The Bostonians* is a strange instance of a writer of power so possessed by his material that he loses his mastery of it. . . . Something in the very nature of the story, its people, the deep animus James felt for certain aspects of Boston life took hold" (*Life of Henry James* I, 738–39). While *The Bostonians* has found its defenders, especially Lionel Trilling and F. R. Leavis, recent criticism has seized on its unusual narratological features and thematic intensities, and registered them as hysteria. Given that the failure of mastery is, as we shall see, closely related to a thematics of gender, this term strikes me as particularly felicitous, and all the more so since it can applied as well to James's stylistic performance.

As for the author, he related his failure to an absence of knowledge, and it is in light of this awareness that I discuss first his narratological choices. The structure he chose for his novel relies heavily, on the one hand, on scenes and, on the other, on a narrator who analyzes the characters from a detached, often ironic and even sarcastic standpoint. *The Bostonians* is very different in this respect from James's later novels. We are not faced with a "reflector," who, as a reflexive consciousness, can be both actor and spectator in the scenes of the novel, and whose experience is also the subject of the narration; this narrator, on the contrary, is the instrument of a distanciation and separation between the writer and the scene represented.

The novel seems in fact to hark back toward James's earlier conception of representation, which he presents in his autobiography. Recalling his first attempts as a writer, James recounts how he used to build his text on an alternance between text and picture: three pages of narration, one page where he would draw a picture of his written text. Every fourth page of that early text, one must surmise, would freeze into a tableau:

I also plied the pencil, or to be more exact the pen—even if neither implement critically, rapidly or summarily. I was so often engaged at that period, it strikes me, in literary—or, to be more precise in dramatic, accompanied by pictorial composition—that I must again and again have delightfully lost myself. . . . When the drama itself had covered three pages the last one, over which I most laboured, served for the illustration of what I had verbally presented. Every scene had thus its explanatory picture, and as each act— though I am not positively certain I arrived at acts—would have had its vivid climax. Addicted in that degree to fictive evocation, I yet recall, on my part, no practice whatever of narrative prose or any sort of verse. I cherished the 'scene' . . . I thought, I lisped, at any rate I composed, in scenes; though how much, or how far, the scenes 'came' is another affair. . . . It took me longer to fill the canvas than it had taken me to write what went with it, but which had on the other hand something of the interest of the dramatist's casting of his *personae*, and must have helped me to believe in the validity of my subject. (Quoted in Matthiessen, 76–77)

Writing in this instance can be summarized as, or goes back to, a visual perception; it begins as (or leads to) something offered to the eye. While James's reliance on the "pictorial" as a mode of representation and of knowledge is of course not unique, it deserves more than a cursory comment.

James's scenic method can be envisaged profitably from the perspective that emerges from Freud's own reliance on the same model. For the analyst too, working on a case history, knowledge and hence the ability to narrate the subject's history go back to the scene. Thus, in his introductory remarks to the case of the Wolf Man, where he discusses the general method of analysis, Freud claims that he wants to avoid pure speculation and give epistemological priority to examples and to his concrete experience as an analyst. The secret of the analytical method resides in the particular case, and the analyst must rely on his perception—to see is to know: "A single case . . . might teach us everything, if we were only in a position to make everything out, and if we were not compelled by the inexperience of our own perception to content ourselves with a little" (*SE* XVII, 10).[7] For the analyst, knowledge can apparently be brought back to perception: what is needed is an eye or senses that are sharp enough to collect (*auffassen*) and to perceive (*wahrnehmen*) the totality of elements that put together constitute a case or a lesson (*eine Lehre*). On the one side is the observing gaze, and on the other the subject, framed off for a stronger definition. Analytical discourse, just like James's novelistic discourse (as the form taken by representation), depends on the scene or the "spectacle" provided by the subject under observation. Vision, meaning both the faculty to see and the object offered to sight, should present the conditions for knowledge and for representation. This explains why James would naturally privilege the scenic method in a novel like *The Bostonians*: as the site of epistemological investments, the scene is the most natural form or setting for a subjectivity or, more encompassing, for a history of the

7. "Ein einziger Fall könnte alles lehren, wenn man nur im Stande wäre, alles aufzufassen und nicht durch die Ungeübtheit der eigenen Wahrnehmung genögtigt wäre, sich mit wenigem zu begnügen" (Freud, *Gesammelte Werke* VII, 32).

subjective conditions that James calls "social life" to be placed under observation.

But the terms of Freud's original formulation, *die Ungeübtheit der eigenen Wahrnehmung* (literally, our lack of practice in observing), also evoke a possible obstacle to a pursuit of knowledge that relies so much on (visual) perception. Sometimes the inexperienced gaze cannot gather enough evidence. But this cannot account fully for James's failure, which he owes as much to the fact that his object was held off from his sight (how much can a man see of a woman's life?) as to a "congenital" inability to see, like some "disease of the retina."[8] This failure might be replaced by speculation, but in both cases the notions of fantasy and of countertransference are just as relevant. Indeed, as Freud came to recognize in the case of Dora, the absence of knowledge produces scenarios of desire. What James's *Bostonians* shows (just like the scenes of passion around Sand) is that this absence becomes the site of hysterical identification and projection. To speak of James's hysteria in his novel is then to address the fantasies of gender that are produced in the work of representation. Such fantasies are the product of a hysteria that is both private and collective.

What must have attracted James to the scene, meanwhile, is that it seemed to offer the guarantee of mastery. For the writer, who unlike the analyst is not bound by the existential status of his subject—his creatures are papermen and paperwomen—the scenic method, as a free construct, appears to ensure authorial control. A process of construction and selection must enable him to stage or frame the "spectacle of life" in such a way that it conveys not simply, according to his theory, the welter of impression or facts that make for "information," but some deeper "truth." In this discussion, too, James uses the figure of the house: "My face was turned from the first to the idea of representation—that of the gain of charm, interest, mystery, dignity, distinction, gain of importance in fine, on the part of the represented thing (over the thing of accident, of mere actuality, still unappropriated); but in the house of representation there were many chambers, each with its own lock, and long was to be the business of sorting and trying the keys" (quoted in Matthiessen, 77). The house of representation, constructed by the writer and for which he owns the key, holds and defines the depths that can be achieved in the act of representing.[9] It is a closed space, marked by a threshold;

8. The phrase is borrowed from George Eliot's narrator, in his/her account of Dorothea Casaubon's visit to Saint Peter's in Rome during her honeymoon (*Middlemarch*, 226).

9. The image of the house of representation holds a prominent place in the preface to *The Portrait of a Lady* (*Literary Criticism*, 1075), with an emphasis this time on what

crossing this threshold is an intentional move, the result of a choice. One finds the key, opens the door, and, remembering James's early admirative words for Sand, there lies the inward drama, the psychological mystery, and the "truth" or "validity" of the subject. In other words, writing consists in this delimitation and appropriation of a space where the scene can be staged. Built on such a principle, *The Bostonians* should offer neither illicit revelations nor untoward confessions.

"I cherished the scene," James writes, "the picture, the representative design, directly and strongly appealed to me, and was to appeal all my days" (Matthiessen, 77). Thus, forgetting about the voice, his voice, he began *The Bostonians* with the conviction that he could impart disinterested knowledge in the shape of the scene. And yet, although it is conceived like a theater for the reader's enlightenment, representation in *The Bostonians* cannot avoid the return of a personal, subjective dimension: the stage where the protagonists perform opens up onto another stage where the author's private hysterical drama gets enacted. James's divided and ambiguous allegiance—to the question of woman and to the loss of the sentiment of sex—triggers, as we shall see, a double identification: the writing is thus uncomfortably caught between a feminine and a masculine line of desire. For this novel, like James's late text on Sand, brings together two irreconcilable positions: a sympathy for woman's conquest of a wider subjective range, and a distrust of the loss of difference that this entails. James's style, uneasily caught between the two impulses, is doomed to lose its poise. Meanwhile, the author's repeated and visible attempts to establish mastery, rather than confirming the values of sexual difference, end up showing their very precariousness.

This precariousness is manifest in the plot as well, which seems to waver between two perspectives sustained by conflicting identifications. A shift of perspective reveals, as in a case of anamorphosis, two very different pictures. From the first position, assuming a retrospective glance and aligning our vision with James speaking of the "decline of the sentiment of sex," one sees the following:

The narrative finds its articulation around a (Girardian) triangle that describes the relations of eros and power among the three protagonists, Verena Tarrant, Olive Chancellor, and Basil Ransom.[10] The main actors,

---

might be described as the writer's voyeuristic stance. Thus, for instance: "They are but windows at the best, mere holes in a dead wall, disconnected, perched aloft; they are not hinged doors opening straight upon life. But they have this mark of their own that at each of them stands a figure with a pair of eyes, or a least with a field-glass, which forms, again and again, for observation, a unique instrument."

10. See René Girard's *Desire, Deceit, and the Novel.* When viewed from the perspective

just as the cast of secondary figures, are defined by the place or role they hold in the war of the sexes. The young, virginal, innocent, desirable Verena figures at the center of this drama; she is the ultimate "value" in the sexual, financial, and rhetorical negotiations which define the novel's plot. Verena's father, a mesmeric healer, is determined to make money out of his daughter's oratory talents; the journalist Matthias Pardon also thinks her voice is worth gold. The cast also includes a "doctoress" who takes a cynical view of the woman question, the skilled and confirmed feminist Mrs. Farrinder, and the pathetic Miss Birdseye of the old Transcendentalist breed. The action culminates, however, in the struggle between the southerner Basil Ransom, who thinks home is the only proper place for a woman, and the wealthy Boston spinster Olive Chancellor, who has devoted her life to the great cause of women. The latter has taken Verena into her home to school her so that the girl's spontaneous eloquence might acquire the weight of facts and knowledge that could make her into the spokeswoman for her suffering sex; the hero is determined to save the woman whom he wants to marry from the vulgar gaping crowds, avid for strong sensations.

Told in this fashion, the story of *The Bostonians* evokes a historical and cultural text characterized by the extreme sexual polarization of the characters ("neurotic feminism" and "reactionary masculinism" to borrow Tony Tanner's terms ("*The Bostonians* and the Human Voice," [156]) around questions of eros and power. Indeed, from this standpoint, James's novel appears to depict, in unquestionably dramatic fashion, the age of the war of the sexes.

But from the other perspective, another story emerges, endowed with the more intimist aspects of an *études de moeurs* along the lines of some of Balzac's tales. This other *Bostonians* is a work of "descriptive psychology" centered on "one of those friendships between women which are so common in New England" ("Notebook," in *Bostonians*, 438). It could be summarized as follows:

In late nineteenth-century Boston, the wealthy and committed feminist Olive Chancellor meets the ignorant but brilliantly gifted public-speaker

---

of a heterosexual plot, the novel shows a structure of mimetic desire, with Olive Chancellor as Ransom's rival and model. Because of its unusual gender arrangement—a man desiring a woman through a woman—this structure does not look like an orthodox version of the Girardian model. But in fact, as both Sarah Kofman ("The Narcissistic Woman: Freud and Girard") and Eve Kosofsky Sedgwick (particularly in her introduction to *Between Men: English Literature and Male Homosexual Desire*) have shown, as soon as we begin to examine Girard's structuralist model from the perspective of gender, its simplifications and blindspots become apparent.

Verena Tarrant. Olive, who is deep, intelligent, but so shy as to be virtually voiceless, feels she has found in Verena the woman who can speak for her own haunting awareness of women's age-old suffering. The two women are soon enthralled with each other, so much so that Verena almost promises she will give herself up, body and soul, to the great cause. But the arrival of Basil Ransom, who comes from the Deep South, threatens this romance between the women. Taken by Verena's charm and glamour, he is determined to marry her. A war is henceforth waged between Olive and Ransom: he wants Verena's body; she, it seems, wants her soul.[11] In a dramatic final scene, the girl is brutally abducted by the hero, who feels that Verena's commitment to lecture in the Boston Music Hall (her theme is "woman's reason") represents the ultimate challenge to his manhood. On the strength of the acceptance (by the *Rational Review*) of Ranson's own manuscript, he had indeed proposed to Verena. The scene of hysteria that replaces the expected *scène de passion* suggests that, in the age of such conflicting desires between what a man wants and women may want, a romantic closure exists only as a dream of the past.

An additional perspective on James's novel emerges as we step back from the positions that seem woven into the text, to follow an insight unexpectedly provided by Constance Fenimore Woolson. Sharing her view, we can identify one unified story line, which documents the shift from one allegiance ("the situation of women") to the other ("the sentiment of sex"). Her version speaks simultaneously of an all-too-conventional heterosexual realignment as well as of feminine insight and masculine blindness. Although we have no proof that Woolson wrote this comment on the basis of her acquaintance with James's novel, it expresses her general awareness of the stories of women's friendships. Still there is an uncanny resemblance between the plot that she sketches out here and James's novel: "I myself have seen tears of joy, the uttermost faith, and deepest devotion, in mature, well-educated, and cultivated women, for some other woman whom they adored. . . . But—but! there is a monotonous certainty that follows on, which arouses to laughter the unregenerate masculine mind and makes it deny the whole (which is a mistake; it *is* there), namely, the certainty that once let loose an agreeable *man* in this atmosphere, and, ten to one, the whole cloud structure topples over."[12] I have seen it with my own eyes, "it *is* there,"

---

11. Goethe's *Faust*, where the split between body and soul is emphasized and which is quoted by Olive Chancellor ("Entsagen sollst du!"), is one of the subtexts of this novel.

12. The citation is from Woolson's "Untitled Essay," quoted in Habegger, *Henry James and the "Woman Business,"* 261, n. 35.

writes Woolson about the relation between women, as she depicts a scene offered in evidence of her knowledge. The vignette she draws resembles indeed an early moment in James Ivory's film version of the novel, which shows Olive, played by Vanessa Redgrave, her eyes brimming over with tears, embracing Verena, after she has first heard her give her speech at Miss Birdseye's. It does not resemble, however, what we are given to see in the novel, where the scene is depicted mainly through Ransom's insensitive, self-serving gaze and through the narrator's insistent descriptions. But while Woolson, it seems, knew what James was talking about when he undertook to "study . . . one of those friendships between women," she also anticipated what were going to be the obvious features of the plot, namely, that in *The Bostonians* the "agreeable man," Basil Ransom, would bring to the ground "the whole cloud structure" of the other relationship. But surely, given the precarious conditions of the original theme (which can be witnessed in Woolson's insistence on "I saw it," "it exists"), Woolson does not show prophetic insight. A story like that of Basil's conquest of Verena is all too banal or predictable; it is that of her "natural destination." Claire Kahane evokes it under the label "Oedipal resolution" (294–95), Alfred Habegger speaks of the victory of philogeny over ontogeny (208), while Tanner ("*Bostonians* and the Human Voice") suggests that it shows the victory of gender over identity. On the other hand, what Woolson had not anticipated in her remarks is the violence, both in the representation and in the writing, that would attend such a *retournement*. This violence, registered as hysteria, is what I shall address, but first it must be placed in context.

A Work of Psychology, Descriptive and Moral

The case of Miss Birdseye, and the debate between Henry James and William James that surrounded it, offers precious insight into James's working methods. Here is the writer defending himself against the accusation that he had, in his novel, borrowed from life and drawn his caricature from the real Miss Peabody:

Miss Birdseye was evolved entirely from my moral consciousness, like every other person I have ever drawn, and originated in my desire to make a figure who should embody in a sympathetic, pathetic, picturesque, and at the same time grotesque way, the humanitary and *ci-devant* transcendental tendencies which I thought it highly probable I would be accused of treating in a contemptuous manner. . . . I wished to make this figure a woman, because so it would be more touching, and an old, weary, battered and simple-minded woman because that deepened the same effect. I elaborated her in my mind's eye. (Quoted in Matthiessen, 326)

In addition to the scene, another principle presides over James's system of representation: his discussion of "a character evolved entirely from [his] moral consciousness" lays bare a cultural and ideological framework that was not present in his aesthetic and epistemological considerations. This passage also highlights the importance of the "female subject" when it comes to creating pathos: "a woman because so it would be more touching." The slip of the pen, which speaks both of causality ("because") and consequence ("so"), shows the overdetermined position held by the women when it comes to creating pathos. There is nothing unusual in the idea that woman constitutes the ideal victim and object of sympathy, except that in this case the woman is not the typical sentimental heroine, but is "old, weary, battered" (this may be taken as a sign of James's acquiescence with a naturalist aesthetics). Nevertheless, the principle of "a woman because it would be more touching" also applies in the case of the beautiful Verena, who is removed from the stage and faces "in tears" the prospect of a union which looks to James's narrator "far from brilliant" (435). It is true too of the hard-earned tears that Olive, singled out for her capacity to suffer ("they rarely suffer as she suffered" [396]), sheds over the loss of her friend. There is abundant evidence that *The Bostonians* relies on the age-old association between femininity and pathos, tears and sentiments or sentimentality.

The unusual term "moral consciousness" needs further commentary. Why not speak simply of "conscience," the term that usually describes an awareness infused with a sense of right and wrong? It seems James wants to dissociate the moral, ethical dimensions involved in the act of representation from their purely cognitive aspects. Morality is one thing, knowledge another, this compound notion suggests. Unlike the term "conscience," this phrase distinguishes between the awareness of the right or the wrong, and the sense of an obligation, of an imperative that, in the Kantian fashion, is associated with conscience. As a result, James's notion of a moral consciousness opens up a space for the individual endorsement or rejection of the ethical imperative that a moral consciousness will, by definition, perceive. Meanwhile, with knowledge, vision, and insight there comes a general benevolence, a desire to do well by the other. This indeed must be James's best defense when accused of mishandling the subject that he imagined and constructed or "represented" in the figure of Miss Birdseye: in spite of all he saw and knew, he meant no harm.

This interpretation of Henry James's words is amply borne out when we consider his brother's enthusiastic response to the novel, character-ized by a startling image which seems like a reminder of some of the figurations that the writer had developed around Sand:

You seem to acknowledge that you can't exhaust any character's feelings or thoughts by an articulate displaying of them. You shrink from the attempt to drag them all reeking and dripping and raw upon the stage, which most writers make and fail in. You expressly restrict yourself, accordingly, to showing a few external acts and speeches, and by the magic of your art making the reader *feel* back of these the existence of a body of being of which these are casual features. You wish to suggest a mysterious fullness which you do not lead your reader through. It seems to me this is a very legitimate method, and has a great effect when it succeeds. (Quoted in Matthiessen, 318)

The image offered by William James's text is characteristically that of the stage; it evokes the writer's pictorial and scenic method. Its true destination is not the exhibition, however, but the possibility of repre-senting "a mysterious fullness." For this reader then, James's novel on "the decline of the sentiment of sex" involves a feat of imaginative cre-ation or re-creation, such as gives a kind of existential if not ontological solidity to his creatures: "by the magic of your art making the reader *feel* back of these the existence of a body of being." Thus one might say of such a character that "it exists, it has come to life, it must be true," because, it would seem, the act of representation has produced a creature that corresponds to a certain model of psychological truth. This is pre-cisely how F. R. Leavis, another admirer of this novel, expresses his sense of the psychological knowledge or truth that James achieves in his novel: "And James's genius comes out in a very remarkable piece of psycho-logical analysis, done in the concrete (and done, it is worth noting, decades before the impact of Freud had initiated a general knowingness about the unconscious and the subconscious)" (135). Singling out James for having anticipated Freud's topology of the psyche, Leavis highlights what turns out to be James's success at evoking a "psychological core." This is achieved, if we believe William the psychologist, as the knowl-edge about feelings and thoughts, and the insight into "passion" (re-membering what James learned from Sand) are brought together, without, however, doing violence to the privacy, intimacy, and mystery that gives the subjectivity its fullness. In this light, *The Bostonians* seems to fulfill the theory of representation that James was at pains to erect around the case of George Sand.

A number of textual elements confirm this. The journalist Matthias Pardon, for instance, is the vivid embodiment of the prurience and indelicacy that the writer stigmatizes from his moral point of view: "indelicacy was his profession; and he asked for revelations of the *vie intime* of his victims with the bland confidence of a fashionable physician inquiring about symptoms" (*Bostonians*, 134). The Naturalists' exhibition of privacy, Dr. Toulouse's physiological *enquête*, the journalist's curiosity for scandal—these are the terms of James's 1897 critique of Sand, which the project for *The Bostonians* seems to have foreshadowed: "There must, indispensably, be a type of newspaper man—the man whose ideal is the energetic reporter. I should like to *bafouer* the vulgarity and hideousness of this—the impudent invasion of privacy—the extinction of all conception of privacy, etc" (438). The description in *The Notebooks* offers the confirmation that James conceived of his "moral consciousness" as the principle sustaining an act of representation that privileges truth at the expense of vulgar information: "mysterious fullness" as against unseemly revelations. But here again it turns out that the project cannot be dissociated from what one might call a sexual politics, or to use the term derived from the earlier inquiry into James's reading of Sand, a sexist vision, where, for instance—and the case is amply illustrated in Verena—woman must embody the virtues of intimacy, interiority, and modesty.

This is where the Jamesian model of representation in *The Bostonians*, as well as the theory that he develops around Sand intersect with a wider cultural text which relates, in a similar fashion, questions of gender and questions of morality. The resistance to woman's exhibition, the desire to maintain the "sentiment of sex" and the sense of the "distinctive," these are the defining elements of James's own attitude toward the contemporary scene. But they also identify the site where his theory of representation, uneasily caught between the descriptive, epistemological project and the work of cultural, ethical valuation, comes to a crisis or, to use the more charged term, grows to a hysterical climax.

In this case again, the text's stylistic as well as thematized hysteria enables us to register, beyond the individual case of James, a wider phenomenon concerning the representation of a gendered subjectivity. Gender is brought to the foreground of James's novel, as an element of culture and of history, but it depends mainly, in its representation, on two aspects: first, on the fiction, insistently sustained by James's descriptions, of a "psychological core" brought back to its sexual determinations (evidenced in the "feminism" and "masculinism" that Tanner singled out as a characteristic trait of the novel), and second, on the sometimes violent imposition of sexual difference, which, as we shall see, is a characteristic rhetorical feature of the novel. It might be useful, however, in order to show how closely the work of representation in James's *The Bostonians* fulfills this masterplot, to quote in full Judith Butler's description, in the abstract language of philosophy, of the compact between gender, interiority, and regulation.

That the gendered body is performative suggests that it has no ontological status apart from the various acts which constitute its reality. This also suggests that if that reality is fabricated as an interior essence, that very interiority is an effect and function of a decidedly public and social discourse, the public regulation of fantasy through the surface politics of the body. . . . In other words, acts and gestures, articulated and enacted desires create the illusion of an interior and organizing gender core, an illusion discursively maintained for the purposes of the regulation of sexuality within the obligatory frame of reproductive heterosexuality. . . . The displacement of a political and discursive origin of gender identity onto a psychological "core" precludes an analysis of the political constitution of the gendered subject and its fabricated notions about the ineffable interiority of its sex or of its true identity. (Butler, 136)

A Scene of Hysteria

The most spectacular evidence that the novel offers concerning "the public regulation of fantasy through the surface politics of the body" is surely the last scene of the novel, the scene of hysteria that brings the story of Verena, Olive, and Ransom to a close. This emotional crisis, with its convulsions, screaming, and tearful intensity, defines the failure of the traditional heterosexual romance. Here the ending does not hover at the bedroom door, hinting at connubial bliss: it presents the sorry spectacle of a future husband wrenching away "by muscular force" his bride to be, with a mother in attendance who "burst into violent hysterics" and a friend, Olive (the bridesmaid?), "on the threshold of the room . . . upright in her desolation" (432). If William feared the kinds of representations that would bring their subjects "reeking and dripping and raw" onto the stage, then he may well have been disappointed in this brutal finale, which seems to perform precisely this, and is moreover described as "a convulsive scene" by the narrator or "a sickening scene" by one of its victims, Verena.

The regulatory function is conspicuously entrusted to Basil Ransom, who takes it upon himself to lead the true woman back into the fold: he embarks on a conquest of Verena with "merciless devotion" (369). This oxymoronic formulation anticipates the final revelation, where the needs of the "sentiment of sex" determine heroic actions that verge on outright physical violence or sheer cruelty.[13] How else, in this age of woman's emancipation, would it be possible to ensure that she keep her orthodox feelings for intimacy and for her husband's pleasure? "The use of a truly amiable woman is to make some honest man happy" (228), the hero exclaims. The novel shows indeed clearly who should ultimately benefit from this regulation. The last scene, where the hero, substituting physical force for his usual eloquence, gets his intended "bodily out of the place," looks like an age-old plot of abduction or (to play weakly on names) ransoming. In this instance, *The Bostonians* is not only, as wisely suggested by Habegger, about the "preeminence of sentiment over thought" when it comes to defining the true woman (this would at least suggest that Verena is swayed by her sentiments), it also demonstrates, in the most vivid terms, in the gestures and attitudes that are akin to those of a war of the sexes, the victory of ancestral force over the will and voice of a woman. That much is needed, it appears, to bring the heroine back to the babies she adores; the coincidence in one scene of her growing passion for the hero and the apparition of babies in a perambulator hints unmistakably at such a proper convergence. "The regulation of sexuality within the obligatory frame of reproductive heterosexuality" can indeed only be achieved at a certain cost. Thus Ransom, covering Verena's face with a hood, takes her away from Boston Music Hall as she is about to deliver her speech on woman's reason, but not before a last battle, a last feat of resistance has taken place:

There at the farther end of [the room], beyond the vulgar perfunctory chairs and tables, under the flaring gas, he saw Mrs. Tarrant sitting upright on a sofa, with immense rigidity, and a large flushed visage, full of suppressed distortion, and beside her prostrate, fallen over, her head buried in the lap of Verena's mother, the tragic figure of Olive Chancellor. Ransom could scarcely

13. Tanner speaks of rape ("*Bostonians* and the Human Voice," 159), and Kahane of rape and castration ("Hysteria," 294–95). As for Habegger—who emphasizes the biographical dimension of James's text as well as its uneasy relation with a "female tradition" of writing—he detects in it the ghost of aggressive masculinity (*Henry James and the "Woman Business,"* 208–9), and remarks on "the sustained act of silencing [of women's speech]," which is represented both in *The Portrait of a Lady* and *The Bostonians* (230).

know how much Olive's having flung herself upon Mrs. Tarrant's bosom testified to the convulsive scene that had just taken place behind the locked door. (425)

[Olive's] face and voice were terrible to Ransom; she had flung herself upon Verena and was holding her close, and he could see that her friend's suffering was faint in comparison to her own. "Why for an hour, when it's all false and damnable? An hour is as bad as ten years! She's mine or she isn't, and if she's mine, she's all mine!"

"Yours! Yours! Verena, think, think what you're doing!" Olive moaned, bending over her.

. . . Mrs. Tarrant had burst into violent hysterics. (428)

The "convulsive scene" takes place behind closed doors, and James leaves it to the reader to fill in with more detail a hysterical scenario that a description after the fact has merely conjured up. Nevertheless, these expressive bodies and increasingly shrill voices seem to somehow answer offstage the need for strong sensations that a gaping crowd, stamping its feet in front of a closed curtain, has been demanding. So much then for the sentiment of sex.

James unquestionably experienced difficulties in bringing his scenario of engendering to a proper close, and this scene of hysteria is the climactic form taken by the narratological uncertainties, gaps, and contractions that pervade his novel. Claire Kahane has appropriately related *The Bostonians* to a hysterical discourse that she defines as "fragmentary, digressive, and full of gaps," and, she adds: "I would suggest that a good many late nineteenth-century texts can profitably be called premodernist and hysterical, that as symptomatic narratives, they articulate the problematics of sexual difference, a difference challenged in great part by nineteenth-century feminism" (286). But the concept of hysteria applies here in an even more specific sense and is related to the quandary with which James began his work, namely, how to account simultaneously for the situation of woman, and the decline of the sentiment of sex.

Our incursion into James's last text on Sand has shown how irreconcilable these two statements turn out to be. The feminist conquest is precisely about the loss of the difference that the sentiment of sex would want to promote. *The Bostonians* was thus bound to become a divided, fractured text, which, relying on opposite identifications, would inevitably show both discreet and more blatant signs of hysteria. If the story of woman takes the form of ultimately passive victimization of the kind that is most acutely shown in tongue-tied Olive, while the sentiment of sex, is entrusted to Ransom's virile, aggressive style, the narrative necessarily relies on two opposed perspectives or, to move beyond formalism, two antagonistic libidinal economies.

The ending can thus be envisaged as the climactic confrontation of the two concepts of femininity and masculinity, or as a last desperate attempt to save one (masculinity) by saving the other. When applied to Ransom's "physical intervention" on Verena, the word "saving" can only be understood ironically. There are enough inflated statements in the novel to show that Ransom's heroic mission is ultimately of a self-serving and egotistical nature: "That was the way he liked them [women]—not to think too much, not to feel any responsibility for the government of the world. . . . If they would only be private and passive, and have no feeling but for that, and leave publicity to the sex of tougher hide" (8); "their business was simply to be provided for, practise the domestic virtues, and be charmingly grateful" (191); "she was meant for something divinely different—for privacy, for him, for love" (258). This surely justifies Olive's admonitory words, "Yours! Yours! Verena think, think, what you are doing!" (428), which give us a glimpse of the other, "feminist" point of view. Ransom's insistent and ultimately violent conquest of the woman offers the vivid confirmation that she, the pure, innocent, and empty-headed Verena, is no more than the necessary and thus valuable counter in an enterprise of self-definition concerned with maintaining the meaning of masculinity: "What he wanted, in this light, flamed before him and challenged all his manhood" (426). Indeed, Virginia Woolf and Luce Irigaray have spoken in nonambiguous terms about the mirror function that devolves upon women. Thus Woolf: "Women have served all these centuries as looking-glasses possessing the magic and delicious power of reflecting the figure of man at its its natural size" (*Room of One's Own*, 35). And Irigaray: "In order for this [masculine] ego to have its valor, there has to be of course a 'mirror,' which give it assurance and reassurance of its valor" (63).

The closing moment of *The Bostonians*, with the figure of Ransom embodying the force or violence that brings about proper gender alignments, is thus symptomatic of the "disciplinary practices" that entail and produce the proper kinds of engendering or "a coherent gender." Whereas, as Butler suggests, these regulatory forces are usually kept from view, the work of representation of James's fiction stages them in the most spectacular fashion. The last of the novel expresses the desire and the anxiety produced by the recognition that, with the disappearance of a "true gendered identity," gender no longer corresponds to some "ineffable interiority." The consequences of such "a decline" and "repudiation of the distinctive" can first be perceived at a narratological level, but they are ultimately of a wider theoretical importance. As the fate of sexual identities now depends on creating a scene of hysteria, where the future of masculinity and femininity depend on their melodramatic enactment, gender becomes legible, inevitably, as surface, as the outward appeareance of theatrical gestures.

Meanwhile, the ending, which I take to be the paroxysm or the moment of crisis of such a theatricalization of gender, has left many readers uneasy because of its thematic ambiguity, its stylistic excesses, and overall lack of poise. As James appears to lose mastery over the narration, it seems that his own voice surfaces under the hero's. This is Leon Edel's argument—"In the final scene, in which Ransom insists that at this crucial moment Verena must make her choice, there is an urgency and a shrillness that may bespeak the author's own shrill anxiety" (*Life of Henry James* I, 144)—as well as Alfred Habegger's, who suggests that "*The Bostonians* was James's ultimate ghost story" (209). In the wake of these two comments, I pursue the idea that the hysterical shrillness of these last pages can be traced back to some private stage of the writer's own gender anxiety. A brief examination of the text of James's autobiography that describe his delicate, difficult initiation into the "sacred connection" of literature and his decisive endorsement "of the rites of that chapel where the taper always twinkled" will help us understand why the scene represented at the end of the novel bears so visibly the marks of the painter's brush.

But while this attempt to get at the roots of James's hysterical narration seems to take the form, at times, of a physiological *enquête*, where like a Dr. Toulouse I "draw a catalogue of [M. James's] outward and inward parts," my interest does not really lie in uncovering the author's secrets.[14] The case study is meant to enable me to develop a theory of representation that can account, in narratological terms, for the cultural, historically bound phenomenon of a sexual identity or "gender core." Lest my readers believe I am promoting, in the course of this book, the myth of James's masculinity, let me add that this demonstration has a counterpart in the next chapter, where I discuss in detail the author's feminine identification.

The Painter's Touch

In 1862, after the Civil War had already begun, Henry James, aged nineteen, was looking for an occupation, for, he wrote fifty years later in "Notes of a Son and Brother," in his *Autobiography*, "mere inaction

---

14. These terms are reminiscent of James's indictment of naturalism, discussed in the previous chapter.

quite lacked the note." He chose to study law at Harvard, but with little commitment, for his real interest lay in literature: "what I 'wanted to want' to be was, all intimately, just *literary*." These few lines represent a summary of the first part of chapter 9 of James's autobiography which leads to the account of (and James's prose deserves to be quoted here as an instance of a style that has become dense to the point of obscurity or obfuscation) "a passage of personal history the most entirely personal, but between which, as a private catastrophe or difficulty, bristling with embarassments, and the great public convulsion that announced itself in bigger terms each day, I felt from the very first an association of the closest, yet withal, I fear, almost of the least clearly expressible."[15] The very private event that James relates to the war ("the great public convulsion") is "a physical mishap," which befell him in the spring of 1861, leaving "a horrid even if an obscure hurt." The wound came upon him "in twenty odious minutes" but is part of "a single vast visitation" which affects the country at large. The "ache" extends beyond the personal: James's "poor organism" cannot be separated from "the enclosing social body, a body rent with a thousand wounds and that thus treated one to the honour of a sort of tragic fellowship." Nevertheless, the writer adds, to "have trumped up a lameness at such juncture could be made to pass in no light for graceful," for indeed, when thousands, including two of James's own brothers, were enrolling in the war, the conjunction might be construed from a different perspective as a little too timely.

This wound does not go away, and, writes James, "I came to think of my relation to my injury as a *modus vivendi* workable for the time." Called upon to express his opinion, the great surgeon produces the mystifying, "strange fact of there being nothing to speak the matter with [him]." Following his visit, the patient chooses, however, to abide by this illness, which after all might be beneficial from the point of view of his literary career. For somebody who is preparing himself for an intellectual "ordeal" requiring "studious retirement," there may be some advantages in being forced by illness to adopt, "book in hand," "a supine

15. The ensuing commentary bears on chapter 9, "Notes of a Son and Brother" in James's, *Autobiography*, 411–27.

James C. Cox singles out this passage as representing the ultimate challenge to James's style: "In confronting the multitudinous deaths out of which his life as an artist took shape, James faced the deepest necessities of his narrative. . . . The elaborateness of the conversion is sufficient to exceed the resources of the celebrated later style. For although the obscurity of the wound is made to order for the style, there is more convergence of forces than the style can negotiate" ("The Memoirs of Henry James: Self-Interest as Autobiography," 19).

attitude"—unless one were to argue the other way, that for somebody ill in this fashion, only a literary vocation seems possible. Meanwhile (for the narrator wants several arguments in this defense), to fight against the illness represents its own kind of combat, "something definitely and firmly parallel to action in the tented field." The narration concerning the wound stops on this note, and James resumes the earlier thread of his life as a student at Harvard.

The history of James's obscure wound is well known, and has been painstakingly documented by Edel, but James's late, deferred attempt to narrate the event offers interesting insights into his own case. The manifold associations presented in his belated account hint at a mechanism of conversion and male hysteria, with clearly evidenced primary and secondary benefits. Elaine Showalter, in a chapter on male hysteria in *The Female Malady*, documents a number of such cases, mostly during the First World War—"malingerers" who, it turned out, were affected with spectacular conversions. Similarly it might be easy to assume that a young man, dropping out of active life in order to fulfill his literary vocation, might hold in the home the feminine of the lady hysteric expecting a rest cure. But the point is not to come to a diagnosis. A narrative offering such easy psychoanalytical resolutions would in any event appear suspicious: the obvious interpretation is only a screen, the real stakes are elsewhere. Furthermore, the question I raise is literary and not overtly biographical, since it concerns James's ghostly voice in the body of Ransom.

In Basil Ransom, the southerner who has fought in the war and lost two brothers, the author seems indeed to have invented a figure symmetrically opposed to the invalid writer who is laid up because of a wound and whose role in the great conflagration cannot go beyond sympathetic identification with the wounded. Ransom's life remains heroic, a life of assertive, virile conquest, even when the object is only a woman: "What he wanted, in this light, flamed before him and challenged all his manhood, tossing his determination to a height from which not only Doctor Tarrant, and Mr. Filer, and Olive, over there, in her sightless, soundless shame, but the great expectant hall as well, and the mighty multitude, in suspense, keeping quiet from minute to minute and holding the breath of its anger—from which all these things looked small, surmountable, and of the moment only" (426). As the champion in the war of the sexes in a battle that is presented in epic terms, Ransom is the very image of a combative, conquering masculinity who faces the challenge of an immensely seductive, but resistant female.

But here, from his autobiography, is how the young Henry James encountered his own adventure, while waging a battle against a fire in a neighbor's stables:

Jammed into the acute angle between two high fences, where the rhythmic play of my arms, in tune with that of several other pairs, but at a dire disadvantage of position, induced a rural, a rusty, a quasi-extemporised old engine to work and a saving stream to flow, I had done myself, in face of a shabby conflagration, a horrid even if an obscure hurt; and what was interesting from the first was my not doubting in the least its duration—though what seemed equally clear was that I needn't as a matter of course adopt and appropriate it, so to speak, or place it for increase of interest on exhibition. (415)

Whereas the fire, only "a shabby conflagration," remains in the background, the wound, "a horrid even if an obscure hurt," stands out in all its epic dimensions, sizable and nothing short of portentous. In his attempt to document the case, Edel found the account of a fire, which on October 28, 1861, burned down the stables of a certain Mr. Tennant.[16] He writes: "in a few minutes the entire stable was in flames amid the screaming of horses and the scramble of an altered town that rushed to give aid and to see the spectacle " (*Life of Henry James* I, 149). But James's autobiographical account is noticeably different from this: the spectacle of the event, as for instance described by the witnesses, has faded into the background, replaced by the description of an intensely subjective bodily experience. Fifty years separate the event from the account on the page, and what remains are the somatic impressions: against the indistinct background of the fire, the rhythmical motion of the arms and the stream of water gushing from the pump, and then the horrible wound. The vividly remembered physical description speaks of a trauma, and the sexual symbolism is pervasive and unmistakable. With its dreamlike aspects, the scene of the fire harks back to a scenario of bodily passion, where the wound would have designated a failure in the symbolization of that desiring body.[17] The fire could be that of passion,

16. "The most logical explanation," writes Edel, "of Henry James's blurring of the date of the hurt (the 'same dark hour' as the outbreak of the Civil War) served to minimize his failure during the first six months to spring to the colors with other young men" (*The Life of Henry James* I, 149).

17. My own formulation of the case relies on David-Ménard's definition of conversion in *Hysteria from Freud to Lacan*. But the definition given by Laplanche and Pontalis in *Vocabulaire de la Psychanalyse* seems equally appropriate: "Mechanism of symptom-formation, which consists in the translation of a psychic conflict and an attempt to resolve

the liquid, semen, and the wound, the sign of a complex of castration, at least this is what interpreting this scene along the lines of Freud's unraveling of Dora's first dream would suggest.[18] And the fire, of course, is endowed in the James family chronicle with powerful evocations: it was in a fire that James's own father lost a leg, while this diminished member and the limping figure would inevitably suggest an impaired virility. Clearly the fire at Tennant's house would have come upon James charged with significations and with uncanny premonitions concerning the fate of his body.

"What he wanted, in this light, flamed before him and challenged all his manhood," James writes about Ransom, as he evokes the climactic and strongly physical moment in the hero's conquest of Verena Tarrant. In the name given to that object of desire lies, I believe, the key to the more private aspects of James's hysteria. As is shown in his *Notebooks*, which are dotted with lists of evocative names susceptible of eventually befitting a character, the author seems to have had a predilection for proper names. But the heroine of *The Bostonians* remains long without a name, until all of a sudden James makes his choice and christens her: "The heroine is to be called Verena—Verena Tarrant." While her first name might have been chosen because of its obvious connotations, the surname is in fact present in one of the inventories of patronymics which precedes the notebook entry by a few pages. But in this instance this name cannot have been chosen merely for its phonemic qualities nor for its general symbolism; it surges up in James's imagination already filled with certain representations, as a word bearing the trace of his private history. Indeed, from a psychoanalytical perspective, words, like objects, are the bearers of libidinal investments and can be subject to displacements and condensation.[19] And the heroine's name, VERENA-TARRANT, is like Freud's well-known *Autodikasker*, a compound, a portmanteau word (see *SE* IV, 299–300). The

---

it through symptoms that can be somatic, motor (such as paralysis) or sensory (anesthesia or localized pain for instance)" (104).

18. This interpretation has long been "in the air," in spite of Edel's spirited defense in the biography (*The Life of Henry James* I, 154). See Freud, *Fragment of a Case of Hysteria* (*SE* VII, in particular, 72): "The antithesis of 'water' and 'fire' must be at the bottom of this. . . . So that from 'fire' one set of rails runs by way of this symbolic meaning to thoughts of love; while the other set runs by way of the contrary 'water.' "

19. "The work of condensation in dreams is seen at its clearest when it handles words and names. It is true in general that words are treated in dreams as though they were concrete things, and for that reason they are apt to be combined in just the same way as presentations of concrete things," Freud writes in *The Interpretation of Dreams* (*SE* IV, 295–96).

name carries then the traces of Tennant, the owner of the stable where, in the course of extinguishing a fire, James underwent his "vast visitation," got his "horrid even if . . . obscure hurt."

Thus, with the heroine's name marked by the author's own signature, *The Bostonians* could be said to carry, like a painting, the writer's touch.[20] At the point where the protagonist, gathering all his strength, with a burning desire ("light" and "flame" are here the revealing figures), saves the woman, the writer is brought back to his own story, the story of his defection and failure, the story of a debilitating hurt. Ransom's voice is haunted by a ghostly presence that speaks a writer's anxiety in an age when women are strong and men are feminized, and where the passivity associated with writing and the large "mob of scribbling women" makes of literature a feminized profession.

In *The Bostonians*, as in James's writing on Sand, the question of representation (meaning both the object of representation and the work of representation) and that of gender (the question of masculinity and femininity) cannot be separated. This is also the theme of one of his letters, where, putting on the guise of a master, he sends to his nephew sonorous words of advice about gender and style, words that, moreover, could remind us of Ransom's style of utterance: "If you go in for literature be a man of letters. You have probably an heredity of *expression* in your blood (from your father through *his* father), and I see symptoms in your stories of the sense and gift for that. So gird your loins and store up your patience. Take the most important subjects you can, and write about the most human and manly things. We live in a frightfully vulgar age; and twaddle and chatter are much imposed upon us. Suspect them—detest them—despise them" (*Selected Letters*, 298). And one feels like adding in Ransom's voice, "the whole generation is womanized; the masculine tone is passing out of the world; it's a feminine, a nervous, hysterical, chattering, canting age, an age of hollow phrases and false delicacy and exaggerated solicitudes and coddled sensibilities, which, if we don't soon look out . . ." (*Bostonians*, 322).

---

20. James's *Notebooks* and *Selected Letters* provide two links in the associative chain between the trauma and the formation of the name. In Jan. 1884, a few months after James had sent his outline for *The Bostonians* to his publisher, he dines at the house of a certain Mrs. Tennant (whom he first met in 1877) (*Complete Notebooks*, 23). Given James's recurrent positioning as the *deuxième homme* in an erotic triangle, the description he gives of his first encounter with Mrs. Terrant is particularly interesting: "a very handsome and agreeable Mrs. Tennant, a friend and flame of Gustave Flaubert" (*Selected Letters*, 154).

The Bostonians

The Sentiment of Sex

One could argue, in a reversal of perspective, that the convergence between the writer's personal voice and that of his hero is not due to some inner compulsion but marks the influence of a *doxa* where the discourses of gender naturally tend to repeat each other and to form one orthodoxy of vision. This phenomenon can be demonstrated by using the idealization of Verena as a textual starting point but bearing in mind the definitions of femininity that we owe to Mary Poovey: "the epistemological term *woman* could guarantee men's identity only if difference was fixed—only if, that is, the binary opposition between the sexes was more important than any other kinds of difference that women might experience" (80), and Julia Kristeva: "the feminine function . . . always constitutes the edge against which the process of signification [*signifiance*] aligns itself as text" (*Révolution*, 614). In James's novel, however, the gender alignment founded on the idealization of woman takes the form of an explicitly thematized discourse of sexual difference, whose spokesman is Ransom. There is otherwise so little play or margin for "signification" that the sexual identities are represented as an unambiguous image of "what a man is" and "what a woman ultimately is." In *The Bostonians* the theatricalization of gender, far from being subversive, is limited to reproducing or mimicking, as an exterior phenomenon, the traits that are grounded in the semblance of an anatomical difference.

"There isn't a hair wrong in Verena, you've made her neither too little nor too much—but absolutely *liebenswürdig*," William James writes to his brother, responding to Verena's charm in the same way as the hero, who is equally held under the spell of this feminine figure evocative of *das ewig Weibliche*:

Her splendid hair seemed to shine; her cheek and chin had a curve which struck him by its fineness; her eyes and lips were full of smiles and greetings. She had appeared to him before as a creature of brightness, but now she lighted up the place, the irradiated, she made everything that surrounded her of no consequence; dropping upon the shabby sofa with an effect as charming as if she had been a nymph sinking on a leopard-skin and with the native sweetness of her voice forcing him to listen till she spoke again. . . . her glance was as pure as it was direct, and that fantastic fairness hung about her which had made an impression on him of old, and which reminded him of unworldly places—he didn't know where—convent-cloisters or vales of Arcady. (*Bostonians*, 214)

Verena in Arcady, as she appears here, seems to embody, true to her name, either eternal spring or renewal, and her mythical femininity, stronger than the threatening corruption of modern times, is associated with the redemptive power of nature. The focal point of all desire in the novel, she holds, in a culture increasingly swayed by malign and destructive influences, the secret of spontaneity, of virginlike purity, and of nature. Seen in this light, her theatricality and preternatural eloquence are but surface features, the imprint of her time, while in essence she remains untainted by the surrounding process of loss and decadence. The paradox of Verena's original purity, which exists beyond all corruption and contamination (essentially present, but yet subject to change, to falling away), is not unlike that which we evidenced around the notion of *pudicité*. It is the theme of one of the narrator's explanatory statements: "And yet there was a strange spontaneity in her manner, and an air of artless enthusiasm, of personal purity. If she was theatrical, she was naturally theatrical" (*Bostonians*, 48). Indeed the final oxymoron designates what is ultimately Verena's true function: to "represent" in the strong sense of the word—since the values attached to a sexual identity are no longer naturally present but must henceforth be represented, theatricalized or "hystericized"—against the loss and deperdition of the contemporary age, the eternal, redemptive value of the feminine. Given these conditions, it should not surprise us that all of Ransom's virile heroism (and even so much violence) should be enlisted to preserve this precious object from the tarnishing touch of a grasping, gaping crowd. This requires that she, like any treasure for display, be kept in "a box with glass sides," as the heroine herself puts it in one of her more insightful utterances (257). The figure speaks, appropriately, of the uncanny visibility given to the woman in this system of representation, it expresses too her entrapment on the inside, as container of "ineffable interiority."

Verena's abduction from the stage in the final scene takes us back to a familiar conception—that the woman who exhibits herself "on the market-place," "on the broad highway," or in front of a crowd of eager listeners (or readers) faces her own undoing. Ransom's plan for the heroine is, when expressed most violently, to "strike her dumb." It takes otherwise the form of a general trimming of her eloquence to adjust it to the dimensions of his drawing room (376), and work as a strategy destined to reposition her in the proper place, the home: "At the end of a moment she made another inquiry: 'Am I to understand, then, as your last word that you regard us as quite inferior?' 'For public, civic uses, absolutely—perfectly weak and second rate. I know nothing more indicative of the muddled sentiment of the time than that any number of men should be found that they regard you in any other light. But privately, personally, it's another affair. In the realm of family life and the domestic affections——' " (327). The narrative of *The Bostonians* shows indeed exemplary concern in mapping out the respective territories of men and women and enforcing the proper alignments, where "naturally" woman's place is at the fireside. This aspect of the gender question was woven into James's text from its very inception in his *Notebooks*: there already the emancipation of woman was related to the threat on privacy, to the loss of the sentiment of sex. Held at bay from James's literary discourse yet part of his awareness (as, for instance, is shown by his outburst about Sand's existential conquests taking place while she was "supremely voteless" ["George Sand," in *Literary Criticism*, 779]) is the question of women's suffrage. In the late nineteenth century the "emancipation of women" meant for some women professional work that would take them into the marketplace and away from the domestic sphere; for all of them it meant the vote. James wrote at a time when the map of gender was undergoing a significant shift. With woman's entry into the public sphere and into the polis, a whole compound that she sustained—domesticity, inward-looking femininity, interiority—seemed to come under threat. Keeping her in that proper place—home, the hearth, the heart—and thus ensuring that the center would hold, might have seemed like the best strategy against the extinction of gender differences. "Women at home became, ideally, specialists in emotional and spiritual life, protecting tradition and providing a stable refuge from the harsh, impersonal public sphere that men now entered in increasing numbers," writes Erna Hellerstein, suggesting that woman's sphere is that of "being," not "doing" (118). Perhaps then, woman's emancipation from the home, by taking her away from the values of interiority, initiates a change whose consequences are not only political or psychological but ontological. As Lionel Trilling wrote, in his commentary on *The Bostonians*: "A movement of sexual revolution is to be understood as a question which a culture puts to itself, and right down to its very roots. It is a question about what it means to be a man and what it means to be a woman—about the quality of being which people wish to have" (110).

Such then are the stakes of the drama James undertook to represent in his novel, where the scene of hysteria is symptomatic of a crisis of gender which must be envisaged in its collective dimensions as part of some wider history, even though it is related to the writer's personal predicament. The collective, ideological sources of James's attitude can be revealed, for instance, in the surprising coincidence between, on the one hand, the novel's main themes, also expressed in the condensed form of his notebook entry dated April 1883, and, on the other, the terms of a letter that Sigmund Freud sent his fiancée, Martha Bernays, in November of the same year.[21] Here we find the young doctor Freud realigning gender around Martha Bernays in the same way we saw the writer make Verena or George Sand the centerpiece and stake of his attempt to write about gender. Freud's letter reproduces the strong lines of *The Bostonians*: the separation of spheres ("It seems a complete unrealistic notion to send women into the struggle for existence in the same way as men. Am I to think of my delicate, sweet girl as a competitor?"); the desire to keep the woman in her house ("I dare say we agree that housekeeping and the care and education of children claim the whole person and practically rule out any profession; even if simplified conditions relieve the woman of housekeeping, dusting, cleaning, cooking, etc."); and the desire to take her back to the natural role of a wife and mother and to idealize her ("earn[ing] a living like men [would lead] to the disappearance of the most lovely thing the world has to offer us: our ideal of womanhood"). But in light of these final remarks, one particular statement in Freud's letter concerns the very notion that lies at the heart of James's project of representation, namely, the decline of the sentiment of sex. Noting the absence of the sexual dimension in John Stuart Mill's *Autobiography*, Freud comments:

All this he had simply forgotten, as he altogether forgot all the phenomena that are connected to sex. This is a point where in general one can simply not consider him as human. His autobiography is so prudish or so eerie that one would never learn from him that humanity is divided into men and women, and that this difference is the most important that exists among them.[22]

21. I am referring to Freud's well-known letter to Martha Bernays, written in Vienna and dated November 15, 1883 (*Letters of Freud*, no. 28, pp. 74–76).

22. I quote the passage in the original so as to highlight the decisive terms of Freud's pronouncement, namely, *menschlich* (human) and *die Menschen* (human beings, humanity). Sexual difference (*der Unterschied, die Teilung in Männer und Weiber*) is thus, for Freud, the determining factor of our human condition: "Daran hatte er einfach vergessen, wie überhaupt an alle mit dem Geschlechtlichen in Zusammenhang stehenden Beziehungen. Das ist im Ganzen ein Punkt bei Mill, in dem man ihn einfach nicht menschlich finden kann. Seine Selbstbiographie ist so prüde oder so unirdisch, dass man aus ihr nie verfahren könnte, dass die Menschen in Männer und Weiber geteilt sind, und dass dieser Unterschied der bedeutsamste ist, der unter ihnen besteht" (*Briefe, 1873–89*, 82).

In this same letter, Freud dismisses Mill's perspective, which brings together gender and race: "he finds an analogy for the oppression of women in that of the Negro. Any girl,

Mill provides Freud with the opportunity to assert his own conviction that the "true" representation of subjectivity is inconceivable without taking into account the sexual (*das Geschlechtliche*). Held back by prudishness or by some unrealistic or idealistic (*unirdisch*) notions that prevent him from acknowledging this sexual dimension, the philosopher is said to fail in his very humanity.

In this example, Freud ascribes to the notion of *Geschlecht* both the older sense of the term, meaning the division or separation between man and woman, and the modern sense of sexuality. The word refers to the signifying function of sexual difference (as what distinguishes men from women) as well as to "all the phenomena that are connected to sex," where Freud seems to define sexuality as the "phenomena" that pertain to or spring from the original evidence of the difference. The letter is thus not only a personal, or a cultural document; it announces the turn of thought that characterizes the analyst's later work: whereas in its traditional sense, *das Geschlechtliche*, just like the French word *sexe* or English "sex," defines in the physical characteristics that pertain to biological reproduction the notion of a difference, in its new meaning and later developments the term acquires a meta-physical meaning and participates in the development of a theory of the subjectivity based on a sexual ontology. One does not "have" a sex; one "is" a sex. The maxim that lies behind the nineteenth-century doctor's attempts to ground the traits of feminine gender in the female body defines as well the substance of the position that Freud defines here in contradistinction to Mill.

No longer veiled by ideological obfuscations, the phenonema that derive from the signifying function of sexual difference will come into their own. But beyond this, they must, according to Freud, ground our knowledge or understanding of what constitutes our human condition. Lecturing his fiancée in a letter, Freud sketches out a new theory that claims that the representation of a self is necessarily associated with a "grammar of the sexes" and that the language of "true subjectivity" must always be gender-marked. And, as a woman, Martha Bernays is, naturally enough, the first addressee as well as the true object of this discourse. But the convergence of Freud's early pronouncement on *das Geschlechtliche* with James's literary project in *The Bostonians* is re-

___

even without a vote and legal rights, whose hand is kissed by a man willing to risk his all for her love, could have put him right on this." This statement should be quoted not only as an instance of Freud's heroic conception of masculinity—not that different from Ransom's—but because it foregrounds what is visible in the earlier quote too, namely, the absolute preponderance, in the Freudian "ontology," of sex as a factor of difference.

markable: it offers proof of a cultural configuration, involving a theoretician and a writer, where the "quality of being" (to borrow Trilling's
term) can no longer be defined outside of an awareness of gender. For
indeed, if the "fact" that is central to such representations of subjectivity
is that of sexual difference (or of "sex" in its older meaning), the phenomena that become the object of a narrative and epistemological inquiry (which are also, as we have seen, the very sites of anxiety and of
regulatory moves) are those of gender, where gender is defined as a
meaning of sex.

After our brief incursion into Freud's text we are now in a better
position to give substance to the elusive term James used to describe in
his *Notebooks* the project for *The Bostonians*—the "sentiment of sex."
For the formulation is unusual indeed: given what we know of the nineteenth century's resistance to sex and its tendency toward sentimen-
talization, the two terms seem antagonistic and the expression seems
incomprehensible. If sex means body, and sentiment refers to the mental
and affective domain, what can be the relation between the two terms?
In one of James's texts on Sand, where he discusses George Eliot, we
had encountered an analogous construction, "erotic sentiment," which
describes the novelist's ability to represent passion. We can assume that
like this term, "sentiment of sex" expresses James's literary commitment
to breaking away from a mere spiritualist or intellectualist conception.
The full representation of subjectivity must include the bodily dimension
of the erotic or sexual. Putting a different emphasis on this notion and
highlighting its moralistic aspect, Alfred Habegger relates it to the family
chronicle and glosses it in the following way: "By 1870 the distinction
[of the sexes] had become the basis of the Jameses' family life, their
individual identities, their deep intellectual commitments, their writing.
Men had the 'sway-power,' and women were affectionate, selfless, and
yielding, and the 'sentimental' consequence of this natural difference was
a powerful feeling of attraction between the sexes" (51). Sex would then
have consequences at the level of sentiment, but conversely, sentiment
(and the term would here be opposed to brutality, violence, vulgarity)
would also be defined as sexual morality, as a regulation of family mores
founded on a gender differentiation.

But the best gloss is doubtless provided by the novel itself. What the
social conditions of modern America reveal is that the sentiment that
belongs to each of the sexes is muddled and under threat: man loses his
heroic and virile dimensions ("it's a feminine, a nervous, hysterical, chattering, canting age," Ransom exclaims in one of his rantings), whereas
the "true woman" is being replaced with the "new old maid" or the

hysteric, nervous and sterile creatures such as Olive ("unmarried in every implication of her being"). But the term is given yet another inflection when the novel shows so blatantly that the two sexes are no longer bound by a code of manners but by sheer violence. The brutality that brings Verena back to the fold or the crowd's avid seizing on the woman as an object of sensational emotions reveals an irremediable loss; a certain delicacy of sentiment that in the "old days" would have determined the relations with the weaker sex seems gone forever. This may well be the most insurmountable problem that James faced in his novel: despite the work's powerful, lingering nostalgia for an age that knew and felt differently about men and women, the sentiment is irrevocably lost. The violence needed to return to the previous state (a situation demanding that woman remain woman, that man be man and act as man) has become the very negation of the value it is meant to sustain. The violent forms given to the representation of what should be the reassuring plot, the plot of reassurance (to pursue Irigaray's notion), shows more clearly than ever that James is firmly anchored in an age of sexual anxiety and of "gender trouble." The novel's hysteria reveals a longing for the now-vanished romance where men were naturally men and women were just women, without any need for such violent stagings and hysterical masquerades as those in James's novel. Such then is the spirit of this age haunted by the reminiscences of clearly defined sexual identities. For indeed, if the discourse that the novelist develops around the sentiment of sex is, as I have tried to show, not only a literary and psychological construction but also one deeply embedded in a wider historical context, it becomes possible to argue that James's *The Bostonians* is not only and merely the product of "male genius" but also the creation of its time.[23] The "sentiment of sex" becomes then the memorable term for an ethics of representation or a "truth" concerning subjectivity haunted by gender. This relentless pursuit of the meaning of sex is the motor and principle that define James's literary performance in his writings about Sand as much as in *The Bostonians*. These works offer then the evidence of a (literary) consciousness of gender that pervades the works of nineteenth-century theoreticians and writers on hysteria.

23. I apply to James what Felman says about Freud: "Freud is a male genius. This may sound like a simple statement. Yet I contend that we do not yet know what this statement really means. It certainly *does not mean* that Freud's stupendous insight is disqualified as far as women are concerned, or that his genius is irrelevant to women (or to feminism); it *does mean* (but in what way?) that his insight is inhabited by certain systematic oversights, and that the light it sheds also casts shadows" (*What Does a Woman Want?* 82).

CHAPTER FOUR

Engendering the Mind: James, Freud, and George Sand

There may, however, be something accurate about this repeated dramatization of woman as simulacrum, erasure, or silence. For it would not be easy to assert that the existence and knowledge of the female subject could simply be produced, without difficulty or epistemological damage, within the existing patterns of culture and language.

—Barbara Johnson, *World of Difference*

In its literal classical sense, the word "simulacrum" refers to the statue of a divinity, but more currently it designates a figure or representation that stands in the stead of the genuine object, replaces it like a trompe l'oeil. A simulacrum thus embodies an illusory presence when the divinity cannot be reached or the real or authentic object is lacking. In the scene of extreme unction in *Madame Bovary*, Emma is a simulacrum since the text presents us with the image of a body in agony, destined to die, which yet speaks of life and eros. The dying Emma represents a desire meant to transcend death, an ideal of passion that is, it seems, the privilege of femininity.

The priest rose to take the crucifix. Reaching forward like one in thirst, she glued her lips to the body of the Man-God and laid upon it with all her failing strength the most mighty kiss of love she had ever given. The priest recited the *Misereatur* and the *Indulgentiam*; then he dipped his right thumb into the oil and began the unctions: first on the eyes, that had so coveted all earthly splendours; then on the nostrils, that had loved warm breezes and amorous perfumes; then on the mouth, that had opened for falsehood, had groaned with pride and cried out in lust; then on the hands, that had revelled in delicious contacts; lastly on the soles of the feet, that once had run so swiftly to the assuaging of her desires, and now would walk no more. (335)

Such a description might explain why nineteenth-century readers of Flaubert persisted in denouncing the scandalous immorality of the novel in spite of its seemingly moral conclusion: the deathbed scene evokes all too persistently the pleasures of the flesh. The holy gestures of the priest bring back to life the sites of the heroine's all too physical, sensual *jouissance*. Thus Emma's dying body carries the fragments of a life driven by eros, with a narration that is staged, at death's very door, as a unique, unparalled scene of passion showing what in this novel is nowhere else to be seen: images of a woman's pleasure, desire, and freedom without the inhibitions of censorship or the ironist's skepticism.

The idealization is perceptible too in Flaubert's style: this is one of the rare moments where the writing "expands with longing and desire" in a text that, if we believe Baudelaire, tends to borrow its elements much more conventionally from "the prop room of the Second Empire" (*Art romantique*, 646). Emma's body has thus become the precious receptacle of all the dreams and desires that belong to the imagination and to the senses: "In Flaubert," Jean Starobinski writes, "the fleshly substance of the novel . . . rekindles an inner perception of the self, linked, to the point of ecstasy, to the production of the imaginary" (*L'échelle*, 179).[1] In attributing to the text itself, namely, to the very substance and texture of the writing and not to the representation only, the qualities of the sensuous, the fleshly (*le charnel*), and suggesting that this phenomenon is related to some subjective experience, Starobinski identifies and describes the features of Flaubert's prose that have led me to single out this passage. The scene of passion staged in and around Emma's death is the site of a "trans-subjective process," that is, of a phenomenon of literary transference, where the words on the page have become the substance or rather the site of a sensory and emotional transaction that can be brought back neither to the figure represented nor to its creator, but where some immaterial substance belonging to the body and desire (the product of the "imaginary"?) comes to life on the page. To conceive of this phenomenon purely in terms of representation and to say, for instance, that Flaubert represents himself in Emma Bovary would be to deny to writing its rhetorical force and to tame (in the name of "form" or "intention") a textual performance that is essentially dynamic and must be envisaged for its peculiar intensities.[2]

---

1. The term *imaginaire* does not refer to Lacan's model, but is used here in the sense ascribed to it by the Geneva School critics, where it describes the writer's creation (or re-creation) of representations and images as a defining trait of his or her fictional and autobiographical writing.

2. On this subject, see Roland Barthes's "Question de tempo": "The shortcomings of structuralism—at least as I perceive them now, after a necessary phase of preparation and simplification—, the great absence in our first analyses was the notion of 'force,' 'intensity,'

However, from the perspective of sexual difference a discussion of representation appears unavoidable, for it cannot be denied that this "writerly" performance uses the woman's body as a simulacrum. This body becomes the privileged site of a literary experience and of the creation of some ineffable difference or value. Thus, true to the conventions of an age that associates femininity with the emotive domain, Emma Bovary ends up "embodying" (and the term must be taken at its most literal as "giving a body to") a subjectivity defined as passion, affect, and desire. The scene we have examined is the climax of the "hystericization" of the heroine which is at work in Flaubert's novel.

In his critical essay on *Madame Bovary* Baudelaire invokes the notion of hysteria in what may appear to be ambiguous terms, since he relates it both to the heroine and to the author and defines it differently in both instances. "Voilà le poëte hystérique," he exclaims, having commented on Emma's pseudomystical phase, and then adds in the same vein: "Hysteria! Why wouldn't this mystery become the matter and the substance of a literary work, this mystery that the Academy of medicine has not yet solved, and which is expressed in the case of women by the sensation of an ascending and asphyxiating lump (I am only talking about the main symptom) and which translates itself in the case of excitable [*nerveux*] men into powerlessness and a capacity for excesses of all kinds" (404). For the poet, hysteria is a meaningful term of representation (where it describes Emma's behavior, actions or moods), but it refers also to a mode of writing, a stylistic performance (in her mystical phase, Emma conjures up the image of the author's own symptoms). But hysteria also evokes sexual ambiguity: the term describes a male author projecting himself onto a female body, which is, however, endowed with masculine traits ("this strange androgynous creature has kept all the seductions of a virile soul and of a seductive feminine body," he writes about Emma). Yet although it enables such a gender crossing, hysteria works differently in men and in women: "powerlessness and excesses of all kinds" for him, "an ascending and asphyxiating lump" for her. The division and corresponding choice are surely not fortuitous: the hysteric's lump in the throat strangles her voice, condemning her to silence and crushing her existence (an image Flaubert himself uses in his ending as he evokes the enormous weight that crushes Emma on her deathbed).[3]

---

or 'energy-flow' ("flux"). . . . Thus your work teaches us that in the margins of the structuralist system—whose beauty is far from being exhausted—there was an inevitable *opening* toward the region of intensities" (11).

3. "It seemed to Charles that there were infinite masses, of enormous weight, pressing down upon her" (*Madame Bovary*, 341).

Hysteria signifies then a return to a body which is the matter of his writing: Emma's death scene, where the heroine's insistently physical agony gets rewritten in a last flight of the imagination as a lyrical *blazon amoureux* (celebrating her lips, eyes, nose, mouth, hands, and feet), epitomizes a process of hystericization of the woman. Her mute body bears his writing and speaks for the male imagination. While, according to Baudelaire, hysteria affects her as a negative and destructive force, it seems to instigate in men the very opposite process: instead of freezing, paralyzing, or striking dumb, it initiates a dynamics made of lack and of excess, synonymous with vitality, creativity, overreaching. It seems thus doubly true, bringing together the insights of Flaubert and Baudelaire, that this "mystery" is destined to provoke a feat of the male imagination: the hysteric's silent body becomes, through writing, the precious object that enables his mental or imaginary (re)creation.

Thus the joint voices of Flaubert and Baudelaire reveal, implicitly or explicitly, some crucial insights concerning woman's place in the creation and representation of subjectivity in the nineteenth century. In this instance, hysteria becomes the revealing sign of a particular textual dynamic, which links the silencing of woman to the elaboration of a discourse of knowledge concerning the subject. My inquiry is inflected so as to respond to the provocation of Barbara Johnson's more elaborate formulation of what constitutes my theme: "There may, however, be something accurate about this repeated dramatization of woman as simulacrum, erasure, or silence. For it would not be easy to assert that the existence and knowledge of the female subject could simply be produced, without difficulty or epistemological damage, within the existing patterns of culture and language" (*World of Difference*, 40). With James and Freud I examine "the dramatization of woman as simulacrum, erasure and silence." Later in the chapter I invoke an exemplary text by George Sand to address the question of an alternative epistemology intent on producing a "female subject."

The Simulacrum

As I retrace the steps of James's theoretical reflections on what constitutes an appropriate subject for fiction, my aim is to give a literary echo to some of Luce Irigaray's philosophical interrogations concerning subjectivity, consciousness, and sexual difference. The philosopher thus speaks of woman's appropriation by a masculine ontology—"Borrowing her made it possible to elaborate the problematic of being" (*Speculum*, 20)—and argues further that "the enigma of the feminine guarantees the progression toward the knowledge of a history of male sexuality" (138). Indeed, the idealization of the feminine which characterizes James's discussions of *Madame Bovary* and his preface to *Portrait of a Lady* must ultimately be brought back to a construction of subjectivity that is firmly anchored in a "history of male sexuality" and contributes, to a greater extent than is perhaps usually granted, to the aggrandizement of masculine knowledge and mastery. The nineteenth-century project of writing and representation, which aims at defining subjectivity in its inner manifestations but focuses on the female subject, thus participates in a process of partitioning and allocation of knowledge that constantly replays the stakes of sexual difference.

James's own provocative, abrupt questioning concerning the validity of Emma as a heroine for *Madame Bovary* and consequently her value as an object for representation and a subject in representation provides a difficult but interesting entry into my theme.[4] In his criticism of Flaubert's novel, Henry James unites again, as with his texts on Sand, a theory of representation and a conception of femininity, while his explicit aim is, as always, to develop an aesthetic discourse. However, the critic puts less emphasis this time on the primarily moral question ("What is representable?") and takes a freer and more speculative turn by raising the question of "representativity."[5] For James, this new reflection on representation is clearly not a political issue but presents rather an occasion for a theoretical exploration of the notion of subjectivity and of the necessary conditions for "subjecthood." His letter to Paul Bourget on the novel *Mensonges* exemplifies, meanwhile, both the critic's detachment from moral concerns and the new direction taken by this thoughts on representation: "What kind of a moral 'inside' could such a creature possess? I pity you when I see you working at constructing her one—as if there were only this in the world. Life gets reflected poorly in such a nature and the reader feels all outraged and betrayed when you invite him to take this kind of a walk under pretence of offering him a psychology of suffering" (*Letters* III, 221). Indeed, while James still uses the term "moral," it is now divested of its normative sense and designates

4. All subsequent references to James's writings on Flaubert are to Henry James, *Literary Criticism: French Writers, Other European Writers and the Prefaces to the New York Edition*.

5. The term "representativity" is used in a feminist context by Naomi Schor: "The very fact that the bourgeois feminists gathered at the Club . . . could have misunderstood the nature of Sand's involvement, the extent of her *representativity* clearly demonstrates how difficult it is to classify Sand when it comes to what she calls 'the women's cause' " (*George Sand and Idealism*, 71).

rather that sphere of presence, existence, or "being" that, beyond the objectified, objectifiable body, defines the subject's interiority or consciousness. This is precisely the central theme of James's criticism of Emma Bovary:

Our complaint is that Emma Bovary, in spite of the nature of her consciousness and in spite of her reflecting so much that of her creator, is really too small an affair. . . .

. . . When I speak of the faith in Emma Bovary as proportionately wasted I reflect on M. Faguet's judgment that she is from the point of view of deep interest richly or at least roundedly representative. Representative of what? he makes us ask even while granting all the grounds of misery and tragedy involved. The plea for her is the plea made for all the figures that live without evaporation under the painter's hand—that they are not only particular persons but types of their kind, and as valid in one light as in the other. It is Emma's "kind" that I question for this responsibility, even if it be inquired of me why I then fail to question that of Charles Bovary, in its perfection, or that of the inimitable, the immortal Homais. If we express Emma's deficiency as the poverty of her consciousness for the typical function, it is certainly not, one must admit, that she is surpassed in this respect either by her platitudinous husband or by his friend the pretentious apothecary. The difference is nonetheless somehow in the fact that they are respectively studies but of their character and office, which function in each expresses adequately *all* they are. It may be, I concede, because Emma is the only woman in the book that she is taken by M. Faguet as *femininely* typical, typical in the larger illustrative way, whereas the others pass with him for images specifically conditioned. Emma is this same for myself, I plead; she is conditioned to such an excess of the specific, and the specific in her case leaves out so many even of the commoner elements of conceivable life in a woman when we are invited to see that life as pathetic, as dramatic agitation, that we challenge both the author's and the critic's scale of importances. ("Gustave Flaubert," in *Literary Criticism*, 326–28)

Taking his cue from Faguet's appreciation, James is led to exclaim "Representative of what?" The formulation is blunt, the question seems almost rhetorical, but "representative of what" launches a discussion of the limitations of the heroine's consciousness and an examination of the conditions that determine the representativity of a particular Subject.[6]

6. In his preface to *The Portrait of a Lady*, James dwells, in relation to Isabel Archer, on the question of "high attributes of the Subject" (1077). Imitating him so as to dispel any possible ambiguity, in this chapter I capitalize "subject" whenever it means subjectivity rather than theme.

Just before, the critic had commented on the small claims that could be made, in this light, for Frédéric Moreau, the hero of *Education senti-mentale*. But there seems to be more potential in Emma Bovary. Thus it is not enough, James's words suggest, that she, the heroine, be a "pres-ence" or that she embody some historical or psychological truth. She also needs to correspond to a certain idea or ideal of subjectivity. It is not enough that the figure in the fiction elicit in the reader the kind of recognition that gets expressed in such a statement as "it looks true, she is alive on the page," which, as James shows in his essays on *Madame Bovary*, is the first, instinctive response to the novel.[7] Nor is it enough to be able to say that the fiction is moral, and that it recognizes the differences (if not all the decencies) that determine the representations of nineteenth-century subjects.[8] But, the critic claims, the question being that of the vessel's "capacity" to hold a "consciousness," the figure must have the qualities necessary to carry such an investment.

But what is this investment? James speaks explicitly and openly about an increase in knowledge but the figures he uses in the course of his theorization show only too well that the stakes of this literary under-taking are inevitably fraught with erotic as well as political dimensions. The scene of knowledge cannot be separated from the scene of passion, and the act of appropriation and valorization of the feminine Subject necessarily involves questions of mastery and power. Representation—defined here as the production or creation of subjectivity in writing—remains political, although in the looser sense of the term: it calls for a critical examination of the local, textual gains and losses that correspond to each created gender and asks that we envisage, from an epistemo-logical perspective, the power struggle or hegemony that opposes a masculine construction to a feminine "being" which exists only in the negative, as the impossibility of its own description.[9]

The figure that stands out in James's discussion of Emma Bovary's representativity is that of the vessel, which of course carries the biblical

7. See his description of the novel ("Bernard and Flaubert," in *Literary Criticism*, 173–4) as well as his passing remarks: "Flaubert as a painter of life" ("Flaubert," 325) and "There is life, there is blood in a considerable measure in *Madame Bovary*" ("Flaubert," 298).

8. Unlike the nineteenth-century "Philistines," James does not seem to object to the supposed immorality of the novel. His quarrel with the male author is not of the same order as his critique of George Sand: there the indecencies of her writing and living were systematically foregrounded.

9. As Irigaray has pointed out, woman is "the borrowed item thanks to which the problematic of Being was elaborated. It is then rigorously impossible to describe being a woman" (*Speculum*, 20).

overtones of women as the "weaker vessel."[10] The critic questions "the dignity of Madame Bovary herself as a vessel of experience" (*Literary Criticism*, 325) and stigmatizes "the small capacity of the vessel." The image evokes a conception of the literary character that is not anchored in the mimetic notion of a type (as James insists when he differentiates Emma from Charles and Homais), but relies on notions of substitution and projection. Accordingly, the Subject produced in the text is figured as an object that collects, contains, or carries whatever "thing" is poured into it, but it can be defined also as a conveyor of meaning (the vehicle of a semantic investment), namely, a textual metaphor. The question of representation must meanwhile be brought back, as we shall see, to the notion of "transfer," both as a feature of rhetoric and as a dialectic of affects and desires (of the kind psychoanalysis has taught us to envisage). But whether we consider her a metaphor or the object of a projection, the heroine's "value" can still be assessed under a single rubric or question: Does she constitute the fit vehicle for the "tenor of the message" she is meant to carry?

James's preface to *The Portrait of a Lady*, with its emphasis on the value of the heroine, shows him tackling this very question in a more expansive and striking fashion, but circling repeatedly around the unexplainable: what is the mystery that lies behind her attractiveness, how come she, "the mere slim shade . . . of a girl," should encounter so much interest? How is it possible, he asks, to "organi[ze] an ado about Isabel Archer"? George Eliot's own words in *Daniel Deronda* concerning girls and their blind visions seem destined to help him, as will the image of "a vessel," which she used to justify Gwendolen Harleth's importance and which James now quotes: "Challenge any such problem with any intelligence, and you immediately see how full it is of substance; the wonder being . . . as we look at the world, how absolutely, how inordinately, the Isabel Archers, and even much smaller fry, insist on mattering. George Eliot has admirably noted it—'In these frail vessels is borne onward through the ages the treasure of human affection'" ("Preface," in *Literary Criticism*, 1077). In fact, the importance of the female Subject cannot really be explained beyond what Eliot says; meanwhile the incommensurability between the object ("the small fry") and its overreaching significance (its "mattering" to the world) can be witnessed, James suggests, in her creations as well as in Shakespeare's. The critic thus proceeds to list the names of the famous heroines of Eliot's

10. The phrase is found in the King James translation: "giving honour unto the wife, as unto the weaker vessel" (1 Peter 3:7).

novels and Shakespeare's plays and, taking comfort from such illustrious precedents, resumes his attempts to explain why he ended up promoting another of those "mere young things," Isabel Archer, to the status of a Subject.

But a few pages earlier, James had already attempted to describe how the figure came to be born—in his own words, how it came about that he recognized "the intensity of suggestion that may reside in the stray figure, in the unattached character, the image *en disponibilité*" (1073). Here too he had emphasized the paradox: the smallness of the object against the high claims it is made to carry or embody: "By what process of logical accretion was this slight 'personality,' the mere slim shade of an intelligent but presumptuous girl, to find herself endowed with the high attributes of a Subject?" (1077). The answer to such a question is naturally deferred, since it might reveal that there is after all no "logical accretion" but just the spontaneous form taken by a desire—she, the stray figure, being merely the recipient of his fantasies. Rather than envisaging this solution, James remains content to defend instead the value of his creation; in his own words she is a "treasure," "a precious object," "the particular 'value.' "[11] However, if the cornerstone of the novel consists in "the conception of a certain young woman affronting her destiny," then it remains imperative to show how she, Isabel Archer, the feminine product of the writer's mind, can aspire to the glorious status of a Subject. James thus chooses to defend the heroine's "representational value," and he attempts to convince his readers that she is worth the expense of spirit that went into the making of her.

From the general perspective of this project, the answer to this question exceeds by far its local value (what it shows, for instance, about James's conception of the heroine), for what we discover here is how fiction gets woven into history, how the imagined Subject becomes part of a history of subjectivity. Let us then follow closely the writer's ar-

---

11. James's elaborate figure provides a particularly interesting description of the mind, infused as it is with the notion of value and "intensities": "The figure has to that extent, as you see, *been* placed—placed in the imagination that detains it, preserves, protects, enjoys it, conscious of its presence in the dusky, crowded, heterogeneous back-shop of the mind very much as a wary dealer in precious odds and ends, competent to make an 'advance' on rare objects confided to him, is conscious of the rare little 'piece' left in deposit by the reduced, mysterious lady of title or the speculative amateur, and which is already there to disclose its merit afresh as soon as a key shall have clicked in a cupboard-door" ("Preface," *The Portrait of a Lady*, in *Literary Criticism*, 1076). In light of my later discussion of Freud's use of the figure of the key, the last image of this passage is highlighted as another instance of the strategy of possession and appropriation which defines this epistemology.

gument as he weaves together fiction and history in his apology for the heroine: if historically woman's claims to subjecthood (namely, to those "high attributes of the Subject") remain precarious, then it becomes necessary to find honorable antecedents for Isabel Archer's case in the world of fictive creations. There James draws his list of literary heroines (Juliet, Cleopatra, Portia, Hetty, Maggie, Rosamund, Gwendolen) in whom, remembering George Eliot's words, his readers should recognize "the vessels of human affection." In other words, the affection (love, passion, or pity) that, through a process of identification, circulates between the reader and such figures, will locate them, the women of fiction, in him or her, the reader in history. In this way, James shows that Isabel Archer and her likes come to occupy in the reader's imagination or consciousness so significant a place that the figures of fictions have become real, historical presences. Provided then it is loaded with the proper charge of meaning, knowledge, and emotion, the figure created in his writing is able to sustain a historical consciousness and to embody some historical truth concerning woman or the Subject in general. This, for James, provides sufficient justification for his heroine.[12]

But this is precisely where the heroine of Flaubert's novel is found wanting—the expense of spirit seems wasted. According to James, "Our complaint is that Emma Bovary, in spite of the nature of her consciousness and in spite of her reflecting so much that of her creator, is really too small an affair" (*Literary Criticism*, 326). And, he repeats, she is "proportionately wasted" (327); she and Frédéric Moreau are "limited reflectors and registers" (326). But she remains, somehow, "*femininely* typical"; the critic pursues while adopting again Léon Faguet's critical view, but with an emphasis on the word "feminine," which does not dispel the ambiguity. Are we to believe that Emma is the embodiment of woman, and must, as such, be read as typically representative of a female existence? Or is it rather, as is suggested in the preceding lines, that she, in her woman's disguise, represents an aspect of an identity that goes beyond her sex; while Homais or Charles Bovary are "but a character and a office," she is "typical in a larger illustrative way?" She would, in this case, embody consciousness beyond her gender. James's

---

12. " 'Place the centre of the subject in the young woman's consciousness,' I said to myself, 'and you get as interesting and beautiful a difficulty as you wish. . . . Make her only interested enough, at the same time, in the things that are not herself' " ("Preface," *The Portrait of a Lady*, in *Literary Criticism*, 1079); James's explanations give further insight into his own vision of what constitutes subjectivity. Here, for instance, he looks at the subject's "relatedness." The heroine's curiosity reflects James's vision of the ideal mind which is not egotistical.

critical prose sustains both versions; the simple interpretation "she is but a woman, what more could we expect by way of a consciousness?" is subverted by the intimations of that other possibility, that she, Emma, in her feminine guise, could represent consciousness at large and as such be, although a woman, the true and only Subject of the novel. But how could this be the case, since the critic has repeatedly expressed his desiderata about Flaubert's enterprise of promotion of such a limited Subject? Her "deficiency" lies after all, according to James, in "the poverty of her consciousness for the typical function." Although James declares in his preface to *The Portrait of a Lady* that such a problem is full of substance, he has not envisaged, it appears, that this "substance" could be so slippery as to finally escape his intellectual grasp and keep him in dim, insoluble contradictions.

It may be that only a more general theory can account for the inexplicable, seemingly unjustified hold that the female figure exerts in these nineteenth-century novels. When, in her interpretation of Balzac's tale "Adieu," the critic Shoshana Felman addresses this problematic of the heroine's status in the fictional text, she suggests that the question must be answered in the more abstract terms of an allegory where the woman is but a namesake for a general questioning of identity ("Women and Madness"). This sheds some light on the obscurities or obfuscations of James's thinking on the status of a feminine identity in relation to models of subjectivity and consciousness. The value of the feminine figure cannot be ascertained and remains necessarily enigmatic, because in such a textual system she embodies the question of identity, of the subject, or of consciousness. But not because such a fiction can claim any knowledge about the particularities of some feminine experience or about what is "femininely typical." "The mere slim shade of an intelligent but presumptuous girl" is simply a ploy that lures the reader into participating in the elaboration of a fictive subjectivity. Emma Bovary and Isabel Archer are the incarnation of a quest for the definitions of "the high attributes of a Subject" or alternately, but also in this context, almost indifferently, of a questioning about femininity as a subjective value, as the form given to identity. In these circumstances, it might be appropriate to consider them as mere simulacra. How indeed could the unknown quantity, the enigma, which is the other in a system of sexual difference whose originating pole is so irreducibly coded as masculine, come into her own or come into her own meaning? This, I believe, constitutes the central paradox of such representations. Reading James on a woman writer or a female protagonist can only confirm Irigaray's impression as she reads Freud, namely, that she witnesses "the process of a consciousness in the making where woman remains the site of the inscription of the repressed" (63).

We think through figures, and the evocative power of Eliot's and James's "vessels" is still with us. For instance, Jessica Benjamin writes in "A Desire of One's Own": "the idea of inner space or spatial representation of desire can be associated with subjectivity only when the interior is not merely an object to be discovered or a receptacle to put things in" (94). Benjamin's comments offer further confirmation that a fictional discourse that conceives of its women as "receptacles to put things in" works first and preeminently at objectifying them and ends up offering to the reader's gaze only the lure, allure of the feminine. For her, "the space should be understood as a receptacle only insofar as it refers to the receptivity of the subject" and "should not be equated with passivity and absence of desire." Benjamin's discussion of subjectivity, founded on the same terms as James's, reveals the lastingness and the validity, for the psychologist at least, of the questions raised by nineteenth-century discussions of representation. But beyond that, it provides, in its new conception of the vessel, a necessary counterpoise to the process I have analyzed here, where precisely the feminine "inside" is above all a receptacle of certain representations, ideas, projects which involve, as actively as has been witnessed in James's texts, a man's desire.

The Erasure

It seems important to focus more narrowly on the gender crossing that this transfer of knowledge and affect onto the feminine figure entails in order to consider the phenomenon of erasure of the female subject. It seems especially important since it might be possible to sketch out in the process a counterpart to James's discussion of the woman writer, which would evoke the kinds of myths that go into the making of a male author. James's fascination with the act of literary creation and his expatiations on this question in his writings on Flaubert will help us outline more sharply the figure of the male writer. Meanwhile, another look at *The Bostonians*, focusing on the question of representativity, will enable us to discuss some of the anxieties attached to women's appropriation of language and of the literary field.

Flaubert's famous declaration "Mme Bovary, c'est moi. D'après moi," whether apocryphal or not, bears precisely on the phenomenon of appropriation and identification that I wish to discuss here. If this statement still haunts our readerly imagination, no doubt it is because it manages to express in an emblematic fashion a somewhat embarrassing topic for critical discussion—the "intensity of life" which certain fictional figures seem to convey ("there is life, there is blood in a considerable measure in Madame Bovary," James writes). "Mme Bovary, c'est moi. D'après moi" takes us back to all the cases where the heroine of a work of fiction, bearing the inscription of the writer's desire, "lives" in the reader's imagination through the emotional and affective charge that she conveys.[13] While Flaubert expresses his romantic longings in Emma, Tolstoy enacts his own conflicting allegiance to passion and morality in *Anna Karenina*, and James endows Olive Chancellor with his own women-haunted consciousness. Such crossings are frequent in nineteenth-century writing; they are vivid reminders of the lure that drew the male writer to the female figure, which was then not only his muse but became his alter ego. From the perspective of literary representation, these forms of fictional transvestism, which produce a female body to fill it with masculine projections, constitute the privileged site for an examination of the more subtle forms of power and violence that sustain the nineteenth-century gender system. This is where the heroine's "representativity" becomes political: to examine the forms of mastery and appropriation that come to bear upon the female creations of Flaubert or James is to examine the politics of the textual-sexual crossings that characterize the nineteenth-century fictions of sexual identity.

When, in his 1893 article, James wonders what place Emma Bovary occupies in the imagination of her creator, he too seizes on the notion of identification—"Madame Bovary c'est Flaubert":

He of course knew more or less what he was doing for his book in making Emma Bovary a victim of the imaginative habit, but he must have been far from designing or measuring the total effect which renders the work so general, so complete an expression of himself. His separate idiosyncrasies, his irritated sensibility to the life about him, with the power to catch it in the fact

13. The phrase may well be apocryphal. Albert Thibaudet quotes a book by René Descharmes, *Flaubert avant 1857*: "Une personne qui a connu très intimement Mlle Amélie Bosquet, la correspondante de Flaubert, me racontait dernièrement que, Mlle Bosquet ayant demandé au romancier d'où il avait tiré le personnage de Madame Bovary, il aurait répondu très nettement et plusieurs fois répété: 'Mme Bovary c'est moi!—D'après moi' " ("A person who had known Mlle Amélie Bosquet, Flaubert's correspondent, very intimately was telling me recently that, as Mlle Bosquet was asking the novelist where he had found the character of Madame Bovary, he had answered very distinctly and repeated several times: 'Mme Bovary c'est moi—D'après moi' " [*Gustave Flaubert*, 92]). In the spirit of this anecdote is Flaubert's letter to Louise Colet, dated April 6, 1853: "For the last six months I have made platonic love (*je fais de l'amour platonique*), and just now the chiming of the bells fills me, in true catholic fashion, with exaltation, and I feel like going to confession" (*Oeuvres complètes: Correspondance* III, 156).

and hold it hard, and his hunger for style and history and poetry, for the rich and the rare, great reverberations, great adumbrations, are here represented together as they are not in his later writings. . . . M. Faguet has of course excellently noted this—that the fortune and felicity of the book were assured by the stroke that made the central figure an embodiment of helpless romanticism. Flaubert himself but narrowly escaped being such an embodiment after all, and he is thus able to express the romantic mind with extraordinary truth. (*Literary Criticism*, 322)

The female Subject, James aknowledges here, is the reflection of a writer who is himself "a victim of the imaginative habit." The idea that *Madame Bovary* expresses the contradictions of Flaubert's romanticism and realism had gained wide currency in James's days, but the critic gives it a more interesting turn when he shows that Emma embodies Flaubert's very own desire to escape from the constraints of realism: her body holds his own writerly investments; he writes herself into her, and he wears the garb of her romantic longings. For James, Emma Bovary is therefore truly the author in disguise.

In their sometimes startling figurations, James's critical reflections on Emma Bovary allow us to catch glimpses of the tacit assumptions that are part of this identification. What these figures reveal are the workings of desire and power that come to bear upon the female figure. James speaks in each of these cases from behind the screen of the words spoken or written by a fellow writer. Discussing the creation of Isabel Archer in the preface to *The Portrait of a Lady*, he invokes Turgenev: "I have always fondly remembered a remark that I heard fall years ago from the lips of Ivan Turgenieff in regard to his own experience of the usual origin of the fictive picture. It began for him almost always with the vision of some person or persons, who hovered before him, soliciting him, as the active or passive figure, interesting him and appealing to him just as they were and by what they were. He saw them, in that fashion, as *disponibles* . . ." (1072). The images of this passage speak suggestively of an encounter with a figure who, like the famous Baudelairian *passante*, is an occasion for desire. The quest for the Subject reads here like a scene of seduction. She (for the figure in question is still the heroine of James's novel) appeals to curiosity, to the imagination, but is also, as the word "solicit" suggests, involved in an economic transaction. Like a prostitute on the sidewalk, she beckons the writer as a body to be used at will.

If this interpretation may appear extravagantly tendentious, the second example can only confirm that in these reflections the scene of sex and passion is never far from James's mind. He cites one of Flaubert's letters to Louise Colet: "How I would have talked with the Greek rhetors, travelled in the great chariots on the Roman roads, and in the evening, in the hostelries, turned in with the vagabond priests of Cybele! ... I *have* lived, all over, in those directions: doubtless in some prior state of being. I'm sure I've been, under the Roman empire, manager of some troop of strolling players, one of the rascals who used to go to Sicily to buy women to make actresses, and who were at once professors, panders and artists" (*Literary Criticism*, 309). Flaubert's *orgie de la littérature*—for literature, the critic thinks, supplies the "'radical absence of the feminine element' in his life"—is James's general theme here, while this letter is presented as a curious and pleasant example of that "sensibility to a *frisson historique*" characteristic of Flaubert's writing. The image of a romantic Flaubert, projecting himself in the world of his own *Salammbô*, must have appealed to James. But the words of the French writer also evoke, in emphatic terms, the desire for a vicarious existence, and they speak of a life in the imagination which is a recurrent Jamesian theme. This form of imagination, which must be understood in the active, Coleridgean sense, stands at odds with the "depersonalization" promoted by Flaubert in the name of a realist aesthetics: here the imagination represents, on the fictional stage, actors who embody the writer's desires.[14] As a stage director, the author becomes a "maker of representations" and produces fictions of sexual identity; he also takes on the role of "a professor, pander and artist" and "buy[s] women to make actresses." Flaubert speaks in unambiguous terms of a gesture of creative appropriation that is necessarily intertwined with scenarios of sexual desire.

The absence of women in the writer's life is answered by their vivid presence in his imagination: James's real concern here is the phantasmic dimension of writing. The value of Flaubert's words lies for him in the fact that they hold a truth that could not otherwise be acknowledged—that the writer's text compensates for an existential lack and carries, metonymically, an erotic investment. The *frisson historique* designates then, beyond the more banal pleasure of escapism (an excursion into another history), the intimate and erotic aspects that are projected, in the name of a history of consciousness, onto the figures of fiction. James and Flaubert call up a theater where the women—prostitutes or ac-

---

14. "The author, in his work, must be like God in the universe, present everywhere, and nowhere visible" (to Louise Colet, in *Oeuvres complètes: Correspondance* III, 61–62). "The artist must work things out so as to convince posterity that he has not lived" (II, 380). This is not unlike James's resistance toward the confessional mode. (See, for instance, my discussion of "Our experiments are quite timid" in the Chapter 2.)

tresses—perform the writer's desires. There the female Subject acts as a decoy: what gets spoken is *his* desire while *she* remains voiceless. As a body devoid of consciousness, desire, or voice, she may as well be called an object. It is in this light that we can now answer James's question with which we began, "Representative of what?": she represents the crossing of a textual and sexual economy whose feminine position is inevitably an ersatz for what cannot be said of men.

Here a reading of *The Bostonians*, centered on the problematic of the voice, might further elucidate the articulation of body, desire, and consciousness in relation to gender. Woman's relation to language and her faculty of utterance are a central concern in James's novel: they are present in Verena's preternaturally gifted eloquence; in Olive, who is haunted by the silent text of women's suffering; and in Ransom, for whom woman's ability to speak out (or to speak up) constitutes the ultimate challenge. James endows Verena with a gift for spontaneous utterance which seems modeled on what he saw in George Sand. The words seem to flow naturally from her mouth; she knows it all by heart, "like an actress before the footlights, or a singer spinning vocal sounds to a silver thread" (252). "She speechifies as a bird sings" (217), and birdlike again, she is said to "emit charming notes" (57). In James's representation, woman's style of utterance is characterized by its spontaneity and facility; it is never the result of work, of thinking, nor is it the effect of truth. The seductions of a feminine voice are opposed to the the hero's naked, blunt assertions of truth, and Verena's powers of persuasion are not the result of her intellectual mastery but the effect of a "form that would render conviction irresistible" (253). George Sand's admirable style and the heroine's rhetorical skills clearly derive from one single conception, which opposes the graceful shape taken by her words to the unadorned rhetorical force of his truth. Indeed the personage is cut in the very same material that covered Sand's lack of "a sense of particular truth" ("George Sand," in *Literary Criticism*, 759). To speak then, in the feminine mode, is merely to exhibit, as seductively as possible, the gaudy silks and trimmings that can best attract the other's gaze. Taken to their furthest reaches, the figures that James associates with woman's speech evoke some hysterical masquerade: when they are not simply a bird's song, the heroine's words conjure up a seductive spectacle, the parody of truth.

In her relation to things of the mind, Verena resembles Sand as well: she too, like the writer, receives, reflects, expresses what is "in the air," but does not produce her own ideas, thoughts, or words; George Sand herself was compared to an aeolian harp. With Verena, James changes registers. She is a reflector, but not of the kind that can think: "Verena's genius was a mystery, and it might remain a mystery; it was impossible to see how this charming, blooming, simple creature, all youth and grace and innocence, got her extraordinary powers of reflection. When her gift was not in excess she appeared anything but reflective, as she sat there now, for instance, you would never have dreamed that she had had a vivid revelation" (78). Not that James deprives women of knowledge altogether, but while he concedes intelligence and even mastery over facts to Olive Chancellor, he simultaneously deprives her of feminine traits: "She had absolutely no figure, and presented a certain appearance of feeling cold. With all this, there was something very modern and highly developed in her aspect; she had the advantages as well as the drawbacks of a nervous organization . . . he saw that she was a woman without laughter; exhilaration, if it ever visited her, was dumb" (15). Nervous or neurotic, cold or frigid, Olive carries within her only the pathological aspects of her femininity and, in stark opposition to Verena, is so unsexed as to have become unfit for marriage. In the narrator's humorous words: "Olive Chancellor was unmarried by every implication of her being. She was a spinster as Shelley was a lyrical poet, or as the month of August is sultry" (15).

Trapped within this inauspicious shell, however, lies buried an exquisite, excruciating awareness of the predicament of her own sex. Thanks to her extraordinary empathetic imagination Olive remembers during her long vigils "their silent suffering," and "the image is always in front of her mind," that of "the unhappiness of women" (33). But Olive, the fragile vessel of a knowledge and anguish that fill her with feminine pathos, is silent. And while she identifies with all the suffering women of the past, she is likewise dumbstruck and ends up posturing in the guise of a silent victim. If anything gets said about women or their condition in *The Bostonians*, it is then necessarily as a joint text produced by the two complementary figures of Verena (the voice) and Olive (the mind).

"My own friend," Olive replied, "you have never yet said anything to me which expressed so clearly the closeness and sanctity of our union."

"You do keep me up," Verena went on. "You are my conscience."

"I should like to be able to say that you are my form—my envelope. But you are too beautiful for that!"(149)

"This sacred and intimate union" between, on the one hand, an intelligence and consciousness and, on the other, a body endowed with a pretty voice evokes a more conventional picture (the kind of marriage that, for example, Ransom would like to promote). But this marriage remains of course sterile: such an association between the "eternal feminine" and a pathological femininity does not engender a Subject; it sanctions rather its effacement. For no single utterance can speak her knowledge, let alone her desire, as long as the novel works on the principle of such dissociation—a mind and a consciousness on one side and a voice and a body on the other. As a form devoid of content (Verena) or as content deprived of a form (Olive), the ghost of the hysteric haunts the pages of James's novel.

It would be absurd, however, to claim that *The Bostonians* is a novel filled with silence: Ransom's words, describing the speeches of women as "windy iterations of inanities," linger too much in our minds. Indeed, the text as a whole resounds loudly with women's words, but they do not express knowledge, only emotions. In his commentary on Sand, James dwells abundantly on her talent for finding words when called upon by circumstances. Her weapon, he claims, is neither logic nor intelligence (she is deprived of both) but her ability to talk: "George Sand is judged from our point of view by one's saying that for her discretion is simply non-existent. Its place is occupied by a sort of benevolent, an almost conscientious disposition to sit down, as it were, and 'talk over' the whole matter. The subject fills her with a motherly loquacity; it stimulates all her wonderful and beautiful self-sufficiency of expression—the quality that we have heard a hostile critic call her 'glibness' " (*Literary Criticism*, 727).

James's description thus identifies a use of language that is proper to woman, where Sand's eloquence is brought back to the typically feminine dimensions of fireside chat or gossip or of intimate *bavardage* between women, where passion, no longer sublime and inexpressible, can be talked about, talked over. Thus Olive and Verena are often shown in conversation, but the narrator confesses that he finds himself unable to represent with a semblance of reality that aspect of their relation. Why indeed attempt to represent what seems so unnatural, namely, Verena's "familiarity with the vocabulary of emotions, the mysteries of 'spiritual life'?" And yet this is part of her "essence": "the extraordinary generosity with which she would expose herself, give herself away, turn herself inside out, for the satisfaction of a person who made demands of her" (366). "Turning herself inside out"—in James's colloquial phrase the revelations of an intimate self acquire strangely physical overtones. How much greater and nobler for James is the kind of suffering from which one can only "avert [one's] head," the tragic silence of Olive, immured in her body, like Antigone in her tomb. Woman's propensity to unveil her feelings with too much eloquence is met here with a resistance that defines its transgressive nature.

Picking up James's disenchanted statement about the need to write another *Bostonians*, Elaine Showalter comments:

Another version of *The [Other] Bostonians*, however, requires a
transformation in the reader rather than in the author; like the Don Quixote
of Pierre Menard, it is *The Bostonians* read otherwise, through the prisms of
poststructuralism and gender theory, in ways that reveal James's own fears of
female literary competition. In this sense, James's novel remains a very
American tale of the 80's, but it is also about the situation of men, especially
literary men, and the agitation on *their* behalf at the fin-de-siècle, a parable
about the struggle over the Word at the end of the century. ("Other
Bostonians," 180)

The novel raises indeed the question of women's relation to the Word, not only as a theme but as a literary performance: the story of Ransom's abduction of Verena from the platform of public speaking cannot easily be separated from its allegorical counterpart. The figures of the text are involved in a struggle between mastery and hysteria, and what is at stake is sexual difference itself. What will happen when women have full access to public speech or to the literary field, and when they speak for themselves?

Her description of the convention put the scene before him vividly; he seemed
to see the crowded, overheated hall, which he was sure was filled with
carpetbaggers, to hear flushed women, with loosened bonnet-strings, forcing
thin voices into ineffectual shrillness. It made him angry, and all the more
angry, that he hadn't a reason, to think of the charming creature at his side
being mixed up with such elements, pushed and elbowed by them, conjoined
with them in emulation, in unsightly strainings and clappings and shoutings,
in wordy, windy iteration of inanities. Worst of all was the idea that she
should have expressed such a congregation to itself so acceptably, have been
acclaimed and applauded by hoarse throats, have been lifted up, to all the
vulgar multitude, as the queen of the occasion. (227)

This passage occupies a central position in the novel, not only from the point of view of the drama (where it gives the impulse to Ransom's aggressive conquest of Verena) but also in the wider context of James's project concerning "the situation of women, the decline of the sentiment of sex, the agitation on their behalf." The passion, agitation, and hysteria of such a scene seems to contaminate the very language of its representation. An alliterative string such as the "wordy, windy, iterations of inanities. Worst," rarely finds its way into James's prose,[15] and the rhetoric invoked here gives us the measure of the writing's (or the writer's?) hysteria when faced with the prospect of a vulgar mob of speaking women.

The Bostonians also provides an alternative but double answer to the question of women's language, where the author appears to take a more sympathetic stance toward women. On the one hand, he sketches a picture of the women's convention in a descriptive mode that oscillates between sympathy and satire. But the words we are given to hear are no more than "a thin tissue of generalities," as if a woman's text were necessarily covered over by the spectacle of her performance ("I listen to your voice, not to your ideas," Ransom tells Verena). He weaves, on the other hand, the text of Olive's intimate sufferings, as if he were listening at the door of her soul. But the figure of the woman who has obtained "wonderful insight . . . into the history of feminine anguish" is but a surrogate, it turns out, for the author himself. There may be more than a hint of self-parody in the description of Olive's silent vigil for suffering women: "the voice of their sufferings was always in her ears" (33); "She sat with them at their trembling vigils, listened for the tread, the voice, at which they grew pale and sick, walked with them by the dark waters that offered to wash away misery and shame, took with them, even, when the vision grew intense, the last shuddering leap . . . she knew (or she thought she knew) all the possible tortures of anxiety, suspense and dread" (175).

Indeed, Olive seems haunted here with the ghostly presence of a writer who can imagine Isabel Archer's "trembling vigils," and who was later to give shape in his novels to the Charlotte Stant, Milly Theale, Madame de Vionnet, or Maggie Verver that Olive Chancellor seems miraculously to have dreamed up, imagined for him. Behind the "conscious anxious silence" (146) that marks Olive's fate lies the shadow of the author, seized with mingled pity and his *frisson historique*, as he envisages the "interminable dim procession" of women bearing "the intolerable load of fate."[16] *The Bostonians* thus tells the story of a double subjection:

15. In the same vein, compare this string with Miss Birdseye's "delicate, dirty, democratic little hand" (*Bostonians*, 24).

16. This is the explicit theme of the final debate in James's *The Golden Bowl*. In this novel James sets up the Prince's benevolent (?) humanism against the heroine's feminist plea: "Maggie recalled—she had memories enough. 'It's terrible,'—her memories prompted her to speak. 'I see it's *always* terrible for women.' The Prince looked down in his gravity. 'Everything's terrible, *cara*—in the heart of man.' " (534).

that of the silencing of Verena in the name of aesthetic and cultural values, but also, more insidiously, that of Olive's "aphonia."[17] But in delineating a heroine who, in her blushes, stammers, and nervousness is made to embody the consciousness and history of women's suffering, James appears to hint dimly at the more familiar figure of the hysteric.

Reading Her Silence

A woman whose suffering body covers up, as in a veil, the mysteries of a feminine soul constitutes the centerpiece of many narratives of sexual identity. James's Olive Chancellor, Flaubert's Emma Bovary, Sand's Lélia or Valentine, Eliot's Gwendolen Harleth, but also Dora, Emmy von N., and a number of other figures of Freud's case histories obey the same conventions of representation. In each case, the female subject embodies a secret meaning related to gender or sexuality, which must be uncovered in the process of narration. From a narratological perspective, these nineteenth-century novels and the case histories belong to the same genre, not only because they strive for what is perceived as a truthful, that is, a psychological representation of subjectivity, but also because this project naturally converges on a female figure endowed with a meaning and a knowledge that exceed her language, but which are yet legible in the history of her bodily symptoms.[18] While the hysteric is enlisted to sustain an epistemological project intent on reconceptualizing subjectivity as inevitably marked by sexual difference, her symptoms define the rules of gender in their application to the mind.[19]

Here, then, the process of engendering does not begin in the body as

17. For this particularly felicitous description of Olive's complaint, I am indebted to a conversation with Peter Brooks.

18. The term "psychological" is used here in a loose sense as referring to the "inner" mental or psychic qualities, and in opposition to "moral." In the course of the nineteenth century, the mind or psyche was gradually divested of its moral dimensions, still so present in the descriptions of nineteenth-century medicine (see Chapter 1) or in James's discourse around George Sand (the woman writer somehow calls for such conservative, retrograde strategies of containment).

19. In articulating this statement, I rely on the two crucial notions, presented by Freud, of the *Hysterika* and *das Geschlechtliche*. The latter is discussed in the last section of Chapter 3; on the question of the *Hysterika* in Freud, see "The Pleasures of the Alcove, or Hysteria According to Freud" in Chapter 5.

Freud was strongly discouraged early in his career from working on male hysteria, as he recounts in his *Autobiographical Study* (*SE* XX, 15–16). In this chapter, however, I am not so much interested in the age-old association of hysteria with femininity: I want to examine, from a historical perspective, the place held by hysteria in the elaboration and definition of the concept of gender, and more particularly, of a gendered mind.

was the case with the medical narratives I studied. Nor does it begin in the social and cultural space, as could be evidenced in James's texts on Sand and *The Bostonians.* What I am tracing here is the gendering of the mind, a process that the various literary scenes concerned with the creation of the Subject could only vaguely adumbrate, and which I pursue in my reading of *Fragment of a Case of Hysteria.* The case history of Dora holds, of course, a conspicuous and problematic place for psychoanalysis, but it can constitute as well a precious document for this historical enquiry. On this account, it can be read indeed in the same way as the "precious text-book" that James deciphered in Sand, as a myth, fable, or merely an example that enables us to examine certain aspects of gender. But the main theme is not so much passion (although it plays an important role), but rather knowledge and science. Dora can be seen as another revealing instance of a female Subject held in the thralls of an observer-analyst as the indispensable object of the quest for an inward knowledge, for the charting of the psychological and mental domains. Indeed, in his article "Naughty Orators," which develops the theme of the hysterical woman (much represented in film melodrama), Stanley Cavell writes that "by the turn of the twentieth century psychic reality, the fact of the existence of mind, had become believable primarily in its feminine (one may say passive) aspect" (352). The hysteric, as we have seen, epitomizes femininity, and she embodies moreover, in a spectacular fashion, a passive and helpless stance with regards to some inner, reflexive knowledge. Her body may speak, but what it projects outward is merely the blank text of her ignorance, which only her counterpart, the physician or analyst, can fill. But, like a screen or mirror, she sends back the gaze of him who peers into her. The gaze of the inquirer defines, as we shall see, the outline of a figure that will have for substance his dream, while his pen will all too often lead him to sketch his own autobiography.

The theme of this new gender fable is the narrative compact that unites the hysteric and the observer-analyst-writer. When she says "read me," he responds, "you are a mystery." This is, in substance, the meaning of this unusual episode in the story of Freud and Dora's reciprocal involvement in hysteria. And my commentary leads me to highlight the place of gender in a scene of knowledge and desire that speaks of a feminine secret and a masculine curiosity.

There is a great deal of symbolism of this kind in life, but as a rule we pass it by without heeding it. When I set myself the task of bringing to light what human beings keep hidden within them, not by the compelling power of hypnosis, but by observing what they say and what they show, I thought the task was a harder one than it really is. He that has eyes to see and ears to hear may convince himself that no mortal can keep a secret. If his lips are silent, he chatters with his finger-tips; betrayal oozes out of him at every pore. And thus the task of making conscious the most hidden recesses of the mind is one which it is quite possible to accomplish.

Dora's symptomatic act with the reticule did not immediately precede the dream. She started the sitting which brought us the narrative of the dream with another symptomatic act. As I came into the room in which she was waiting she hurriedly concealed a letter which she was reading. I naturally asked her whom the letter was from, and at first she refused to tell me. Something then came out which was a matter of complete indifference and had no relation to the treatment. It was a letter from her grandmother, in which she begged Dora to write to her more often. I believe that Dora only wanted to play "secrets" with me, and to hint that she was on the point of allowing her secret to be torn from her by the doctor. (*SE* VII, 77–78)

The narrative progression and articulation between these two paragraphs highlight what is the obvious purpose of this fable—a demonstration of the fact that no thing (symptom, dream, or object) the patient produces can defeat the analyst's perspicacity. An event that occurred during the analytical session is thus meant to provide indirect confirmation for his skill at getting the truth out of his patient. The story takes the following course: the hysteric, having just denied Freud's interpretation of a symptomatic act (which accounted for Dora's playing with her reticule), comes to her session the next time with the "gift" of a letter, which announces her next gift to the analyst, the all important First Dream. The discourse, on the other hand, is made of the following sequence: having just brilliantly interpreted the patient's first dream, the narrator congratulates himself on his powers of observation and interpretation ("the task of making conscious the most hidden recesses of the mind is one which it is quite possible to accomplish") and tells, by way of an example, the story of Dora's wanting "to play 'secrets'" with him. Story and discourse, in this case, entail a strongly polarized distinction between the events the hysteric provokes in the course of the analysis and the analyst's display of his ability to make sense of these events in light of his theoretical project. The distinction is, of course, of crucial importance: the story that she tells or, in this instance, literally enacts on the analytical stage must guarantee the claims of his theory. In other words, her story becomes the text of his investigation and knowledge. Although Freud often emphasizes the contrast between the seemingly haphazard, meaningless events of her story and his discursive ordering which aims at confirming his mastery and lucidity as a theoretician, in this instance the claims he makes for his percipience verge on extravagance.

A case history obeys two narrative conditions: it must tell a particular story whose aim is to retrace the history of the hysteric's symptoms, but it needs to provide as well the theoretical frame for which the subject in question is the prime example and illustration. The single event the fable recounts has to be read, therefore, on two levels. Within the unfolding of the analysis, the letter functions symbolically as a gift (whose value is, moreover, prophetic) to the analyst. From the perspective of theory, meanwhile, this episode presents an allegory of the analytical stage, with its three elements: the woman, the secret, and the analyst. There, the letter is destined to tell the secret of her availability for his decipherment. It cannot be read as a signifier or text, but must be understood as a sign that invites the analyst to do his work as a reader-analyst; as such it confirms, this time in an affirmative fashion (this is important, for Dora had again just said no), the compact that brings them together. What the letter says here, in place of Dora (through a metonymic displacement), is "read me," "pierce my secret," or rather, considering the overall dynamic of the analysis, "I allow you to tear a secret from me." From a psychological perspective, which is the one chosen by Freud, the patient plays a game of seduction involving a secret.

But this narrative and therapeutic compact raise, of course, the question of Dora's strategy. For the hysteric makes here the kind of appearance that could easily be described in the words of James's account concerning "the origin of the fictive picture": as an "active or passive figure," she seems to appeal to his imagination or knowledge, she "solicits him." To ask in this instance whether the figure is active or passive means deciding whether the patient knows (or does not know) what she is doing. It also means choosing where we want to put the emphasis in the compound term *Symptomhandlung* (symptomatic act). Must the letter be compared to a symptom, like something that speaks against the patient's consciousness? Or does it reveal, as a gesture (*eine Handlung*) expressing, symbolically, the patient's trust and confidence in the doctor's perspicacity, the desire for an active recovery? There is, of course, no way to tell, and from an orthodox psychoanalytical perspective, the difference is not of crucial importance: whatever the degree of recovery or illness the event may bespeak, it still belongs to Dora's hysteria since it lies beyond language in the realm of bodily signs.

The question of the hysteric's passivity or, on the contrary, of her active and knowing endorsement of her role in the game of analysis only begins to matter when there is a lingering suspicion that passivity means victimization, powerlessness, or erasure. From such a perspective, activity and passivity are not indifferent terms, even though they seem to coexist in one event; they define the ambivalence that characterizes the hysteric's stance. The fable could be said then to display Dora actively endorsing her passive role as a hysteric exhibiting herself under the analyst's gaze.[20]

Meanwhile, from the point of view of its mise-en-scène or dramaturgy, this story epitomizes what must be the hysteric's fate: she is doomed to produce on her body signs that call for his elucidation. The enigma consists in a body that offers itself, with various degrees of resistance (or perversity), to the analyst's decipherment. Analysis then begins to look like the scene of a seduction, whose object is not so much bodily possession as the possession of a knowledge of the body. This aspect can surely not have gone unnoticed by Freud himself; the fact of exhibiting a letter is not that different from handing over a box—this being the example of a symptomatic act that Freud had presented just before the fable. In both cases it falls to the doctor to "open" the object. But as we assume that the letter is offered to the analyst as a provocation, a question arises whose implications are inevitably moral: Must Dora's gesture be understood as a perversion, of an epistemological as well as an erotic nature? It could then be argued that she, willingly and deliberately (but how much so?), offers this new *Symptomhandlung* not as an expression of her affect or suffering but as a ploy that shows her awareness (or call it her "instinctive perception") of the rules of the game; the fable would then exemplify the patient's struggle to resist. Dora's analytic session looks then increasingly like a battleground where a fight is waged between the patient's stubborn resistance to being cured and the analyst's repeated attempts to weaken her defenses, or phrased differently, between her willing ignorance and his knowledge.

It seems now difficult to keep at bay the question of simulation. The symptomatic act may be feigned: in a gesture of ostentatious generosity,

20. With both the hysteric and the criminal "we are concerned with a secret," writes Freud. "In the case of the criminal it is a secret which he knows and hides from you, whereas in the case of the hysteric it is a secret which he himself does not know either, which is hidden even from himself" (*Psycho-Analysis and the Establishment of the Facts in Legal Proceedings*, SE IX, 108). As my commentary indicates, the question is not only one of activity versus passivity but of knowledge versus ignorance. What happens when the hysteric willingly, deliberately, produces a secret? Is Dora on the side of the hysteric or the criminal? Or is she merely Freud's accomplice? On this subject see Kofman, "Narcissistic Woman," 222–25.

she gives him one more sign or symptom, namely, this letter which, like a sacrificial offering, is in fact destined to fuel his ardent desire for knowledge. At this point the scene of her hysteria becomes a masquerade. Not only does Dora play her role as hysteric to perfection; she also sustains, by the sheer power of her performance, the analytical stage itself since she ensures, through her willing provocation, that the play that brings together the two actors does not run out of text. Thus when he says "you are such a mystery," she answers, "look at me, read me, just like a letter."

But how "authentic" an illness is hysteria? The question has arisen repeatedly and in various forms, and is certainly not negligible. "And one knows," Irigaray writes, "how much incredulity, repression, derision came to bear upon the hysteric because of this 'malingering' " (70). What is it that takes precedence? The hysteric's relish for performance, her desire to create spectators or an audience for her troubles, or some genuine suffering that knows no other means than body language (even when it resembles seduction) to arrest the other's compassionate attention? Nineteenth-century doctors repeatedly had to fend off the objection that hysteria was a simulated illness. Contemporary vade mecums of psychiatry still warn doctors against the dangers of confusing a certain typical feminine theatricality with the symptoms of a real hysteria.[21] But in the case of Dora, now a paper creature, how will we ever know? There is indeed no way of ascertaining how much control and mastery went into such a performance and whether, in this instance, the patient achieved a small victory over the analyst (having identified the rules of the game), or whether, on the contrary, she confirmed in this symptomatic act her willingness to collaborate in her treatment. This dilemma foreshadows another radical uncertainty, that which lies in the patient's resounding choice to abruptly terminate the analysis. As Cavell argues, it is impossible to know whether her walking out on Freud and out of the analysis signals her triumph or her ultimate acknowledgment, in the form of the most spectacular resistance, of the truth of his claim (352).

Nor shall we ever know what Dora's grandmother (paternal or maternal, the story doesn't tell) said in her letter beyond the fact that "she begged Dora to write to her more often." It is a tantalizing thought that this fable could provide yet another instance of Freud's blindspots. It may be indeed that Dora, taking a more active part than I have so far imagined, was trying to seduce Freud—into taking a different intellectual

21. See Chap. 1, n. 8.

track. She may have been trying to redirect the path of the analysis. What does it mean when the grandmother, belonging to the side either of maternal silence or of patriarchal command, asks Dora to write, in spite of her "dyspnoea, *tussis nervosa*, aphonia, migraines, depression, hysterical unsociability, and *taedium vitae*"?[22]

The gender fable does not answer this question, but it reveals why the story of the grandmother and granddaughter does not matter to Freud. When he claims in the preceding paragraph that no secret can escape him, he also designates in unambiguous terms the object of his epistemological quest: *das verborgenste Seelische*, literally, "what of the soul is the most concealed." Thus for the theoretician, the body of the hysteric is not read for its suffering, nor really for its history, but is pressed for the knowledge that it can offer about the secrets of the human soul. Freud's language is here definitely "ungendered," as borne out by his choice of the plural, collective term *die Sterblichen* (the mortals) and the impersonal and neuter form *wessen* (whose), when it would have been possible in German to mark the statement as feminine (using *deren*). The analyst thus refers to a psychic space not marked by a sexual difference. Nonetheless, the body that has been represented throughout is unquestionably Dora's, the hysteric's.

This discrepancy suggests that hysteria is here a trope, as the immanent, visible figuration of that inner psychic space which is the object of Freud's quest. In other words, from the point of view of analytical theory, Dora "produces" in her hysteria that which needs to be brought to consciousness and which stands in the place of consciousness. The spoils will be *his*, just as this knowledge extracted from *her* will constitute the foundation of *his* science of the mind. Meanwhile, this polarization leaves open the question (as my emphases should make clear) whether the subjectivity or consciousness produced here can still be considered genderless. One thing is certain, however: the structure on which this epistemology relies is unquestionably polarized in terms of gender. Her hysterical (or hystericized) body, since it has become the receptacle of his own knowledge and science, is instrumental in the construction of a consciousness of which she is the blindspot. This process of simultaneous valorization and negation of the woman's experience is what has led Irigaray to suggest that women have been made into "wardens of the negative" and to write that "the *enigma* of femininity is the token of a progression toward his absolute knowledge. He would then need to

22. Dora's symptoms are enumerated in this fashion by Freud (*SE* VII, 24).

bring increasingly into the actuality of his consciousness this 'nonknowl-edge' that she perpetuates, this 'unconscious' that, without her knowl-edge, has been attributed to her" (138).

Keys and Boxes

But I want to return to my earlier theme—woman as a vessel—in the wake of Irigaray's discussion of woman's ascription to "nonknowledge" and to the "unconscious." For while the theme plays, in a predictable fashion, a female body against a masculine mind, Freud's *Fragment of a Case of Hysteria* constitutes, because of its complex elaboration of a discourse on the Subject, an exemplary text for inquiry into gender and knowledge. Indeed, in this case history, the female Subject is represented in the familiar form of a vessel and its variations. Pill boxes, reticules, jewel boxes, little chests, rooms that must be locked: all of these are considered by the analyst to represent woman. Every object that can be defined as a cavity susceptible of holding or containing "things" ex-presses, by metaphor or metonymy, a female body—it too built around a hollow space, a void that can be filled. Each of these objects, defined by its boundaries, instigates a spatial dynamics between an inside and an outside: each can be opened or closed; each invites or denies (when it is closed or locked) investigation or exploration. In this respect, it could be said of Dora and of the "woman of a certain age" (who asked Freud to open her pill box) that they too, like the boxes they carry in their hands or in their dreams, are such receptacles, filled with an inside which demands to be explored.[23]

Indeed, the discursive pattern (or the logic of Freud's exposition) that leads to (or produces) the fable of Dora's letter suggests as much. The sequence begins with a paragraph concerning women and boxes, fol-lowed by another where the analyst speaks of his ability to read what spills out of the hysteric's body, and ends with the fable about the patient and the letter (both of these wanting to be opened). By the power of these synecdoches, the analyst's progress is mapped onto his object, the woman, in such a way that a container (box, bag, body, letter) is likened to the woman's sex, which in itself stands for what she offers to his penetrating, perspicuous gaze (or his alerted ear). Freud remarks,

23. On this subject see Teresa de Lauretis's suggestive remarks about the elaboration of a mythical structuration around sexual difference, with a hero who "crosses the bound-ary and penetrates the other space. . . . Female is what is not susceptible to transformation, to life or death; she (it) is an element of plot-space, a topos, a resistance, matrix, and matter" (*Alice Doesn't: Feminism, Semiotics, Cinema*, 118–19).

" 'Where is the key?' seems to me to be the masculine counterpart to the question 'Where is the *box?*' They are therefore questions referring— to the genitals" (*SE* VII, 97). This statement, which belongs to Freud's interpretation of Dora's second dream, offers further confirmation: from a psychoanalytical perspective, objects can function as symbols, and they are endowed with a gender that is not merely grammatical. In the "symbolic geography of sex" mapped out in Dora's dreams, a box, as a receptacle, a hollow space, is naturally feminine. But no explanation is given for this gender attribution beyond a number of linguistic associations: "Is not 'jewel-case' [*Schmuckkästchen*] a term commonly used to describe female genitals that are immaculate and intact?" (*SE* VII, 91). Or, "*Zimmer* [room] in dreams stands very frequently for *Frauenzimmer* [a slightly derogatory word for 'woman,' literally, 'women's appartment']. The question whether a woman is 'open' or 'shut' can naturally not be a matter of indifference. It is well known, too, what sort of 'key' effects the opening in such a case" (*SE* VII, 67). It may be, to follow Freud, that language bears the traces of our unconscious wisdom, and perhaps it is true, as Octave Mannoni suggests, that language reproduces "the, for man, signifying function (or nature) of the *marks* of anatomical difference" (62). The kind of attention the analyst pays to language would then offer the confirmation that we constantly reinvest our world with gendered meanings. If we hold the conviction that the "difference between men and women is the most important one" and that it characterizes our human condition, then to affirm, as Freud does, that keys are masculine and boxes feminine (a fact part of common knowledge, he suggests) constitutes a meaningful insight not only into our relation to objects and language but into our mental lives. But if we accept these premises, we are naturally led to interpret every phenomenon in terms of sexual difference: not only the objects in themselves but also what one does with them and the analyst's doing itself. This takes us back precisely to the question of gender and knowledge, and beyond that, to the gendering of knowledge.

Freud's interpretation of Dora's second dream has become in recent years the predestined text for such an inquiry. Kaja Silverman, for example, speaking of "Freud's insistence that Dora occupies the position of a young man in the first part of her second dream," singles out Freud's interpretation as an instance of his inability to conceive of a feminine subjectivity (*Acoustic Mirror*, 246, n. 41). Neil Hertz has demonstrated as well, with incontrovertible brio, how "the suggestion that Dora's imagining of the female genitals is bound to be from a man's point of view is of a piece with Freud's persistence in characterizing Dora's love as 'masculine' " ("Dora's Secrets," 236). In Hertz's analysis, it is unquestionably under the sign of masculinity that the dreaming Dora embarks on a quest for knowledge of her sexual body: it is "the phantasy of a man seeking to force an entrance into the female genitals." The reconstruction of the sequence *Bahnhof—Friedhof—Vorhof* (which leads Freud to exclaim, in a self-congratulatory fashion, "Here was a symbolic geography of sex") and, before that, his ability to discern in these images their sexual undertones presuppose a knowledge of anatomy and of a descriptive language, referring to the sexual body, of the kind that would precisely have been his prerogative as a doctor. Indeed, the technical, latinate words that the images of Dora's dream conjure up in his mind could have sprung from the pages of his very own anatomical textbooks or encyclopedia. To many readers, Freud's interpretation resembles here a little too much the "phantasy of a man."

But I may be going too fast here. Let us go back to Freud's moment of triumph, just as he wonders whether his intuition might not have been *ein witziger Irrtum*, that is, an error that looks like a joke:

At this point a certain suspicion of mine became a certainty. The use of *Bahnhof* ["station"; literally, "railway court"] and *Friedhof* ["cemetery"; literally, "peace court"] to represent the female genitals was striking enough in itself, but it also served to direct my awakened curiosity to the similarly formed *Vorhof* ["vestibulum"; literally, "forecourt"], an anatomical term for a particular region of the female genitals. This might have been no more than a misleading joke. But now, with the addition of "nymphs" visible in the background of a "thick wood," no further doubts could be entertained. Here was a symbolic geography of sex! "Nymphae," as is known to physicians though not to laymen (and even by the former the term is not very commonly used), is the name given to the labia minora, which lie in the background of the "thick wood" of the pubic hair. But any one who employed such technical names as "vestibulum" and "nymphae" must have derived his knowledge from anatomical textbooks or from an encyclopedia—the common refuge of youth when it is devoured by sexual curiosity. If this interpretation were correct, therefore, there lay concealed behind the first situation in the dream a phantasy of defloration, the phantasy of a man seeking to force an entrance into the female genitals. (*SE* VII, 99–100)

An "imaginary walk" across dark woods leading to a more open peaceful ground is part of Freud's own itinerary as well. In a study of the myths that informed Freud's own vision of his intellectual progress, titled "Acheronta Movebo," Jean Starobinski quotes a passage from one of Freud's letters to Wilhelm Fliess concerning *The Interpretation of*

Dreams, where the same dense woods of Dora's dream make a striking appearance: "The whole thing is planned on the model of an imaginary walk. First comes the dark wood of the authorities (who cannot see the trees), where there is no clear view and it is easy to go astray. Then there is a cavernous defile through which I lead my readers—my specimen dream with its particularities, its details, its indiscretions and its bad jokes, and then, all at once, the high ground and the open prospect and the question: 'Which way do you want to go?' " (Freud, *Origins of Psychoanalysis,* 290). Not only do the hysteric and the analyst show an analogous familiarity with anatomy and the vocabulary of sex, but they conceive of their quest for knowledge through the same figures. This letter, dated August 6, 1899, precedes the analysis of Dora by about one year. But, as noted by the editors of the Standard Edition, it seems that Freud repeatedly, and erroneously, associates Dora with his own *annus mirabilis* 1899, the year that was decisive for his conception of *The Interpretation of Dreams.* It is possible that the analyst had "read himself" into Dora's dream even more literally than has ever been suspected: he might have been mapping out, in the course of interpretation, his own dreams onto her dream. Or, more specifically, the interpretation of Dora's dream uncovers primarily Freud's desire and his dependence on the hysteric to fulfill such a desire.[24]

What if, moreover, we apply Freud's own conception of "a symbolic geography of sex" to this "cavernous defile"? What does this say about the analyst's relation to the object of his knowledge—to the mind, to the hysteric's unconscious, to the woman's "nonknowledge"? The figure reveals here again that a masculinity complex can shape not only the scene of desire but also that of knowledge: reading his desire into the hysteric's text, the analyst repeatedly remodels her in the shape of a hollow core, as the negative of his own, insistently present masculinity.[25]

The gendered plot of knowledge can be summarized in a few sentences. When, in an attempt to gain access to "the most hidden recesses of the mind" (*das verborgenste Seelische*), the analyst bends "with sharpened attention" over the hysteric's text, he holds the key to his own

24. Julia Kristeva, in *Histoires d'amour,* writes about "the young Freud's phallic desire to penetrate the psychic space and . . . [his] debt toward the all-powerful hysterical femininity" (157, n. 2).

25. In line with my earlier discussion of the fabrication of "a gender core" (in the section "A Work of Psychology, Descriptive and Moral," Chap. 3), here we are witnessing not so much the "public regulation of fantasy through the surface politics of the body" as the *private* regulation of fantasy through the cognitive exploration of the hysteric's body. What I am arguing then is that a gender core is also the effect of a private, intimate "consciousness" and not only of some generalized, socialized public morality.

knowledge.[26] Dora's dream constitutes a pretext for him to exercise his judgment, perspicacity, penetration. To enter into a dense wood, to penetrate the secret of books, to enter into the woman's body, this is the masculine undertaking. The search for the key to the enigma (as a masculine activity) and for the knowledge of the sexed body (as a masculine privilege) leads him, the analyst, inevitably to that surface or veil that defines her as a body, container, vessel of his secret. The exploration of the secrets of the psyche in Freud's quest for consciousness can indeed not take place outside a discourse of gender: at the very heart of this intellectual undertaking we meet again *das Geschlechtliche*—as the representations of eros, as an indissoluble link between power and sexuality. Freud's undertaking to read the human soul through the exemplary case of the hysteric can never be divested of its gendered inflections, and in this map of *das verborgenste Seelische*, there can be no zones of epistemological neutrality. This analytical quest for a knowledge of the Subject brings in its trail another wager on the meaning of sexual difference.

Stanley Cavell has written that in psychoanalysis, countertransference means "the theft of woman's knowledge, that knowledge, which, suppressed, caused the conditions psychoanalysts were first asked to see, conditions of hysteria" (352); Monique David-Ménard's project can be understood as an attempt to retrieve the loss of that knowledge. In her analysis of the case history, she tries to uncover woman's subjectivity before it is caught in a network of sexual difference, that is, before Dora's active role in the quest is inevitably understood as a "masculine position."[27] For in the Freudian interpretation, there is no space for a consciousness or knowledge on the other side of sexual difference: to look for a key to the great enigma of the difference between the sexes is always already a masculine gesture; the quest for femininity can, paradoxically, only be understood within a masculine subject-position. Within such a model, a feminine consciousness—as an awareness or

26. In the original the phrase is *Geschärfter Aufmerksamkeit*; Alix and James Strachey translate it as "awakened curiosity" (*SE* VII, 99). However, as David-Ménard (*Hysteria from Freud to Lacan*) has shown, *Aufmerksamkeit* (attention) is an important element of hysteria, but is understood differently, as a form of thought, in the intellectualist tradition. Freud's description typically creates an implicit opposition between the hysteric's "attention to bodily positions" and the analyst's attention, which is purely intellectual.

27. In her feminist approach, Silverman wants to argue against this specific alignment; she suggests that in the girl's case, "desire and identification may be strung along a single thread in the female version of the negative Oedipus complex" and that "Freud's account of the Oedipus complex—positive and negative—is predicated upon this assumption as is his reading of Dora's homosexuality" (*Acoustic Mirror*, 150).

comprehension of the desires that originate in the female body or a knowledge concerning sexual difference and its meanings—cannot exist. However, working beyond this Freudian frame, David-Ménard allows us to catch in the story of Dora glimpses of a feminine consciousness. We see merely glimpses because, as Irigaray suggests, "We are familiar with the fragility of the hysteric's ego, its fragmentation, that it constantly risks exploding, bursting into pieces. Its fleeting, secretive relation to 'consciousness' " (109).

"They must have neither eyes nor ears nor words nor thoughts for this 'evil,' the knowledge in itself is here already evil," Nietzsche writes on the question of women's modesty (*Gay Science*, 429). The philosopher's awareness of the interdiction that bears on woman's knowledge of sexual matters, which forces her to deny the evidence offered by her eyes, ears, or thoughts, offers a sobering counterpart to Freud's exhilarated awareness of the powers of his own eyes, ears and thoughts: "for him who has eyes to see, ears to hear." If, as I suggested earlier, the hysteric's relation to knowledge is defined by such a denial, her counterpart, the analyst, prides himself on his ability to derive knowledge from such sensory, and especially visual, evidence. The juxtaposition of Nietzsche's statement with that of Freud highlights what are the philosophical but also the cultural and political implications of the gendered scene of knowledge that informs the analyst's undertaking. Hysteria becomes the revealing symptom of a crisis in knowledge brought about by the enforcement of gender on the woman. The hysteric thus carries thus the stigma of woman's inability to pursue her quest for self-knowledge— for consciousness—and of a feminine *pudor* that has neither eyes nor ears nor thoughts.

In her detailed analysis of Dora's second dream, David-Ménard, who insists on reading Dora's hysteria (and not, as has often been the case in recent years, Freud's countertransference), uncovers the fleeting and fragile elements of the hysteric's progress toward a knowledge of sexual difference. With her father dead, Dora can now proceed freely to read and learn. The philosopher thus evokes Dora's "rejection [of men] and the desire to chart her own course—or else to be a guide for the others who are exploring the city." She highlights too that the "solution to the crisis is conceived only in the element of form, gaze and immobility: paintings, a statue" (125). Dora's progress toward a knowledge of the "sexual order" seems arrested at the stage of *Schautrieb* (her desire to contemplate, to gaze) but cannot be articulated as fully as *Wisstrieb* (a desire to know).

This is where Dora's passion for images and the admirative, contemplative stance it entails become emblematic: in that "plastic suspension of her body," her curiosity ends and her hysteria begins. The dream bears the trace of this moment in the indication "two hours," which leads to a scene at the Dresden Museum where she "remains *two hours* in front of the Sistine Madonna, rapt in silent admiration" (*SE* VII, 96). The moment of arrest and intense attention stands out in this representation of a quest that is evoked in terms of constant motion and progress, until the end (*der Friedhof*) is reached.[28]

But what does Dora see in the Madonna that makes her want to stop in silent identificatory admiration? A femininity that remains immaculate in spite of the Virgin's having known, experienced the full bodily mystery of maternity. Untainted, destined to perpetual virginity (*Aieparthenos*), but a mother, the Virgin represents the perfect woman—she who remains untouched by the evil of sexual knowledge (for this knowledge *is* always evil for women, as Nietzsche reminds us). In other words the Madonna is the very emblem of a *pudicité* that represents the acme of femininity: she is endowed with an innate purity that no "sexual event," no bodily experience or manifestation, can ever trouble ("incapable of failing, [she] soars above any blame like an angel on earth," to quote a definition of *pudicité* discussed in Chapter 1). Defined in this way, the object of Dora's admiration is not a private idol, but can be identified as the ideal of femininity that the nineteenth century imposed on women. It is then Dora's virtue, defined as *pudor* or sexual ignorance, that stands in the way of her knowledge. This where the cultural and social regulations concerning woman's knowledge, reinforced by her analyst's prejudice (sexual curiosity can only be a masculine trait for him), determine the failure of her consciousness. For indeed this "seeing" of herself that the dream reveals can hardly be identified as her consciousness, for she does not know what she sees.

Had she been able to know it, she might have been cured. But we are left with a patient who, identifying with the Madonna, experiences a form of mystical *jouissance* (to speak the Lacanian language) that stands in place of a desire for truth.[29] David-Ménard warns us as she begins

28. David-Ménard's conception of hysteria is indebted to a phenomenological approach, which enables her to analyze closely the bodily aspects of hysteria, focusing on movement and immobility and the forms taken by the body's "attention." The evocative phrase "plastic suspension of the body" appears on page 159 of her volume *Hysteria from Freud to Lacan*.

29. On this subject, see Doane's suggestive remark in "Veiling over Desire": "As Stephen Heath points out, the 'more' of the woman's *jouissance* in Lacan's work compensates for the absence she represents in relation to the scenario of castration. And one could add that the price to be paid for visual immediacy and the 'more' of *jouissance* is the absence of knowledge" (132).

her discussion of Dora's exploration of the sexual order: "We do not mean to suggest that from this moment on everything is clear and that at last she discovers and accepts sexual difference" (125). Indeed, Dora remains a hysteric, and remains so precisely in her failure to acknowledge femininity and thus sexual difference itself. The pursuit of knowledge has been arrested, on her side, in the scene of her gazing at the Sistine Madonna, "rapt in silent admiration." But while she was remembering that scene—which may have been the key to her enigma—her analyst was more deeply concerned about mapping out a masculine model of subjectivity, where she figured as "an inverted, reversed projection of the aim (or telos) of the history of male sexuality" (Irigaray, 138). The footnotes Freud added to *Fragment of a Case of Hysteria* show him working belatedly to interpret this "nodal point in the network of her dream-thoughts" (*SE* VII, 96). It seems that until then, analyst and analysand had been talking on this particular matter at cross-purposes. But no, not even that: Dora had long stopped talking; she had been gone for a long time, having closed the door on her silence after the third session of discussion of this very dream.

Between Women

If, in James's novel and in Freud's case history, the representations of sexual identities remained bound by the most rigid conventions, they would not hold much interest for a discussion of the female subject: the hysteric would be kept so firmly in the place of the other that she would inevitably be an object—the passive term and center of a discursive system ruled by a masculine theory.[30] But the Jamesian and Freudian texts owe their appeal as much to their innovative and prospective aspects as to their exemplary historical and cultural dimensions.[31] These authors not only reproduce the conventions of gender; they also delimit and begin to explore the margins and unexpected clearings that define the

30. Here I differ from Irigaray, who cannot conceive of a theory of the subject that would not be inherently masculine. She develops this idea in the first paragraph of "Toute théorie du sujet," where she claims that "any theory of the 'subject' will always have been appropriated in the 'masculine gender' [au masculin]" (*Speculum*, 165). Using Sand's *Lélia* as my first example, I argue that a number of nineteenth-century women writers developed in their writing the first elements of a theory of the female subject.

31. Juliet Mitchell speaks about the dangers of approaching Freud as if his theories had never evolved: "the end supersedes the beginnings. . . . These beginnings are the conventions and ideologies which we found inadequate and which in *apparently* confirming by trying to understand, he overthrew" (*Psychoanalysis and Feminism: A Radical Reassessment of Freudian Psychoanalysis*, 49).

territory of another kind of epistemology, where a representation of the female subject becomes possible beyond the "simulacrum, silence or erasure" we have encountered so far.

Thus *The Bostonians* and *Fragment of a Case of Hysteria* sketch out the premises of another configuration, where knowledge is not the product of sexual difference but derives from the relationship between women. Present in so many nineteenth-century novels, the relation that links two heroines is usually envisaged in contrasting terms, as part of a long tradition that opposes two different, often antagonistic versions of femininity whose aesthetic features correspond to moral traits. The fair-haired against the dark lady, virtue set off against the wiles of the rakish woman, innocence against experience—this doubling of the woman is a commonplace of literary representations and has existed at least since the Middle Ages. In George Eliot's *Mill on the Floss*, the predictable moralization of the dark lady and the fair (the latter always wins) becomes the subject of a conversation between Maggie Tulliver and Philip Wakem. The novels of George Sand and George Eliot show indeed a number of emotionally charged encounters between women, and while such scenes occupy a secondary role in relation to the main erotic plot, they are nonetheless endowed with powerful emotional evocations. The representation is often melodramatic: it relies on a bodily language made of gestures and signs of emotion, at the expense of dialogue and especially of discursive commentary. It looks then as if, placed under the rule of a heterosexual plot, the novel could merely hint at but not really develop the stories of the relation between women.

For James and Freud, however, the relation between women plays a crucial role in the exploration of the enigma of femininity: it is the object of an explicit discursive commentary which attempts to imagine, narrate, and probe into its significations. Their narratives thus take a crucial turn when the heroine is shown to possess a secret: brought together, Verena and Olive do not embody some female mystery; they are the proud possessors and inheritors of some knowledge that concerns their sexual identity. Similarly, Dora becomes a knowing subject as soon as Frau K. comes onto the stage. Moreover, if there is some substance to the secret that she carries like a letter, she must hold it from somewhere or somebody. Where then did she gather that knowledge which she suppresses and yet displays for the benefit of her observer-analyst? Many nineteenth-century narratives seem to offer the same answer to this question as they pair together two women: the worldly-wise, older woman and the girl on the verge of adulthood, moving in and out of her innocence. The general characteristic of these doubles is that they participate in the sexual initiation that is sketched out in the narrative as a transmission of knowledge or the imparting of experience. While the heroine is typically endowed with what Freud calls *Gedankenunschuld* (innocence of mind), the other woman knows from experience: she has lived "at first hand" and has had immediate access to the mysteries of sexuality. In Sand's early novels, Indiana, Valentine and Lélia owe their knowledge to Noun, Louise, and Pulchérie. In Eliot's *Daniel Deronda*, Gwendolen Harleth's mind, imagination, and memory are invaded by Lydia Glasher's stories about "a woman's life." Verena Tarrant and Olive Chancellor or Dora and Frau K. thus have a long ancestry of similar doubles telling the story of sexual initiation.

The notion of sexual initiation must be understood here from the general perspective of an inquiry into woman's knowledge. I am not primarily concerned with its homoerotic aspect, even though this aspect is undeniably a factor in the pedagogical relation that unites the two women: how could the transmission of knowledge be severed from the affective ties that make it possible? But what I want to put to the test, given the impasse of knowledge that arises with the gendered scenarios that oppose him to her, is the alternative epistemological model that *The Bostonians* and *Fragment of a Case of Hysteria* seem to sketch out, unwittingly, as they speculate on the relation between women. Also, through these examples, I examine a model of subjectivity where sexual difference holds a significant place, and I trace the elements of a gendered consciousness, which is created by this line of female transmission. Here again, a gender fable is destined to provide the evidence for my argument and theory. This particular fable, however, which I take from George Sand's *Lélia*, is not about hysteria; on the contrary, it focuses, somewhat immodestly (using bodies as metaphors), on the contents of a woman's mind, on what she knows. It is not about hysteria, because, as we saw, hysteria is about the ignorance of such knowledge. What Sand shows, in an amazing episode of her novel which Naomi Schor labels a "primal scene of sexual differentiation," is that a woman can have a theory of subjectivity, and that this theory must account, by definition, for her gender (*George Sand and Idealism*, 66). However, in order to bring out the full implications of the Sandian narrative, the construction of the theme needs to be examined first in the exemplary texts of James and Freud.

A relation between women figures, of course, prominently in *The Bostonians* as a counterpart to the plot of sexual difference involving Ransom and Verena. The narrative that reflects on the "decline of the sentiment of sex" is equally concerned with the "friendship between women," as James announces in the project of the *Notebooks*: "The subject is a strong one, with a large rich interest. The relation of the two girls should be a study of one of those friendships between women which are so common in New England" (438). The theme is highlighted in his discussion of the title: "I have displeased people, as I hear by calling the book *The Bostonians* . . . [I] meant only to designate Olive and Verena by it as they appeared to the mind of Ransom, the southerner and outsider looking at them from outside" (quoted in Matthiessen, 329). The emphasis on the external stance held by the observer or witness of such a relation is revealing—"an outsider," "from outside"—for it corresponds to the typical dramaturgy of the scene between women when, as is the case here, the spectator is male. The male gaze is here defined by its exteriority, yet paradoxically, as has been shown in criticism of pornography, this exteriority does not lead to disinvestment from the scene. On the contrary, the scene involving two women serves to enhance the voyeuristic impulse. The increase of desire produced by a sense of transgression ("what these women do is perverse") and exclusion ("this scenario excludes me as a man") holds the promise of an even more secret knowledge of what women "do" or what women "are."[32] This phenomenon is naturally sublimated in the Jamesian text, but it might explain the peculiar intensity of Ransom's quest: Verena's "possession" by another woman greatly increases the epistemological and sexual stakes for a hero cast in the role of an observer from outside of their relation.

Lillian Faderman suggests that Boston marriages had become a theme of general sociological interest in the 1880s, and for the contemporary historian, such as James imagined himself to be, the relation between Verena Tarrant and Olive Chancellor would have seemed topical.[33] But given the private history of the James family, such a theme must have held for the author more personal and intimate meanings: his sister Alice, who was "delicate" and "nervous" (and who, at eighteen, had developed, in her mother's words, "genuine hysteria"), ended up sharing her life with her nurse and loving companion Katherine Loring; their relationship seemed to have troubled the writer. In this respect, the hero

32. See Kuhn, *Power of the Image*, 32–33, and Solomon-Godeau, *Photography at the Dock*, 235.

33. See Lillian Faderman, *Surpassing the Love of Men: Romantic Friendships and Love between Women from the Renaissance to the Present* 190. Her description seems to echo the words James ascribes to Olive Chancellor: "My own friend . . . you have never said anything to me which expressed so clearly the closeness and sanctity of our union" (*The Bostonians*, 149).

might have functioned, typically, as a screen for the author's own interest: an early curiosity soon gives way to an obsessive desire to come between the two women and to pull Verena away from an unnecessary influence. A few times James expressed his bewilderment at his sister's preference for such a relationship and seemed, on the whole, to have been made uncomfortable by it (see Lewis, *The Jameses*). The plot may represent the extreme and uninhibited enactment of an impulse related to the "awkward circumstances" that surrounded his sister's life. And yet, hovering at the door of his sister's sickroom or facing the prospect of representing a friendship between women, the author remains in the same overall stance: he is a disappointed observer ("I had the sense of knowing terribly little about the kind of life I had attempted to describe" [quoted in Matthiessen, 319]). It seems then that far from dispelling the mysteries of the feminine, the image of a "between women" works, tantalizingly, to undo the certainties that might have been constructed around or projected onto the myths of femininity.

Fragment of a Case of Hysteria has in recent years become a cause célèbre in the critique of Freud. Neil Hertz, for instance, speaks of "a politics of visibility which renders feminine desire invisible to Freud" ("Dora's Secrets," 176). But Freud, like James, expresses belatedly his sense of failure and the lack of mastery over his subject, mostly in the notes he added during the five-year gap that separated the analysis from its first publication. The case history, like a palimpsest, is inscribed with the successive layers of a reflection that unfolds over several years until the work's publication in English in 1923. Hertz's criticism bears on the text's second layer produced five years after the termination of the analysis; drawing the consequences of the process of transference and countertransference of which Freud has acquired a new awareness, it highlights the failure of a knowledge that overlooks the analyst's desire as well the confusion that characterizes Freud's discussion of Dora's "gynaecophilic currents of feeling" ("Dora's Secrets," 231). The long note Freud added to his postscript, where he begins by emphasizing the time lapse that separates him from the analysis and displays the knowledge that he gathered in the interval, reads almost like a recantation. It emphasizes in an unmistakable fashion the importance of the "homosexual," "gynaecophilic" theme in the patient's mental life and the analyst's failure to take it into consideration:

The longer the interval of time that separates me from the end of this analysis, the more probable it seems to me that the fault in my technique lay in this omission. I failed to discover in time and to inform the patient that the homosexual (gynaecophilic) love for Frau K. was the strongest unconscious current in her mental life. I ought to have guessed that the main source of her knowledge of sexual matters could have been no one but Frau K.—the very person who charged her with being interested in those same subjects. Her knowing all about such things and, at the same time, her always pretending not to know where her knowledge came from was really too remarkable. I ought to have attacked this riddle. (*SE* VII, 120)

Indeed, for Freud as for James, the relation between two women, in spite of the visibility it acquires in their texts, remains mostly unexplored. As a supplement that offers a radical challenge to the earlier vision, it threatens the totality of the analyst's or the writer's epistemological project and determines the defeat of a certain kind of knowledge. Thus if, in the earlier stages, Dora's relations with Frau K. occupied a marginal position in the analysis, it is now the enigma, that particular knot where the work should have begun. Freud's "an dieses Rätsel hätte ich anknüpfen müssen," which relies tellingly on the image of a knot, acknowledges the failure and the regret.[34] It simultaneously identifies what should have constituted a recognizable, meaningful strand in his text, but never did.

But the reasons for this failure derive not only from the analyst's imperfect technical knowledge; they might also be related to narrative conventions that privilege the heterosexual plot. This is revealed in the original narration of the case, not as a footnote but in the body of the text: "I must now turn to consider a further complication, to which I should certainly give no space if I were a man of letters engaged upon the creation of a mental state like this for a short story, instead of being a medical man engaged upon its dissection" (*SE* VII, 59). If literary representation conventionally values a "fine poetic conflict," whereas the relationship between women represents a flaw or complication, it might be tempting for the writer to overlook this motif. In what seems an incidental observation, Freud allows us to glimpse his authorial stance; he also expresses, indirectly, a literary awareness or desire that may have inflected his analytical work in a decisive way. The denial—I am not a writer but a "medical man"—is concerned with the desire for an orthodox, immediately satisfying story: a straight erotic entanglement and its natural solution, marriage. The elements of such a plot can easily be

34. "I ought to have attacked this riddle," is Alix and James Strachey's translation, but the phrase could be rendered more literally: "I should have unknotted this riddle first." The same notion is present in *Knotenpunkte* (nodal point), the term Freud uses to describe the importance of pictures in Dora's second dream (*SE* VII, 96).

discerned in the case history: Dora's marriage with Herr K. would have been "the most satisfactory solution for all the parties concerned," writes Freud, and more than once we see the analyst working on the elements of such a happy ending.

The case history, like the novel, relies then on a double plot which, as it foregrounds the conventional story of a marriageable girl, also evokes the uncharted narrative of a relation between women, whose complexity lies in the fact that it is not simply erotic, but that inevitably it is infused with epistemological elements. It stands there, still to be known, observed, understood, written. Moreover, it is about women exchanging secrets and sharing their knowledge. Not only is Frau K. the object of Dora's erotic desire (as revealed in Dora's evocation of her "adorable white body"), she must also be "the main source of her knowledge in sexual matters" (*SE* VII, 120). For the analyst, the question concerning the origin of Dora's knowledge is solved (all too easily, if we consider his dismissive attitude) by her *gynaecophilia*. But what if the relation between these two women were reconsidered from a pedagogical point of view, as an instance of teaching, as a situation that enables the transmission of knowledge from woman to woman? On this aspect, *Fragment of a Case of Hysteria* offers no further insights; on the contrary, Freud's lack of awareness and ease concerning the gynaecophilic theme and his overriding interest in the heterosexual plot have thrown a pall of darkness over the scene of desire and knowledge that united Dora and Frau K. But while the problematic is beyond the scope of Freud's analytical project, it is an essential aspect of this reconsideration of epistemological patterns.

James's novel, however, gives more scope to the exploration of the desire and knowledge that the relation between women appears to chart. Not that James succeeds in representing the scene: a comparison between James Ivory's film and the novelist's text is revealing here. The script of the film remains close to the text, and yet most of the scenes between women seem to have been freshly invented, or, to put it differently, they enable us to visualize a relationship that in the novel is somehow lacking in consistency and visual credibility. James must have been right about his own text: the obsessive "pencilling out" is part of a failure of vision. It is then not at the level of a representation, but in the discursive commentary that belongs to the narrator's recording and explanatory voice that the relationship is thematized, and most prominently around the notion of passion.

Thus, commenting on the attraction Verena increasingly feels for Ransom, the narrator distinguishes passion according to its object: "It was always passion, in fact; but now the object was different" (369). Ransom is the object of what is now, unmistakably, an "erotic passion" or the "passion of love" (as James calls it in his early texts on Sand). And such passion renders Verena incapable of saying no to the man who asks her to give up what she has thought or felt so passionately in the other relationship: "She loved, she was in love—she felt it in every throb of her being" (369), "a force she had never felt before was pushing her to please herself" (371). Indeed James's text invites us to conceive of this passion as corresponding to the erotic drive and as a force that transcends individual will. And passion is naturally going to be the fate of the "true woman."

Yet in his depiction of the relation between Olive and Verena, the narrator had used the term with a different meaning, where, deprived of the sexual connotations that it holds in the heterosexual plot, it spoke of sublimation. "The pure, still-burning passion that animated her" (253), "a passion as high as ever found shelter in a pair of human hearts" (396)—the word "passion" designates here the exchange of words and knowledge that belongs to woman's mental life, her *Seelenleben*. The first half of *The Bostonians* shows us—before "the whole cloud structure topples over"—glimpses of several such moments of shared intellect and emotion. Olive initiates Verena, the "new England Corinna," into the facts and figures of history (137) and tries to impart her knowledge and her love for ideas. "Consuming the midnight oil," the two women are involved in studies where they peruse the books of history in hopes of understanding their fate, their "sex" (168–69). How indeed could James have ignored this aspect of a woman's desire? He had after all met it in George Sand. What better example for such a "passion" than the woman writer's relentless pursuit, in her "life at first hand" and her writing, of the limits of femininity? There too, as in the gynaecophilic plot of James's novel, passion does not mean a passive submission to her gender, but evokes a life of the mind not severed from its affective ties.

But, as we know, the novel takes a more cynical turn: the transformation in the meaning of passion, from the spiritual to the physical, overlaps with the silencing of the heroine. Together they reinstate the orthodox plot of gender. Woman is thus subjected not only to erotic passion, but to a silencing and erasure which, in the name of sexual orthodoxy, condemns her to convert into bodily symptoms—usually as hysteria but here merely tears—the knowledge that she might have owned but needed to relinquish. For his plot, James cannot give up the sense of distinctions founded on a rigid differentiation between the sexes, and his resistance to the idea of a "knowing woman" seems to redouble as he closes his narrative with a heroine not only carried away by passion, but silenced by masculine will. There is no place in *The Bostonians* for a passion that would allow the ideal woman to be a speaking, knowing subject as well as a subject in an erotic plot. That the heterosexual plot is ultimately tied to physical violence (the force that ultimately pushes Verena out of Olive's sphere of influence is that of Ransom's muscles) shows meanwhile that the "fine poetic conflict" was, for James, no longer an easy solution. The ending leaves two victims: Verena shedding her tears, and Olive sacrificed on the altar of a lost cause, a belated revolutionary, a philosopher sacrificed to the mob (433). That *The Bostonians* ultimately represents the demise of gynaecophilia could hardly have been signified more clearly.

A Knowledge of Gender

The scene by the river which tells of an exchange of words, love, and knowledge between Lélia and her half sister, Pulchérie, is presented here as an alternative to James's failure of imagination and as an attempt to fill, fictively, the gaps of Freud's case history. This topic must be broached cautiously, for to read such a text in light of questions of gender and consciousness (and, moreover, reading it as a gender fable) may seem like a provocation. It is so much easier to read Sandian representation for its erotic frisson than for the more elaborate, less immediately perceptible ideas that her text offers, that to examine the bower scene between Lélia and Pulchérie from an allegorical perspective, as part of a history of woman's knowledge, may look at times like sheer blindness or obstinacy.[35] Why look so hard for the ideas when we are faced with images of sensuality and a text that seems to overindulge in sexual fantasy?

But maybe we are doomed to encounter such quandaries. In her discussion of woman's silencing and of the erasure of the female subject, Barbara Johnson hints at the fact that the search for alternative patterns to a masculine epistemology, such as might eventually lead to a "dramatization" of the "existence and knowlege of the female subject," will necessarily entail difficulties and bring in its trail "epistemological dam-

35. As Naomi Schor points out in her essay on Sand's idealism (in *A New History of French Literature*, 769–73): "Yet so massive, so crushing has been the triumph of realism that at least in literature . . . idealism has all but vanished from our critical consciousness, taking with it the reputation of its most eminent French representative, George Sand" (771).

age." The interpretation that follows, however, finds its justification in Johnson's notion.[36] It takes what may appear to be a paradox (if not an inconsistency or absurdity)—that bodily scenarios represent a quest for knowledge and consciousness—as proof that the alternative to a masculine theorization is different in a nonsymmetrical way and in fact works against traditional epistemological models. It is not so much that Sand offers bodies and their "experience" of eros as an alternative to an abstraction from the physical *donnée* or "pure" rationality, but that Sand's writing works against such a separation or opposition and goes toward mending the gap between the body and the mind. Desire makes for knowledge, and knowledge is embedded in scenarios of desire: the consciousness her text defines cannot conceive of itself outside of an awareness of what sexual difference does to our bodies and minds. Reading Sand for a theory of sex and gender depends on a belief in allegory (where character and events stand for ideas). More concretely, it means looking for signs of awareness and for a theoretical knowledge in what is insistently represented in bodily forms and sensations, and as sight and vision rather than discursive analysis. Bearing these preliminaries in mind, the reader is invited to follow me in this seemingly perverse attempt to read in George Sand's *Lélia* a scene of knowledge over or against what looks so much like an erotic encounter between women.

From a structural perspective, the encounter between Lélia and Pulchérie, which extends over many pages, is put into prominence: it occupies the central section of George Sand's narrative as if, in a novel notorious for its narratological inconsistencies, this were meant to be its stable focal point. Embedded in this part, one episode stands out which recounts in the form of a dreamlike and visionary recollection—imparted by Pulchérie to her sister—another scene between women.[37] Gender is the central theme of this encounter, and it is the explicit subject of the fable. In this, Sand's gender fable differs from the others we have encountered so far. In these earlier instances the valorization of gender

36. I have also found support for this reading in Naomi Schor's excellent, but brief comments on this passage. The fact that Schor and I end up reading these pages in a similarly "original" fashion, and this when there had been no exchanges between us, not only strengthens the validity of this interpretation but says something about a contemporary feminist awareness. What should we make of this instance of telepathy between women?

37. My interpretation bears on pages 155–58 of the 1960 French edition of Sand's *Lélia*, cited in the bibliography. From my mainly literary perspective, this is unquestionably the stronger text, whereas the 1839 version is possibly more interesting from a feminist point of view, since in her revision Sand emphasizes the ideological aspects of her narrative.

was the fable's ultimate purpose, but it had to remain hidden: the stories told by Brachet, James, or Freud go back to a hidden desire or a latent anxiety concerning sexual difference, which cannot be resolved in an explicit fashion. What mattered in these cases was the performative force of the tale. But Sand's gender fable does not, in its telling, perform the work of making sense of sex; it presents, albeit in an allegorical form, a theory of sexual difference and gender: gender is now the acknowledged object of a discourse.

Because it is never explicitly stated, the morality of my earlier fables depends on an act of interpretation performed under the aegis of a feminist suspicion or resistance. But when the fable reads gender as a matter of fact, as is the case with Sand's story, this resistance no longer applies. It is replaced, however, by a masculine resistance. The cast of this gender fable thus includes a protagonist who stands outside its frame: a male reader, an "outsider" looking at it "from outside." Pierre Reboul, the commentator to whose impeccable scholarship we owe the rich, learned, and (in many places) insightful Garnier edition of the novel, seemed predestined to take on this role: his readerly science does not allow him to read the signs and take in the knowledge that the Sandian text offers him, and he occupies the characteristic role of the puzzled reader or disappointed observer of the scene between women, like James and like Freud. Trapped in the older epistemological patterns, this reader repeatedly conveys the sense that this text is illegible, and while he tries hard to fend off the impression that it is merely "immoral," he cannot extract any substantial meaning from it. But what better proof could there be of "the difficulty" that, if we believe Barbara Johnson, inevitably arises with any attempt to produce "female subjects"?

But now for our fable. A ball at the Villa Bambucci has brought together Lélia, the heroine, devoid of power, afflicted with an irrevocable coldness of mind and body, and her sister, a courtesan. Lélia tells the story of her unhappiness to the pleasure-seeking, pleasure-loving Pulchérie and concludes with what looks like a rhetorical question: "Do you know what has been my fate since we have been separated?" To which Pulchérie replies: "All I have known is that you have had a problematic existence as a woman." She then offers to tell her sister about a memory and one of her dreams, thus replacing the predictable answer—which no doubt would speak of misery or unhappiness—with the account of an earlier scene that had brought the two women together. The scene Pulchérie recalls for her sister takes place on the bank of a river, under an "ardent" sky, in an idyllic landscape that evokes a mythical bower of love. The two women had fallen asleep in each others arms, and, says Pulchérie, this is "where God revealed to her, for the first time the power of life."

In his first note, Pierre Reboul refers his readers to the romantic writer Nodier, who "insists at length on the innocence of the first incests," and he adds, in his own voice: "this description of the first emotions [*troubles*] of puberty is truly original [*ne doit à aucun autre texte*]." These comments, seemingly destined to frame the tale with an explanation, are remarkable above all for the conflicting signals they give: this is innocent, says the commentator, but it is also filled with sexual evocations (*troubles* is used here, as often in French, as a euphemism for sexual desire); it may seem incestuous, but must be innocuous. Faced with the signs of female passion, this reader settles for the typical attitude of modesty and tries to throw a veil over the (too) physical evocations of Sand's text so as exculpate them (or her, the woman writer) from the guilt associated with a knowledge of the sexed body and of sexuality. But the scene is indeed unmistakably suffused with eroticism, and it does depict what can only be taken as a sexual awakening: "nothing revealed itself to me through suffering. I did not wear myself out like you in trying; it is because I did not look for it, that I found." However, the pleasure garden offers its revelations not only to the senses; through the images of a dream, it also speaks to the mind.

"That day, happy and calm as I was," Pulchérie pursues, "a dream, strange, delirious, unheard of, revealed to me a mystery that so far had remained impenetrable and quietly respected." In this dream, "a man with black hair was leaning toward me to lightly touch my lips with his own warm and ruby lips," she recounts, and she remembers how she woke up at this point with a dim understanding of the dream's meaning—what had been revealed to her was "the sense of beauty in another creature." Whereas earlier Pulchérie, like Narcissus, could only love her own image ("I wished then to kiss myself in that mirror which reflected me and which inspired me with an insane love"), she now finds beauty in another being. Although it is coined in aesthetic terms, the scene of awakening is in fact about the discovery of the other's "truer," that is, sexual identity. Waking out of her dream, Pulchérie discovers Lélia who is asleep next to her and yet seems to belong to the dreamworld. With her thin muscular arms covered with down, she resembles the "dark-haired child of the dream" and, says Pulchérie, "there was something masculine and strong in you that almost prevented me from recognizing you."[38] The narrative thus sketches out a progress that takes her from

38. Sand's *Valentine* presents a similar scene of awakening, where the heroine discovers

self-love to loving another, where the other is endowed with the discrete marks of the other sex.

When Lélia opened her eyes, explains her sister, she, Pulchérie, was seized by an "unknown shame" and "turned aside as if she had committed a guilty action." Indeed, while it seems to have taken place in a such a state of "benign aloneness" as characterizes for Carol Gilligan the typical stage of such female awakening, a woman's accession to sexual knowledge cannot remain devoid of guilt.[39] Desire is associated with shame, and the recognition of sexual difference calls for the typically feminine gesture of modesty. This revelation is a transgression; it sketches the path from that innocence described as "long-respected ignorance" to a knowledge that throws an irrevocable shadow over consciousness. "You look like a man"—these are the last words spoken in the scene Pulchérie recalls for the benefit of her sister.

Sexual difference is the theme of the pedagogical narrative, where one woman tells the other about her vision. The story recounts too, in an allegorical fashion, the breaking out of the narcissistic circle; it defines a relation that is different from the self-seeking, self-pleasing scenario of feminine doublings. This scene between women represents thus the transmission of sexual knowledge: in spite of its focus on the representation of the body and its sensuousness, it is not merely an account of erotic passion, and the acknowledgment of the erotic and sensual sphere (of a pleasure-body) is tied to this coming into awareness of sexual difference. For how could the *Wisstrieb* (the desire to know) expressed here be distinguished or separated from a desire and a consciousness that begin in or with the body? In fact, the Sandian fable recounts precisely the story of such a binding between the sensual body and a consciousness of gender. Here Sand reveals her unexpected sharpness of vision. It will, for instance, take many decades before Freud, in his turn, considers the stages of intellectual development while identifying a similar overlap between the sexual drive and the epistemophilic drive. It will take Simone de Beauvoir or Denise Riley to think philosophically about this kind of phenomenology of the gendered body.

Meanwhile, in this quest, the heroine of George Sand's fiction comes closer to being a subject on her own terms than any of the feminine figures invented by Flaubert, James, or Freud. For Sand's gender fable tells the story of woman's engendering as a coming into consciousness

---

her lover's body ("a neck velvety in its darkness and perspiration," a shirt that showed "a skin tanned by the sun").

39. Quoted by Jessica Benjamin, "A Desire of One's Own," 97.

predicated upon the recognition not of her sex (there would be nothing new in that) but of her necessarily gendered condition. Read allegorically, the scene between women confirms the truth of sexual difference as an arbitrary and not an essential fact, in what appears to be its smallest syntagm: the other (*tu*) looks like (*ressembles*) a man (*un homme*).[40] It offers then the vision of an engendering that ties the notion of desire to sexual difference and, paradoxically, teaches in the scene between women the orthodox lesson of heterosexual desire. Naomi Schor explains:

In this scene, where desire for the other is shown to spring directly and immediately from the mapping of sexual difference onto sexual identity— seeing Lélia as masculine, Pulchérie abandons her earlier self-directed narcissistic eroticism for heterosexual anaclitic love—Pulchérie ceases to be a type, the courtesan, an allegory of *jouissance*, to become an individual female subject, coming under the sway of the phallus. . . . Like that of Lélia, the allegorization of Pulchérie collapses under the pressure of the vicissitudes of female sexuality under patriarchy. (*George Sand and Idealism*, 66–67)

Produced under the impulse of what must be the same desire, namely, to retrieve from Sand's writing its share of ideas or the possibility for a feminist theory, Schor's interpretation and mine for this gender fable converge around the same lesson or "morality." What Sand's text presents here is an image of a sexual identity (as an "individual female subject") and a consciousness of gender. Gender is understood here as a principle of difference that subsumes a "female sexuality" under the rule of heterosexuality.

Seemingly troubled by the scene depicted by the woman writer, Reboul attempts to find the explanation in her life and writes, "No doubt, Pulchérie remembers here the life or the thoughts of George Sand." Here again the attribution of an autobiographical meaning aims at dispensing the critic from truly reading the scene. And yet the question was stated explicitly enough: what can be said in response to the heroine's *mal d'être*? The memories and dreams that Pulchérie presents to her sister provide the answer and dispel the secret of the woman's destiny. Lélia's comment illustrates her new understanding: she had not seen ("je ne

40. I quote Naomi Schor's comment in full: "Sexual difference is then arbitrary, not essential. It is applied onto sameness to institute difference where difference is lacking. It is not the founding difference of the symbolic order but merely *the difference of differences*. Indeed, invariably in Sand, distinctions between same sex doubles are isomorphous with sexual difference" (*George Sand and Idealism*, 145).

devinai pas") what her sister had wanted to show her but now she knows. " 'I had not realized,' Lélia answered, 'that a destiny had been accomplished for you, whereas for myself no destiny would ever be accomplished.' " It may be that Lélia's unhappiness anticipates that of the hysteric, who, in her failure to acknowledge sexual difference, is haunted by her inability to assume her feminine gender. Arrested, frozen in her predicament, Lélia, unlike her uninhibited, pleasure-seeking sister, redefines a woman's existence as a female complaint.[41]

The morality of this fable, which Lélia draws spontaneously from her sister's story, thus speaks of gender not only in epistemological and philosophical terms, but also at a more general historical and cultural level. It suggests that the assumption of one's sexual identity and the recognition of the roles and properties that derive from one's gender determine the conditions of existence. They give to Pulchérie, the courtesan who seems reconciled with her own pleasure-seeking, pleasure-giving body, what her sister does not have: a destiny. Meanwhile Lélia's predicament surely finds an echo in Judith Butler's remark: "The cultural matrix through which gender identity has become intelligible requires that certain kinds of 'identities' cannot exist—that is, those in which gender does not follow from sex and those in which the practices of desire do no 'follow' from either sex or gender" (17). Indeed, Lélia's metaphysical inclinations do not meet with the requirements of her sex; they might possibly correspond to her masculine gender, but even then, a desire that can be so insistently sublimated and is relentlessly projected into the intellectual sphere would make of her precisely what she is shown to be in Sand's fiction, an outcast, a monster, an insoluble mystery—"an angel, a demon, but not a human creature" (*Lélia*, 7).

"It goes without saying," writes Reboul, "that such a passage does not appear in the 1839 edition" (155). It is easy to see why this scene was omitted from the revised, bowdlerized later version of the novel: it represents, to quote Sand's text, "a mystery that so far had remained impenetrable and quietly respected" (156). The revelation of such a secret, told by one woman to another, would have to leave its trail of scandals and could only be communicated to the initiate. Reboul tells us that the *Europe littéraire* of August 1833 issued the following warn-

41. "*Lélia* is not a book: it's a scream of pain, or a bad dream, or a bad-tempered discussion full of truths and paradoxes, injustice and warnings. . . . You cannot ask Lélia for a moral code any more than you could ask for intellectual work from someone who is ill. . . . You must have understood this, Mademoiselle, since in that book you saw only a woman to be pitied" (George Sand to Marie Talon, quoted by Reboul in Garnier edition of *Lélia*, 595–96),

ing: "On the day when you open *Lélia,* lock yourself up in your study so as not to contaminate anybody. If you have a daughter, whose soul you would like to remain pure and naive, send her out to the fields to play" (589). The scene between Lélia and Pulchérie speaks of the fundamental difference, at the level of the body, between the sexes. Pleasure gives way to knowledge, to a knowledge which is exchanged between women, and which bespeaks an awareness of sexual difference that, unlike the scene that was orchestrated around the bed of the woman in confinement, is not veiled by modesty. Not that the novel can represent without disguise the revelations of a male body. Lélia is cast in the role of a man, and Pulchérie's gaze is displaced metonymically onto what are the more innocuous physical parts, which yet express sexual difference: those arms that should have been round and soft, but are muscular and hairy.

The bower of love pictured in Sand's tale of engendering finds its echo in the Freudian *alcôve,* which holds the secrets of sex and hysteria.[42] But while in Sand's text it represents, unabashedly, the stage of an initiation into sexual knowledge, for James or Freud it remains above all a predestined setting that promises to reveal the ultimate mysteries of femininity. The best known nineteenth-century representation of a *scène d'alcôve* between women is perhaps Courbet's notorious painting *The Sleepers,* in which two women—one russet-haired, the other dark-haired—lay sprawled on a bed, entangled in each other's arms, naked.[43] Freud's case history too shows a glimpse of Dora sleeping in Frau K.'s bedroom, Verena moves into Olive's house,[44] and at the heart of her connubial bedroom Gwendolen meets with the figure of the other woman, Lydia Glasher. Meanwhile the bedroom that holds the tantalizing picture of two women has become, for Freud, James, and George

42. For a discussion of the *scène d'alcôve,* see my postscript, "Always Secrets of the Alcove."

43. This picture, which Courbet painted for the private delectation of the collector Khalil Bey, has been given two titles: *Le sommeil* and *Paresse et luxure.* Meanwhile, the scene represented in Sand's *Lélia* offers not merely the sensual delights of an *hortus deliciarum,* but also the benefits of shared knowledge. This does not mean, however, that the Sandian depiction is meant for women only. Yet the male reader-viewer of the scene, Reboul, responds only to its erotic overtones and remains blind to (or resists) the knowledge that it conveys.

44. Going much further than the writer, James Ivory pictures some bedroom scenes, with very interesting results: as they skirt around the expected or predictable lesbian scenario, these scenes bring out very forcefully the ambiguity that, in James's text, surrounds Olive's relation to Verena. "What is the nature of her passion?" one is left wondering. By not providing us with the obvious or cliché picture of homoeroticism, James Ivory ends up remaining very close to the Jamesian text.

Eliot as well, the place of the last secret of hysteria.[45] Watching at the door of the private, intimate room or house that the women share, they hope to uncover the mystery of the feminine, the secret of her sex. But the scene between women can only disappoint the male observer— Henry James, Sigmund Freud, or Pierre Reboul—and while it defeats his attempts to see what makes the difference, at the same time it urges him to hear it, in its consequences: " 'Et je ne devinai pas,' répondit Lélia, 'qu'une destinée venait de s'accomplir pour vous, tandis que pour moi aucune destinée ne devait s'accomplir' " ("And I did not guess," answered Lélia, "that for you a certain destiny had now fulfilled itself, when for myself there would never be a destiny").

Thus in George Sand's text—but then she, as James exclaimed, "was never hysterical" (*Literary Criticism*, 721)—the door opens onto a stage where the scene between women can speak of pleasure, of passion, but above all of knowledge. George Sand's text makes us hear in the murmurs of women's conversations not so much the sounds of some transgressive pleasure, but the shared memory of some visionary experience of an "engendering." Thus the knowledge that this exemplary representation of a scene between women conveys is that of sexual difference, of sexuality, and ultimately, taking the woman's side, of the price one pays for one's gender. But whereas Sand can still envisage in this relation a knowledge that is devoid of guilt and suffering, in the later instances the "sexual initiation" of the "between women" situation inevitably institutes a relationship of possessiveness or rivalry instead of the transparent sorority represented by Sand. The negative coloring given to the relationship is simply a reflection of the evil associated with sexual knowledge in a woman. It is revealing in this context that the same image appears in Eliot's and Freud's texts: the two women are compared to Medea and Creusa, and the gift of one woman to the other is like a poison which burns its recipient.[46]

To tell the story of the "between women," whether as a fiction or in

---

45. Or should we say, at the risk of mixing metaphors, its "navel"? "There is at least one spot in every dream at which it is umplumable—a navel, as it were, that is its point of contact with the unknown" (*Interpretation of Dreams*, SE IV, 111).

46. " 'It's rather a piquant picture,' said Mr. Vandernoodt—'Grandcourt between two fiery women. . . . It's a sort of Medea and Creusa business. Fancy the two meeting! Grandcourt is a new kind of Jason' " (Eliot, *Daniel Deronda*, 403).

"When Dora stayed with the K.'s she used to share a bedroom with Frau K., and the husband used to be quartered elsewhere. She had been the wife's confidante and adviser in all the difficulties of her married life. There was nothing they had not talked about. Medea had been quite content that Creusa should make friends with her two children" (*SE* VII, 61).

the course of analysis, is to imagine (in the strong sense of "giving shape to," "finding figures for") the narrative of a female relation and transmission when the only evidence offered the writer or analyst consists in overheard noises and whispers, or the ephemeral traces of dreams and symptoms. But the exploration of such a territory requires that the writer-analyst relinquish a certain kind of knowledge, such as belongs to textbooks or is inscribed in the conventions of a "fine poetic conflict"; he needs to turn his attention to the scene. But not as a curious observer, for the lure of this spectacle is more likely to seduce him than to enlighten him. What remains then is to listen, listen in the fashion that James evokes when he attempts to provide a remedy for Flaubert's nerves (or should we say his hysteria?):

For it was not that he went too far, it was on the contrary that he stopped too short. He hovered forever at the public door, in the outer courts, the splendor of which very properly beguiled him, and in which he seems still to stand upright as a sentinel and as shapely as a statue. But that immobility and even that erectness were paid too dear. The shining arms were meant to carry further, the other doors were meant to open. He should at least have listened at the chamber of the soul. This would have floated him on a deeper tide, above all it would have calmed his nerves. (*Literary Criticism*, 314)

Would it be excessive to suggest that here James is talking about a new epistemology, of a kind that might, concerning "the existence and the knowledge of the female subject," make some difference?

CHAPTER FIVE

Reading Sexual Difference:
The Case of George Sand

> I do not doubt that woman is different from man, that heart and mind have a sex. The opposite will always be an exception.
> —George Sand, *Histoire de ma vie*

Nohant, 1st May 1837

It is seven o'clock in the morning. I am not yet in bed. I spend the nights working so that I can spend the days with you. Tomorrow night, I'll see you! And as if heaven, in war with the earth, became more human only for the sake of our love, the weather is magnificent today, for the first time since some interminable storms. The color gets reborn with the sun; the greenery, wrapped in mist, is bursting this morning as if it had been born last night. The nightingales are singing in full throat. There have never been as many in my garden as this year. The horizon is pure, the air is sweet, the smells are rising. I am going to see you! I am coming to you full of sadness and love, sure of the present and not of tomorrow, feeling devoured, devoured by you. (*Correspondance* IV, 23)

This is how George Sand writes to Michel de Bourges: in the language of passion, bringing together, unrestrainedly it seems, body and text. Among her letters to her lover are other versions of such encounters where the prose meets the emotions and the emotions the prose. The writer's variations on the theme of passion are sometimes more emotional, sometimes more erotically charged, but they are all endowed with the irresistible eloquence and spontaneity that, to a critic like James, were the mark of her style. On absence: "I have often sat down alone and apart, with a soul filled with love and knees that were trembling with voluptuousness" (III, 564). On lovesickness: "When a fever troubles me, I have the doctor take a pint of blood. The doctor says it is a *crime*, a *suicide*, that in any case it does not relieve me much, that I should have a lover or that my life is threatened by its very excess" (III, 734). The declaration: "The leaves are growing in the woods, the acacia revives, the sun is warming the young grass. Come, let us be happy, if I die on the next day, *I, I* only can say: what matters life! I have only one passion in the world, and it is you. Tell me the day and the hour, I'll go and wait for you at B." (III, 785). Desire: " I love you, yes, I love you, I suffer and I delight in it fiercely, bitterly; I am devoured by a thousand snakes, consumed by a thousand desires, burned by a thousand transports" (III, 814). Remembrance: "I cannot bear to think that this body that is so beautiful, so adored, so impregnated with my caresses, that this body so often broken by my embraces and revived by my kisses, several times made sore and weighed down by our desires, several times healed and revived by my lips, my hair, by my burning breath . . . But alas, my memories are going astray" (III, 735).

Sand works during the night and makes love in the daytime, and the diurnal setting of her passion speaks eloquently of a sexuality that is neither closeted nor buried in the dim Victorian dusk:[1] "My head seems broken by the work of this long arid night, it was the cigars and the coffee that sustained my poor style that's worth two hundred francs a page. My body is all broken because of a terrible, but delicious tiredness, whose marks I carry in a thousand places" (IV, 38). Sometimes, as the anecdote of her involvement with Mérimée suggested, loving takes place at night, while writing begins in the early hours of the morning. But what is the difference? George Sand loves, lives, writes freely and intensely, so much so that she exclaims that her "life is filled to excess." The same body that is broken by love wears itself out in the writing; she maintains between her life and her text an immediate, spontaneous relation which, it will be recalled, deeply troubled her observer and critic, James. The scandal arises not merely with her appeal to the senses and the experience of the flesh: it seems inconceivable that the passage from the lover's bed to the writer's page should occur so easily. Nor is it conceivable that the imagination should so spontaneously take on a bodily, sensual shape. The woman writer offers the revelations of a troubling and tantalizing freedom that challenges the notions of intimacy and privacy and the social conventions: love enacted so to speak

---

1. Michel Foucault has written eloquently about this "Victorian" dusk in "Nous autres, victoriens," the introductory section of *La volonté de savoir* (9–22). I use the term "Victorian" in the extended sense that it carries in Foucault's work on sexuality.

on the public stage, and moreover outside the marriage bonds. This is how the critic responds to the representations that he reads in the woman writer's text.

When, however, remarking on the expansive mode that characterizes her literary performance, James identifies the proximity between desire and language, he reminds us usefully of another aspect of Sand's stylistic performance, which is in the domain of not only representation, but writing. Commenting on her style, he declares: "She has all a woman's loquacity, but she has never a woman's shrillness; and perhaps we can hardly indicate better the difference between great passion and small by saying that she was never hysterical" ("George Sand," in *Literary Criticism*, 721). It seems that the absence of shrillness and the equipoise of voice that characterize her writing are related to this continuity between desire and language that James admired, envied, and feared. And the letters to Michel de Bourges are only the most telling instance of "a writing of longing and desire," where she writes her passions, experiences her loves, and lives and loves in her writing. From the general perspective of style and, more specifically, from that of the relation between sexuality and textuality, hysteria would then be the symptom of a rupture between passion and expression. This chapter pursues James's insights and tests his theoretical model in an examination of the representation and the textuality that characterize her writing.

George Sand is here not merely the object of an inquiry into stylistic and generic questions; she is also part and substance of a certain history of subjectivity where her texts constitute an exemplary body for what James called "the computation of the feminine range" (779). She appeared earlier in this project as a test case for questions of gender and representation, but here I wish to retrieve from her writing—so as to test James's claim about her not being hysterical—her subjective stance in relation to desire, sexual difference, and knowledge. From a literary perspective, this means charting the limits of the writer's discourse to see whether or when the veil of hysteria has fallen between a desire, a mind, and their language. But from a wider historical and philosophical perspective, the history of Sand is destined to illustrate the fate of the thinking and writing woman at the beginning of the gender-conscious era that this project attempts to define. In what follows I analyze the scene of hysteria in her early novel *Valentine* and some relevant moments from Sand's autobiography *Histoire de ma vie*. While in the first part the emphasis is on the representations of sexual identity which can be elicited from her texts, the second part highlights the play of gender, desire, and knowledge in her writing.

Valentine and Its "False Notes"

When James talks about *Valentine*, he begins by praising the text but highlights, nevertheless, its "false notes" and "startling confusions" ("George Sand," in *Literary Criticism*, 729). Indeed, a summary of the novel can only confirm this impression and make us wonder whether such a plot is comprehensible or even legible in light of our modern readerly expectations.

Bénédict, a young man of modest extraction, is passionately in love with Valentine, who, on her mother's cruel insistence, is destined to marry an aristocrat. But she loves Bénédict passionately. The dilemma seems almost Cornelian—must she choose *l'honneur* or *le coeur?*—but it applies to a young woman, and the conflict is inflected with a new element of class. The uneasy choice between duty and passion is represented a second time in a retrospective narrative, when Louise (the heroine's half sister and a mother substitute for Valentine) relates her own ill-fated passion for Monsieur de Neuville, which produced an illegitimate offspring and led to the death of the loved man. But *Valentine* tells the strangest of family romances: it turns out that Louise's lover is killed by her own father in what appears to be overdetermined revenge, and it is both his daughter's virtue and his own honor (since his wife has had an affair with the same Monsieur de Neuville) that the father avenges. The fact that Bénédict had loved the dark-haired Louise before falling passionately in love with the fair, pure, and noble Valentine is another aspect of these doublings that are insistently present in this text. The struggle between virtue and love, with Louise as an alter ego to Valentine and serving as a conscience and as her initiator into the affairs of the heart, constitutes the novel's focal point. Morality seemingly wins over passion: the consummation of Bénédict and Valentine's love is deferred until she is a widow. But this does not bring about a happy ending: already guilt-ridden, sad, and tormented, Valentine is precipitated into an early death when she hears that her lover has been mistakenly killed by a jealous rustic, the husband of a peasant girl who had herself been infatuated with Bénédict. The novel ends by holding up the picture of an idyllic and innocent love that flourishes on the ruins of the earlier passions: Valentin, Louise's son, blissfully loves Athenais, Bénédict's jilted country love.

Valentine is George Sand's second novel, written in 1832 in her grandmother's boudoir in Nohant and, as she specifies in her autobiography, in a "petite armoire qui me servait de bureau" (*Histoire de ma vie* II, 146). The description of this writing space speaks tellingly, if metaphorically, of the domains that the novel will explore, namely, femininity (as *le boudoir*), the closet (as *l'armoire*), as well as the thinking mind (*le bureau*).[2] Moreover, it places the text under the sign of a female lineage, which is manifest at an intradiegetic level, with a grandmother who is Valentine's best protector, but also extradiegetically, since it is to her grandmother's own story that Sand owes the main elements of her plot. The story of Valentine and her husband, M. de Lansac, mirrors that of the unhappy union of the author's own grandmother with the comte de Horn.[3] But the female ascendancy is also an intertextual element, for one of the models for *Valentine* seems to have been Mme de Lafayette's *La princesse de Clèves*.

George Sand's text also announces the theme and the form of the later realist novel of manners centering on the life of a young girl or woman. This may account for the attraction it held for James, who praises the representation of the heroine for its "sweetness" and "generosity." Its central theme, which it shares with many texts of nineteenth-century realism, is a young woman's foray into existence, but within the constraints of bourgeois morality. Valentine appears to foreshadow a line of female heroines whose stories are typically that of a growth into consciousness and conscience; caught between innocent girlhood and knowing womanhood and exposed to wide influences outside the parental sphere, they experience life "at first hand" and must learn to tread their way into a moral existence. Sand's heroine thus resembles Isabel Archer, Dorothea Brooke, Gwendolen Harleth, Jane Eyre, and Lucy Snow, or on the French side, Mme de Morsauf and Emma Bovary. Indeed, a comparison with *The Portrait of a Lady*, *Le lys dans la vallée*, *Daniel Deronda*, *Jane Eyre*, or *Villette* would show that *Valentine* represents, with similar ambiguities, an interrogation of subjectivity and sexual identity. Here too the novel makes of the hero-

2. The "closetedness" (see Eve Kosofsky Sedgwick, *The Epistemology of the Closet*, 3) I discuss is not that of a gay identity, but one attached to this nineteenth-century woman's attempts at self-definition through her writing.

3. In *Histoire de ma vie*, George Sand tells the story of her grandmother's unhappy marriage to the comte de Horn: "On the eve of the wedding, which was attended by the abbé de Beaumont (my great uncle who was the son of the duc de Bouillon and of Mademoiselle de Verrières), a devoted manservant came to ask the young abbé, who was still almost a child, to prevent at any cost the young countess of Horn from spending the night with her husband. They sought advice from the count's physician, and the count himself was eventually persuaded." The marriage remained unconsummated, and the comte died some time later in a duel. The plot of *Valentine* thus owes a number of its features to the story of the author's paternal grandmother, who was the main person responsible for Aurore Dupin's education.

ine's feminine identity the staple of a questioning of social and moral codes, but with a particular emphasis on her passion. The conflict between the affections of the heart and the demands of social class falls into the background, at the expense of a struggle which is staged within and around the heroine's body and mind. There, the pursuit of a subjective identity that encompasses a woman's desire meets with the laws of gender.

But the principles that determine the representations in Sand's work are not merely historical and cultural; they are also internal and thus generic. As an early work, *Valentine* gives a good indication of Sand's inventiveness and spontaneity but also reveals an uncertain grasp of the narrative conventions meant to sustain a system of verisimilitude and psychological realism. While in its general style of utterance the novel is unquestionably the product of a "poetic" imagination and of an inner vision, it appears to abide, in its representations, by the laws of the genre and strives to offer to the reader's critical gaze a text that is not only meaningful but also "acceptable" in the moral and aesthetic sense. But as the writer strives toward a moral and sexual conformity, she also produces some of her worst writing in the mode of bourgeois sentimentality and, as we shall see, tea making. James, our "archcritic," while admiring the composition and the eloquence of this novel, could not grant it his unqualified assent—here again the woman writer lacks a sense of discrimination. Indeed, as a feminist plea, *Valentine* exposes, even more bluntly than *Indiana*, the conflicts or ambiguities that inform a vision that, although sensitive to the "sentiment of sex," still seems unable to sustain its principles without its share of melodrama and transgression.

A high moral ideal runs repeatedly against the vagaries of passion. James's comment is of particular value because it reproduces, with the critic in the moralist's guise and the writer offering a narrative of passion, what is in effect the crux of the novel. To read James on Sand is to be confronted unremittingly with the paradoxes of Sand's text:

There is something very fine . . . about "Valentine," in spite of its contemptible hero; there is something very sweet and generous in the figure of the young girl. But why, desiring to give us an impression of great purity in her heroine, should the author provide her with a half-sister who is at once an illegitimate daughter and the mother of a child born out of wedlock, and who, in addition, is half in love with Valentine's lover? though George Sand thinks to better the matter by representing this love as partly maternal. After Valentine's marriage, a compulsory and most unhappy one, this half-sister plots with the doctor to place the young wife and the lover whom she has had to dismiss once more *en rapport*. She hesitates, it is true, and inquires of the physician if their scheme will not appear unlawful in the eyes of the world. But the old man reassures her, and asks, with a "sourire malin et affectueux," why she should care for the judgement of a world which has viewed so harshly her own irregularity of conduct. Madame Sand constantly strikes these false notes; we meet in her pages the most startling confusions. (*Literary Criticism*, 728–29)

James ends here on a familiar note. Sand is wrong, and more wrong than ever when she does not make the proper family discriminations, when a healthy, decent family should be the natural stage for the bourgeois romance. The same criticism had been raised earlier, and in strong terms: "she had a very imperfect knowledge of family life" and "her observation of family life was particularly restricted and perverted" (715). And the doctor, who promotes the lovers' happiness by putting them *en rapport* (note the use of the French word chosen for its erotic overtone), is wrong too: in James's description he ressembles a go-between, like Pandarus to Troilus and Cressida. In short, to James's taste, *Valentine* seems too uncomfortably caught between an ideal of purity and the overtransparent manifestations of a polymorphous and perverse eros.

The lovemaking scene shows most tellingly the contradictory impulses of Sand's narrative. Desire seizes on the image of a wounded foot: that of Valentine, burned by scalding tea—for how else could the sexual act be represented, if not by a displacement?[4] As an instance of "female fetishism," this scene has been analyzed from a psychoanalytical and feminist perspective by Naomi Schor ("Female Fetishism," esp. 364). The different stages taken by the mutual seduction highlight, meanwhile, the kinds of contradictions that haunt *Valentine* when the principles of gender and the constraints of the genre are met with the Sandian impulse to write of desire. One day Bénédict, burning with passion, catches Valentine unawares in the midst of her prayers and can no longer resist his strong inclinations. He takes her into his arms, but she resists in spite of her own passionate feelings: " 'Listen,' she said to him in a fiery tone and leading him up to her madonna, 'I had sworn that I would never see you again, because I had imagined that I would never be able to do it without crime. You must now swear to me that you will help me to

4. "The sacred penetration remains sacred by virtue of its ineffability," writes Nancy K. Miller (in "Writing from the Pavilion: George Sand and the Novel of Female Pastoral," in *Subject to Change: Reading Feminist Writing*, 210).

respect my duty: swear it in front of God, in front of this emblem of purity.' "[5] Thus the heroine speaks eloquently for her virtue, holding up, significantly, the emblem of the virgin. But Bénédict's "ardent nature" can no longer bear the strain of this struggle between virtue and passion, and he faints. Valentine pulls him into her room and proceeds to make tea, "she becomes again," the narrator intervenes, "the active and zealous housewife whose life is devoted to the care of others" (*Valentine*, 304). As an angel of the hearth, Valentine serves tea, her sublimated passion converted into virtuous, motherly instincts. But not for long. Waking abruptly from his swoon, the hero spills the tea on her foot. She is wounded and, fatally, they fall into each other's arms: "Indeed, as she walked away, she was limping. He threw himself on his knees and kissed her little slightly reddened foot through her transparent stocking, and he almost died again; and Valentine, overcome with pity, love, with fear above all, did not this time tear herself away from his arms. . . . This was a fatal moment, which had threatened to happen sooner or later" (304).

This indeed is another one of those "false notes." Although he does not distinguish between a moralist's objection and a negative aesthetic response, James must have been right. Where then lies the offense—in the strange morality of such a passage or in its stylistic awkwardness? What are we, modern readers, smiling at? At the qualms of their conscience or at such bad writing? The question may seem pointless: we have been aware for long enough of the ideological and, in the nineteenth century, specifically moral assumptions that underlie aesthetic processes. But in order to unweave the thread of the Sandian representations, we must suspend for a moment such a resolution and examine *Valentine* from the point of view of genre.

In focusing on desire in relation to the "real" or the law, *Valentine* does not differ much from the texts Tony Tanner examines in *Adultery in the Novel*. But compared to *La Nouvelle Héloïse* (another likely model), Sand's novel seems to have interiorized further the struggle between the two entities: it is now fully and almost exclusively inscribed in the psychological sphere. The obstacles are only seemingly patriarchal—cruel marriages driving unhappy wives to adultery; in this novel are found neither a Wolmar nor an abusive father, but rather a solitary guilt-ridden conscience which must meet its destiny. Furthermore, Sand seems to have translated the aristocratic codes that motivated the actions

5. George Sand, *Valentine*, 302. All subsequent references to *Valentine* are to the Slatkine Reprints edition.

of *La princesse de Clèves* into their bourgeois equivalents. The heroine's noble father is dead, her mother is of common stock, and her husband, more concerned about pleasure and money than honor, resembles a derelict Balzacian hero rather than the aristocratic souls who haunt the pages of Madame de Lafayette or Goethe. Sand's novel offers then a domestic version of the aristocratic novel of manners, and desire, as James saw very well, circulates in a restricted circle of the family and around incest.[6] *Valentine* represents, moreover, the femininized and sentimental version of a bourgeois dream: in the privacy of their homes the protagonists are involved in such typically feminine activities as reading, painting, music, conversation, and the education of children. This ideal coalesces in the tableau of an idyll which, lasting for fifteen months, unites in a "secret pavilion," equally removed from Balzac's cities and Madame de Lafayette's aristocratic mansions, Valentine and Bénédict, and their foster child, Valentin, who is Louise's son. Their aspirations are never toward the public sphere and heroic action; instead they are centered on the domestic virtues: "le ménage et les enfants," and those "modest and inward-looking pleasures" (105).

George Sand's creative imagination and eloquence develop within the confines of such representations. Meanwhile her writing, which never ceases to "expand with longing and desire," meets the constraints of representation with varying degrees of unease or clumsiness. The text's "false notes," such as the awkwardly staged scene of seduction, the utopian space of the pavillion that accommodates the lovers just like husband and wife, and the scene of hysteria all reflect, in varying degrees, the tensions between the élan of her writing and the restricted economy imposed by the choice of a genre.

Like *The Bostonians*, *Valentine* refracts the history of a gendered subjectivity through its generic commitments; the model of sexuality that it presents cannot be separated from the assumption of a preferred narrative mode and a commitment to the conventions of representation sustained by a certain model of femininity. Indeed, hysteria overlaps here again with the question of gender: it singles out the heroine, as the choice victim of an internal, interiorized struggle between the law and desire. The unrepresentable which, as we shall see, haunts Sand's novel comes into existence with the writer's acceptance of narrative conventions and orthodox representations. How else could one make sense of the startling discrepancies between the voice of Sand the letter writer, which

---

6. On incest in relation to nineteenth-century narrative, see Zwinger, *Daughters, Fathers, and the Novel*.

speaks of a desire "beyond gender," and the representations and figurations of sexual identities so insistently present in a novel such as *Valentine* (but also, as could be shown, in *Indiana* or, in a lesser degree, in *Lélia*)?

The scene of hysteria, with Valentine at its center, is like a primal scene in that it stages the subject's encounter with sexual difference. But when the emphasis falls on its literary and historical aspects, it takes on the appearance of yet another kind of gender fable, where gender has become the principle that determines the act of representation, because in Sand's writing of fictional desire there can be no meaning outside of the subject's insertion in the sexual difference. Representation is my main concern in the first part of this chapter, while in the second part I examine the hysteria of Sand's text from a psychoanalytical perspective. For this "literary hysteria" does more than draw its veil over the heroine's illicit desires; it is manifest at the very heart of Sand's writing, where it threatens to cover up and fully obscure the passion and the knowledge that sustain it. The later inquiry into Sand's autobiographical text thus reveals the woman writer's dutiful daughterly compliance with an imperative of blindness and silencing that makes of the author, inevitably, a hysteric.

Valentine, or Hysteria According to Briquet

Among a number of troubling and confusing scenarios represented in Sand's novel, the heroine's wedding night stands out as a climactic moment of passion expressed in the intensities of the writing but also in the subject that is represented. Passion means here that Valentine is in love and suffers for it; it is the matter of her subjective experience, and the form it takes is hysteria. Here then the contradictory impulses of Sand's text—the urge for expression and the need to abide by generic conventions—are reflected in the heroine's pathological, hystericized body. This unremitting struggle to preserve feminine *pudeur* is dramatized in a body held in the thralls of passion and a mind seemingly intent on virtue, while Valentine's hysteria transforms the guilt associated with woman's desire into purificatory suffering.

Thus the heroine can spend her wedding night dreaming about love, without her husband, but in her lover's presence. Heightened to a paroxysm of passion and modesty, the representation speaks of a "dialectic between sexual indulgence and sexual abstinence" which, according to Carol Richards, is characteristic of the writer (13). As it is inhabited by hysteria, the nuptial bedroom becomes the stage for a scene of passion that can be represented the more graphically because it exists as an impulse outside of the heroine's will or consciousness. Here then Sand effects what appears, for Simone Lecointre, to be a general characteristic of her writing—"a split between an enamored subject and part of her representations, which are then rejected to the imaginary and poetic spheres" (52). As a trope and mode of representation, hysteria can indeed speak of a forbidden, unspeakable desire; it maintains in a state of maximum intensity the oxymoron of "pure female passion" which is central to Sand's *Valentine* through a process of dissociation, displacement and confusion of gender roles.

The scene of hysteria marks the conformity of Sand's representations of female subjectivity with the discourses of the nineteenth-century *médecine morale*. Woman's passion and her knowledge are reinscribed as hysteria, and the hidden recesses of her soul (*das verborgenste Seelische*, to use Freud's term) are put on display under the form of bodily pathology, which is charted like a "progress" that takes the heroine through a feverish state, torpor, delirium, convulsions, and reaches its climax as a cerebral stroke. Hysteria salvages morality in Sand's fiction in keeping with the belief best represented in Briquet's scientific project, where woman is shown to convert her secret and inexpressible emotions into symptoms destined to show her virtue. Recall that in the theories of Voisin, Virey, and Brachet, *pudeur* represents a counterforce and an inhibiting factor that prohibits the expression or even experience of feminine passion, and as such acts as a prophylactic. For Briquet, however— and this is where his representations and those of Sand begin to look alike—hysteria is not the alternative or negative counterpart to pudor: it is pudor itself, in its most acute and painful manifestations. His theories can thus provide a frame of reference for the unusual scenario of *Valentine*'s wedding night.

In the first pages of Briquet's treatise *Traité clinique et thérapeutique de l'hystérie*, he writes: "To me, hysteria is a neurosis of the encephalon whose apparent phenomena consist principally in the disruption of the vital acts that enable the manifestation of affective sensations and passions" (3). The signs of hysteria correspond to "the apparent changes through which sensations, passions, needs are manifested," and the symptoms are under the direct influence of "the moral affections," which would normally be expressed through "the voice, gestures or facial expressions." The illness is related to an affective sphere irrevocably tied to morality, which seems to act as a censor; it re-presents, that is, it mimes, without the mediation of language but through a bodily gesture, what is of the domain of passion or affect: "Hysterical phenomena are the more or less troubled repetition not of all these actions, but of those through which painful sensations, sad or violent affections, and passions are rendered manifest" (4).

In this model, hysteria corresponds to the inhibition of an affect, which remains unpresentable except through bodily tropings. It is the bodily trace of an affective process, where the symptoms are correlated to a psychic content. This theory foregrounds, unlike any of the others examined so far, the expressive and figurative nature of the disease. While modesty corresponds to a withdrawal from the sensations and emotions that the true and pure woman is unable to express, hysteria is related, both in terms of etiology and therapy, to a need for expression. And in his handling of the cases, the physician is naturally led to privilege the act of verbal communication with his patient. It could be said indeed that in Briquet's conception, hysteria is a question of language. Under the rubric of "treatment according to the causes," he recommends that the doctor lend his ear to his patient's verbal complaint, for "most often [the hysterics] are unhappy women who are very glad to find in a doctor a confident for their sorrows" (633). With a model that relies so visibly on the heterogeneity of body and mind and that comes very close to defining mechanism of conversion, Briquet, of all four doctors, comes closest to the early Freudian model of the illness.[7] For him, as later for Freud, hysteria is closely related to the failure of representation and can be alleviated, if not cured, through an act of narration. This might explain why Briquet's theories can be shown to have such affinities with Sand's fiction. The following pages, in which I draw analogies between his medical treatise and her novel, represent then, among other things, the counterpart to the first chapter of this work: they are about the convergence, on the subject of woman, of the discourses of medicine and literature, but with a shift of emphasis, toward the ideological underpinnings of literary representations.

Briquet's notions overlap indeed with Sand's fictional representations in the early 1830s: an extreme sensibility, overpowering emotions, the stringent demands of feminine modesty, the bodily symptoms of a moral suffering, and the intervention of a well-meaning, perceptive physician. In *Valentine* the writer represents a female subject in a way that seems to anticipate the doctor's work on hysteria; this can only confirm the

---

7. Remember that Briquet's theories establish the most tenuous of connections between the symptoms and the organic cause, and they repeatedly fail to identify the entity of the brain that provokes the illness (see Chap. 1). For discussions of the early Freudian model as well as the question of the dissociation between body and mind, see David-Ménard's lucid exposé in the first chapter of *Hysteria from Freud to Lacan*, 24–27.

earlier impression that the fictional and medical representations are constructed through a process of mutual enhancement. From this combined perspective, hysteria becomes a figure or trope for the constructions of sexual identities, and a telltale sign for a certain conception of subjectivity. If the term does not appear in Sand's text it may be that it had not yet acquired the kind of currency it enjoyed by the middle of the century, or that the woman writer, always inclined to downplay her knowledge, had deliberately chosen to skirt it.[8] But the representations, meanwhile, fictional and medical, contribute to our perception of a sexual identity, which is defined in both cases in this discrepancy between the bodily sphere on the one hand and the affective and mental domain on the other. Hysteria is the paroxystic form taken by such a division. Thus one can see how the distinctive dramaturgy that enables the representation of Valentine's *affections morales*, with its emphasis on bodily symptoms, maps out a feminine version of a psyche and of a mental life.

To dwell on the actions and figures that belong to the scene of passion and hysteria in *Valentine* is to uncover those "psychological mysteries" for which James had singled out the writings of George Sand. It also means deciphering, in the scenario made up of actions, gestures, and words that lead to the crucial moment of hysteria, the elements of an inner mental stage.[9] As her marriage to the feared comte de Lansac draws near, Valentine is taken so ill that on the day of her wedding she hardly looks like herself. Her grandmother intercedes on her behalf and asks that the husband give up, for that one night, his conjugal rights. Thanks to her protection and with the help of the old matronly nurse, the heroine is left alone, locked in her nuptial chamber without the incommodious presence of an unwanted husband. Bénédict, however, having witnessed a double marriage (while Valentine is united with de Lansac, Athenais, his former fiancée, is married to a peasant), cannot refrain from expressing his feelings and exclaims that without love the conjugal act is simply a rape: "Yes, a rape, repeated Bénédict overcome with anger (and one must not forget that Bénédict was endowed with an excessive and exceptional nature). . . . And there, in full view of so-

---

8. To my knowledge, the term "hysteria" does not appear in Sand's early fiction, but she uses it in her letters (see the introduction to Chap. 1), perhaps merely to respond to Flaubert's provocations.

9. This is indeed where the excesses and confusions of Sand's narrative can be interpreted as "failures of thought" characteristic of a hysterical attitude. In this, I attribute to the texture of Sand's writing displacements that are analogous to those described by David-Ménard on an existential plane. On the transformation of thought into movement, see, for instance, *Hysteria from Freud to Lacan*, 182.

ciety, which approves and ratifies, a modest and fearful woman, who has known how to resist her lover's transports, falls branded by the kisses of a hated master" (183). These words define, in an unusually explicit fashion, the stakes of Valentine's story. In a voice that may seem autobiographical, the writer makes her plea for the (erotic) sentiments of the woman, and she provides moral justification for what may appear, from the point of view of bourgeois moralism, the most improbable or immoral action: a lover eavesdropping on his beloved's wedding night.

Indeed, in the absence of the lawful but hated husband, Valentine's lover takes his stand at the side of Valentine's bed. Hidden behind a curtain, Bénédict spies on Valentine and becomes in this way the spectator of the scene of passion or, rather, of hysteria that seems staged for his own benefit. The consummation of the love is, as we know, deferred (by two years or fourteen chapters) until it is no longer adulterous. The scene that takes place in the alcove speaks unquestionably of passion,[10] and hysteria is here neither a veil nor a defense against bodily, erotic scenarios but rather, it enables them. Thus the hysteric draws from her illness a double benefit: she avoids an ill-loved husband and expresses her sexual passion in a dissociated form that exempts both her conscience and her consciousness.

But this is not the inspiration of a moment: the heroine's illness develops gradually at the rate of the overpowering yet suppressed emotions she experiences in her love for Bénédict. And thus her first symptoms—her paleness, torpor, generalized pain, and fever—testify not only to her sensibility and impressionability but also to the growing intensity of her passion. It is in the heroine's body that her affects can be deciphered, just as for the physician, sensibility and emotions can be measured in the soma:

In women, this feeling machine [*appareil de sensibilité*] is endowed with its own thermometer which the physician can handle so as to judge precisely the degree of intensity that this sensibility has reached. It can be found in the effects produced by the emotions: every woman must feel under their influence, to varying degrees, a compression of the epigastrium, a tightening of the throat, and disturbances in her limbs. In the case of women endowed with a limited sensibility they are hardly marked; in those who are impressionable,

10. The word *alcôve* denotes in French, more specifically than the English term, a niche or recessed part in a larger room, containing one or several beds, which can be closed off during the daytime. The *alcôve* is thus also defined as "le lieu des rapports amoureux." The English term is henceforth used in the more specific French sense. For a more detailed discussion, see my postscript, "Always Secrets of the Alcove."

they show to a high degree, and the hysterics experience them at their maximum. (49)[11]

Reading the correlation between an experience of the psyche and its bodily transcription leads us to hysteria as the point of maximum intensity of woman's affective experience: the point where her bodily reaction to emotions becomes pathological. The older metaphor of a lovesickness (presented under the heading *affections morales tristes*) is now reinscribed in the guise of a pathological body: in Briquet's vision, hysteria literalizes what was before only a figure.[12] The body takes over, truly and fully, as the site of the painful enactment, which to the noninitiate speaks merely of illness or madness, while for the perspicuous doctor it is the textbook of the woman's emotional state. Valentine bears the impress on her body of the text of her passions; this sanctions her ignorance and innocence, and moreover protects her from social stigma. Only the doctor can tell that this is love, of which she is a victim and not a culprit. A natural progression takes her along the path of her emotions, with increasing degrees of sensibility and impressionability, toward a suffering that makes of her the quintessential victim of her moral and psychological frailty.[13] But the body and mind are so sharply dissociated that the hysteric appears to carry no mental or rational awareness of her actions or feelings.[14] In its place, she experiences her bodily pains, until she finally drifts into total oblivion: such is the case with Valentine's *con-*

11. On the image of the thermometer in medical discourses on women, see Terry Castle's "The Female Thermometer."

12. In the chapter "Symptomatologie de l'hystérie," Briquet evokes the process of symbolization that characterizes hysteria as he establishes a first chart listing the "bodily impressions" felt by "an impressionable woman" who has been submitted to a "moral emotion." He then asks that these be compared to the corresponding chart, which describes the different elements of a hysterical attack. The descriptions of the "impressions affectives" are thus shown to correspond to bodily phenomena, and the emotions are returned to the body. We owe to Freud's linguistic awareness the notion of a "demetaphorization" characteristic of certain hysterical symptoms. He discusses symbolization in *Studies on Hysteria* (*SE* II, 178–81), where he writes, "the hysteric is not taking liberties with words, but is simply reviving once more the sensations to which the verbal expression owes its justification" (181).

13. *L'impressionabilité* is a key notion in Briquet's conception of hysteria. It figures abundantly in the clinical charts as well as in the chapters devoted to its etiology and in the case histories he presents. The defining feature of Briquet's hysteric is thus her impressionability.

14. In this dissociation between body and mind, the difference between lovesickness and hysteria can be foregrounded again. The American Psychiatric Association's *Diagnostic and Statistical Manual of Mental Disorders* gives as a defining feature of hysteria the notion of "dissociation" or "dissociated state."

gestion cérébrale, which sanctions the death of her mind. For when it meets with passion, woman's delicate, highly sensitive emotional and moral sphere is in danger of disappearance; in its place we find the rawest of materials, a body meant to suffer.

"It is because women feel so vividly that they become fatally the prey of hysteria," writes Briquet in his chapter "Physical Constitution, Moral Disposition." While the *cause prédisposante* of Valentine's illness lies in her sensibility, one could also, in the chart titled "Determining Causes according to Contemporary Science," recognize the origin of Valentine's symptoms: a disappointed love. Briquet draws an impressive list of causes, some of which can be internal: "The affections of the soul and principally, anger, envy, jealousy, love and especially thwarted love, boredom, sorrow, terror, prolonged atttention, vexations. In general, all the circumstances which can excite a sensibility while efforts are being made to hide this excitation" (164). Some are external, when they correspond to such passion-provoking events or situations as "Music or such entertainment are as likely to arouse strong passions: the reading of novels . . . lascivious paintings, the pleasure a woman feels at the sight of the man she loves, a kiss or even simply being touched by the loved one, frequenting the public walks tóo regularly . . . the sight of all the objects connected to luxury or the fine arts, hope for an impossible union, being abandoned when love was reciprocated . . . venereal desires excited but not satisfied, masturbation, venereal excesses" (164–65). The presence of the beloved, a desired union that is impossible, venereal desires, these are all present in Sand's fiction. Like the scenes of passion in Sand's novel, they are a reminder that the nineteenth century did indeed ascribe sexual desires to women.[15] But such is the urge to purify her from these sexual aspects that the links between woman's erotic life and the symptoms of hysteria do not appear in the physician's theories, but are only present in the margins, buried among a list of examples. For him as for the novelist, hysteria marks woman's exculpation from the sins attached to her sensuality, and doubly so. Since the "expression of passions" is ascribed to the illness, she cannot be held responsible for them. "Her suffering brain," so sensitive to the *affections morales*, has created "the pathological state necessary to the production of hysteria" (116) and provides in the form of symptoms an additional proof of her

15. This is true in spite of Briquet's disclaimer in the introductory pages of his book (see Chap. 1). As has been shown often enough, nineteenth-century discourse concerning women's sexual desire is fraught with contradictions. See, for instance, Nancy F. Cott, "Passionlessness: An Interpretation of Victorian Sexual Ideology, 1790–1850," and Peter T. Cominos, "Innocent Femina Sensualis in Unconscious Conflict."

moral sense. Fifty years later, following the same lines of reasoning, Freud wrote in *Studies on Hysteria* about the consolations he can offer the hysteric: "we are not responsible for our feelings, and . . . her behaviour, the fact that she had fallen ill in these circumstances, was sufficient evidence of her moral character" (*SE* II, 157).

In short then, while hysteria can define a conscience which is experienced as bodily stigma and is thus made visible for the gaze of the physician-moralist, it also sanctions the erasure of the subject's consciousness. Feminine virtue depends, as we know, on woman's ignorance, and this is true as well of Sand's heroine. When in the first love scene Valentine blushes under Bénédict's innocent kiss, she shows her *pudeur*; the later hysteria is just a more intense form of the same quality. In both situations, the expression of passion is detached from the will or consciousness of the subject, who cannot then be held responsible or accountable.[16] Haunted by the symptoms of hysteria, the heroine is delirious, acts in her sleep, and is seized with hallucinations, but she is preserved from the contamination of desire in the noblest of fashions, which corresponds to her remarkable nature. Delirium is, for Briquet, a privileged manifestation of hysteria, given to "young subjects, principally those endowed with a precocious intelligence, a very sharp imagination and impressionability" (428).[17]

But delirium, in Sand's fiction, not only adds to the heroine's imaginative, poetic nature; it is also a narrative device whereby words can be attributed to the heroine's desire, but words which are foreign to her consciousness.[18] In this case hysteria is not the underside of silence but offers, on the contrary, the possibility of filling the gaps of the unpresentable through the aberrations of the illness. While the body bespeaks, most visibly, the struggles and the sufferings of virtue, it is this same body that, in its diseased state, gives to woman's passion its voice:

16. See *Valentine*, 66. On blushing as a bodily phenomenon analogous to hysterical symptoms, see David-Ménard, *Hysteria from Freud to Lacan*, 59–63.

17. Under the rubric *hystérie*, Larousse's *Grand dictionnaire universel du XIXème siècle* describes delirium in a fashion that resembles Valentine's behavior: "There are some who are in ecstasy or somnambulic, some faint or have delirious ideas and begin to scream. In certain cases, delirium takes the form of inspiration and is accompanied by various hallucinations." As for Briquet, he writes on the same subject: "Fits of delirium are rather frequent among hysterical patients . . . sometimes they constitute the dominant fact . . . they are in themselves the attack and are not accompanied by the usual hysterical occurrences" (*Traité de l'hystérie*, 428).

18. In George Sand's conception, hysteria is vocal. When Olive Chancellor suffers from aphonia, or George Eliot conveys the notion of inexpressibility ("words were no better than chips," she writes in *Daniel Deronda*, 558) and evokes the silencing of the heroine, George Sand endows Valentine with the words that express her passion.

"Valentine, floating between reality and illusion, sometimes waking sometimes sleeping, told Bénédict candidly all her secrets." She addresses her lover as if he were her husband: "kiss me, but do not look at me. Turn off this light; let me hide my face on your chest" (194). This hysteric is, for a while, not tongue-tied. But on discovery of a letter by Bénédict, where he confesses his presence during the night and his intentions to commit suicide, the heroine's emotions reach such a paroxysm as can only lead to further symptoms: delirium gives way to a seizure, followed by such deep prostration that the doctor diagnoses "a cerebral congestion."

"An affectionate old man," "a good old country doctor, a humble scholar, who many times in his life had had an opportunity to dry tears or blood"—George Sand's Monsieur Faure resembles the family doctor as Angus McLaren defines him in his study of French medicine between 1800 and 1850: "he could make himself an indispensable fixture of bourgeois society by becoming, in addition to its medical consultant, its moral counsellor and confessor" (39).[19] In the tradition of Cabanis and Pinel, Faure practices *une médecine morale*: having uncovered the secret source of Valentine's complaint, "he undertakes to calm these two erring hearts, and to heal one through the other" and "applies to them a more efficient moral treatment" (*Valentine*, 213).[20] When the causes are so clearly moral, then the treatment cannot be truly physical but must deal with the patient's affections: "let us hasten the paroxysm of this passion; without me, it might burst out in a way that could be even more terrible; my presence will sanction it and we might then be able to assuage it" (215–16). The idyll in the pavilion thus takes place under the doctor's prescription.

There is no priest in *Valentine*, but the doctor will hear her confession. The remorseful heroine sometimes prays alone in her chapel dedicated to the Virgin, or else she whispers into his ear the secrets of the alcove. The physician is now called upon to listen to the complaints and confessions of suffering women, and, Briquet writes, "he will need to rely on the full resources of his intelligence, his tact and his perspicacity."

---

19. Both Angus McLaren ("Doctor in the House") and Jan Goldstein relate the increasing "medicalization" of the mental and emotional sphere to the rise of the medical profession and the reaction against the Church. "As the medicalization of emotional life progressed, and the label 'hysteria' (or 'neurasthenia') became more firmly affixed to this female 'fog in the head,' the choice of counsellor became clearer—and the new clarity no doubt pleased psychiatrists and leaders of the early Third Republic alike" (Goldstein, *Console and Classify: The French Psychiatric Profession in the Nineteenth Century*, 374).

20. Goldstein's *Console and Classify* is an indispensable book on this subject.

He must be "well informed on the moral causes that have given rise to hysteria, and provided he frames his questions skillfully enough . . . he will find that ordinarily, the hysterics are only unhappy women, who are only too glad to find in their doctor a confident for their sorrows" (633). "One works to the best of one's power, as an elucidator (where ignorance has given rise to fear), as a teacher . . . as a father confessor who gives absolution, as it were, by a continuance of his sympathy and respect after the confession has been made," Freud seems to echo in *Studies on Hysteria* (*SE* II, 282).

In the early work of Freud, or in Briquet's treatise, or in Sand's novel, the hysteric tells the same story of impossible passions and existential unhappiness. Indeed, it looks increasingly as if the social and cultural situation that determines her experience is the cause of her illness as much as her inner constitution is, even though the medical theories and the fictional narrative focus insistently on the latter. It is then understood that hysteria marks the conflict that arises when woman's susceptibility to passions meets with a moral imperative that requires her to suppress them. The axiom that lies behind Briquet's medical discourse and George Sand's fiction alike is not primarily that of "anatomy is destiny," but rather, in a secondary and more complex articulation of a "moral" sphere around bodily difference, the notion that woman is held under the sway of an extreme emotional and moral susceptibility which corresponds to her bodily condition. The correlation between body and mind is an unspoken assumption of Sand's text and remains unexplained, as I showed earlier, in medical theories. But while it becomes in this fashion the theater of passions, woman's moral sphere is bound to be reappropriated by the soma. Such indeed is the weakness of her mind that she is doomed to meet in her flesh the slings and arrows of fortune and thus to bear in her hysteria the stigma of her mental predicament.

But while my reading of *Valentine* has so far insisted on the novel's combination of realism and romance, from another perspective (beginning for instance with the inevitability of the novel's ending) it could be shown to belong to the genre of tragedy. There, hysteria would signal a fatally predetermined unhappiness whose principle is expressed, unwittingly, by Charles Bovary in Flaubert's novel: "C'est la faute de la fatalité" ("It's the fault of Fate" [360]), and is confirmed by Olive Chancellor, when she claims that the "load of fate" weighs on women more intolerably (*Bostonians*, 175). That in his early days as a physician and therapist Freud should come to similar conclusions suggests there may be some truth in such visions: " 'No doubt fate would find it easier than I do to relieve you of your illness. But you will be able to convince yourself that much will be gained if we succeed in transforming your hysterical misery into common unhappiness' " (*SE* II, 305). The repetitive nature of stories of hysteria would merely confirm a historical fact (or is it merely a construction?), namely, that nineteenth-century women, and among them preeminently the hysterics, were after all simply the victims of their sexual identities.

The Pleasures of the Alcove, or Hysteria According to Freud

Read through the prism of a bourgeois realism imbued with moral concerns, hysteria can salvage the heroine's morality: it represents woman's nature brought to a paroxysm of feminine modesty, and it participates in what could be termed the "orthodramatization" of feminine sensibility. It reinforces or confirms her difference; it establishes her sexual identity. But when read against the grain, the scene of hysteria in *Valentine* signifies, in a hallucinatory mode, the undoing of proper gender attributions: as the spectators of the hysteric's private theater, we are privy to a complex scenario of repeated reinscription and dissolution of sexual identities enacted under the sway of desire. The alcove is then the stage for an "inward drama," where desire and knowledge are brought together or opposed in a complex script of subjective inscription. Whereas the earlier reading of Valentine's wedding night focused on the representation of hysteria in order to elicit certain cultural formations, a closer examination of Sand's hysterical writing, while taking some distance from the represented, foregrounds the processes of signification. In this textualized form, hysteria becomes a feature of Sand's style, and it enables us to achieve a better understanding of what is the particular and recognizable stamp of her writing.

Meanwhile, it is with a lover's gaze (like that of Bénédict, who, hidden behind the curtains of the heroine's bed, spies on the secrets of the alcove) that I undertake this other reading of Valentine's scene of hysteria. But also, like an analyst, I turn the alcove into an amphitheater: "All of this is taking place in the hysteric's imaginary room converted into an amphitheater," Catherine Clément writes (*La jeune née*, 108). Leaving behind the qualms of Briquet concerning the erotic nature of hysteria, I turn to Freud, who examines unblinkingly, in two closely related essays, *Hysterical Phantasies and Their Relation to Bisexuality* and *Some General Remarks on Hysterical Attacks*, the rituals of seduction of the *Hysterika*.[21] I thus hope to lay bare in *Valentine* the desire that George Sand

21. The hysterical woman is a recurrent term in Freud's discussion in these two essays.

took care to hide in her representation but that inevitably transpires from her writing. Writing participates in a libidinal economy that reveals the drives and the fantasies that the representation of *Valentine*'s scene of passion, using hysteria as a screen, seemed intent on denying: representation involves veiling, while writing has to do with the revealing hand. If George Sand is hysterical, sometimes, it must be in her fiction, which, when it meets with the sexed body, is constituted of such splitting or division. For as we shall see, although this other perspective on Valentine's bedroom offers the spectacle of a representation freed from moral constraints and from the need to sustain the realist conventions of sexual identity, there too desire and knowledge are met with the resistances of gender. The need to abide by the law of gender overrides the other impulse, which impels Sand to write of "longing and desire" and of "passion."

Thus, if I refer to Freud as a theoretical model for this alternative reading of the scene of hysteria, it is not merely because his theories enable me to make sense of the figurations of seduction, which can hardly be overlooked when reading *Valentine*. It is also because the major elements of his reflections in these two essays—the hysteric's body, masculine versus feminine, daydreaming, expression and repression— seem to converge with the main themes of the Sandian text. Moreover, in these texts, Freud reads the hysteric's body not only as a set of symptoms but for its representations, like a text that tells the stories of her desires. The analyst's focus on bodily representations can profitably be redirected at Sand's *Valentine*, the more so since in both cases the hysteric's body appears to perform within a gendered scenario.

There is also much for the literary critic to learn from Freud's brief exposé, at the beginning of *Hysterical Phantasies and Their Relation to Bisexuality* (written in 1908 at the same time Freud was working on *Creative Writers and Day-Dreaming*), of his conception of *Wahndichtung*. The term describes the imaginary figures that haunt the minds and sometimes the performances of the pervert, the paranoic, and the hysteric (*SE* IX, 159–60), and the notion leads to an elaborate semiological model which associates hysteria with daydreaming and relates the phantasies of the mind to their enactment in hysterical symptoms. Freud's concept of *Wahndichtung*, of a creative, literally "poetic" process proceeding from illusion or desire, provides an interesting insight into Sand's textual performance. As it dwells on the relation between phantasy and

---

Like his predecessors, he establishes his typology of hysteria by focusing exclusively on a female subject; his use of the *Hysterika* strikes me here as emblematic.

its enactment as bodily gesture, it enables us to conceive of a similar relation in the literary text: the gestures and actions that the bodies perform in Sand's narrative correspond to certain authorial desire.

The sheer theatricality—the melodramatic nature of the scene of hysteria in Sand's text—not only looks outward, as a response to a moral imperative where a heroine's femininity must be rendered visible in a spectacular enactment. It is determined as well by some inner compulsion, of which writing is the form, where an imaginary body, held in the thralls of certain gestures and movements, represents a female subject. Within such a conception, the particular bodily dramaturgy Sand ascribes to the protagonists of her novel in the crucial scene of hysteria becomes a telltale sign of a certain conception of the body and of its engendering: it marks the subject's imaginary insertion or positioning in sexual scenarios.

The scene of hysteria in *Valentine* is inscribed with George Sand's imaginary investments; the textual irregularities, intensities, repetitions, and figurations—the text's symptoms—that show through the frames of representation belong to the author's private text. Writing opens a gap or a space for experience and memory. We hear in her fiction, projected as voice and transferred into the very web and force of textuality, echoes of the same passion we encountered in her love letters. At this point the figurations of hysteria come as close as can be to what Freud described as *Wahndichtung*: the literary process gives way to the representations of a desire and knowledge that define a subjectivity.

Let us then reexamine the scene of hysteria in *Valentine* from a Freudian perspective and with renewed suspicions. "Lock me in, take the key, and only go to bed when the house is shut," Valentine tells her nurse (189). While it serves as a reminder of the external threat (the husband may be lying in wait), the emphasis on a closed space and the insistance on enclosing the heroine define a setting whose symbolic evocations are unmistakable. A woman's solitude may speak of virtue and renunciation from worldly pleasures, but it is often suspected, by moralists and doctors alike, to promote the uncontrolled expression of passions and phantasies. As a closed, inner space and woman's secret preserve, the room where Valentine spends her wedding night has been transformed into a boudoir: the predestined space for her erotic reverie and for the secret rites of feminine sexuality.[22] Erotic, because everyone knows (or at least

22. In the section "Theory in Practice: The Woman's Place," in *The Discourse of the*

our nineteenth-century physicians do, starting with Virey and ending with early Freud) that a solitary or idle woman tends to lapse into day-dreaming, and that her daydreaming is typically made up of erotic thoughts. Thus the heroine's encasment in her room calls for suspicion: it signals not so much a defensive gesture as a dangerous occasion.

Indeed, locked up in her room, and unware of another presence, Valentine speaks and performs her passion under the eyes of her lover. The boudoir is now an alcove, and hysteria a disguise for erotic activity. Thus, pushing back her bedclothes, "[Valentine] was drawing closer, and seemed to invite his caresses with a naive and trustful air" (195). Taking her imagined lover into her arms, she embraces him: "She drew him toward her with an extraordinary feverish strength. Her cheeks had taken on a vivid hue, her lips shone brightly. A fleeting fire suddenly showed in her dull eyes, clearly she was delirious" (196). Placed emphatically at the beginning of the clause, the adverb "clearly" (*évidemment*) works as a disclaimer—only her illness can explain such a behavior—for what is too much like an erotic scenario. This is not delirium, but sexual desire, and moreover, desire displayed for another. Discussing hysterical attacks, Freud singles out a characteristic form, which is of particular use to the patient because it brings her pleasure: "the attack is directed at particular individuals; it can be put off till they are present, and it gives an impression of being consciously simulated" (*Some General Remarks on Hysterical Attacks*, SE IX, 232). Sand's text represents then a phantasy that is staged for its chosen spectator, like a seduction; the heroine's hysteria answers her lover's desire as if by contagion: "As she was no longer excited by her lover's burning breath, Valentine lapsed again into a motionless and peaceful torpor" (195).

There are models for such a bedroom scene: the *scène du cabinet* in *La Nouvelle Héloïse*, where de Preux experiences a moment of ecstasy on discovering Julie's garments scattered in her room, or Raphaël's spying on Foedora as she undresses in her room in Balzac's *La peau de*

Sublime: History, Aesthetics and the Subject. (252–78), Peter de Bolla analyzes the meanings associated with the lady's intimate apartments. They are the predestined site for peculiarly feminine perversions such as the reading of novels, narcissistic contemplation in a mirror, and more dangerous still, solitary pleasures.

"A common source and normal prototype of all these creations of phantasy is to be found in what are called the day-dreams of youth. . . . They occur with perhaps equal frequency in both sexes, though it seems that while in girls and women they are invariably of an erotic nature, in men they may be either erotic or ambitious," writes Freud in *Hysterical Phantasies* (SE IX, 159), repeating what he had asserted in *Creative Writers and Day-Dreaming* (SE IX, 146–47).

chagrin. But the hysteria of Sand's text elicits a more complex and ambiguous scenario than merely the male discovery of the female body. It represents two subjects, but in a great confusion of actions and motivations, particularly in light of the two principles which, as I showed earlier, determine the representation in this novel—those of modesty (as virtuous passion) and of sexual identity ("she" is feminine, "he" is masculine). For instance, Bénédict appears at the beginning of the scene in the guise of a virile defender of the heroine's virtue: his presence in the room is meant to save her from her husband's advances; he is even ready to kill her if she should no longer defend her virtue (188). Later he attempts to cover the heroine's denuded body in what appears to be a gesture of feminine pudor. But, "having gently lifted the curtain of her bed," he succumbs to (male) voyeurism, "intoxicated by the bliss that his untroubled looking affords him" (192), and can barely "master [love's] passionate thrills" (190). And yet he falls one more time into the attitude of feminine (?) modesty: "contemplation remained for a long time without danger, the angels are less pure than the heart of a man of twenty when he is passionately in love" (193), until his resistance breaks down and he finds himself drawn fully into the scene, this time as an actor and not merely as a chosen spectator:

"Yes," she said, while raising herself, "*you* are my husband; I know it, my Bénédict; I too love you. Kiss me, but do not look at me. Put out the light; let me hide my face against your chest."
    As she spoke, she embraced him and drew him toward her with an extraordinary feverish strength . . . clearly she was delirious. But how could Bénédict have distinguished her agitation due to the illness from the rapturous passion that was devouring him? In a gesture of despair, he threw himself on her and, on the point of yielding to his violent, agonizing desire, he could no longer hold back his nervous, heart-rending screams. (196)

The hero's nervous, heart-rending screams reveal the pleasure he takes in the scene of hysteria; they are, like the hysteric's scream, caught between pleasure and pain.[23] But at this point the door must imperatively be opened, to prevent the worst from happening: "But immediately some steps were heard, and a key turned in the lock." The scene had begun

23. On this subject, see Freud's discussion of Fraülein von R. in *Studies on Hysteria*: "if one pressed or pinched the hyperalgesic skin and muscles of her legs, her face assumed a peculiar expression which was one of pleasure rather than pain. She cried out—and I could not help thinking that it was as though she was having a voluptuous tickling sensation." (*SE* II, 137).

with similarly indistinct sounds which came from Valentine's closed room, and, listening at the door, the hero knew he had found his destination. Valentine's audible breathing and the distinct and indistinct words that emerge from the room serve as a prelude to a scene that, under such auspices, cannot be mistaken and must be stopped short, because the hero and heroine are becoming too involved in a pantomime that looks like . . . But let us hear, rather, Freud's words in *Some General Remarks on Hysterical Attacks*. "What points the way for the motor discharge of the repressed libido in a hysterical attack is the reflex mechanism of the act of coition—a mechanism which is ready to hand in everybody, including women, and which we see coming into manifest operation when an unrestrained surrender is made to sexual activity. Already in ancient times coition was described as a 'minor epilepsy.' We might alter this and say that a convulsive hysterical attack is an equivalent of coition" (*SE* IX, 234). One might want to object to an interpretation that overlooks the difference between "her agitation due to illness" and "his passionate rapture," and that endorses the hero's own confusion, when the narrator calls insistently upon us readers to discriminate between pathology and passion, between hysteria and sexual desire, between her and him. Sand's text thus attempts to sustain in its representations the proper gender distinctions: in a woman, desire takes on the appearance or at least the name of hysteria, whereas in the case of a man this displacement is unnecessary—although, as the phrase "how could he have distinguished?" shows, it may be difficult to make the orthodox difference between a symptom (hers) and an affect (his). In this alcove, the difference between the hero and the heroine is not signified at the level of an innate and visible bodily difference, but through the figurations of hysteria: woman is to man as the hysteric is to the "healthy," conscious mind. However, the writing works against these sharpened delineations and distinctions, and threatens to dissolve the sexual differences: Valentine and Bénédict look increasingly like one and the same body in the thralls of a hysterical desire or delirium.

Hysteria marks here, as it did in *Fragment of a Case of Hysteria*, the imperative of gender. As we saw, in the Freudian perspective (relayed by Lacan in "Intervention on Transference"), Dora's history takes the shape of an uneasy, contradictory progress of a subject who, unable to endorse her gender attribution, oscillates between the poles of activity or passivity, subject of desire or object of desire, masculinity or femininity. In *Valentine* too, hysteria designates the subject's insertion in the system of gender, but it signals simultaneously the price to be paid for the proper gender ascription—that of her "mindlessness" or unconsciousness. If Valentine "is" what her sex means her to be, that is, *if she is her gender*, it cannot be at the level of her mind, but, paradoxically, in the enactments of her body. The fiction thus endows her with a sexual identity at the expense of an awareness of her desire. Because it relies on such a split between body and mind, hysteria marks then a resistance to gender.

The example of Sand can thus be added to the earlier cases. We saw, with Freud and Dora and with James and George Sand, how the epistemological imperative that requires that the scene of "her passion" be read in terms of a grammar of the sexes (while enforcing the proper gender alignments) invariably produces a hysterical scenario. James's encounters with the epicene George Sand, while provoking ceaseless attempts to identify her as a man or a woman, grow to an unparalleled climax of gender confusion and illegibility. At the level of knowledge, of a desire for knowledge and its attendant epistemology, the Freudian case history reveals a similar collapse of differences: the analyst ends up projecting his own masculine quest for knowledge onto the analytical stage while the patient (as the gender fable of Dora's secret shows) can be suspected of parodying her own hysteria for his benefit. As for George Sand's novel, while it expresses (more transparently than the critic's or the analyst's text) a desire to obey the laws of gender, it leads to the same impasse where masculine and feminine have become truly indifferent, indistinguishable—were it not for the heroine's hysteria.

Difference as a Theme

Scenes of hysteria always point to questions of sexual difference; this is shown in the representations of George Sand's novel as much as in the texts of psychoanalysis. Freud's incidental remark about "a mechanism . . . in everybody, including women" quoted in the previous section—taken from a text that begins by focusing on the hysterical woman patient, *die Hysterika*—is the most striking example. In his two articles *Hysterical Phantasies and Their Relation to Bisexuality* and *Some General Remarks on Hysterical Attacks*, he often reverts to the opposition between women and men, feminine and masculine, but above all singles out one image that shows in an emblematic fashion the gender split that for him characterizes hysteria. Thus in *Hysterical Phantasies* he states, "Further counterparts of [the bisexual nature of hysterical symptoms] are found in certain hysterical attacks in which the patient simultaneously plays both parts in the underlying sexual phantasy. In one case which I observed, for instance, the patient pressed her dress up against her body with one hand (as the woman), while she tried to tear it off with the other (as the man)" (*SE* IX, 166).[24] In his discussion of multiple identifications in the other text, Freud refers as well to the hysterical performance of that "patient [who] tore off her dress with one hand (as the man) while he pressed it to her body with the other (as the woman)" (*SE* IX, 230). One single example provides the only illustration in both texts, as if this image constituted a visual matrix, an icon, for the analyst's reflections. No other example in the Freudian corpus on hysteria shows so clearly that sexual identity relies on the assumption of a particular role, on the performance of an action or behavior that can be identified as masculine or feminine. The hysteric plays alternately, but in the course of one performance, the "man" and the "woman." Thus, tearing off their clothes or veils, the hysterical subjects are made into men; holding them back in a gesture of *pudeur*, they are like women, "feminine." Sexual identity is thus produced in a bodily performance, through the imitation of certain gestures, attitudes, traits.

But what do we learn from George Sand's fiction if we examine it from a similar perspective?

Seated on the edge of that bed, whose fragrant and delicate linen sent shivers through his body, he would suddenly throw himself on his knees, seeking to regain mastery over himself, and restrict himself to gazing at her. He wrapped her chastely in the embroidered muslin that protected her young bosom, so peaceful and pure; he would even pull back the curtains a little over her face so as to avoid seeing her and to find the strength to leave her. But Valentine, with the longing for fresh air characteristic of sleep, would push these obstacles away and, drawing closer to him, seemed, with a naive and confident air, to want to attract more caresses. (195)

Thus Valentine and Bénédict rehearse, under the cover of hysteria, a scene of seduction which, as the choice of the imperfect tense suggests, can be repeated ad libitum.[25] One hand pressing back and the other

24. In the next sentence Freud discusses the plastic nature of the hysterical phenomenon ("so plastically portrayed"). This "plastic quality" is indeed present in Sand's representations of her female subject in the scene of hysteria: the emotions are systematically displaced onto gestures, and the emphasis falls heavily on a "body language." David-Ménard's general remarks on this question are illumating: "What are called form and content in the plastic arts correspond to material and content in dreams and symptoms. The formal material that the hysteric uses—*movements that can describe a scene that is on display*—are the same thing as the content of the symptom: thinking of incest as possible, wanting to actualize sexual difference in a spatial order, and through the body, so as to avoid having to express it" (*Hysteria from Freud to Lacan*, 171).

25. "Assis sur le bord de cette couche dont le linge odorant et fin le faisait frissonner,

tearing off—Sand's novel presents a replica of the Freudian figure, but using two actors, a woman and a man. When, in the troping of hysteria, Sand's writing of passion represents this double scenario of "masculine" seduction and "feminine" modesty, we are faced with a representation of bisexual desire.

Sand then, just like Freud, writes here again the conventional distribution of sexual roles, where activity belongs to men and resistance and passivity to women (as late as 1908 Freud still needs to insist that hysteria can signify active seduction even for women). Not only does she represent "erotic passion" in its moods, motions, and gestures, but the initiative of the seduction is ascribed to a woman. Speaking of the confusion in sexual roles that characterizes Sand's writing in general, Mireille Bossis concludes that "the roles are interchangeable or misappropriated" (186). Sand's writing of desire can indeed break the frames of conventional representation, but not completely. Although *Valentine* expresses feminine desire, it is only with respect to the bodily sphere, as movement and sensations.

But, as the pathological turn given to "this impressionable soul which cannot follow its duties" (*Valentine*, 161) and the mise-en-scène of her mind's demise, hysteria confirms the fragility of woman's "moral" sphere, of her psyche. While she loses all consciousness, the hero is endowed, characteristically, with lucidity, knowledge, will, and mastery: he protects and defends her. She is delirious, but he remains clear-minded, conscious; he resists while she gives in; he writes down the narrative of a scene of hysteria of which she is, by definition, the unconscious actress. He knows, sees, understands, while she remains the blind victim of her *affections morales*—of the affects that invade her mental space, the locked room, the alcove. She may experience erotic sensations, but does not know of them. Valentine's hysteria is a "compromise formation"; while it endows woman with the text of a bodily passion, it ensures, in conformity with nineteenth-century models of female subjectivity, that the heroine's desire not be inscribed as knowledge and remain outside of woman's consciousness.

If indeed, as suggested by Jean-Claude Vareille, George Sand's writing results from "the never ceasing search for a middle term between sen-

---

il se jetait rapidement à genoux . . . , et il se bornait à la regarder. Il l'entourait chastement des mousselines . . . ; il ramenait même un peu le rideau sur son visage. . . . Mais Valentine . . . repoussait cet obstacle, et . . . semblait appeler ses caresses" (*Valentine*, 195). If it were meant to describe an action that occurred once only, this passage would be in the *passé simple*.

sation and knowledge" (135), we are forced to recognize that in *Valentine* this search can only be represented as the marriage of his knowledge with her sensations. More needs to be said, however, on the theme of knowledge, because it applies not merely to the represented (as the depiction of the protagonists and their actions) but also determines the scope of the representation. The question is then what is there to be seen or known in her text of the sexed body? A rhetorical reading reveals a split between discursive knowledge and a figurative enactment analogous to what we witnessed at the level of the represented. Indeed, a complex play of recognition and censorship sustains the representations and marks the author's own resistance to sexual knowledge: she sees and does not see, she knows and does not know the sexed body.[26] The hysteria that characterizes the author's writing can then no longer be overlooked; it must be examined as a revealing case history in the exploration of a feminine epistemology.

Thus from the point of view of its figurations, the alcove reveals a gendered scenario and yet expresses a denial of sexual difference. It might indeed be tempting to say, paraphrasing Naomi Schor, that *"gender* is here applied onto sameness to institute difference where difference is lacking."[27] Unlike Valentine's husband, Bénédict, the man of her dreams and the ideal of her passion, is a femininized figure deprived of phallic attributes, as is clearly shown in the following hallucinatory scene: "For an instant, she thought she could see M. de Lansac pursuing her with a sword raised in his hand; she threw herself on Bénédict's breast, and [put] her arms around his neck" (194). While Lansac thus figures as a sexual threat, Bénédict, his antidote, defends her virtue by covering her body. The "other's other" has become, in this phantasmic scene, just the same: like a woman, the hero enacts the defensive gestures of modesty; like a woman, he is castrated.[28] "He was her safeguard and defender against himself" (192): from the perspective of gender, the play of pronouns and possessives speaks tellingly of a shift away from the masculine into a feminine stance. Working "against himself" he is on

26. Here I paraphrase Zwinger's apt formulation: "the hysteric's response—I tell and don't tell you that I know and don't know what I can't and can tell" (*Daughters, Fathers, and the Novel,* 122).

27. Cf. Schor's discussion of *the difference of differences* in *George Sand and Idealism,* 145.

28. "It seems opportune now to turn to the question of the representation of the Other's other," writes Naomi Schor ("The Portrait of a Gentleman: Representing Men in (French) Women's Writing," 144).

her side, realigned in the feminine gender. If this *scène d'alcôve* is indeed, as I argue, a version of the Sandian primal scene, what it reveals is the conspicuous absence of the other sex.

But the peculiar intensities with which this scene is invested are sustained by another text, and another alcove casts its shadow over Valentine's wedding night. As she writes in her autobiography, *Histoire de ma vie*, about her "very impressionable memory," Sand remembers one of her early dreams. The little Aurore Dupin, as was her name then, is about four years old. She still sleeps in a cot, "which every night gets moved out of the alcove," and, Sand remembers, "her favorite game while going to sleep was to let her finger wander over the screen made of brass wire that was on the door of the alcove next to her bed (*Histoire de ma vie* I, 538). The main actor in this story is "a beautiful sparkling punchinello all gold and scarlet," a newly received gift. For the child, however, this toy seems, in an obscure fashion, to threaten the doll; at her urgent request, the punchinello is placed on the stove instead of being put to sleep as usual with the doll in the closet. Meanwhile, the author recalls:

I had a terrible dream during the night: the punchinello had woken up, the bump in front, dressed with a bright red waistcoat, had caught fire on the stove, and he was running around, everywhere, pursuing sometimes me and then the doll, who was running away frantically, while he would reach us with long jets of fire. I screamed so much that my mother woke up . . . the imaginary impression that I had received as a child remained for quite a while, and instead of playing with fire as had always been my passion, the mere sight of fire would strike me with terror. (I, 539)

The burning fire that terrifies the child, the threatening bump, the colorful puppet pursuing alternately the doll and the child, Aurore's nightmare—all bear unquestionably on what takes place in the alcove, and the answer provided by the dream symbolism corresponds to a castration complex: the threat of that protruding burning thing, the fear of being wounded. Indeed George Sand's account of a dream, with the dreaming child lying in its own bed, next to a screen that separates her from her mother's bedroom, gives us the elements of a primal scene offering the simultaneous revelation of the sexual act and of sexual difference.

"The fear of man," which is expressed metaphorically in *Valentine*, is thus the fictional reenactment of the author's earlier fear and goes back to a traumatic event: the terrifying husband holding his sword resembles the punchinello with its burning bump; Valentine and Bénédict fleeing from his raised sword resemble Aurore and her doll fleeing from a threatening burn. The scene of hysteria represents then, like the dream in the autobiographical narrative, a phantasmic scenario whose central concern is sexual difference. Indeed, David-Ménard's analysis of hysteria and castration in the last pages of her book strikes me as a particularly appropriate comment for Sand's representations of the primal scene, fictional and autobiographical; it has an unexpected explanatory power in relation to her writing:

One might even say that, by seeking the impossible, by seeking to represent sexual difference and thus spending her life wondering if he (or she) is a man or a woman, a hysteric is "closer" to castration than an obsessional patient, who displaces the specific question of difference toward the question of hierarchy and aggression. Freud first differentiated hysterics and obsessionals by positing that the obsessional symptoms represented the reality of a sexual experience and its prohibition, whereas hysteria would be limited to the rejection of *jouissance* in the mode of disgust. (166–67)

The repetition of the scenario of sexual fear in Sand's texts is not obsessive, but must be related, rather, to a streak of hysteria that, contrary to appearances, is present in her writing of feminine desire. Both her dream and the fiction testify to a turning away from sexual difference, to a disgust with the other sex and an unwillingness to acknowledge masculinity which can be put on a par with Dora's own famous rejection of her male suitors (*SE* VII, 28–29). Indeed hysteria does not as a rule entail a denial of desire, but rather an unwillingness or inability to conceive of desire with respect to sexual difference. Thus George Sand can write of passion, of a woman's passion, and yet never find an object, its object, outside of the solipsistic, narcissistic world of a sameness that holds sexual difference at bay.

The scene of hysteria depicted in *Valentine* is about modesty, passion, and seduction—the hand that veils being at the same time the hand that reveals. For if, on the one hand, Sand displays in her writing the sensual, bodily marks of a feminine desire and gives to the heroine a language (albeit that of madness) for her desire, she ensures on the other hand by the means of representation that the knowledge or consciousness of the sexual scenario be attributed to a masculine mind. At this point in the novel, Valentine is ambiguously the object (on a mental plane) and the subject (as a body) of passion, while the other, Bénédict, mirrors her own castration. Only the troping of hysteria, because it dissociates the mind from the body, allows then for the expression of passion in a woman. But this should not surprise us: the conformity of the Sandian representations with nineteenth-century models of sexual identity as evidenced in the texts on hysteria suggest there may be historical reasons for such a phenomenon.

The myth of a feminine modesty holds such sway in nineteenth-century representation that in a writer like Sand, woman's desire exists only in the shape of bodily symptoms while she learns, like the hysterics at Brachet's bedside, not to see the sex that makes the man. In its representations of modesty, this scene of hysteria brings together the two aspects that were explored in the medical treatises on hysteria: the familiar conception that saw in modesty an aversion to a pleasure body as well as the more elaborate model of a denial in relation to the knowledge of the sexed body—where woman's modesty was shown in her ability to close her eyes, to pretend that she had not seen, and so gloss over his masculinity. It is because Sand's text obeys the requirements of this second type of masculinity that her hero remains, even at the very heart of passion, "a ladies' man."[29]

Speculations on Difference

Examining George Sand's own vision of passion and knowledge will give us not merely a better understanding of her own writing but more general insights into writing and sexual difference. For there, as I have suggested, hysteria as the manifestation of a prohibition on sexual knowledge occupies a significant place. Indeed, as James had rightly seen, passion remains a fact or, better, a principle of George Sand's writing in spite of the difficulties and hence oblique moves and tropings that intervene in the process of representation. One of the rare passages in *Histoire de ma vie* where the writer presents a theory for her writing confirms this: "According to this theory, novels would be works of poetry as much as of analysis. True situations, true characters would be needed; they even would have to be real and should be grouped around a type destined to epitomize the main sentiment or idea of the book. This type usually represents the passion of love, since almost all novels are love stories . . . this love, and the type itself, must be idealized, and one should not be afraid of endowing it with all the powers to which one's own self aspires or with all the suffering one has seen or experi-

29. This notion appears in James's critical essay "*Daniel Deronda*: A Conversation," where it is used to depict Eliot's failure to represent a properly masculine figure; the hero is criticized for being "a ladies' man." Schor uses the term as well in her article "Portrait of a Gentleman," 114.

enced" (II, 161). The originality of Sand's conception of writing lies, as has been shown by Naomi Schor, in its idealism—the notion that representation must not strive to imitate the real, but should rather offer a symbol or figure (a "type") for an idea. Her works are not autobiographical in the narrow sense: it is not that its protagonists reflect the writer's experience, but Sand's passions get translated into the figurations of her writing, which express a desire or a suffering which has been witnessed or experienced. Thus she can claim that the origin for the idea, or the idea itself, is passion—as has been amply borne out by our examination of Sand's writing through the lens of James's criticism.

Histoire de ma vie envisages in several ways the relation between the "passion of love" and writing, but most obviously as part of the writer's intellectual development. Passion and knowledge, both related to sex, are refracted through the diverse and conflicting pedagogical models promoted by the convent, the mother, and the paternal grandmother, who all exerted their influence on the writer. On the subject of her adolescent years spent in a convent, which coincided with her first attempts at writing, Sand tells us: "The great error of a monastic education is to want to exaggerate chastity. We were not allowed to take walks in pairs, we had to be at least three; we could not kiss each other; our innocent correspondence aroused concern, and all of this would have planted ideas in our heads if we had had in ourselves the germ of those bad instincts that people suspected in us. As for myself, I know I would have been deeply hurt if I had understood the motif of these strange prescriptions" (I, 939). The defects of an education that restrained the "impulse of human affections" and kept the young girls in ignorance about sexual matters exerted a decisive influence on the writer's beginnings. As she retraces in *Histoire de ma vie* her emergent literary vocation, Sand emphasizes how incapable she felt of inventing love scenes. Even after she created Corambé, the country of her dreams and phantasies, where she would project, without ever writing them down, her imaginary fictions, the young Aurore always expressed the same feeling, devoid of erotic elements: "in this kind of enchanted world what prevailed were filial or brotherly affection, sympathy, an attraction of the purest kind" (I, 840). Meanwhile the other, less sublimated forms of love, not yet understood or deciphered (they were, the author claims, "like hieroglyphs"), are not represented: "Since I did not feel in myself anything that could have explained why a creature could develop an exclusive attachment to another, in this order of unknown affections which were so to speak like hieroglyphs, I was careful not to carry my novel onto a terrain that remained frozen to my imagination" (I, 839). Aurore Dupin began to write fiction while still at the convent, and her mother, Sophie, read her work and suggested that she try writing about love: "On Sophie's advice, I had decided to lead them to the experience of love; but when I got to that point, when I had described them both as beautiful and perfect, in an enchanting spot, at sunset, at the entrance of a gothic chapel under the shade of imposing oaks, I still found myself incapable of depicting love's first emotions. It wasn't in me; not a word came . . . the damsel became a nun and the hero, a priest" (I, 940). Thus, even as she sketches her first novels, Aurore feels incapable of representing passion: "it was always a fiction that stood outside of me and that I felt I could not paint." "Nothing prevents you from inventing what you do not know," Béatrice Didier echoes, and she concludes that the autobiography appears "to account for a hidden mechanism of prohibition" ("Femme—identité—écriture," 570). Indeed, the scene of hysteria in *Valentine* shows that even though the fiction begins with "a sentiment or an idea" devoid of moral claims, the originary prohibition does not vanish. The Sandian novel can represent the "sentiment of sex" and its idealization, but not, Sand herself claims, with "la vérité de la peinture" (II, 161). My initial historical, contextual reading of the scene has shown how Sand's fictional representations remain aligned within the conventions of sexual identity and abide by the prohibitions that, in Sand's days, bore on the expression of a feminine sensuality or desire. The rhetorical and Freudian reading has revealed, on the other hand, a narcissistic scenario where the masculine other is abolished and the love scene is represented as a mirroring of feminine desire, of a desire whose object is fantasized but not acknowledged in its otherness. The prohibition on passion seems to have loosened its hold since passion can now be represented figuratively. In its place, however, we find another prohibition that bears this time on the knowledge of sexual difference. What the alcove reveals then is not only a "passionate denial" of the other but an inherently narcissistic self-sufficiency.[30]

But why look so insistently for sexual difference or for representations of masculinity in fiction written, after all, by a woman writer? Why not be content to say that all writing is inherently narcissistic? The answer is found in the Freudian model which establishes that progress toward knowledge, and hence the subject's intellectual development, necessarily

---

30. "Un refus passionné" is, as Ned Lukacher shows in the foreword to David-Ménard's book, a key notion in her project: "This characterization of hysterical disgust as 'a passionate denial' stands at the heart of *Hysteria from Freud to Lacan* as well, for it describes the desiring energy, the force, the nonsubjective, nonpsychological will that compels the subject onto the field of jouissance and maintains her there" (xvi).

depends on a prior recognition of sexual difference: the recognition of such a primal, originary otherness constitutes the indispensable premise of an epistemophilic drive that will henceforth lead the subject in his or her quest for knowledge. In other words, entrapment in the narcissistic libidinal economy of hysteria ensures, as Irigaray writes, that "woman's self remains largely unconscious": "the hysteric's self is fragile, splintered, always risks exploding, bursting, and has only a fleeting, tenuous relation with consciousness" (108–9). If the woman writer is trapped in the narcissistic circle of her hysteria, she may never create, invent representations other than those that are dictated by the conventions of a sexual identity, and particularly those that bind the female subject to a fateful repetition of ignorance and passivity in the name of rigid sexual differences.

Another last critical glance at *Valentine* and at Sand's autobiography should offer a local, more specific answer to this theoretical questioning. For indeed, while in her fiction George Sand turns insistently around sexual difference, in her autobiography she faces more squarely, on a few occasions, her own understanding of sexual difference and by implication sexuality. The question I raise here is thus not simply the result of my own modern feminist awareness, it was addressed long ago by George Sand in or rather through her writing.

Masculinity is represented, or at least acknowledged, in one scene in *Valentine* which connects an erotic discovery to specularity by bringing together the heroine and the hero on a riverbank.[31] This scene is constructed in a fashion similar to the encounter between Pulchérie and Lélia, and yet it differs in two significant ways: its two protagonists are a woman and a man, and it turns away, in a typical gesture of modesty, from the decisive revelation.[32] It deserves close attention because it highlights so sharply, in its narrative progression, the moment of veiling, the abrupt assumption of the prohibition that makes for the hysteria of Sand's writing.

As Valentine seems totally absorbed in her daydreaming and unwittingly loses herself in contemplation of the man she loves, she recognizes in Bénédict "a man with a manly breast, which could be throbbing with a violent passion." The word *un homme*, repeated four times, is here unquestionably gendered and denotes masculinity, just like the physical traits highlighted in the description. As if to dispel any misunderstand-

---

31. In "George Sand, la rêverie et la vision transformante," Marcel Raymond analyzes in a more general way the relation between water and specularity (198–200).

32. My commentary bears on pages 108–16 of *Valentine*.

ing, the narrative voice adds: "in her husband, Valentine had never seen the man." Indeed the emphasis on sensuous elements in Valentine's vision of Bénédict sketches out a body that is unmistakably erotic and masculine: the hair is "in disarray," "the neck naked and sunburnt," his posture appears careless. Carried away in her musing, Valentine responds to his "masculine otherness" which, writes Sand, "sets throbbing the ignorant and pure heart of the young countess." Her blood, seized with "magnetic emanations" and "mysterious emotions . . . was gradually aroused." Unlike the later scene in the alcove, which celebrates Valentine's unconsciousness and figures her erotic arousal as hysteria, the heroine is in this instance endowed with the ability to see her lover; she is neither estranged from herself in a hallucination nor is she the object of the hero's gaze. In other words, this scene represents for a brief interval the convergence of erotic feeling and the consciousness of sexual difference. Thus the heterosexual plot that constitutes the idea or "ideal" behind this particular fiction emerges for once fully if only briefly.

But this is true only for a short spell. The heroine's vision is soon troubled, she reverts to ignorance—"the ignorant girl did not understand what troubled her so"—and, with characteristic feminine modesty, she turns her gaze away. The young woman has learned not to see: "Benedict and Valentine, totally unaware, remained alone on the bank, a few steps away from each other. Valentine remained seated pretending to play with the daisies. Bénédict, lying on the grass, kept pressing a burning handkerchief to his brow, his neck, his chest, and was looking at Valentine with a gaze whose fire she could feel *without daring to look*" (115, emphasis mine). The scene by the water, which could have signified transparency, enlightenment, knowledge, shows now a benumbing and a clouding over of the mind. As a screen that, as well as rendering the lovers' perception of each other less immediate, creates the necessary distance for perception, the water of that river could have mirrored their consciousness of each other as a man and a woman. And in fact it does so, but only fleetingly and in a fractured way: the counterpart to the first image, where Bénédict gazes at Valentine, occurs belatedly, in the bedroom scene: "Bénédict stood beside her, with even more liberty to contemplate her than when he had adored her image reflected in the water" (192). For while in Rousseau's famous "Cinquième promenade" the reverie by the water leads to a recentering of the self and creates consciousness, in Sand's writing, on the contrary, it initiates a drift into unconsciousness and signifies ultimately the heroine's dispossession and alienation. She is impelled by a feeling she does not know and driven by a power that escapes her, which is described as a "fluid" or as "magnetism." Indeed, in George Sand's writing, the confrontation with sexuality and sexual difference creates such blindnesses: in her representations, gender and consciousness can only exclude each other.

In the third part of *Histoire de ma vie* titled "De l'enfance à la jeunesse," which is shaped like a Bildungsroman, Sand writes about the education given to young girls and specifically about sexual knowledge. Mentioning "the eternal attraction held by the mystery of her emotions," she adds, in the form of a note and using again water as a metaphor:

This attraction for mystery is not a phenomenon that is peculiar to my own organization. Let all the mothers recall their childhood, which they too easily forget when they raise their daughters. This state of the soul that searches itself is inherent to childhood and particularly to women's childhood. One should neither brutally counter this inclination nor allow it to develop excessively. I have seen mothers, whose surveillance was indelicate and jealous, always suspecting some impurity in their daughters' chaste daydreams, and they have thrown stones or filth in this quiet and pure lake, which still reflected only the sky. I have seen others that would let all the dirt fall in from outside without the slightest suspicion. It is truly difficult and sometimes impossible to see the bottom of those still waters, and this is why one should not worry too much about it [c'est à cause de cela qu'on ne saurait trop s'en préoccuper]. (I, 811)

The abrupt and ambiguous ending of this passage, untranslatable because of its radical ambiguity,[33] performs, indeed mimes the very thing it describes, namely, the interruption of thought, the relinquishing of a particular reflection. This phenomenon, related to the thinking mind, is a manifestation of hysteria: "hysterical theatricalization, the conversion of the conceptual into a display by way of a linguistic pirouette that suddenly subjectivizes the 'rigor' of a development, would be one version of hysterical metaphor, in the field of discursive practices," David-Ménard writes (166). Sand's note reveals not so much a linguistic pirouette, as the philosopher would have it, but rather a kind of letting go, an "abandonment" of thought to the errancies of language. Supposing that at a certain stage of her development, of the growth of her consciousness, the young girl ceases to see only the purer reaches of the sky. What is it she sees? What is she looking for? How does the passage from

33. The most recently published translation of Sand's *Histoire* says: "It is certainly difficult, at times almost impossible, to see to the bottom of those still waters, and for this very reason they deserve our constant attention" (*Story of My Life*, 1130). From a grammatical point of view, the two meanings are equally possible. Only a rhetorical emphasis, perceptible when the text is voiced, would mark one or the other possibility.

chastity and purity take place? If the young feminine soul is like still water, what is it that lies dormant, what knowledge? Pondering this "introspective consciousness" that seems to characterize girls above all, Sand raises implicitly the question of its object. But she does not identify let alone name the object of the girl's curiosity.

Furthermore, only the emphasis of a speaking voice, which by definition is absent from writing, would make it possible to distinguish between the two possibilities of meaning that the grammar permits here. Does the concluding statement mean that "one should not care too much about these things" or rather that "one never cares enough"? While the preceding statement, with its emphasis on the difficulty or even impossibility of the task, suggests that one should stop worrying, the theme of this note—that mothers should take care of their daughter's developing minds—suggests the very opposite. Such a passage, whose central concern is still women's pursuit of knowledge, performs what it thematizes, the impossibility of knowledge: the bottomless mystery cannot be unveiled for it undoes itself, vanishes in the pursuit. The Sandian narrative anticipates here in an uncanny fashion the figurations Virginia Woolf employs when she speaks in *Professions for Women* about the prohibition that bears on woman's writing: "Her imagination had rushed away. It had sought the pools, the depths, the dark places where the largest fish slumber. And then there was a smash. There was an explosion. There was foam and confusion. The imagination had dashed itself against something hard. The girl was roused from her dream. She was indeed in a state of the most acute and difficult distress. To speak without figure, she had thought of something, something about the body, about the passions which it was unfitting for her as a woman to say" (quoted from Gilbert and Gubar, 1387). In both instances, probing into the depth of still water—the modern metaphor for reflection or speculation—leads the writer to a stumbling block, an insurmountable obstacle. And she, the writer or thinker, renounces because she is faced with an impossibility of thought, of writing.[34]

But to come back to Sand, our case history and, as James calls her, "our precious text book." This example shows again her awareness, or rather (for how can we tell that she knows, since she performs in her writing the very absence of knowledge that she represents or thematizes?) her compliance with the law of gender which casts a veil over

---

34. While Woolf speaks of a failure of expression, I am tempted to claim, in narrowing the margin between thinking and writing, that the phenomenon described is not only of the same order, but truly the same. By not writing, Woolf's fisherwoman stops thinking.

woman's self-reflexive knowledge. While this prohibition determined the hysterical representations of her fiction (there the female subject's experience and knowledge could only be dissociated), it is endorsed as well in Sand's autobiographical note, where thinking stops short in front of the body. The writer herself acknowledges in other parts of her Bildungsroman that she too often, too easily has let the veil fall over her mind and has thus renounced knowledge. "I shall die in the thick cloud which surrounds and oppresses me. I have torn it only for brief moments" (II, 303), she declares peremptorily at the end of *Histoire de ma vie*.

Sand also reveals in her autobiography the point of origin of this *via negativa* and the cause that led to this "choice" of not looking, not asking, not wishing to know. The interdiction on sexual knowledge was issued, characteristically, by Aurore Dupin's aristocratic grandmother (her father's mother and the rival to Sophie, Sand's mother), and, also characteristically, its impulse is moral outrage. Falling from the lips of the woman who stands on the father's side, the prohibition begins with the revelation that Aurore's mother is a fallen woman—*une femme perdue*. Led to believe that her beloved mother is doomed irrevocably because of some mysterious unspeakable sin, the child now experiences her existence differently. Here again, the image of water is summoned to describe a troubled consciousness: "Life began to flow again like a quiet stream, but for me the stream was now troubled and I no longer looked into it" (I, 858).[35] No explanations are given, the initiation into the secrets of sexual life is denied the child, and, Sand writes, she is left with "a painful enigma about which nobody had wanted to speak a word." Such is the traumatic force of the unexplained that it casts an undefinable, irremovable veil over the child's whole mental existence and that it throws the shadow of a spiritual death: "I tried to live without thinking about anything, without fear and without desire" ("J'essayai de vivre sans songer à rien, sans rien craindre et sans rien désirer" [I, 860]). The repeated *rien* speaks vividly of the negation entailed by this new life.

Later, in a moment of crisis, Aurore, by now a young woman, is tempted by suicide:

This temptation was sometimes so strong, so sudden, so bizarre that I could well see that I was sick with some kind of madness. It would take the form of an *idée fixe* and came close at times to a monomania. It was water above all that attracted me like a mysterious spell. My only walks would be along the

35. "Trouble," *troublé*, a frequent word in Sand's vocabulary, is often endowed in French with sexual connotations. Thus the very figures used to describe the denial of sexual knowledge go back, uncannily, to the body.

river, and as I no longer thought of looking for pleasant spots, I would follow it without thinking until I found a deep place. . . . I could then no longer tear myself away from the bank, as soon as I had defined my purpose I would gradually say to myself: "Yes" or "No?" so often and for so long that I risked being thrown in by the "yes" to the bottom of that transparent water that hypnotized me. (I, 1095–96)

The water here is neither troubled nor still, for it is meant to save, to purify, and to give rest to her mind. But it is still that mysterious element which contains the elusive significations, the inarticulate perceptions, and the denied knowledge which constitute, according to Sand, a woman's identity. "Woman is, generally, a nervous and restless creature, who transmits to me in spite of myself, some eternal unrest (*trouble*) which bears on everything," George Sand wrote by way of a preface to her friendship with Marie Dorval. Meditating on the "contempt" in which "dear Montaigne held her sex," she attempts to define what makes her strength ("my willpower had become used to often dominating nature's weaknesses"), and she also denounces her weaknesses: "I was then not quite a woman like those that the moralists censure and mock; I had in my soul enthusiasm for beauty, thirst for truth, and yet I was after all a woman like all the others, sickly, nervous, dominated by my imagination, childishly susceptible to tender feelings and to the worries of maternity. Would this relegate me to a secondary rank in the creation and in the family? . . . *I do not doubt that woman is different from man, that heart and mind have a sex. The opposite will always be an exception*" (II, 126–27, emphasis mine).

Illness, imagination, affections, maternity: only the most conventional views on female identity emerge from Sand's apology for woman. The only claim the author makes in the course of her discussion is to state that the difference between the sexes cannot justify "a moral inferiority." Indeed, in her moments of depression, in her nervousness and headaches, she all too easily returns to the fold, despite the myths that saw her as a conquering Amazon.[36] George Sand's entry into the adult world of morality and *pudeur* was marked indelibly, it seems, by her grandmoth-

36. For, as I showed in the introduction to Chapter 1, Sand says elsewhere, "il n'y a qu'un sexe," expressing a conviction that stands in absolute contradiction to the belief, stated here, in a sexual identity. I take these waverings in her thoughts, on the question What is a woman? which after all seems to have preoccupied her throughout her life, to be another sign of her tendency to relinquish thinking, which enables her to endorse, even if only superficially, the conventions of gender.

er's oracular pronouncement: she was the strongest, most respected of censors, bringing her voice to what was, after all, a cultural imperative. The scene of hysteria in *Valentine* goes back to such a beginning: it preserves the appearances of pudor; it casts its veil over the troubling, impure consciousness of a sexed body. The heroine is therefore merely a figure for the author's knowing ignorance.

These readings of *Valentine* and of some key passages in *Histoire de ma vie* have shown well enough how Sand's writing disavows sexual difference, although she was sometimes only too willing to hold to the belief of sexual identities. In her fiction, passion or desire are insistently represented—this James had known from the beginning—and what remains impossible, except for one brief moment, is the representation of sex as the fact of difference. The hysteria that marks Sand's work designates then this thing for which neither thoughts nor words can be found: the subject's insertion in sexuality. "I did not look for the word of the sphinx" (I, 859)—the words that mark in Sand's autobiography the watershed between childhood innocence and an unhappy consciousness resonate significantly with Freud's own words concerning the mystery of sexuality. He indeed refers to the subject's questioning about his or her origin (Where do children come from?) and identity (the question of the difference between the sexes) as the "riddle of the sphinx."[37] It is not that Sand did not know the answer to these questions, but rather that, like the hysterical women of Brachet's tale, she did not want to seem to want to know: she too closed her eyes and glossed over the difference. As the prisoner of this willed ignorance, George Sand may have believed that she justified and salvaged in her mind a desirable female identity. But this surely also defines the limits and the limitations of her writing. She was, after all, condemning that mind, in spite of its love for beauty and truth, to dwell in a philosopher's limbo. Reading the words of Julia Kristeva, one might think George Sand had missed, but only narrowly, by the breadth of that hysterical negation, becoming a "creator of speculative fictions."[38] "In fact, Narcissus was not wholly

37. Freud himself uses this phrase in *Three Essays on the Theory of Sexuality* (*SE* VII, 195–96) and *Introductory Lectures on Psycho-Analysis* (*SE* XVI, 318).

38. On the subject of Sand and philosophy, see Schor's discussion in *George Sand and Idealism*, 77–81, as well as 233, n. 37. My conclusions, which differ from Schor's, depend on a different conception of philosophy, but also on a different approach to this question. While I have tried to gauge Sand's "abilities" as a feminist philosopher by examining her writing, Schor has chosen to discuss Sand's feminist ideas or theories as expressed, for instance, in her *Lettres à Marcie*.

deprived of an object. Narcissus's object is the space of the psyche; it is representation itself and fantasy. But he does not know it and he dies. If he knew, he would be an intellectual, the creator of speculative fictions, an artist, a writer, a psychologist, a psychonanalyst. He would be Plotinus or Freud" (*Histoires d'amour*, 148).

CHAPTER SIX

"Girls and Their Blind Visions": George Eliot, Hysteria, and History

> What in the midst of that mighty drama are girls and their blind
> visions? They are the Yea or Nay of that good for which men are
> enduring and fighting. In these delicate vessels is borne onward
> through the ages the treasure of human affection.
>
> —George Eliot, *Daniel Deronda*

The scandal and transgression associated with George Sand's name lie
for the nineteenth century not so much in her works, where in spite of
certain "confusions" morality is preserved, as in the apparent immorality
of her existence. In her pretensions to virtue, Valentine outdoes her creator: Sand's realism endows her heroines with more conformism than
the author herself ever achieved. Our archcritic, meanwhile, seems to
pursue with a certain *frisson historique* the story of the woman whose
"life . . . at its most active may fairly be described as an immunity from
restrictive instincts more ably cultivated than any we know" ("George
Sand," in *Literary Criticism*, 787). What ultimately draws Henry James's
most passionate interests is the story of Sand's passions, because it
speaks of the forbidden, of the extraordinary, and to borrow one of his
images, of "soiled linen." The phase "soiled linen" belongs to his theory
of representation which links Sand to Zola; it appears again as the critic
greets the publication of her biography: "a tub of soiled linen which the
muse of history, rolling her sleeves well up, has not even yet quite begun
energetically and publicly to wash."[1] The figure shows James making
the distinction between the clean and the dirty; what it does not reveal,
however, is the fascination, the thrill—the frisson—that the spectacle of
such corruption held for James. That fascination is expressed in a letter

---

1. James, "George Sand," in *Literary Criticism*, 741; the letter is quoted by Leon Edel,
The Life of Henry James II, 313–34.

to Edith Wharton in which he remembers their joint visit to Nohant, Sand's home: "that wondrous day when we explored the very scene where they pigged so thrillingly together. What a crew, what *moeurs*, what habits, what conditions and relations every way—and what an altogether mighty and marvellous George, not diminished by all the greasiness and smelliness in which she made herself (and so many other persons!) at home" (James and Wharton, 215). Or, differently, in the writerly glee with which the critic plays, in his 1897 essay, with sexual innuendo: "nothing is more striking than their convulsive effort either to reach up to it or to do without it. They would have given for it all else they possessed, but they only met in their struggle the inexorable *never*. They strain and pant and gasp, they beat the air in vain for the cup of cold water in their hell" (*Literary Criticism*, 745) or, later, not mincing his words: "so much publicity and palpability of 'heart,' so much experience reduced only to the terms of so many more or less greasy males" (773). Dirt, the impure, the immorality, all of this in the woman's quarters, when she should have been responsible for the rituals of purification. "Die quälende Reinmacherei der Mama"—these are Freud's words describing the mania for cleanliness that characterized Dora's mother (*SE* VII, 90). Indeed, in the shadow of Dora's involvement in the sexual traffic of fin-de-siècle Vienna, stands her mother, the instrument, martyr, and telling emblem of the nineteenth-century ideal of feminine purity.[2] Zola regularly fell in love with *blanchisseuses*, which, as James might have said, shows his fascination with dirty linen, or else his need for redemption.[3]

But enough of these scenarios of passion and perversion. This last incursion into Jamesian territory is intended above all to provide a context—the underside—for a discussion of a writer whom the nineteenth century would have singled out precisely for "her restrictive instincts" and dispassionate intellect. In *The Bostonians*, George Eliot makes an appearance as a deity presiding over woman's intellectual pursuits—a picture on the wall of the female academy gathered in Cape Cod. The

2. In the words of Freud: "I never made her mother's acquaintance. From the accounts given me by the girl and her father, I was led to imagine her as an uncultivated woman and above all as a foolish one, who had concentrated all her interests upon domestic affairs. . . . She presented the picture, in fact, of what might be called the 'housewife's psychosis'" (*SE* VII, 20).

3. The detour through the German text shows more palpably what is at stake in such figurations, namely an attempt to project onto woman the burden of reinstating a pristine purity (of the kind invoked in the concept of pudicity [*pudicité*]). It is not merely a question of cleaning, but of purifying and making white, as is conveyed so well by the French term for laundresses: *blanchisseuses*.

dying Miss Birdseye, the skeptical "doctoress" Prance, Verena, and Olive (who like Eliot reads avidly the German philosophers) have taken up cloistered quarters to prepare Verena for her great public appearance at the Boston Music Hall. Olive has brought her lares: the complete works of George Eliot and—twice—the image of the Virgin: "Olive had taken her cottage furnished, but . . . the paucity of chairs was such that their little party used almost to sit down, to lie down in turn. On the other hand they had all George Eliot's writings, and two photographs of the Sistine Madonna" (344). Here James alludes teasingly to George Eliot's well-known admiration for Raphael's painting. These then are, in James's (satirical?) conception, the ornaments and effigies that adorn the altar of female knowledge. But there may be more truth than appears in this fictional play. While Olive's admiration for Eliot and the Virgin directs our gaze at Eliot's admiration for the Virgin, it also conjures up the image of Dora held in passionate absorption before the picture of the Madonna at the Dresden Museum, and even of Sand's Valentine praying to the Virgin in her private chapel. What emerges repeatedly from our nineteenth-century readings is a tableau—the woman gazing at the Virgin—which is like the matrix around which desire, knowledge, femininity, and moral purity find their articulation. And this tableau must be remembered as the emblem and memento of a scene of hysteria, whose actress is a woman.

Here then, briefly, is the account, according to George Eliot's biographers and critics, of another scene of hysteria.[4] In 1858, George Eliot spends six weeks in Dresden with her companion, George Henry Lewes. This is her second trip to Germany following what to her friends and acquaintances appeared to be a scandalous elopement: on the July 20, 1854, Mary Ann Evans had traveled to Weimar, semiclandestinely, with Lewes, a married man and father of a large family. During her second stay in Germany, she goes to the Dresden Museum almost daily, and on each visit pays homage to the Virgin, lingering for a long time in front of Raphael's Sistine Madonna. "Vor der Madonna verweilte sie zwei Stunden lang in still träumender Bewunderung," (she remained *two hours* in front the Sistine Madonna, rapt in silent admiration [*SE* VII, 96]), writes Freud about Dora's visit to the Dresden Museum; and his prose is infused here with phonemic patterns as if he had to convey his own writerly rapture in front of this tableau of femininity. For, it seems,

4. See in particular Mary Jacobus, "*Dora* and the Pregnant Madonna," in *Reading Woman: Essays in Feminist Criticism.* The rapprochement she establishes between Eliot and Dora greatly helped my own understanding of these instances of hysterical admiration.

while women admire the Virgin, men admire the picture of a woman "rapt in silent dreamy admiration" of the Virgin. Thus in the case of George Eliot and G. H. Lewes: "All other art seems only a preparation for the feeling of superiority of the madonna di San Sisto," she writes in a letter, and in her diary: "I sat down on the sofa opposite the picture for an instant, but a sort of awe, as if I were suddenly in the presence of some glorious being, made my heart swell too much for me to remain comfortably, and we hurried out of the room." Meanwhile, in his own diary, Lewes writes about his own contemplations of the Virgin and mentions his hysteria (the result of identification maybe, for it seems to answer Eliot's own "swelling of the mother"): "I looked at the Raphael Madonna di San Sisto, till I felt quite hysterical."[5]

The veneration for the Virgin—which creates an unmistakable resemblance between the Jamesian and the Sandian heroines as well as between George Eliot and Dora—speaks of a desire for purity and of knowledge made of guilt. Always already fallen, the hysteric gazes passionately at the figure of a femininity that, in spite of its involvement in biological, bodily sexuality, has remained pure, serene, intact. For she has learned that while guilt should always be inscribed in the woman's body (unless her sex be hallowed by the marriage sacrament and destined to procreation), when it comes to her soul, redemption, as a return to an original purity, is impossible. This is the knowledge recounted in George Eliot's *Daniel Deronda*, in the story of Gwendolen Harleth: its theme, treated in the tragic mode, is "the growth of [a woman's] conscience." Henry James's words concerning the heroine remind us aptly that her story might profitably be envisaged from the perspective of hysteria: "The universe forcing itself with a slow, inexorable pressure into a narrow, complacent, and yet after all extremely sensisitive mind, and making it ache with the pain of the process" ("*Daniel Deronda*: A Conversation," 990). Indeed, hysteria shows that (or explains why) against all intentions and desires, Eliot's narrative, whose originary impulse goes toward the representation of the "consciousness of a girl," ends up sacrificing the heroine to the rituals of conscience. "After all," writes Catherine Clément, "hysteria is the simplest of solutions, for to hold oneself in a state of permanent guilt is to constitute oneself as a subject" (*La jeune née*, 90). The following pages chart across Eliot's novel the path of an ethical and textual choice, that is, of a discourse, in which woman

5. Eliot's remarks are quoted from *George Eliot Letters* II, 471–72 and from J. W. Cross, *George Eliot's Life* II, 58. Lewes's words are quoted in a note by Gordon Haight (*Letters* II, 472n). These passages are discussed by Jacobus, *Reading Woman*.

is shaped through a process of sublimation so as to embody, in her very hysteria, the harrowing pains of a conscience and beyond, a subjectivity whose characteristic mark is a state of expectancy and of suffering that is best described in the French expression *un être en souffrance*. From this perspective, Gwendolen's story becomes the nineteenth-century allegory of, and for all the waiting women, of all those whose story or history holds as yet only the promise of another beginning.

Woman as Spectacle

Daniel Deronda opens with an insistent peal of questions:

Was she beautiful or not beautiful? and what was the secret of form or expression which gave the dynamic quality to her glance? Was the good or the evil genius dominant in those beams? Probably the evil; else why was the effect that of unrest rather than of undisturbed charm? Why was the wish to look again felt as coercion and not as a longing in which the whole being consents? (3)

Framed in the hero's mind, these questions set the tone for the aesthetic, epistemological, and moral examination of the heroine. George Sand's *Lélia* starts with a similar set of questions:

"Who are you? and why is it that your love causes so much evil? There must be in you some terrible mystery unknown to men. Surely you are not a creature made of the same clay and inspired with the same life as we are! You are an angel or a demon, but you are not a human creature. Why hide from us your nature and your origin? Why live among us, if we are found lacking and we cannot understand you. If you come from God, speak, and we shall adore you. If you come from hell . . . You, from hell! You, so beautiful and so pure!. . . . And yet, Lélia, there is in you something infernal. Your bitter smile belies the celestial promises of your glance." (3)

Indeed, whether as a conscious imitation or not, Eliot's novel begins where Sand began in 1832, with the question of woman. While it might have been interesting to pursue a comparison between the two texts to examine, for instance, how in both texts the conventions of narration break down under the pressures of such a question, my purpose here is more limited.[6] If I quote *Lélia*, it is in the interest of historical accuracy,

6. "I would suggest that a good many late nineteenth-century texts can profitably be called premodernist and hysterical, that as symptomatic narratives, they articulate the problematics of sexual difference, a difference challenged in great part by nineteenth-

to show how, with such a beginning, Eliot's novel seemingly abides by a traditional mode of representation: a woman is on display, her identity is put into question, and the gender of the viewer is predictable. In *Lélia* it is the poet Sténio who voices these questions. *Daniel Deronda* begins more subtly: the absence of quotation marks turns them into free indirect speech which typically enables the merging of the voice of narrator and protagonist. This ambiguity is resolved, however, at the beginning of the second paragraph, which begins, "She who raised these questions in Daniel Deronda's mind." The gaze is thus clearly identified as masculine, while the spectacle, inevitably, is that of woman.

The first paragraph sets the stage for a specularization of the heroine that constitutes a steady and easily identifiable strand in the whole novel. Gwendolen can be said to "exist" as surface projection of the images held in the gaze (and in the mind) of the men who shape her destiny: Deronda, Klesmer, Grandcourt, and a more undifferentiated group (made up of Mallinger, Gascoigne, and their likes). In this system of representation, the masculine gaze holds an overdetermined position: her image is sustained by those several men who observe and judge her, the unknown woman, the mystery. The novel produces, however, its hierarchy of gazes: while Deronda holds the highest position in this scale, the lowest level is occupied by those who, like Gascoigne, pronounce on "what maidens and wives are likely to know, do and suffer, having had a most imperfect observation of the particular maiden and wife in question" (*Daniel Deronda*, 704). Three types of gaze come into prominence, and they determine the heroine's *Bildung*: the hero's knowing and sympathetic gaze, Klesmer's aesthetic assessment (she is for him "a bit of *plastik*"), and Grandcourt's gaze of erotic possession and domination. Here *Bildung* means literally "shaping"; the multiple gaze bearing upon the woman seems to determine her outward shape. From a thematic perspective, the heroine's Bildungsroman, as her outward history, is clearly "male-authored": read for her actions, her acts, and for the way in which her body moves across time and space, Gwendolen is not more and not less than passive feminine matter moulded by the different perspectives of a masculine vision.

In this structure, Daniel holds a privileged position: "his grave and

___

century feminism," Kahane writes suggestively ("Hysteria, Feminism, and the Case of *The Bostonians*," 286). Indeed we should not be surprised that the narrative conventions break down under the pressure of a questioning, which, as I tried to show in Chapter 4, challenges the conventional epistemological frames. But *Lélia* more than *Daniel Deronda* generally subverts the generic conventions of the novel.

penetrating gaze" (302), "his activity of imagination on behalf of others" (162), and his general interest in female pathos ("those tragedies of the copse or hedgerow" [172]) designate him as an avatar of the perspicuous nineteenth-century moral doctor. The epigraph to the second chapter tellingly evokes the ghost of a Briquet who claimed he could, by the force of this gaze, tame or heal his hysterical patients. It announces too Freud's "keen, probing eyes" and his "piercing gaze" (Gay, 156–57, 613).

> This man contrives a secret 'twixt us two,
> That he may quell me with his meeting eyes
> Like one who quells a lioness at bay.
> (Daniel Deronda, 11)

The emphasis on a specular mode of knowing and of narrating the subject, so present in Eliot's novel, belongs to a pre-Freudian epistemology. Reading *Daniel Deronda* from the perspective of representation, it seems that the shift from gaze to voice, from the visual observation of the subject to the dialectic of narration and reconstruction that characterizes psychoanalysis is still to come. The notion that to see is to know, the idea that truth can be extracted from visible phenomena and that the gaze can be the finest instrument of intellectual mastery are some of the epistemological claims that this text tries to sustain.[7] Indeed, the femme fatale who figures at the center of *Daniel Deronda* ends up appearing to us modern readers as a forerunner of the heroines we are used to seeing in classical cinema. The fascination exerted by the feminine has had such a lasting hold on representation that, from Lélia to the modern actress, the woman as "icon: an image to be looked at by the spectator" (de Lauretis, 139) and as the object of endless interrogations, projections, and phantasies has undergone countless incarnations.[8]

The heroine inevitably occupies, to slip into Stanley Cavell's discourse about cinema, the focal point of the camera; she is that around which

7. The limits of this epistemology of the visible are shown in the episode of Grandcourt's death, where the meaning of Gwendolen's action (who throws the rope a little too late to save her husband) cannot be subsumed under its outward appearance. Thus Deronda's unresolved, unanswered question: "And it has all remained in your imagination. It has gone on only in your thought. To the last the evil temptation has been resisted?" (*Daniel Deronda*, 644). The narrator probes this question as s/he discusses the heroine's desire (648–49).

8. For a particularly enlightening discussion of this topic, see Doane, "Veiling over Desire."

the spectacle turns.[9] Yet from the very beginning, Gwendolen's "iridescence" (36) challenges this structure: her aspect changes and, like a reflector, her image diffracts and refracts the look that tries to see her as one stable image. While she is endowed with an aura that draws the gaze to that which stands on the other side of the visible, the essential instability of her image signals that appearances might be deceptive. Her "iridescence" thus reinforces the suspicion that the first, strongly polarized questioning might have aroused: there may be more to this woman than meets the eye; vision, in the case of Gwendolen, cannot guarantee "epistemological certitude" (Doane, 107).

But the uncertainties that the representation of Gwendolen provokes do not merely derive from the changeable, unpredictable qualities of this "iridescent" object. As several critics have shown, *Daniel Deronda* reveals, when it comes to representing the heroine, a problem with the language of fiction which not even metaphor can solve.[10] If the specular image does not in fact give the "truth" about what is represented, the logical move would be to give representation an inward turn. One could indeed imagine that metaphors could be found that would render legible what the images hide or cannot say.[11] But at this point the narrator's critical stance, who speaks for "girls with their blind visions," and the general philosophical prejudice best known through Nietzsche's maxim that "woman closes her eyes to herself" seem to stand in the way of such a representation.[12] If girls are blind, and moreover only seem to know themselves as surfaces reflected in the gaze of the other, then to represent, even metaphorically, the substance that lies behind the surface becomes impossible. To enter the heroine's mind is, as the narrator claims repeatedly, to remain in the realm of appearances. Her mind is haunted by the ghostly and the phantasmal, and the questions raised at the beginning cannot be answered by another visual spectacle which would offer a truer vision of Gwendolen, one that would drive inward and provide a psychological anatomy of this particular woman. And yet,

9. See Stanley Cavell's discussion of the genre, which he calls, in "Naughty Orators: Negation of Voice in *Gaslight*," the "melodrama of the unknown woman" (340).

10. Richard Freadman in particular emphasizes George Eliot's "interest in the powers and limitations of language" and the "semiotic concern" perceptible in her novel (*Eliot, James and the Fictional Self*, 63–64). See also William Myers, *The Teaching of George Eliot*, 224–25; and Elizabeth Ermath, *George Eliot*, 129–30.

11. Here we might be faced with a case of anasemia—an irreducible difference of nature between what the figure might say and what it is destined to describe. On this question see Derrida's "Me-Psychoanalysis."

12. The phrase is quoted by Doane, "Veiling over Desire," 123. See also the last section of Chapter 1 where I raise the question of woman's blindness to herself.

as Jacqueline Rose argues, "it is the dramatic staging, the spectacle itself to which the story seems ineluctably to return" (107). One could add that the spectacle threatens to engulf the process, if not the very possibility, of narration.

Indeed, the narrative voice ultimately fails to compensate for what the original investment in specular representation entailed, namely, a loss of inner vision or of psychological depths and shadings. There is then much that remains unsaid and unspoken, and also unknown, in this novel. But this is precisely where my interest begins, with the sense that the silences of Eliot's text are not empty, but rather that they demand to be read. The hold that the figure of Gwendolen has on the readers' imagination may well originate in our subliminal realization that there is much about her that calls for interpretation. This is where a new aspect of the fictions of hysteria comes to the fore.

Reversing the Gaze

From a narratological perspective, the several scenes of hysteria represented in the novel constitute spectacular instances of the predominance of representation over writing and voice, since they essentially rely on the violence and shock value of the image, as against the capacity of language to chart cohesive explanations or expressive descriptions of a subjectivity. Free indirect speech, for instance, is conspicuously absent in these scenes, while the words of direct speech (when they are not merely screams) are endowed with a phatic quality that places them almost beyond meaning: the narrator presents a description but seems to have lost all didactic or interpretative powers. The urge toward expression seems to override the ability to express. Like the reader, the narrative voice is faced with the notorious illegibility of hysteria, and this inevitably affects our reading: the sense-making process is brought to a halt by the sudden irruption of a spectacle. The scene of hysteria is a form of melodrama where the representation focuses on the body at the expense of the inner registrations of thought or consciousness expressed discursively. This scene opens up an abyss of incommensurability between the visible and the knowable, which in turn creates a desire to lift the veil, to go beyond the mere surface to probe into the depths. But it is a paradoxical figure, since it calls for a reading of depths and yet prohibits such reading because it is primarily spectacle and surface.

Working with representations of women in film, Mary Ann Doane argues that a discrepancy between the visible and the knowable is so often present in representations of women that it has created its own form of compensation: "the blindspot . . . is compensated for by an *over-sight*, a compulsion to see her, to imagine her, to make her revelatory of something," she writes (133). Neither an aesthetic concern nor a structure of desire can fully account for the fascination elicited by a *diva*; an epistemophilic drive is inevitably present as well, but only subliminally. But the hysteric is different since, in the spectacular and violent display of passions and pathos, she cries out to be heard, she demands to be understood and known. Hysteria always proclaims a secret and necessarily assumes a desire for knowledge. This is true as well, by implication, of a hysterical mode of representation. As we shall see, the hysterical heroine of Eliot's fiction addresses herself to the reader, and she says, just as Dora said to her analyst: "Read me." "Why was the wish to look again felt as coercion and not as a longing in which the whole being consents?" The coercive force of Gwendolen's image is thus the first sign of her unorthodox constitution, of her hysteria. This gaze (which is but a stronger form of the surreptitious or internalized glance that the hysteric always casts at the spectator for whom she performs) wants to obtain confirmation that she exists there, in the gaze of the other. In the dialectic of power and domination, the specular regime institutes the subsidiary position of a "returning" glance and thus instigates a reversal of power.

In fact, the "dynamic quality" of this glance troubled Eliot's readers from the very beginning. Her publisher, Blackwood, finds the term awkward and writes to the author, diplomatically: "I remember pausing at the use of the word dynamic in the very first sentence and I am not quite sure about it yet as it is a *dictionary* word to so many people" (*George Eliot Letters*, November 10, 1875, VI, 183). In the critical debate that James stages in "Daniel Deronda: A Conversation," Pulcheria believes the term reveals the author's pedantry and intellectualism. But maybe Eliot had settled for a word of the wrong register: in her days, "dynamic" belonged essentially to a scientific context and described, in physics, alchemy and homeopathic medicine, a force produced by an immaterial or spiritual influence. If, by definition or convention, woman is perceived above all as passive matter, one can see why, given the force of its original meaning, the term would have seemed out of place. But there may be more to this: a faint memory of a mythical figure, of Medusa's evil look, which blinds (de Lauretis, 110).

The word "dynamic," relayed by the notion of "coercion," is to be taken as the first symptom of a disturbance that promises an interesting reversal in the gendering that usually defines the spectacle of woman. If the structure of representation, as I have implied all along, assumes on the one side of the gender divide a desire to master, to know, to pierce surfaces in order to read depths (and this is precisely Deronda's original position) and places on the other, as the object of the unveiling, the woman as spectacle, then the fact that the woman looks back with a dynamic glance and somehow coerces the spectactor to look back at her will necessarily have an incidence on gender. Gwendolen's dynamic glance, the first sign of her hysteria, brings in its trail a radical questioning of the very foundations of the system of representation and sexual difference.

Gwendolen is entrusted with none of the gifts of vision, insight, or foresight that her "dynamic glance" could have entailed. This first glance, which the heroine returns to him, her spectator or reader, functions as a sign but does not correspond to a text. It belongs to a dynamics of power and desire, but does not elicit any knowledge. Indeed, from an epistemological point of view, it is a blank signifying nothing. But this precisely defines it as a symptom of hysteria, following the crucial distinction between signifiers and signs, which Monique David-Ménard highlights in Lacan's work. The symptoms of hysteria do not function as signifiers bound to other signifiers, but are signs "intended for someone" (194, n. 26). In other words, Gwendolen's "dynamic glance," as part of her hysteria, does not speak; it is merely an appeal to an other. As a particular aspect of Eliot's narratology, the scenes of hysteria must be perceived for what they are: failures in the process of signification; moments of textual absence or semantic void. They are "un-written" and offer no metaphors that could be read as vehicles of a latent content, they do not offer a set of signifiers which, once decoded, could lead us to a hidden or buried text. Hysteria, like its first annunciatory sign, the dynamic glance with which the novel opens, is the name given to a force that works insubstantially yet powerfully to attract us readers to confront under new terms, in a new guise, the object-subject of the spectacle, the uncharted space of what lies beyond the surface of woman's body.

However, the initial exchange of gazes does, in the course of the narrative, give way to a linguistic exchange, where the two protagonists, Gwendolen Harleth and Daniel Deronda, are involved in a reciprocation of affect and knowledge that seems to foreshadow an analytical scene. As has often been noted, the confessional mode of their conversations, where the heroine represents to the hero her beliefs, her emotions, and her fears, and, moreover, her increasing dependence on such moments create a transferential stage similar to that of the Freudian talking cure. The hero's openly declared inability to respond to the intensity of Gwendolen's demand hints at a demise of the analytical mind in front of a woman's desire that takes us all the way to the story of Freud and Dora. Such is, it seems, the benumbing effect of their *hysterica passio* that these hysterical women leave their analysts-counselors with no words to answer: it took Freud four years to overcome the silence that followed Dora's parting words, and Deronda is left speechless in his last encounter with Gwendolen: "[he] could not speak again" (750).

In fact, the dialogue between Gwendolen and Deronda drifts repeatedly into the unspeakable. "There was a long silence between them" (747), "she could not finish" (750): the last scene between them, with its exemplary dramaturgy, is punctuated by similar comments, while the dialogue is regularly supplanted by visual registration or the description of gestures and bodily attitude. "Her withered look of grief" (750); "He met his upward look of sorrow with something like a return of consciousness after fainting" (749); "Gwendolen had sat like a statue with her wrists lying over each other and her eyes fixed—the intensity of her mental action arresting all other excitation" (748): these examples, selected at random from the description of the protagonists' last encounter, show well enough the convergence of bodily representation with mental phenomena. The silence which inhabits them cannot rest as mere void or absence but, on the contrary, puts a further demand on the reader to respond to what remains unspeakable or unanswered in this novel's "struggle of language and consciousness" (Hertz, "Some Words," 283). It has other consequences as well, where a discussion of representation not only raises narratological, literary questions, but also philosophical issues. These can be foregrounded in a critical moment of a scene of hysteria.

Suddenly loosing Deronda's hand, she started up, stretching her arms to their full length upward, and said with a sort of moan—

"I have been a cruel woman! What can *I* do but cry for help? *I* am sinking. Die—die—you are forsaken—go down, go down into darkness. Forsaken—no pity—*I* shall be forsaken."

She sank in her chair again and broke into sobs. Even Deronda had no place in her consciousness at that moment. He was completely unmanned. (646)[13]

This passage is excerpted from the scene of confession that follows Grandcourt's death, where the reader has been asked to "imagine the

---

13. With such dramatic emphases and "mimetic" punctuation, Eliot's style seems here to emulate a theatrical or melodramatic mode. Similar instances occur in *Deronda* on pages 642 and 717.

conflict of feeling that kept [Deronda] silent," as the hero only reluctantly hears a confession that is part of "an exaggerating medium of excitement and horror" and "a state of delirium" (642). It shows the heroine in the thralls of a mental pain and anguish that can only be expressed, it seems, in these theatrical gestures and failed utterances suggestive of hysteria. The sobs that end this outburst foreshadow Gwendolen's "hysterical crying" at the very end of her confession (653).

This moment in Eliot's text is a particularly interesting instance of the failed conversations and the kinds of impasses of knowledge that hysteria can provoke. The confession does not in fact bring relief, nor does it, if we conceive of it as a case of transference, succeed either in achieving the undoing of symptoms or in bringing about knowledge "through the active mediation of signifying language" (Felman, *Lacan*, 56). The divide that opens between the protagonists evokes then almost too literally "the radical castration of the mastery of consciousness": "Deronda had no place in her consciousness. . . . He was completely unmanned."[14]

The implications of such statements can best be understood by comparing the text with one Eliot certainly knew well, since she translated it, and which might have been the model for such a scene:

In another I first have the consciousness of humanity; through him I first learn, I first feel, that I am a man: in my love for him it is first clear to me that he belongs to me and I to him, that we two cannot be without each other, that only community constitutes humanity. But morally, also, there is a qualitative, critical distinction between the *I* and *thou*. My fellow-man is my objective conscience.[15]

14. This phrase appears in Felman's definition of the uncounscious: "The unconscious, therefore, is the radical castration of the mastery of consciousness, which turns out to be forever incomplete, illusory, and self-deceptive" (*Jacques Lacan and the Adventure of Insight: Psychoanalysis in Contemporary Culture*, 57). It could be argued that it is the return of the repressed which renders the conversation impossible.

15. I owe this suggestive passage to Richard Freadman's invaluable study *Eliot, James and the Fictional Self: A Study in Character and Narration*, 64. Singling out two strands of philosophical sources that to him "appear especially germane to such a novel as *Deronda*," he quotes as one of them this passage from Feuerbach's *The Essence of Christianity* in Eliot's own translation (158).

"An dem Anderen habe ich erst das Bewusstsein der Menschheit; durch ihn erst erfahre, fühle ich, dass ich *Mensch* bin; in der Liebe zu ihm wird mir erst klar, dass er zu mir und ich zu ihm gehöre, dass wir beide nicht ohne einander sein können, dass nur die Gemeinsamkeit die Menschheit ausmacht. Aber ebenso findet auch moralisch ein *qualitativer* ein *kritischer* Unterschied zwischen dem Ich und Du statt. Der Andere ist mein *gegenständliches* Gewissen" (Ludwig Feuerbach, *Das Wesen des Christenthums*, 191). Notice the shift of vocabulary: *Bewusstsein* (consciousness), once infused with a moral dimension, becomes indeed *Gewissen* (conscience).

This quotation from Feuerbach's *Essence of Christianity* is echoed, for instance, in the narrator's comment about the insistent demand Gwendolen puts on Deronda's sympathy and understanding: "Those who trust us educate us" (401). The relation between the protagonists, between the suffering woman and her confessor, represents indeed an education into sympathy and otherness. Gwendolen is for Deronda, who in that scene is unmistakably the center of consciousness, the indispensable "other" who determines his humanity. It is possible then that the intense and extreme nature of such an exchange does not merely derive from the author's desire to represent some extreme affective states, but that it signals as well the philosophical stakes that are put into play here. Given the nature of the wager that lies in such an encounter between an *I* and a *Thou*—the very definition of what makes a man, *ein Mensch*— the conversation would naturally have to reach the intensity of melodrama.[16]

As we begin to match the philosopher's text against Eliot's fiction, however, their overall similarity dissolves under the pressure of their differences. "In another I first have the consciousness of humanity," writes the philosopher. With respect to Daniel, it might be accurate to say that he finds in the other, namely, Gwendolen, "the consciousness of humanity." But the hero is so ostensibly denied a place in Gwendolen's consciousness ("Even Deronda had no place in her consciousness at that moment") that the philosopher's statement, which is predicated upon reciprocity, no longer applies: she cannot find in him the same "consciousness of humanity." The theory does not work equally well for the hysteric and the analyst-confessor, for the woman and the man: we must then assume that in Gwendolen's case, consciousness cannot be produced in the intersubjective scenario, but elsewhere and differently. The reciprocity in Eliot's text is merely the physical and affective experience of holding hands, sharing tears, exchanging kisses: but these bodily gestures evocative of shared emotion or sympathy are too obviously at a great remove from Feuerbach's definition of consciousness or conscience. Eliot writes, "Sobs rose, and great tears fell fast. Deronda would not let her hands go—held them still with one of his, and himself

---

16. As Peter Brooks (to whom I am greatly indebted for this discussion of hysterical representation) has shown in *Melodramatic Imagination*: "The site of [the] drama, the ontology of the true subject, is not easily established: the narrative must push toward it, the pressure of the prose must uncover it. We might say that the center of interest and the scene of the underlying drama reside within what we could call the 'moral occult,' the domain of operative spiritual values which is both indicated within and masked by the surface of reality" (5).

pressed her handkerchief against her eyes. . . . She bent foward to kiss his cheek, and he kissed hers. Then they looked at each other for an instant with clasped hands, and he turned away" (749–50). Pathos can blur the boundaries between subjects (whose sobs? whose tears? are they only Gwendolen's?), but consciousness, even though defined by Feuerbach as a sense of belonging, is predicated upon a notion of identity that maintains the separation and difference between the self and the other. This is not to say that Eliot's text wants to hold up this moment of shared sentiment as a new model for (inter)subjectivity, but rather that she, so to speak, stops short in the middle of the impulse that Feuerbach's text could have given her. Body language is not even a substitute for consciousness or conscience; it expresses their demise. Moreover, a true exchange of the kind that Feuerbach imagines is impossible—what can she know of "humanity" in the throes of such hysteria?

Because it fails to imagine or believe in the possibility of such a community of consciousness or cannot conceive of a consciousness constructed communally in shared, reciprocal understanding or love, Eliot's text seems to hint at the failure or at least at the limitations of a theory of sympathy. While her version of a conversation takes this unexpected negative turn, it suggests that some forms of human interraction cannot so easily be resolved into cognitive or moral solutions. This is where the humanist conception promoted by Feuerbach begins to founder. Read in light of the fictional passage, the philosophical text emerges as an insistently universalizing statement. This appears especially in the original German text, where the word *Mensch* (expressing a non-gender-marked humanity) gives to Feuerbach's statement on reciprocity and intersubjectivity its full force. This confident universalism cannot be retrieved in the English translation "man" or, in Eliot's formulation, "fellow-man." Thus the writer's skepticism comes back like a ghost to haunt Feuerbach's theory, and it raises the question of gender: Which of the sexes figures behind the statement "I first learn, I first feel that I am a man"? Eliot's representation of a conversation is bound to raise such questions as Who learns what from whom? Who, of man or woman, is the subject who learns, and which object or instrument?

This pedagogical point is in fact raised earlier in the novel and resolved in an unambiguous fashion—he learns from her: "Young reverence for one who is also young is the most coercive of all. . . . But the coercion is often stronger on the one who takes the reverence. Those who trust us educate us. And perhaps in that ideal consecration of Gwendolen's, some education was being prepared for Deronda" (401). That she should teach him the moral imperative—that the moral sphere of man should be produced by some feminine influence—should not surprise us: the alliance of femininity with some higher moral sphere is a staple of the Victorian idealization of woman, even though we might be left wondering at the meaning of "ideal consecration." Is she going to be his muse? a vestal virgin? Or more like a victim sacrificed on the altar of good moral knowledge? It is true that this passage, unlike the earlier scene, allows us to imagine conversations that do not fail, where conscience now finds a place and maybe even consciousness—although this might mean putting too much weight on the word "education." However, this still leaves burning the issue of gender, and nothing suggests that a man and a woman can exchange positions—that she, for instance, could be the subject of such an apprenticeship.

This incursion into Feuerbach's text has made it possible to identify what is the irrevocably gendered nature of a scene of consciousness predicated upon the needs and urgencies that impel her to go to him as to a fellow soul. It also puts a different, more skeptical light on Deronda's natural sympathy, this spontaneous impulse that leads him to encounter the other in the guise of girls and their tragedies. George Eliot's novel acts as a reminder that such a humanist dialectic more likely than not will stop in the first stage, and it will go only one way, from the man to the woman; it can even be sustained between a man and two different feminine others, as shown in the hero's double allegiance to Mirah and to Gwendolen. It fails to work in the other direction. To then narrow the divide between theory and fiction would be to gloss over what is, after all, the most startling aspect of Eliot's reworking of Feuerbach: that it shows the impossiblity of sustaining the model of a general humanism when it is applied to the "consciousness of a girl." Centered around a woman, the scene of consciousness as it had been sketched or dreamt by the philosopher collapses, and with it the other who, rendered unable to take his "place" and his share in it, is now "unmanned."

The philosophical implications of the closing word of this scene—"unmanned"—may well be the most troubling and difficult to grasp. Within a psychological frame, the term can be accounted for easily enough as a figure, while it could hold pride of place in a feminist reading intent on deciphering in the novel the signs of a power struggle.[17] But what is the meaning of this "unmanning" in light of the previous discussion? What is it indeed to be thrown from the happy, innocent state of being a man "before gender" (like the subject of "I first learn,

---

17. It is between the mother and son, Daniel and Alcharisi, that the struggle for power is explicitly wagered.

I first feel that I am a man") into history that is now gendered and to find oneself "unmanned"? Within such a narrative, the scene's last word could be read as a statement bearing on the consequences of such a conversation or even as a warning. It would say that in that space of intersubjective relations, the masculinist stance must be returned to the neuter; losing the mark of virility, one is neither more nor less than a man (*Mensch*) before men (humanity). A Deronda unmanned would then no longer know or speak as a man (*Mann*) but would, albeit through some painful loss, rejoin the common fold of humanity.

Or are we to envisage a more radical process: a neutralization of the man in Deronda, as a "destruction of the peculiar properties of" and a "counteracting of the effect of"? Another interpretation indeed suggests that the hero's demise implied by this last word is the irresistible effect of Gwendolen's own power. The conversation ends, it will be remembered, with the assertion of her consciousness and the simultaneous exclusion of his: "he had no place in her consciousness." This statement could have far-reaching consequences. If the fictional scenario were to prevail (and not the philosopher's plot), we would see the end of reciprocity of consciousness that Feuerbach imagined. The other vanishes into thin air: what remains, alone, is one sovereign narcissistic subject, who seems immune from lack.[18]

Meanwhile, the negation of *him* induced in the process of constructing *her* consciousness cannot be canceled out and is surely not a matter of indifference: inscribed in the term "unmanned," there is a loss that speaks of a difference, an antagonism, and an inevitable suffering that the philosopher had perhaps never envisaged, but which the novelist recounts in the story of Gwendolen's hysteria. It may be then that Deronda's "unmanning" constitutes the farthest-reaching effect of Gwendolen's dynamic, hysterical glance and of the coercion that it exerts: held frozen within the masculine gaze for her femininity, she can only, like Medusa, evoke the presence of his own lack—and then "neutering"

18. "In other words, does he admit that woman is the only one to know the secret, to know the final answer to the riddle [*énigme*], that she most assuredly does not want to give it away (since she is, or believes herself to be, self-sufficient) and has no need of any complicity? Such is the path opened up by 'On Narcissism,' a painful path for the man who complains of woman's inaccessiblity, of her coldness, and of her 'enigmatic,' undecipherable nature," writes Kofman with regards to Freud ("Narcissistic Woman," 223–24). Kofman's words greatly illuminate George Eliot's novel if we accept that, as the "new Oedipus," Freud offers the paradigm of the masculine position or attitude. It is against this irreducible self-sufficient otherness of the feminine, embodied in Gwendolen, that Eliot's narrative seems to struggle; the ultimate sacrifice of such a "beautiful" heroine testifies to Eliot's deep revulsion against "feminine" narcissism.

would be the better word. Eliot's fictional response to Feuerbach in the form of a scene of consciousness that is now irremediably gendered opens wide, wider than ever anticipated, the divide between the sexes. The image of an easy, tension-free scene of exchange and dialogue vanishes; in its place is violence, pain, and the irretrievable gap that separates him from her, like the end of all conversation.

Consciousness Is Not an Agent but a Symptom

As a fiction of sexual identity, George Eliot's *Daniel Deronda* tells then the story of the differences between a man, Daniel Deronda, and a woman, Gwendolen Harleth.[19] On Daniel's side of the divide is a gradual involvement in the history of humanity and the eventual discovery of a vocation. On Gwendolen's is a coming into consciousness as conscience and a progressive freezing into an immobility suggestive of a state of expectancy and suffering. The extent of the heroine's estrangement can be measured in two comments ascribed to the narrator which appear in the scene that represents the last conversation between the two protagonists:

The world seemed to be getting larger round poor Gwendolen, and she more solitary and helpless in the midst. The thought that he might come back after going to the East, sank before the bewildering vision of these wide-stretching purposes in which she felt herself reduced to a mere speck. (747)

That was the sort of crisis which was at this moment beginning in Gwendolen's small life: she was for the first time feeling the pressure of a vast mysterious movement, for the first time being dislodged from her supremacy in her own world, and getting a sense that her horizon was but the the dipping onward of an existence with which her own was revolving. (748)

At the close of the novel, the heroine is granted an insight into her condition, which, although minimal (no more than a "bewildering vision" and "a sense that"), might yet stand for a newly achieved consciousness. These two passages can be understood to represent the

---

19. The phrase in the heading is a misappropriation of G. H. Lewes's definition: "'Consciousness is not an agent but a symptom,' mind constitutes 'the activities of the whole organism in correspondance with a physical and social medium'" (quoted in Freadman, *Eliot, James and the Fictional Self,* 65). I have given Lewes's words a more literal meaning than they obviously held for him.

inaugural moment of the heroine's growth into awareness of her place in the vaster scheme of things. They sketch a move from a self-centered to a relational positioning in the world; breaking out of the narcissistic circle, she now places herself in a wider plot, which in the second description resembles the grand design of history—"the dipping onward of an existence with which her own was revolving." The move is from outside to inside, from a solitary, useless, single life to the collective, communal project.

The end may thus have brought about the heroine's redemption; this new awareness could then be read as the clearest sign of her "recoverable nature" and thus answer Deronda's fond wish that after the crisis of her husband's drowning, the heroine may yet be saved. It may be that this ending answers as well a more general wish, of the kind expressed in *Lélia*, for instance, where the heroine prays on two important occasions to be released from the exile that has been inflicted on her, as a woman petrified in her solipsistic suffering.[20] We may have to accept that to conclude Gwendolen's story in this fashion is to give her the most moral as well as the most positive of ends: endowed with a place in history, she is saved—for history at least. We might also consider that Gwendolen's last outburst of hysteria, which follows this conversation, differs from all the others in that it precedes some final remission, as the emphasis on "living" suggests: " 'I am going to live,' said Gwendolen, bursting out hysterically, . . . she fell continually into fits of shrieking, but cried in the midst of them to her mother, 'Don't be afraid. I shall live. I mean to live' " (751).

Yet one might be inclined to exclaim, echoing the narrator, "poor Gwendolen," for the knowledge comes very late, and not as a gradual enlightment under the power of reason, but as yet another violent crisis of *hysterical passio*—as a drama of affect combined with pathos, which leaves her "look[ing] very ill" (750). "Poor Gwendolen" too because she has clearly not retrieved the intellectual ascendancy that, earlier on, she had held over Deronda, and which left him helpless and unmanned, with no influence over her consciousness. (But then, had we not been told all along in the novel that it is morally objectionable to "make another's

---

20. Gwendolen is not the first literary heroine to express the burden of woman's isolation from history. The following excerpt from Lélia's complaint evokes the same predicament: "Pourquoi m'avez-vous fait naître femme, si vous vouliez un peu plus tard me changer en pierre et me laisser inutile en dehors de la vie commune?" (Why have you made me a woman, if soon after you would change me into stone and make of me a useless being cut off from communal life? [99]).

loss one's gain"?) Moreover, one might be inclined to respond to this conclusion with the words of Simone de Beauvoir (from *Pour une morale de l'ambiguïté*) and endorse her rebellious stance: "to live is merely not to die, and then human existence is no different from some absurd vegetating state" (quoted in Kruks, 14).

Readerly sympathy will not take us far, however; it is from a logical, narratological point of view that the ending must be examined. This view makes us envisage what constitutes the central paradox of Eliot's novel, a paradox, moreover, that explains the presence of hysteria as the figure that, textually and philosophically, can best represent such a contradiction.

There comes a terrible moment to many souls when the great movements of the world, the larger destinies of mankind, which have lain aloof in the newspapers and other neglected reading, enter like an earthquake into their own lives—when the slow urgency of growing generations turns into the tread of an invading army or the dire clash of civil war, and grey fathers know nothing to seek for but the corpses of their blooming sons, and girls forget all vanity to make lint and bandages which may serve for the shattered limbs of their betrothed husbands. (747–48)

This is how the narrator of Eliot's novel, shifting his/her stance, reconsiders the heroine's predicament: having been "reduced to a mere speck," she figures in the next sentence among those "many souls" now unquestionably aligned within the more orthodox plot of a male-centered history. As "generations" are turned into armies, "grey fathers" look for their sons, and "girls" attend to their husbands, the heroine finds her (proper) place in the common fold of humanity, in a situation where her sex can no longer grant her a special claim on our pity.

This is not the narrator's first excursus into history, however. Earlier in the novel and in conjunction with the memorable discussion of girls as "delicate vessels," the narrator had raised similarly the specter of a war in which women mourn for husbands and sons, and men endure the loss of bread, "a time when the soul of man was waking to pulses which had for centuries been beating in him unheard" (109). "The soul of man," *die menschliche Seele*—Eliot's language when she writes about history inevitably harks back to the ungendered world of a Feuerbach. Yet this happens precisely when the novel raises twice, in the most explicit fashion, the question of woman's place in the vast scheme of the history of humanity. The historical theme is framed by two questions, the first concerning *a* girl, the second girls as a species:

Could there be a slenderer, more insignificant thread in human history than this consciousness of a girl, busy with her small inferences of the way in which she could make her life pleasant?—in a time, too. . . .

What in the midst of that mighty drama are girls and their blind visions? They are the Yea or Nay of that good for which men are enduring and fighting. In these delicate vessels is borne onward through the ages the treasure of human affections. (109)

In this novel the other sex is indeed the object of a relentless examination, which begins, on the first page, with Deronda's questions and is also, as we saw, promoted by the "visual structure" of the representation itself. But here the question mark that first surrounds the "striking girl" (8) has been displaced onto a different, more philosophical level: it is, this time, not the nature of the object that matters, but, at a further remove, the nature of our investment in the object. Why do we care? the narrator seems to say, and the first question is answered implicitly in differential terms: because girls are different they cannot be effortlessly subsumed under the wider, more familiar category of history. The question What are girls? arises then as a difference or supplement that cannot be comprehended under the wider rubric of those "larger destinies of mankind": her story is whatever that history cannot comprehend.

Here the ending ("the bewildering visions of these wide-stretching purposes in which she felt herself reduced to a mere speck") strikes me as providing a puzzling answer to such a questioning: "a mere speck" can hardly meet the demands of "what are girls and their blind visions?" granted even that "a mere speck" might stand closer to Gwendolen's voice than to the narrator's. Common sense suggests that if it had been a mere speck, the "consciousness of that girl" would not have borne 750-odd pages of narration, even shared with the hero. Yet she is described as little more than a speck, a dot that trails into near silence. Indeed, even the ending does not help: when Gwendolen's full measure is taken, we see the startlingly narrow scope of her fulfillment, especially when compared with the heroic promises held by his "wide-stretching purposes." What remains is the thinnest of threads, slender to the point of unnarratable tenuousness, and the question is not answered: what about the girls and their blind visions?

Nor is the question answered in the preceding narration, for it is only at the end of the novel that the notion of consciousness becomes meaningful, when the final crisis brings about the inaugural moment which hints at a "reformed" heroine. Before that the term is insubstantial, a mere cipher that surrounds the inner side, the unrepresentable inward drama. "Pale as one of the sheeted dead . . . a wild amazed consciousness in her eyes, as if she had waked up in a world where some judgment was impending" (638)—when the context reveals such vivid and extreme figures of emotion, the word "consciousness" looks almost like a misnomer, and the more so when "judgment" is experienced in the guise of a moral sanction given by an entity that is so clearly a stranger to the self. How indeed can you identify a consciousness when what is presented is the mere bodily registration of emotion? Thus, although the psychological discourse of the novel seems to rely at regular intervals on the word "consciousness" as a way of designating the heroine's autonomous, individual inner sphere, it is only in the final crisis that we can decipher its fuller meaning and begin to trace its history. But this deferral leaves the question mostly unanswered: the novel has yet to produce the story of Gwendolen's newly acquired consciousness.

The final stage of Gwendolen's story shapes the "consciousness of a girl" within the confines of a mighty closet drama and in the form of negation. In the last scene of the novel, the heroine is the living refutation of the metaphor which, in the earlier stages, appeared to account for her significance: it seems impossible to imagine Gwendolen as a "delicate vessel" bearing "the treasure of human affection." Whatever the level at which we read her, more literally as a "vessel-womb" or as a token within the more complex system of a relational and transferential staging, Gwendolen reveals the demise of the meanings that the narrator earlier located in the history of girls and their blind visions. As the scales fall from her eyes, she can only look at the world through the tears of her ultimate chastisement and renunciation. "To be one of the best women, who make others glad that they were born" is indeed a strange reformulation of the earlier proposition, one that entails such a reduction that it contains none of the forward-looking, creative, perhaps procreative possibilities of her former incarnation as a vessel of human affection. Furthermore, when compared with the earlier passage, this scene offers no resting place to that treasure of affection put into circulation. "The burthen of that difficult rectitude towards him was a weight her frame tottered under" (750): the transfer of conscience from him to her amounts to a moral imperative, an imperative that threatens to crush her. Indeed, after Daniel's departure, the heroine breaks down, or rather breaks into hysteria: such is the expenditure of grief and need in this final, cathartic crisis that it leaves her with no more than a thread of history ahead of her: "I shall live. I shall be better" (750). In its depiction of woman's fate, *Daniel Deronda* works toward entropy. After this last hysterical outburst, the consciousness of the girl, born from her ashes, appears to begin in a new cycle, yet to be written. To be merely living is not much of a story and is surely, in terms of human history, the most minimal of beginnings.

Perhaps the solution to the quandary that Eliot's novel sets up—how can that "mere speck," a girl with her blind visions matter to the world—simply cannot be found at the level of a narrative resolution, and perhaps the secret of Gwendolen's history lies, in fact, in the figuration. "In these delicate vessels is borne onward through the ages the treasure of human affection" appears indeed to provide the most immediate response to the general interrogation: "what in the midst of that mighty drama are girls and their blind visions?" "A vessel," the writer answers, which like a womb is the instrument of generation. The attention paid to such a slender thread would then find its justification because the thread is woven into the great chain of being in which the subject's erotic fate is inscribed. It appears that, conventionally enough, the author holds that "in the case of woman" it is love that matters above all, and the novel could do no more than rehearse the topos of woman's definition and circumscription within the sphere of affect. That woman possesses emotions, feelings, and passions suffices to guarantee that she is a subject: a consciousness would then be the mere recording of those affective impressions related to her inscription within the erotic plot.

Nevertheless, it seems hardly defensible to argue that a woman's consciousness can be defined, solely and completely, within this generational plot. This again would make of "consciousness" a misnomer, for the very definition of the term holds that consciousness is necessarily manifested as judgment and consequently thinking and that it cannot be reduced merely to affect, or to erotic and sexual components.[21] In fact even a cursory glance at *Daniel Deronda* shows the narrator enquiring relentlessly about Gwendolen's ideas and testing her on her ability of make adequate judgments. In order to stand by the notion that a girl's consciousness can be measured merely in affective terms, the author would have had to remain blind to her own performance.

In this instance it might be helpful to bear in mind Freud's analogous pronouncement about woman's desire being primarily erotic and man's turning on ambition: an examination of his case histories shows that

---

21. As Jean Hyppolite has shown in his commentary on Freud's *Verneinung*, even within a model of subjectivity such as the one developed by Freud, which gives crucial importance to "human affections," consciousness is necessarily made of those other faculties, judgment and thinking. See "A Spoken Commentary on Freud's *Verneinung*."

a persistent questioning of woman's knowledge and judgment runs counter to the theoretical emphasis on erotic wishes. Eliot's novel shows the same thing—that it might be easier to discourse on woman's emotional life than on her intelligence. Fortunately, however, *Daniel Deronda* easily convinces us that, as James remarked in one of his letters on George Eliot, "We know all about the female heart; but apparently there is a female brain too!" (*Selected Letters*, 104). Unquestionably, the consciousness at stake here stretches beyond its definition as affect.

It may be then that I have interpreted the figure too literally and that it deserves to be read within a wider symbolic economy. Couldn't we say that the "consciousness of a girl" matters because of the particular dynamic or economy that it enables or triggers? The statement indeed implies that consciousness "means" because it carries, conveys, transports that which as a "treasure" constitutes a precious value in a system of exchanges. Since I have already (in my earlier discussion of James's appropriation of Eliot's formulation) tackled the question of woman as a metaphor for the subject in nineteenth-century writing, I focus here, more narrowly and in light of Eliot's project, on the nature of this symbolic exchange whereby the "consciousness of a girl" becomes the bearer of affective investments.

Critics have often enough used the psychoanalytical model to explain the relation between the hero and the heroine in *Daniel Deronda*,[22] but a phenomenon of transference is involved as well on a different level, providing another answer to the question of the investment carried by the "consciousness of a girl." The analytical frame is not only pertinent for the conversations between Deronda and Gwendolen; it can be shifted to encompass the relation between the reader and the subject of the text as a relation that owes its existence, if we pursue the narrator's claim, to our affective investment in the figure. Our willingness as readers to follow the "insignificant thread" is determined by an interest that indeed mere curiosity or desire for knowledge could not solely warrant. It relies on a closer "'implication' in the symptom observed" (Felman, *Lacan*, 23) and is inseparable from an intersubjective context created by our affective involvement in the heroine's drama. Our interest in "girls and their blind visions" is thus always, just like Deronda's, "personal" and yet "ex-centric" to our conscious readerly self (Felman, 123), and hence simultaneously impersonal. "Girls and their blind visions" are thus the

---

22. "It is a commonplace that George Eliot had anticipated Freud—in her presentation of the urgencies of transferential need as they shape Gwendolen's painful talks with Daniel, and, more compellingly still, in her exploration of repression and of the terrors associated with the return of repressed images and feelings," writes Neil Hertz in "Some Words in George Eliot: Nullify, Neutral, Numb, Number," 291.

instrument in a general "human" (and the term is of course predictable within Eliot's humanism) dialectical process of discovery. Their otherness, termed as insignificance and blindness, works incrementally on a more general, universal history. "*The* treasure of human affection" is, as my emphasis on the definite article suggests, a formulation that is so general as to be beyond attribution either to those men "enduring and fighting" evoked in the previous statement or to some specific interest in the object (such as Deronda's, for instance). In short, the investment in girls and their blind visions is collective and marks a universal dependence on the human affection that is rehearsed between us and them on the transferential stage of our reading.

This alone can explain why the "consciousness of a girl" remains a concept endowed with meaning and value in Eliot's novel, even when it eludes both the representation and the knowledge that come with narration. This is how the most tenuous and smallest inferences that sketch out her life still belong to the web of a history that knows many seemingly mightier dramas. It is precisely because it is so thin or broken that the discourse of the hysterical heroine comes to mean so much; we are drawn by the unrepresentable. Hysteria as the stage of woman's dispossession and as a symptom of consciousness acts here as a vivid reminder of the secret territory that remains to be seen, known, and understood, a territory that escapes the ready perceptions of representation. Hysteria signifies the demise of the heroine's consciousness yet invites us visibly and insistently to read this absence. Read in light of the narrator's comments on "girls and their blind visions," the heroine's hysteria is less a figure of madness or suffering than the sign of a crisis of consciousness which repeats itself until the "terrible moment" of revelation endows the heroine with its substitute—a conscience. Thus I devote the last part of this chapter to a critical exploration of the most spectacular of the scenes of hysteria in *Daniel Deronda*: Gwendolen's wedding night. This is my answer to the invitation to read hysteria. By shifting my perspective from the philosophical content of representation to the performative dimensions of Eliot's writing, I show how hysteria, when it is understood as a textual phenomenon and literary representation, can teach us to read more attentively the text of woman's history and consciousness which Eliot has woven into her novel.

Reading Hysteria

Three scenes of hysteria hold a conspicuous place in *Daniel Deronda*: the first occurs when Gwendolen, playing Hermione in a game of charades, freezes in terror as a sliding panel reveals "the picture of the dead face and the fleeing figure" (91). Later in the novel, the heroine is faced with the same figure, but this time it takes the identifiable form of her drowned husband's face: her anguished memory leads her to rehearse compulsively in her mind a scene (as a memory or phantasy?) that shows "his face above the water," "the dead face—dead, dead," and herself "leaping from [her] crime" (648). Here again, but this time with Daniel in attendance and in the role of confessor and analyst, the heroine, who is held in the throes of some unspeakable, unutterable memory or desire, breaks into "hysterical crying" (653). In Eliot's text, the notion of hysteria, always conveyed in its milder adjectival form ("hysterical") or as a description of a behavior ("hysterics"), is usually associated with the heroine's "discourse of imaginative fears" (394) as what best represents to a late nineteenth-century reader the heroine's unexpected, theatrical behavior as well as mental suffering accompanied by a state of dissociation. In such scenes too, "words [are] no better than chips" (558), and failing to relate discursively the adventures that befall Gwendolen's consciousness, the narrative progression seemingly comes to a halt. The discursive flow is arrested in scenes or tableaux that rely on the reader's visualization of the heroine's condition as a bodily performance. The evocation of gestures, shrieks, and sobs replaces the dialogue or interior monologue, while the description, with its particular rhythms, intensities and figures, alludes to some unutterable or irrepresentable inner drama.

Hysteria could profitably be studied as part of the elaborate moral and psychological discourse of Eliot's novel, but emphasis on its literary aspects shows that it holds much more in store than the mere registration of the subject's positioning within such a frame.[23] As an element in the particular narratology and dramaturgy of subjectivity, it deserves to be scanned for its critical and literary significations. My theme in this last part then is hysteria as *une chose littéraire* (borrowing Shoshana Felman's term), namely, as an aspect of what literature is and what literature only, among other competing discourses such as philosophy, psychology, or history, can perform. The scene under scrutiny is that of Gwendolen's

23. "The moral examination of female psychology—in which we classically locate the depth of George Eliot's fully human perception—is therefore doubly contaminated. By the sexual fantasy which supports it as well as by all the questions of social inequality and misery which this attention directed at the woman serves to displace," writes Jacqueline Rose in "George Eliot and the Spectacle of Woman," (*Sexuality in the Field of Vision*, 113). Built on similar premises, our approaches diverge since Rose endorses a marxist-feminist approach whereas my own theme—the burden gender places on bourgeois Western women (and, by implication, on men)—leads me to focus singlemindedly on the philosophical and historical implications of such a phenomenon, but without taking into account social and economic determinations.

wedding night, in the closing pages of chapter 31 of *Daniel Deronda*, and it provides us with the first elements of a rhetoric and poetics of hysteria organized around the following notions: the letter, dissociation, the signifier, displacement, condensation, and the phantasmatic.

The letter. The scene of hysteria begins—the term must not be understood in its temporal sense, but as origin and causation—with a double injunction to read, which is presented at its center: "It was legible as print and thrust its words upon her" (330). The heroine's receipt of the letter triggers the crisis of hysteria, while "legible as print," the letter of the text, which is addressed to us its readers, implicitly enjoins us with a similar burden of interpretation. But before addressing the question of the statement's figural meaning, I must unravel its elements from the perspective of narrative. Putting their imprint on the heroine's mind ("those written words kept repeating themselves in her"), the words of the letter constitute the *cause provocante* of the illness: they are the text of her hysteria and what determines its performance. The analyst might say that it is because these words, although "legible as print," exceed the mind's ability to interpret them, or because they touch consciousness at a point of lack or failure of symbolization, that they give way to symptoms (David-Ménard, 66). Let it be stated, on the other hand, that the text expresses no such thing, yet it matches the letter, without any transition or mediation, with the representation of a hysterical body. The content of this message keeps recurring under various forms, while the later insistent reappearance in chapter 35 of the very words of the letter is proof that they literally cannot be absorbed by the mind: "The words of that letter kept repeating themselves, and hung on her consciousness with the weight of a prophetic doom" (395). If words are what keeps the heroine in the sphere of visions, of dread, and of the phantasmal, then it can only be true that the letter represents the crux of the heroine's failed consciousness and the secret of her illness. But this letter belongs, at the same time, to the text of which we are the readers. Jerry Aline Flieger tells us that "according to Freud's own view of it as 'compromise formation' or symptom of desire, the literary text may be considered to be a 'letter in circulation,' which is at once metaphoric in nature—as symptom of the repressed tragic conflict between law and desire—and metonymic in function, driven by a never-assuaged *désir* addressed, like the purloined letter, to the other it both reaches and misses" (205). Although it bears on the literary text in general, this statement offers a vivid reminder that the hysteric's letter (as what consitutes her hysteria) is always susceptible to enfold us in its secret. Within the fiction, it is to the heroine that the words appear "legible as print," but print they are for us especially, the readers of Eliot's fiction. The letter is not only the site of the unresolved conflict embodied in Gwendolen Harleth; it is also an injunction to us, readers of the novel, to engage, as if by some compensatory logic, with its demand to be interpreted. "Read me" says the letter of Eliot's text thrust upon us, and where Gwendolen in her hysteria fails, we readers are called on to witness the scene of her trauma and to respond to its provocation of violence and mystery, for such a theater of sensation,[24] with its "spasm of terror," "its tremors of lips and hands," its "hysterical violence," could hardly leave us indifferent.

However, in this instance and unlike what we saw in the Jamesian scenario, the scene is presented in such a way as to prevent our total involvement or identification. A very noticeable, because unique, shift of person that occurs in the middle of the narration positions us, irrevocably, as the readers/viewers of the scene: "But coming near herself you might have seen the tremor in her lips and hands." As it breaks away from the impersonal narrative voice focusing on its object (framing the hysteric in a tableau), the narration resorts to apostrophe and conjures up an "I-you" structure: taking on a voice, the narrator summons the absent reader to be a witness. But beyond its emotive function (as increasing the pathos of the scene), this rhetorical move functions in a deictic fashion, as the marker of the reader's position. Indeed, as he examines the role of person in writing, Roland Barthes speaks of a "mixed system of person and non person," characteristic of discourse, and aligns the pronouns "you" and "I" on the side of the personal, as entailing the speaker's participation in the statement (*Rustle of Language*, 16). He remarks further that "this double system . . . produces an ambiguous consciousness which manages to keep the personal quality of what is stated, yet periodically breaking off the reader's participation in the statement." One could argue, conversely, that a shift of person as emphatic as this apostrophe calling on our participation in the scene of hysteria creates a consciousness in the reader, and this without the usual ambiguity. The reader is separated from the hysteric's nonconsciousness and is yet held in its thrall, and it is then to him that the burden of consciousness falls, unambiguously, and this in the act of reading her hysteria.

---

24. On the question of reading the "sensation novel," see D. A. Miller's brilliant analysis, focusing on the readers' "hystericized bodies," in the introduction to "*Cage aux folles*: Sensation and Gender in Wilkie Collins's *The Woman in White*," 187–88.

Dissociation. The letter, I have argued, is only the *cause provocante* of Gwendolen's hysteria; it is the factor that brings about the crisis, but this is not where the illness truly begins. It is indeed in the use of the reflexive person or pronoun that the first signs of hysterical dissociation can be detected: "Gwendolen . . . threw herself into a chair by the glowing hearth, and saw herself repeated in glass panels with all her faint-green satin surroundings" (329). This formulation, which distinguishes carefully between the agent and the subject of the action, is symptomatic of the increasing dissociation which the heroine is made to experience in her growing hysteria. Earlier, as if in anticipation of the later drama, we see that Gwendolen moves toward her wedding night with a sense of "an insistent penetration of suppressed experience." The heroine's state of mind is represented as an invasive process, and seems to respond to the sway of some inner psychical division. This dissociation is rendered more perceptible in the metaphor that envisages that same mental space in the guise of a theater, the subject having become the bemused, distant witness of her own existence: "Was not all her hurrying life of the last three months a show in which her consciousness was a wondering spectator?" Gwendolen's "seeing herself" is indeed part of a general emphasis on reflexive constructions such as "felt herself," "threw herself," "saw herself." The specular division created in the process is relayed, meanwhile, by another analogous dissociation which relies on the autonomous life or, rather, activity that is given to bodily parts in descriptions of her sensations: "her heart gave a leap," "a new spasm of terror made her lean forward." The choice of language evokes in both these cases, and through a cumulative process, the yawning gap that figures in the place of a unified, masterful consciousness. It should not surprise us then that the onset of hysterical crisis is registered by a combination of the two forms of dissociation, an "act of seeing" conflated with a bodily response: "the sight of him brought a new nervous shock, and Gwendolen screamed again and again with hysterical violence" (331).

The fate of Gwendolen's consciousness in the scene of hysteria can thus be traced in the following fashion: overwhelmed by the perception and its affect, the subject has lost her reflexive faculty, and responds to the trauma with a body in motion, a body as emotion that erupts into screaming and shrieking. The dispersal, splitting, fading of the subject which was initiated even before the fatal letter "thrust its fatal print upon her" assumes the climactic form of a hysterical fit. The only unified knowledge that the heroine holds is that of "feeling ill." Meanwhile, as the specular, reflexive ability is taken away from the hysteric, consciousness becomes also the reader's share: "She could not see the reflections of herself then, they were like so many women petrified white." Who indeed is made to see here, if not the reader, through the agency of the narrator? And what is to be seen? The text answers first with a metaphor, but then, reinstating the stance of the distant, analytical observer, gives up the pretense of mapping out the heroine's inner progress. The scene of hysteria is described from outside, and eventually through her husband's bewildered, critical gaze, but it is no longer enacted in the rhetorical and metaphorical figurations of the writing. The text or letter of Gwendolen's hysteria and of her missing consciousness must then be read in the interval that separates the first specular moment, ascribed to the heroine ("she saw herself"), from its demise and the substitution of the reader ("she could not see the reflections . . . coming near herself"). If here, as so often in nineteenth-century texts, vision is made to stand for knowledge, we can conclude that Gwendolen's entry into the hysterical scenario is matched by the decline of her consciousness.

The literary scene of hysteria is meanwhile inevitably predicated upon a redoubling of vision. The stance of the "wondering spectator," which is initially ascribed to the heroine watching her own self in performance, also defines the reader's position. This structural overlay, where the gaze within the scene is matched by another gaze that is to be located outside of the framed tableau (where, in other words, the action is so insistently drawn back to the "ostensive presentation" or revelation of an "arrested scene") presents, as Alexander Gelley has shown, the "structure of phantasy (or phantasm) as a scene of desire."[25] Expressed intradiegetically as well as extradiegetically, the desire to hold her in focus must necessarily be ascribed to the agent or entity that endorses the act of representation, which expresses in the writing its investment in the contents of the scene. Since the scene mainly shows but does not narrate, it might be tempting to view it from a distance, like a spectacle, and to seize on its obvious melodramatic features and to interpret it sequentially, as a causal interlinking of behavior and action. But the rhetoric of Eliot's writing forbids such an easy move and sustains other exigencies. "Coming near," as we

25. "In episodes of this type the effect is that of an arrested scene, nearly a tableau, since what they consist of is nothing but the ostensive presentation of a figure or setting. The action of such scenes is not an action within the scene but the presenting or disclosing of the scene," writes Alexander Gelley in his analysis of the scene in Hawthorne's short story "Wakefield" (*Narrative Crossings: Theory and Pragmatics of Prose Fiction*, 159). The scene of hysteria in *Daniel Deronda* seems a particularly apt illustration of what his theory of the scene highlights, namely, a shift in representation from the outer to the inner stage.

are invited to do by the narrator, we soon find that the scene of hysteria must be read along an axis that is not merely temporal, chronological, sequential, but requires us rather to decipher positionalities of desire within a field of representation that is envisaged in its specular, metaphorical, or figurative aspects.

The signifier. As a first instance of this demand for an enhanced form of readerly implication, I examine here a grammatical irregularity in a discussion that should mark a noticeable shift of attention from the discourse of representation to the performance of writing.[26] What on the surface may be taken as a slip of the author's pen is examined as a symptom. Thus we find in Eliot's text on hysteria an unusual, ungrammatical occurrence of a reflexive pronoun: "But coming near herself you might have seen the tremor in her lips and hands" (331). What are we to make of this foreign body in the sentence, "herself," whose effect can surely not be reduced to mere redundancy? It might be accounted for easily enough as part of the general emphasis on reflexive constructions: "herself" repeats the pronoun of the previous sentence ("she could not see the reflections of herself then") and also harks back to the moment preceding the crisis, which relies heavily, as we have seen, on such dissociations ("she felt herself being led," "she threw herself"). But "herself" carries as well, like a ghostly presence, the reflexive "yourself." The implied presence, like a modulation or echo of this "yourself" that the grammatical slippage makes possible, reinforces the apostrophe: our identification with the hysteric might then be stronger than acknowledged.[27]

Furthermore, putting the emphasis on "self" this time, we would be able to foreground the covert expression of a "self" or subject that lies behind the hysteric's ostentatious performance. The grammatical error and ambiguity of the reflexive "herself" reveal then the multiplicity of subjective positions involved in the scene of hysteria. Overdetermination, that is, a plurality of meanings but also a plurality of determinations, is the rule as we read the signifier as a symptom. The slip of a pen can also be taken as a reminder of the several desires that converge around

26. Marc Redfield first drew my attention, a long time ago, to this unusual grammatical feature.

27. These are the kinds of "transegmental drifts" that Stewart analyzes in *Reading Voices.* "[In his discussion of *Finnegan's Wake*] Derrida comes as close as anywhere in his work to acknowledging the pressure, however phantasmal, of pronunciation upon script," Stewart writes (245). I argue, similarly, that Eliot's grammatical slip reveals "the pressure, however, phantasmal" of voice upon writing.

the scene of hysteria: the referent of the symptomatic word could be, as I have shown, the hysteric involved in her own subjective drama or the spectator who participates in it in the intersubjective mode of transference. In addition it might also involve the subject involved in the writing: "coming near myself."

Moving away from representation to envisage the transitive meanings of "to write," one is inevitably confronted with such ghostly referents and above all with the figure of the writer. Roland Barthes discusses precisely this literary phenomenon, using the example of the middle voice of the verb "to sacrifice": "in the case of the active voice, the action is performed outside the subject, for although the priest makes the sacrifice, he is not affected by it; in the case of the middle voice, on the contrary, by acting, the subject affects himself, he always remains inside the action, even if that action involves an object" (*Rustle of Language*, 18). His illustration of what writing means, in the guise of a linguistic analysis of the verb "to sacrifice," turns out to be particularly appropriate for this examination of the scene of hysteria: for the victim of "textual" hysteria, just like the victim of sacrifice, invokes a multiple cast of characters and is always apt to provoke their affective involvement. Indeed, Eliot's slip of the pen shows that the difference between the narrator's voice and the author's presence, just like that between the priest who officiates as a sacrificer and the person who makes a sacrifice for himself or herself, might be much smaller than suspected. Under "herself" speaks the "I" that had effaced itself from the representation but returns in the symptoms of the writing. The agrammaticality produced in the writing speaks of affect and desire, when the representation tended on the contrary, as we saw, to contain and to frame affects and desire within the scene of hysteria while establishing, on the outside, the stance of a viewer-analyst.[28] An examination of the signifier in the scene of hysteria is bound to evoke an autobiographical subtext, not as the representation of the author, but rather, to borrow one of Louis Marin's propositions on autobiography, because "the autobiographical text in

28. For the relation between linguistic forms and affect, see Gilles Deleuze's groundbreaking study "The Schizophrenic and Language: Surface and Depth in Lewis Carroll and Antonin Artaud." Given the unusual rhythms, intensities, and displacements of Eliot's writing of hysteria, it could be said that her text produces as well "passion-words" and "action-words" (291) and reveals a tension (and not a radical break) between "language-affect" and "the organization of language" (287).

On the difference between writing and representation, see Roland Barthes, *Le plaisir du texte*, 88–90: "This is representation, really: when nothing gets out, springs out of the frame: of the painting, the book, the screen."

the place of the subject will be haunted [*travaillé*] by an originary, in-audible voice, which it echoes in its signifiers" (43).

Displacement. The symptom represents one element in a general con-figuration, and it remains essential not to lose sight of the general form taken by the illness. This leads us inevitably to ask, in the most blatant fashion, about the outcome of the wedding night. How do the expected erotics of the scene give way to hysteria? While the substitution of hys-teria for the *nuit de noces* has become by now a familiar situation, we are not dispensed from attending to the particular form it takes in Eliot's novel. Ellen Moers describes, in vivid terms, what she thinks happened during the wedding night: "There is of course nothing that could re-motely be called pornographic in George Eliot's treatment of Gwendo-len's deflowering by her husband Grandcourt; the matter is not even mentioned, directly. But indirectly, by means of the jewel-case, George Eliot conveys all that need be told about Gwendolen's hysterical, virginal frigidity: about Grandcourt's sadistic tastes; and about, in addition, mer-cenary marriages, wedding night customs, and sexual hypocrisy in the Victorian age" (253). Another enthusiastic and sensitive reader of Eliot, George Steiner, has praised eloquently this author's uncanny ability to represent, in her use of figurative language, the intimate, private scene of erotic life. Steiner wrote the following comment about *Middlemarch*, but the same would surely hold true for the later novel: "George Eliot's perceptions of sexual feeling, the closeness of observation she brings to bear on erotic sensibility and conflict, yield nothing to that of the mod-erns. In most instances what passes for characteristic post-Freudian in-sight is, by comparison, shallow. But these perceptions and the free play of imaginative recognition are immensely in advance of, immensely more explicit than, the vocabulary available to a serious novelist of the 1870s" (105). James too, it will be remembered, singled out Eliot among all other nineteenth-century British writers for her ability to convey erotic meanings. Indeed there seems to be general agreement among her readers that George Eliot is able to convey in her figurative language the sense of the sexual, eroticized body. This scene is no exception.

In this instance, however, the thread of the erotic is very tenuous. Apart from a first kiss on the lips and Grandcourt's pressing Gwendo-len's hands to his lips somewhat later in the bedroom, no gesture of love is represented. There may be, on the other hand, more than a hint of eroticism in a decor that is warm, glowing, conducive to "creeping lux-urious languor," and is framed with a reference to its ceilings, which show a Spring shedding flowers and Zephyrs blowing trumpets (329). There are then enough indications to suggest that the heroine is entering a bower of love. One might even decipher in the move from antechamber (*Vorhof*) to boudoir a progress within a geography of sex not unlike that which Freud examined at length in Dora's second dream. The sexual symbolism of the adder, of the box, of the jewel is unmistakable, whereas the words "penetration" and "thrust," used at the beginning of the scene to describe the heroine's mental experience, appear in this light as strange equivocations. While undeniably present, the erotic or sexual body is, however, the object of considerable displacements.

But the most visible phenomenon of such a scene is a lack of symbolization of the sexual body and the substitution of hysterical symptoms. The heroine's "pleasure-body" is conspicuously missing, while the affective, expressive charge is displaced on her hysteria. That Gwendolen's erotic body should not exist here, but that meanwhile another body should be drawn—with its tremors, pallors, shrieks, and fits—shows indeed how close the representation comes to the clinical definition of hysteria as "a deficiency in the subject's symbolization of the body" (David-Ménard, 44). In its failure to convey the "perceptual reality" of a pleasure-body, the text reveals the symptoms of hysteria as they are defined by Monique David-Ménard: "It is now clear where this reversal leads: from the omnipresence of the hysterics' body to the eyes of a fascinated observer, the study of sensorimotor functions permeated by language leads us to say that that ostentation is only the obtrusive side of the hysteric's absence with respect to her own body, for want of symbolization. The hysteric has no body, for something in the history of her body could not be formulated, except in symptoms" (66).

David-Ménard's study begins with an investigation into the meaning of Dora's disgust, in the wake of Freud's observation that "I should without question consider a person hysterical in whom an occasion for sexual excitement elicited feelings that were preponderantly or exclusively unpleasurable" (*SE* II, 28). "I hate the touch of woollen cloth touching me" (103), Gwendolen exclaims when asked why she does not dance the waltz. The disgust Eliot attributes to her heroine ("she objected with a sort of physical repulsion to being directly made love to" [63]) may be part of a pattern of hysteria. One is then increasingly tempted to ascribe to Eliot the unerring eye of an analyst and the uncanny foresight into psychological processes that have only been understood in our century. What is one to make then of such an anachronism?

It is precisely because the scene of hysteria presented in *Daniel Deronda* in 1876 comes before Freud, and before the kind of theoretical insight found in case histories such as that of Dora (1905) or Wolf Man (1909), that a psychoanalytical interpretation can work so well. François Roustang in *Un destin si funeste* speaks tellingly of the cultural, temporal gap that constitutes the necessary condition for rendering analysis operational. Analysis can only work, he claims, if "the theory stands ahead of the cultural situation of the symptom by one step"—*en avance d'un temps* (91). In other words, the analytical stance depends on invention: it is predicated upon the fact that there is, in its object, something yet to be known.[29] George Eliot's novel benefits from being read psychoanalytically precisely because it exhibits in its textual "symptoms" a *méconnaissance* analogous to the "ignorance" displayed by the hysterical patient who provoked Roustang's commentary. Our stakes differ, however, in that unlike the analyst who strives for a cure, I rely on a psychoanalytical reading for what it shows in terms of a history of a woman's consciousness. In the fragmentary elements that emerge from a psychoanalytical reading lies the unspoken, unrepresented side of the history of the gendered subject that gets written in Eliot's fiction.

Condensation. The scene of hysteria in *Daniel Deronda* turns upon the letter sent by Lydia Glasher: while it can be read within the narrative sequence as what provokes the crisis, it also constitutes the focal point of the heroine's "discourse of imaginative fears." What it performs, as a curse, is made possible by what it carries as a signifier; this is why we must proceed to unravel the figures and stories that it condenses.

The language speaks here of a desire for knowledge. The overall narrative takes on the appearance, as Peter Brooks has remarked, of "a plot of female curiosity" (*Body Work*, 252). The sequence is revealing: Gwendolen receives a packet, sealed by a paper, which shows a letter that covers a box in which are to be found the jewels: "She knew the handwriting of the address, it was as if an adder had lain on them." A later repetition of the same motive, in the guise of a memory, foregrounds what the narrative sequence, conceived as a progressive unveiling, has rendered visible, namely, the imbrication of the letter with the jewels: "they had horrible words clinging and crawling about them as from some bad dream, whose images lingered on her perturbed sense" (397). "The perturbed sense," of which Gwendolen's hysteria is the sign, lies then at the convergence of a handwriting (Lydia Glasher's), the jewels

29. Or put differently: "The effect of the theory corresponded to what it invented in relation to the cultural coordinates of the interlocutor (or analysand)" (Roustang, *Un destin si funeste*, 91).

(Grandcourt's inheritance through his mother), and those words that kill (the letter on the jewels).

One can detect in the succession of unveiling, unwrapping, and uncovering, just as in Dora's second dream, the representation of an epistemophilic drive. A similar "symbolic geography of sex" makes of the jewel case (*Schmuckkästchen*) the equivalent of the female body, while the unmistakeably phallic symbol of the adder evokes a male body. This complex figure, which in the letter and the box holds emblematically both a female and a male body, looks like the very site of an engendering. And it is this figure which triggers, repeatedly, the hysteria: "It seemed at first as if Gwendolen's eyes were spellbound in reading the horrible words of the letter over and over again as a doom of penance; but suddenly a new spasm of terror. . . ." The adderlike words draw repeatedly Gwendolen's inner and outer gaze, bringing in their trail the whole sequence of bodily symptoms as well as the mental dissociation-dissolution characteristic of hysteria. Indeed, whereas in the first stage the figure holds the heroine in the thralls of a visual fascination, it reverbates in a second stage, described in chapter 35, in the inner space of her mind. The letter, the text insistently proclaims, is what is given to the heroine by way of a consciousness: it "hangs on her consciousness," "gnawing trouble in her consciousness," "the words of that letter kept repeating themselves, and hung on her consciousness with the weight of a prophetic doom" (395).

Between the first trauma and its repetition as memory, the "hysterical violence" has become "violent hysterics." The change in the wording is revealing enough: it registers the fact that the violence has been internalized as symptomatic behavior. The effect of the letter reverberates far beyond the initial shock, as a reminiscence: "the words had nestled their venomous life within her, and stirred continually the vision of the scene at the Whispering Stone." The letter then works proleptically as well as retroactively, taking the heroine back to another moment of terror: "Gwendolen, watching Mrs. Glasher's face while she spoke, felt a sort of terror: it was as if some ghastly vision had come to her in a dream and said, 'I am a woman's life' " (137). What looms behind Gwendolen's hysteria is the image of the rival woman, who, like Medea to Creusa, curses the other woman's marriage with her poisoned gift.[30] This image, moreover, offers Gwendolen a counterpart to the dead face of her husband, condenses in it like a vision, a knowledge that is unmistakeably

---

30. See my discussion in Chapter 4 in the section titled "Between Women."

gender inflected. It seems indeed that the letter of Eliot's text is ultimately about a history peculiar to women and about some hard-earned visionary knowledge.

The phantasmatic. "She could not see the reflections of herself then: they were like so many women petrified white, but coming near herself you might have seen the tremor in her lips and hands" (331). This is hysteria seen from outside, framed by the spectator's gaze. But the simile reveals, simultaneously, an attempt to show from inside, but through the power of an analogy, the loss of identity and the paralysis that affects the heroine: "so many women petrified white." The self-seeking gaze is met, it seems, with a phenomenon of petrification, or, to return to the body, it is supplanted by the movement or position of frozen terror. "I feel petrified" this hysteric says, implicitly. Hysteria here again works by condensation: Gwendolen's stance is another reminder of the encounter with the other woman at Whispering Stone and more pointedly of the later "Medusa-apparition in Hyde Park" of the same Lydia Glasher. Eliot's text of hysteria overlaps in an uncanny fashion with Freud's presentation of the mythical encounter with Medusa: "The hair upon Medusa's head is frequently represented in works of art in the form of snakes, and these once again are derived from the castration complex. . . . The sight of Medusa's head makes the spectator stiff with terror, turns him into stone. . . . The symbol of horror is worn upon her dress by the virgin goddess Athene. And rightly so, for thus she becomes a woman who is unapproachable and repels all sexual desires—since she displays the terrifying genitals of the Mother" (*SE* XVIII, 273). Because it evokes the castration complex—fear of the loss or absence that marks the woman's genitals for the viewer—the image of Medusa strikes the spectator with terror and turns him (or her?) to stone. Would a Freudian interpretation of the myth allow for such a substitution of pronouns? Freud's insistence on Medusa's apotropaic function suggests a negative answer. Eliot's text, however, displays an array of female images that strike another woman with terror and violence: the Furies at the end of this passage, the specular demultiplication of those "women petrified white," the allusion to Medea and Creusa, and finally the encounter between the two rival women under the auspices of Medusa. The text's obsession with the myth of Medusa confirms what is so conspicuously enacted in Gwendolen's hysterical symptoms: that hysteria is the sign of the hysteric's inability to assume her own body. These encounters with Medusa represent another, this time wholly negative, version of the scene of transmission between women. Faced with this specular other who resembles herself, a woman, the heroine cannot bear what she sees, and "closing her eyes to herself," she flees into the terrors of hysteria.

In Eliot's text, the scene of hysteria is not bisexual (unlike what we saw in *Valentine*), but it does resemble Dora's story in the interpretation of Lacan and David-Ménard: it shows the impossibility of sustaining one's gender in the grammar of the sexes and represents "a passionate denial of sexual difference that seeks to attribute to the other a kind of responsibility for having spoiled sexuality" (David-Ménard, 102). The scene of female rivalry that looms behind the scene of hysteria suggests that, as David-Ménard writes about Dora, "the other woman fascinates through the power to swallow up the patient's entire existence, a power attributed to her, when she 'steals' from the patient the heterosexual object of her desire" (100). The hysteria represented in Eliot's text begins then with the story of a woman who attempts to steal back a husband whom the other wants. Glasher steals Grandcourt on the wedding night: "the man you have married has a withered heart. His best young love was mine; you could not take that from me when you took the rest. It is dead; but I am the grave. . . ." (330). And in this it seems, Eliot may not only uncannily have anticipated Dora's hysteria but may also have invented her own. It might be that in writing about her heroine's hysteria she shows her glimpses of her unconscious. Barthes's comments on modern writing seem, in this instance, truer than ever: "Thus, in the middle voice of *to write*, the distance between *scriptor* and language diminishes asymptomatically. . . . In the modern verb of middle voice *to write*, the subject is constituted as immediately contemporary with the writing, being effected and affected by it" (*Rustle of Language*, 19). Neil Hertz has written suggestively on the personal allegory that lies behind Eliot's writing:

To seek an author's personal allegory behind the realistic surface she has woven is often as unrewarding as it is methodologically dubious, but in the case of George Eliot's works, because they are explicitly about the imagining of others—about the status of the image of one person in the imagining mind of another—the play between the imaginer and the imagined, between author and character, and the possibility of a narcissistic confusion developing between the one and the other has already been thematized and made available for interpretations. (*End of the Line*, 82)

The sheer dramatic intensity, the theatricalization of the representation, as well as the writing's overbearing and repetitive investment in figures suggest indeed that the scene of hysteria fulfills in Eliot's novel the role of a phantasmatic, in the sense given to the term by Kaja Silverman.[31] Thus, in my literary interpretation of hysteria, I have not only encountered the "author inside the text" (in the guise of a narrator or as a kind of stage director of a hysterical scenario, with the heroine as leading actress), but I have also found myself reading what Silverman calls the "text 'inside' the author—for the scenario for passion, or, to be more precise, the 'scene' of authorial desire" (*Acoustic Mirror*, 216).

In the heroine's hysterical screaming and in the tremor of her lips and hands, the representation meets with the writing, and the difference between what writes and what gets written vanishes. A moment like this enables us to touch, at some tangential point, the unsayable and unrepresentable that haunts the imagination of the woman holding the pen. In the case of George Eliot, just as was true of George Sand, the "phantasmata" speak of gender. The figures of Gwendolen's hysteria, meanwhile, designate the proximity between the writer and her creation, and they mark the convergence between art and life, between the performance of writing and the enactment of some deeply subjective event or experience. When Gwendolen reads death in the letter addressed to her by Lydia Glasher, when she flees in terror from an impending guilt, the heroine's screaming cannot be separated from the writer's. Hysteria then, sprung from this discrepancy where the will to express meets the impossibility of representing, evokes in the negative mode a desire for consciousness.

But this implies that we resist the lure of the representation that would suggest that the meaning of hysteria lies solely in its pathos and that the heroine's story signifies only in terms of its affective contents. Because Eliot's hysterical writing in *Daniel Deronda* presses upon us the obligation to read its figurations and because, moreover, in this instance "the process of reading is assimilated very tightly to the silent movement of thought within us" (Beer, 214), we can identify this desire for consciousness. As the written and writing figure of knowledge and desire caught between recognition and terror, the scene of hysteria bespeaks a desire that is neither fiction nor reality, but that like any true fantasy might come much closer to identifying a subject than any stories or histories that can be told. If Eliot faces in this novel the impossibility of retracing the "consciousness of a girl," it may be because, coming close to such

31. In her theorization of the "female authorial voice," Silverman suggests there are at least two "points of entry that help to organize the authorial corpus": nodal points (made of the repetition of sound, image, scene), and "a sound, image, scene, or sequence which is marked through some kind of formal excess" (*Acoustic Mirror*, 218).

a theme, she encounters too much forgetting, too much blindness. We have to remember, however, that hysteria is nothing but a sign, an invitation to read, that it does not reveal a code that would enable us to lift the secret; it just spins its own stories. Pulling off the veil, as my psychoanalytical reading has attempted to do, amounts to revealing the undivulged secret and the silence that ultimately lie behind writing.

The Inward Turn

"In the case of Gwendolen Harleth. Eliot seems to equate the necessity of narrative, of biographical meaning, with the woman's life, with the sphere of inwardness—affirming in this manner a fundamental tradition of the novel," Peter Brooks writes suggestively in *Body Work* (255). The concept of inwardness can indeed justify Eliot's interest in representing consciousness in her novel; it explains, moreover, the inward turn that history takes when woman is its subject. It also throws a different perspective on the closure applied to Gwendolen's story: if her life relies on "being" (when his consists in "doing"), then the heroine, in her frozen, but knowing predicament, singled out by her peers "to be one of the best of women, who make others glad that they were born," reaches her apotheosis precisely there, in that absolute inwardness of nonaction that defines her new beginning. Moreover, the old saying remains true *pati natae:* in the feminine mode, to be is to suffer, and to know, for a woman, is to suffer the pains and pangs of a private history written in the body before it emerges, if it ever does, into consciousness.

Read for this "introversion" and as a forerunner of the stream-of-consciousness novel, the story of Gwendolen can be strung consistently and right to its end on the line drawn by this inward progress toward the more exquisite pains or intensities of a fuller consciousness, one that knows how to subsume emotions and affections under the higher categories of morality. Or more appropriately, because of the weight given to the mortifications that come with a moral imperative, her story can be summarized as the denial of consciousness, and the upholding of conscience in its stead. "Her remorse was the precious sign of a recoverable nature," comments the analytical and critical voice belonging to Deronda or to the narrator, after one of Gwendolen's hysterical breakdowns. In this way the tale of her woes never trails far from a story of hysteria, at least as our nineteenth-century doctors identified it. Just as in Sand's *Valentine*, hysteria speaks in Eliot's text of an ethical and aesthetic choice that imposes on woman the pains and pangs of conscience, and models her on a pattern of sublime, ineffable spiritual pain.

"Hysteria"—the words of Clément are worth repeating—"is the simplest of solutions: to hold oneself in a state of permanent guilt is to constitute oneself as a subject" (*La jeune née*, 90).

But, as we saw, hysteria is not only a theme in Eliot's novel; it is also a form of representation. The narrative process, which takes the heroine through the different stages of her *Bildung*, is repeatedly halted by a form of "freeze-framing" which, as a scene or tableau, is insistently visual and yet invites us repeatedly to read beyond the visible. Beyond the spectacle of woman's assumption of a conscience that the novel represents, one is faced then in the scenes of hysteria with a language that seems to work "at the point of fragility of the symbolic" (David-Ménard, 188). As my first, resistant interpretation of the novel's terms and of its ending have suggested, Eliot's project of representing the "consciousness of a girl" is riddled with difficulties and contradictions. A closer examination of the writing that characterizes the scene of hysteria has shown that the sense of such scenes threatens to collapse altogether under the weight of the unknown and the unrepresentable which stand in the place of her consciousness.

The symptoms of such a negation can be seen at a narratological level, as the narration can be shown to shuttle back and forth, repeatedly, between narrative and scene or, to shift registers, between discourse and performance. As a literary phenomenon, hysterical representation mimes in its accents and displacements a signification that cannot be articulated discursively. Indeed, as Lacan has shown, it eludes discourse defined as what is *réfléchi, articulable, accessible* (as thought, expression, and communication) and it exists only as image or hallucination (*Ethique*, 60). The effects of hysteria are not merely linguistic; they also affect our understanding of representation. They are a reminder of a pervasive and insistent negation or repression that, in the nineteenth century, came to bear upon the consciousness ascribed to woman. They show that the inward turn the novel has given to history ultimately leads, like Woolf's fishing line, to some inexpressible, unrepresentable bedrock. Hysteria is here again the equivalent of a veil, which separates this time representation from the unrepresentable. Gwendolen's consciousness, her inwardness, cannot be staged fully as representation and narrative but is mapped around moments of textual intensity which appear to be the figured enactment, in the timeless (because activated in every reading), nonnarratable space of writing, of an unconscious. In her attempt to write the fiction of her heroine's consciousness, Eliot gives her novel a form more radical than has generally been appreciated: she endows her character with a depth of unspokenness and with the kinds of displacements and metaphors that do not really represent a consciousness but rather end up delineating the latter around the borders of a textual unconscious. Indeed, if, as has often been suggested, "George Eliot had anticipated Freud in her presentation of the urgencies of transferential need" (Hertz, "Some Words," 291), not enough has been said about the "struggle of language and consciousness" waged in this text, where Eliot anticipates both modernism, as a style, and psychoanalysis, as a new understanding of subjectivity.

If the project of narrating the consciousness of a girl is halted repeatedly by the fact that no more can be shown or said than this freezing into a screaming, sobbing, or shrieking stance, then these moments of hysterical crisis are for us readers of the "consciousness of a girl" the precious signs of a negativity that cries out to be heard. The hysteria represented and enacted in Eliot's text is then the nodal point of a critical interpretation which analyzes the meaning and assesses the implications of the blindness of vision that affects the heroine. From this perspective, the textualized symptoms of hysteria, which must be understood as failures in symbolization or ungraspable metaphors, constitute nevertheless the realities of the female subject that figures at the center of Eliot's novel; her consciousness can then be mapped out against the backdrop of her hysteria. But it might be more appropriate to reverse the relation between ground and figure, and to say that her hysteria, which is turned toward an unconscious and the play of signifiers, traces the contours of a consciousness, as a secret history of knowledge and desire. "The universe forcing itself with a slow, inexorable pressure into a narrow, complacent, and yet after all extremely sensitive mind, and making it ache with the process—that is Gwendolen's story," Henry James writes ("*Daniel Deronda*: A Conversation," 990). Gwendolen's *pathologein*, her hysteria, deserves more than just a sympathetic or mournful glance ("another one of those suffering women!"); it needs to be interpreted on its own terms, as a figure that defines the "interiority" of woman's history as imagined by Eliot.

The insistence on bodily phenomena that characterizes the scenes of hysteria in *Daniel Deronda* must be understood as the representation by default, as the underside of a gender-marked consciousness. At the same time, I am well aware that hysteria also has a history, in our modern critical times, as "a privileged dramatization of female sexuality" (Irigaray, 70) and that, moreover, its reliance on the body as a site of signification might single it out as ideal terrain for the decipherment of the semiotic, in the sense given to this term by Julia Kristeva. I have chosen, however, to interrogate Gwendolen's hysteria from the perspective of language and consciousness, and I have put the emphasis on the linguistic predicament, the failure of symbolization that defines hysteria *in* literature, but also *as* literature. "Words were no better than chips," the narrator exclaims, when commenting on the failure of language between Grandcourt and Gwendolen ("her passion had no weapons" [558]). I find myself inclined to trust the theoretical insight of the teller of the tale. Reading hysteria against the body, I propose that hysteria is then the symptom of language's inability to answer the writer's need to express some particularly feminine history. That history, while marked significantly by failure in the symbolization of desire and the prohibition of jouissance,[32] cannot be reduced to either pure affect or body language. It accounts for a form of *Aufmerksamkeit*, for a perception and an awareness that are, however, marked by a denial. Working within a model of negation makes it impossible to decipher in the hysteric's body a femininity brought back to its bodily and behavioral components. I have chosen, on the contrary, responding to the philosopher's invitation, to read "the history of the subject's desire, in so far that this history is inscribed on his or her body" (David-Ménard, 59). It can still be said that Eliot's attempts to revise history to include the private dramas and ecstasies of "girls and their blind visions" have taken a peculiar and paradoxical form. But it may be that writers feel more acutely and are able to register more accurately the failures in knowledge because they experience them first hand, confronted as they are with the errancies and lacks that define the languages of the "unsayable" and the unpresentable. It seems crucial to me to grant them this particular insight and to read them by taking the risk of that ambivalent knowledge.

This attempt to reflect on consciousness and gender through the figurations of hysteria constitutes then a variation or modulation of similar projects—by Foucault, Derrida, Felman, and Cavell—which associate the cogito with a scene or play of madness. Because it belongs so typically to the feminine gender, because it became, in the nineteenth century above all, the madness that is peculiar to women, and because it is so charged semiotically, hysteria has enabled me to reflect upon a gender-marked consciousness. It could be argued then that it is precisely there, in the *méconnaissance* of desire and *jouissance*, that a feminine consciousness or history necessarily begins and, simultaneously, threatens to founder in Eliot's project. In that sense Gwendolen's hysteria is about the engulfment of knowledge in the repetitive play of a desire that does

32. This is how hysteria is defined by David-Ménard, in the wake of Lacan, in *Hysteria from Freud to Lacan*, 44.

not know itself. The particular but exemplary predicament embodied in Gwendolen's hysteria is that of a feminine blindness of vision. In her book *Acoustic Mirror*, Kaja Silverman argues forcefully that there can be no subject without the specular and insists on defining woman's subjectivity in its psychic dimensions: "as a projection inward from the surface of the (constructed) body" (147). It also seems to me that much is to be gained (from a feminist perspective but also for a better understanding of Eliot's writing) if we, as readers, attempt to follow the path of this inward turn. The female subject that is held in focus in the scene of hysteria tells stories of a kind that must indeed take their meaningful place in our modern Western history.

"Always Secrets of the Alcove": A Postscript

"These things are always secrets of the alcove"—"Das sind immer Ge-heimnisse des Alkoven"—remarked Breuer to Freud, when imparting his knowledge of hysteria to his younger colleague.[1] The truth of this remark has received ample, and often literal, confirmation from the texts I have examined: hysteria's favorite place is the bedroom, a place that holds the secret of the subject's desire and knowledge, but also a site of re-membrance and of a return to the primal scene. In George Sand's

---

1. The older Freud, in his semi-autobiographical *On the History of the Psycho-Analytic Movement* (*SE* XIV, 13–14), remembers the moment of "enlightenment" (which in fact brings together the experienced physicians Charcot, Chrobak, and Breuer, each imparting his knowledge to the young candidate). Freud had not, at the time, immediately understood Breuer's expression, so Breuer added the gloss *des Ehebettes* (of the marriage bed).

The alcove or bedroom, as the place where, in a bourgeois culture, the body is revealed in its naked and sexualized state, carries a unique weight of symbolic associations in this history of a gendered subjectivity. My own enquiry has thus led me back to Barthes's insight, while highlighting the hysteric's subversion of the structure defined by the critic: "The pleasure of the text . . . is an Oedipal pleasure (to denude, to know, to learn the origin and end), if it is true that every narrative (every unveiling of the truth) is a staging of the (absent, hidden, or hypostatized) father—which would explain the solidarity of narrative forms, of family structures, and of prohibitions of nudity" (quoted in de Lauretis, *Alice Doesn't*, 107–8). From the perspective of the mind and hysteria, Cavell in "Naughty Orators" (335) emphasizes that the "scenes of psychic torture" in *Gaslight* take place in the bedroom. David-Ménard highlights as well the importance of "the bedroom scenes and summonses" in the history of Freud's patient, Elizabeth von R. (see "The Search for the Psychical, or the Importance of the Structure of Scenarios," 30–34 in *Hysteria from Freud to Lacan*).

Valentine and George Eliot's *Daniel Deronda*, hysteria is enacted in the alcove, while the hysterical scenarios of Henry James's critical writings on George Sand return again and again to that space of his imagination which reveals the scenes of her passion. What these various readings of hysteria have shown is the overdetermined form—the structure—that underlies and informs the nineteenth-century representations of the subject that are defined by their "inward turn." These representations go back repeatedly to the alcove, which holds the secret of sex and sexuality; with the revelation of sexual difference, identity is put on trial. It seems then as if the dramatization of subjectivity that leads to the knowledge of the "life of the soul," for which the hysteric is the prime case or model, could only find there, in the alcove, its epistemological grounding. But while the question of sexual difference can be answered as the subject witnesses (in reality or memory or in a dream) the scene in the alcove, the question of gender, which is raised by hysteria, cannot be met so easily. Unlike sexual difference, gender has no ontological grounding and draws its significance from the subject's performance in and around the spectacle staged in the alcove of his imagination, which is unfolded in the process of writing. This is why writing does not merely bear the traces of the subject's quest for a sexual identity but in fact produces different versions of this "inward drama" which aims at retrieving the meanings of sexual difference.

Let me present here one last gender fable, chosen because of its theoretical value, for it could be said that this fable is the key to all the previous stories on gender that were recounted here. Unlike the other texts I have discussed, this one brings into the open and gives away, in one revelation, the secret of gender and of consciousness. Its value for this inquiry lies in the fact that it exposes the fundamental assumption—the theory—that, without exception, determines the shape given to the other gender fables examined in this work, whether they belong to the discourses of medicine, literature, or psychoanalysis. The story that will be recounted here defines then, belatedly, a cultural myth staged in the alcove whose actors are, so to speak, put in the presence of gender. Since I have assumed throughout this work that writing is like dreaming, and that texts, like dreams, can be interpreted to yield their wealth of subjective inscriptions, let me dwell for a moment on the account and interpretation of this famous dream that goes back to the alcove.

This fable then is double: it is made of the dream, which Freud recounts in the case history of the Wolf-Man (*From the History of an*

Infantile Neurosis), but it involves as well the analyst's interpretation of the scene in the alcove that this dream represents:

'I dreamt that it was night and that I was lying in my bed. (My bed stood with its foot towards the window; in front of the window there was a row of old walnut trees. I know it was winter when I had the dream, and night-time.) Suddenly the window opened of its own accord, and I was terrified to see that some white wolves were sitting on the big walnut tree in front of the window. There were six or seven of them. The wolves were quite white, and looked more like foxes and sheep-dogs, for they had big tails like foxes and they had their ears pricked like dogs when they pay attention to something. In great terror, evidently of being eaten by the wolves, I screamed *and woke up.' (SE* XVII, 29)

The dream itself and the detailed analysis that follows testify to a "perceptual passion" that the analyst seems to have shared with his patient to an unusual degree.[2] Freud appears to labor harder than ever, against intellectual disbelief and moral outrage, to make it yield its wealth of individual and theoretical truth, and he warns his readers at this outset, quoting a "wise saying" from *Hamlet*: "there are more things in heaven and earth than are dreamed of in our philosophy" (*SE* XVII, 12). As the analysis will demonstrate, its central theme must be elicited from a sexual scenario destined to reveal the ultimate reality of castration and of its founding value for subjectivity. The analysis reveals, moreover, an interpretative slant that works to bind together the subject's psychological identity and the recognition of gender. Thus this dream needs to be interpreted along the two axes of desire (where the subject is caught in a scene of passion) and of knowledge (where he learns to decipher the "significance" of the scene).

Its beauty (in the sense in which the term would be attributed to a mathematical theorem) lies in the elemental combination of a scenario of desire and a figuration of knowledge. For it bears in itself the traces of passage from the "phantasy world" of dreaming to a waking state that corresponds to "reality": the window that opens, Freud suggests, means the sudden opening of the eyes onto some "real" scene that is remembered in the dream. As for its latent erotic content, it can only be

2. "Perceptual passion" is a term borrowed from Silverman, who writes about Longdon and Nanda's "hyperdevelopment of hearing and vision" in *The Awkward Age*. She adds, in a description that seems to fit Freud very well: "his [i.e., Longdon's] perceptual passions are more fully exercised upon an internal than an external scene" ("Too Early/Too Late," 187).

reached through an elaborate process of reconstruction: "scenes, like this one . . . are as a rule not reproduced as recollections, but have to be divined—constructed—gradually and laboriously from an aggregate of indications" (*SE* XVII 51), Freud insists. The construction developed in the analysis leads to an event that occurred very early in the patient's life: the dreaming child of four had remembered ("dreaming is another kind of remembering," adds Freud [51]) a moment of the past, when, at the age of one and a half, he woke up from a nap in his parents' bedroom on a hot summer's day and witnessed a scene of sexual intercourse between them. This then is the primal scene, as Laplanche and Pontalis define it: "it belongs to the individual's—ontogenetic or philogenetic—past and is an event that is perhaps of the order of a myth, but whose presence precedes any significance that can be later attributed to it" (*Vocabulaire de la psychanalyse*, 433).

Indeed, if in the first interpretation Freud tries hard, very much like a storyteller intent on verisimilitude, to endow the reconstructed scene with the semblance of reality, in a second version he revises his interpretation. How indeed could a child raised in a respectable bourgeois household have witnessed such an unseemly scene? Freud reconceives his interpretation so as to emphasize its fictional nature, partly, it seems, in order to avoid the scandal that a "real memory" would have entailed. In its revised version, the primal scene no longer corresponds to a real event, but proceeds from the child's phantasy, or it traces some philogenic knowledge, in the guise of a prehistoric truth that every subject carries in himself or herself. However, whether it is conceived as a reality or a phantasy, or is the product of some "collective memory," does not fundamentally alter its meaning or value. The vision or myth that was secreted away in the child's and in the adult's mind until it is remembered belatedly as a dream goes back to the alcove.

But my purpose is not to analyze yet again a case history which, under repeated scrutiny, has always yielded precious insights. It is the overall structure of this gender fable which interests me, because of its relevance to the scenes of hysteria and *scènes d'alcôve* that I presented in this work. What matters is that a curtain is lifted or (to use my earlier figure) a veil is pulled off, and that the unveiling reveals a scene enacted in the alcove, which holds a foundational value for the patient's subjectivity and "an extraordinary value for the history of the case" (*SE* XVII, 51). While its effects are unpredictable, its significance must be clear: "The material of the analysis shows that there is one condition that this picture must satisfy. It must have been calculated to create a conviction of the reality of the existence of castration" (36). The repetition of words in the

German speaks emphatically of overdetermination: the child must have been the witness (*Zeuge*) of a scene that is destined to convince him (*überzeugen*) of the existence of castration. The Wolf-Man's dream is then about the fact of sexual difference. This is why the dream constitutes a decisive revelation concerning the patient, while it is also, as Freud insists in his account, the key to the analyst's knowledge. The dreaming child of four understands the perceptions or sees images that he gathered (or possibly fantasized); they show him the secrets of the alcove: "When he woke up, he witnessed a coitus *a tergo* [from behind], three times repeated; he was able to see his mother's genitals as well as his father's organ; and he understood the process as well as its significance" (37). With such a scene (whether fictional or real) firmly imprinted in the mind, the child knows about sexual difference, even if later on he withholds his credence and continually denies this knowledge. From the analyst's perspective, to identify this "passionate denial"—that is, to retrieve the original pattern that shaped the representations as symptoms or dreams—is to hold the key to the patient's hysteria.

Freud takes an unusual interpretative leap when, writing about this crucial discovery, he asserts that the infant "understood the process, as well as its significance." Can the child really interpret the scene, that is, can he gather from the raw material of perception the idea of the difference? Is it not rather that another figure has now been drawn into the primal scene—that of the observer-analyst? For surely it is the analyst's privilege to be aware of the "significance of the difference." The full cast of the spectacle of sexual difference revealed in the alcove thus involves not only the man and the woman (who offer the revelation of the sexual difference), and the witness (who should infer his sexual identity from such a scene), but also the theorist (who recognizes in that visible difference a meaning or a concept).

The weight of the interpretation bears then on a phenomenon that cannot be attested but can only exist through the work of analytic reconstruction: "the question of castration is of course the question of phenomenality, the reality phantasy/question," writes Ned Lukacher (153). The case history of the Wolf-Man leads then, the critic argues, to an impasse that marks the limits of Freud's epistemology: while the patient knows and does not know "of castration," Freud conceives of the primal scene as real or phantasmatic. The truth-value of the primal scene depends then on a belief and, more specifically, on our willingness to credit the Freudian interpretation: "Many details, however, seemed to me myself to be so extraordinary and incredible that I felt some hesitation in asking other people to believe them," writes Freud in the "Introductory Remarks" (*SE* XVII, 12). To credit this interpretation is to acknowledge the primacy of that scene and to attest to its reality. But to blink (the hesitation of *Verleugnung*) or to close one's eyes (the rejection of *Verwerfung*) is to call into question the originary status of the subject of sexual difference. Indeed, this "conviction of the reality of the existence of castration" gave way, in the patient's case, to a fleeting and fragile recognition, while it was produced by the analyst as an interpretative tour de force, a supremely daring act of reading, which puts a high premium on the reader's belief.[3]

The analyst's presence in the alcove speaks tellingly of his own epistemological investment in that symbolic space. But it might also challenge the interpretation which holds that the primal scene is the determinant, foundational "event" that lies behind the patient's individual history. Indeed, while Freud first held by the conviction that to witness the scene is to understand its subjective implications, he communicates later, in a footnote, his own awareness that vision, knowledge, and understanding could not coincide at such an early stage in the subject's life: the significance is a later addition, it came with the dream, and through the mechanism of deferred action.[4] This suggests in turn that the scene, a mere physical, psychic, or metaphysical "fact" (which Freud defines as a "process"), exists outside of any meaning attributed to it, in the words of Jean Laplanche and Jean-Bernard Pontalis: "la scène . . . est déjà là avant toute signification apportée après-coup" (*Vo-*

---

3. The phrase in quotation marks comes up several times, with variations: "a conviction of the reality of the existence of castration" (Freud, *History of an Infantile Neurosis*, *SE* XVII, 36), "a conviction of the reality of castration" (45), and a "conviction that castration may be more than an empty threat" (57).

4. Two footnotes in Freud's text reveal that he had second thoughts on the question: "I mean that he understood it at the time of the dream when he was four years old, not at the time of the observation" (*SE* XVII, 37). A longer footnote dwells extensively on the concept of *deferred action* and provides the following explanation: "At the age of one and a half the child receives an impression to which he is unable to react adequately; he is only able to understand it and to be moved by it when the impression is revived in him at the age of four" (45). But the question of the child's knowledge is not so easily resolved after all; in his concluding remarks, Freud brings it to the fore again: "If one considers the behaviour of the four-year-old child towards the re-activated primal scene, or even if one thinks of the far simpler reactions of the one-and-a-half- year-old child when the scene was actually experienced, it is hard to dismiss the view that *some sort of hardly definable knowledge, something, as it were, preparatory to an understanding, was at work in the child at the time*" (120, emphasis mine). Freud's repeated attempts to (re)construct a temporal sequence for the child's knowledge of gender reveal indeed two contradictory currents; the model of deferred action is met with the competing "wish" that the knowledge be traced back to the origins of subjectivity—that the knowledge come with the vision of the scene.

cabulaire de la psychanalyse, 433). Meaning accrues to sexual difference in a belated fashion, gradually, as part of every subject's history, unless the revelation is so traumatic that it is denied and gives way to symptoms. The growing awareness of what the *scène d'alcôve* signifies is what this book defines with the term "gender." And the narratives, literary and otherwise that I have examined, here represent so many encounters with gender, or so many "cases" where a subject, writing his or her private and cultural history, reflects on the significance of sexual difference, in an attempt to come to terms with the "secret of the alcove."

Thus, a more skeptical outlook on Freud's interpretation ends up highlighting his own overrriding desire to "make it mean" from the outset. The analyst tries to trace the significance of the primal scene back to its initial occurrence so as to bring about the coincidence between sexual difference and the subject's history, as if the spectacle of sexual difference should necessarily (or in the best of worlds) produce immediate awareness of its meaning. The subject's very destiny would then be tied to the assumption of gender.[5] But by conflating in this fashion sexual difference and gender, Freud is led to overlook what is ultimately the question the hysteric addresses to the world at large and specifically to the analyst: Why do I have to choose between one or the other sexual identity? Why, in the scenarios of passion, do I have to give up one or the other of the roles or identifications?[6]

Reading Freud by probing his language for the desire and the knowledge that it holds, one can identify a desire for sexual difference, a concern that it be "true" and answer the riddle of subjectivity, which stands precisely at odds with the hysteric's symmetrical "passionate denial" of the difference.[7] What opposes then the analyst to the hysteric is a shared

5. This seems to be Lacan's conception as well, as shown in his interpretation of Dora: "For Dora to gain access to this recognition of her femininity, she would have to take on this assumption of her own body, failing which she remains open to the functional fragmentation (to refer to the theoretical contribution of the mirror stage) that constitutes conversion symptoms" ("Intervention on Transference," 98).

6. This is the question that Freud faces in *Analysis Terminable and Interminable,* giving it the name *das Gegengeschlechtliche* (SE XXIII, 251), translated as "the attitude proper to the opposite sex." Rather than an "attitude," *das Gegenschlechtliche* is, I would argue, a conception or a belief—for which the hysteric acts as an emblem or effigy—that one sex does not or should not exclude the other gender. The concept of *das Gegengeschlechtliche* shows Freud's later awareness of the subject's deep-seated resistance to the assumption of the proper gender, and thus puts into question his earlier, more confident assertion that hysteria can be "set right," or, to use Lacan's formulation, that there can be "an ortho-dramatization of subjectivity" in relation to gender.

7. In the words of Mannoni: "interrogate language for the desire and knowledge that it holds, and not for its referent" (*Clefs,* 62).

obsession for the spectacle of sexual difference, which is held in the alcove, the site of the primal scene. The infant at one and a half, the dreaming child of four, the adult patient, the analyst, and finally the reader are invited to convene around the spectacle that offers visible evidence for sexual difference and is the site of the subject's engendering. One glimpse, and there is enough truth—the gradual reduction of the phenomenon to that minimal unit of one brief vision speaks evocatively of the foundational nature of the scene.[8] To see it once is to know all there is to know, provided the right conditions are fulfilled, namely, that the bodies show their differences. The posture of the bodies in the alcove and the patient's subjective positioning in relation to them determine the whole sequence that constitutes the patient's history.[9] If the hysteric's passional attitudes tell his or her life story, one posture engenders them all: the posture which, in the primal scene, renders visible "the existence of castration."

It seems indeed that for Freud, the image of sexual difference constitutes the matrix of all representations of subjectivity: the alcove where the subject is the witness (*Zeuge*) of his or her conception (*Zeugnis*) and acquires the conviction (*Ueberzeugung*) of the reality of castration. The bodily (and mental) disorder that characterizes hysteria originated there as well: "Analysis shows, in the case of people with whose life-story the physician will later be concerned, that at such moments two impulses take possession of the immature spectator. In boys, one is the impulse to put himself in the place of the active man, and the other, the opposing current, is the impulse to identify himself with the passive woman" (*SE* XIV, 54). Thus, in *History of the Psycho-Analytic Movement*, Freud identifies, in a recapitulation of the primal scene's significance, the causal relation between the primal scene and hysteria. The hysteric's predicament begins with a double identification: he or she is both at once—the

8. This is contained in an addition signaled by the square brackets on pages 57–60. The child must have seen the scene, once, independent of the bodily positioning; this appears to be the ultimate "grain of truth" to which Freud chooses to hold. He thus writes: "it is true that we cannot dispense with the assumption that the child observed a copulation, the sight of which gave him the conviction that castration might be more than an empty threat" (*SE* XVII, 57).

9. On the importance of positions in this case history, Peter Brooks states, "Postures appear to indicate the joints and interconnections of event, the way one event 'plugs' into another" (*Reading for the Plot: Design and Intention in Narrative*, 275). As for the meaning of positions, attitudes, and movement in hysteria in general, David-Ménard tells us, "To construct her identity, a subject retains—from everything that makes up her life—scenarios in which her body is at stake: not her entire body, but certain of its movements, states, or positions" (*Hysteria from Freud to Lacan*, 40).

active man and the suffering woman.[10] For to have seen is not enough; the scene requires that the subject begin to play there, through an act of identification, the appropriate gender role, that which corresponds to his or her biological sex. The primal scene is thus not only a myth concerned with origins, but also the true beginning, which sets the pattern of all subsequent desire and knowledge. Around this secret then, the hysterical mind is held in suspension and, for that reason, drawn insistently to the threshold of the alcove. The secret of the alcove haunts every hysteric precisely because it is felt more strongly for remaining unresolved. The question of its significance remains for the hysteric an open, burning issue.

This literary study has led us to envisage again and again in the symptoms of hysterical writing a desire that, while holding to the truth of sexual difference, can never fully acknowledge or endorse the laws of gender. And these literary, medical, early psychoanalytical representations of hysteria have acted as vivid and sometimes violent reminders of the repression that is tied to the enforcement of gender. In retrospect, the first gender fable I presented, with Brachet questioning the ladies about their understanding of gender in the room of the woman in confinement, begins to look uncannily like a parody of some primal scene, but one whose significance is not individual but collective. In this (parodic) light, the primal scene is about sexual ideology—the privileging of force over and against sense. Its elements are the valorization of the phallus, the subject's spontaneous, effortless compliance with the rules of the "gender game," and above all, the gradual internalization of a repression that means to deny (particularly in the case of women) the first "intelligence" that we naturally have of what "makes" sexual difference—a mere anatomical divergence. The primal scene as presented in the case history of the Wolf-Man entails, on the other hand, the "reality of castration," a subject's rebellion against the rules of gender, and a constant and shared effort on the part of patient and analyst to understand the far-ranging implications or, to use the analyst's word, the full "significance" of sexual difference. Furthermore, Brachet's desire to

10. Freud thus attributes the Wolf-Man's hysteria to his repudation of the two "feminine" sexual currents that dominate his life (*SE* XVII, 113–4) as well as to a "wavering" between "contradictory libidinal cathexis": "his childhood had been marked by a wavering between activity and passivity, his puberty by a struggle for masculinity, and the period after he had fallen ill by a fight for the object of his masculine desires" (117–19). What then lies at the root of the patient's hysterical conversion is the inability to abide by one consistent and orthodox position within the "grammar of the sexes."

show off through his (hysterical) women looks like a parody of Freud's more genuine and decisive epistemological investment in his hysterical patients for the constitution his own theories of subjectivity. "Where am I? Where is my place?" each subject asks himself or herself when faced with the spectacle of sexual difference.

There is no denying then the heuristic value and the wide-ranging cultural significance of the *scène d'alcôve* for our understanding of subjectivity. The mise-en-scène or dramaturgy of desire and knowledge that it triggers enables us readers, standing at a remove like the analyst in the Freudian scenario, to elicit from it a wealth of subjective inscriptions that belong to a history of modern consciousness. For the analyst, the encounter with sexual difference is meant to constitute the founding event of subjectivity; reading against the grain of such an assumption, I have tried to assess the cost of the repression that occurs when subjectivity is modeled, defined even according to gender.[11] My readings of hysteria have led me to focus simultaneously on the law of gender and on the desire for difference, for a "difference within" that the enforcement of this distinction between the sexes produces. I analyzed, meanwhile, what might be some of consequences, for a history of the subject and for a history of the relations between men and women, of this "grammar of the sexes." This is how, in the wake of many recent studies that have made hysteria the stepping-stone of a feminist inquiry, I have chosen to meet some of the interrogations raised by the figure of a hysteric—she has been made into an effigy of a mind haunted by a questioning of gender.

The law of gender, as we have seen, enforces femininity on the female and, from there, masculinity on the male; it wants symbolically to map the contours of mind according to the traits of the body. In his or her failure to comply, the hysteric is condemned to chart a desire and a knowledge outside of such conventions of representation—in the "pathologein" of symptoms or in the act of writing—and she (or he) speaks thus more palpably of the force of gender than any other subject. Hysteria is then the place where gender is put to the test, the place where, in the nineteenth century, a history and a theory of gender emerged

---

11. "Psychoanalysis represents a twofold movement in its thinking; on the one hand it emphasizes the sexual infrastructure of life, on the other it 'inflates' the notion of sexuality until it comprehends the whole of existence," writes Maurice Merleau-Ponty (*Phénoménologie de la perception*, 185). My own perspective has led me indeed to analyze what the subject might gain from the point of view of the existence of the mind if she (or he) resisted the discriminatory social and cultural structures erected on the basis of sexual difference. In that sense, I too resist the notion that "sexuality integrates the whole of existence."

whose traces are still with us. The hysterics treasure in their symptoms not only the stories of an illicit desire but the knowledge of all that which, in the name of the law of gender, should be given up. As the texts of Flaubert, James, Sand, and Eliot show, hysteria, as a mode of figuration, can sustain their desire and knowledge, but does not name them or give them a palpable form. They are doomed to experience consciousness in the negative, as a secret inscribed in the writing.

But hysteria is my own story as well, or at least the story of a project that hovers between two gendered roles. As a reader of Flaubert, James, and Freud, I have imitated the attitude of the observer-analyst intent on retrieving from the symptoms of representation the subject's position in relation to the scene of engendering. Standing on the threshold of the hysteric's chamber, I have pried into the secret articulations of desire, knowledge, and gender and looked for the traces of consciousness. To stand on the analyst's side—the masculine side—has made it possible to uncover the particular narratology (founded on what James called the "sense of difference") and the dramaturgy (whose staple is the scene of passion and knowledge) that sustains the representations of sexual identity. My various textual encounters with representations of hysteria have repeatedly brought to light the hysteria—as a relentless questioning of gender—that presides over a system of representations intent on seizing the subject's "inner life." This is where Freud's analysis of the primal scene in *From the History of an Infantile Neurosis* is particularly instructive: it reveals not only the analyst's desire for sexual difference, but uncovers the foundational epistemological value of the "existence of castration" for the representations of the subject. The figure of the alcove, which springs from that desire, produces in turn its own epistemological pattern, which is then endowed with a truth-value and a foundational meaning. Here then, says the analyst, lies the secret of *das verborgenste Seelische*—of the subject's most hidden recesses of the mind. As for the philosopher, he might say that this is the matrix of all representation— the form informing all the other forms—and that consciousness necessarily bears the traces of that secret.

But my concern in this project has also been writing, as a space where the utterance can speak beyond the frames of representation. This is where, changing sides, I have moved into the alcove. There, like James's Olive Chancellor haunted by the voices of suffering women, or like Woolf's Lily Briscoe, who imagines the sacred but secret inscriptions that are held "in the chambers of the mind" of another woman, I have listened to the voices issuing from women's texts. The gesture is one of "feminine empathy," while the word "feminine" means no more than an imaginary, readerly alignment with the other subject position, of those (and they don't have to be women) who have internalized some "originary" prohibition on reading, thinking, speaking and became thinking bodies. Because I wanted to acknowledge the depths of unspokenness and the measure of the denial or negation of desire and knowledge that characterize "a woman's text," I have read George Sand and George Eliot with the eyes of a modern rhetorician, attentive to figures and intensities, in hope of sustaining a mode of intellectual and historical exchange that would be intersubjective.[12] But these readings obey as well the other, analytical principle, which led me to uncover the primal scene of a gender inscription staged in the alcove. In George Sand's and George Eliot's alcove, hysteria is present as a representation, but also as a principle or force behind their writing that speaks simultaneously of a knowledge of sexual difference and of a passionate denial of gender.

There, in those traces of hysteria that my readings attempt to decipher, lies the secret in the form of a representation that defines the feminine consciousness. This consciousness carries the marks of its gender precisely when it simultaneously acknowledges, in the forms of representation, and denies, in the performance of writing, a sexual identity that the converging discourses of the doctor, the analyst, and the critic have built around the distinction between the sexes. In this instance, "feminine" must be understood as designating the internalized difference that results from the assumption of sexual difference as gender. A gender-marked consciousness is here not merely a fact of language or one of its effects, but bespeaks the internalization of the prohibition on certain modalities of desire and knowledge and the denial of the free play of subjective possibilities.[13] A gendered consciousness, this study attempts

12. In the words of Lucette Finas (quoted by Roland Barthes in "Question de tempo," an introduction to *Le bruit d'Iris*, 11): "reading as an exchange between the *forces become figure* of the text that is being read and the *forces become figure* of the text that is reading" ("la lecture comme échange entre la *figure des forces* du texte lu et la *figure des forces* du texte lecteur").

13. As I have tried to show, literary texts enable us to document a complex process of internalization of gender, which leaves a mark or a trace that is not merely an element in the functioning of the psyche, but is also a historical fact. My own feminist concerns have thus led me away from psychoanalytical approaches, such as Lacan's or Mannoni's, to document a history whose dimensions are to be seen eventually in the field of the existential or the real. From my perspective then, the expression of sexual difference (*la sexuation*) as gender (*le genre*) in language and in the order of the symbolic not only determines our condition as subjects in language but affects our ways of dealing with the world. On the question of the relation between grammatical gender and sexual difference, see Mannoni's illuminating discusssion in "L'ellipse et la barre," (*Clefs*, 61–62).

to show, is a historical and ideological construct and hence is not an essential fact or constituent of the female subject. Nor is it an immovable structure: Henry James, in his last text on Sand, speaks in persuasive terms of "the removal of immemorial disabilities" ("George Sand," in *Literary Criticism*, 780). One is not born with a consciousness of gender, but grows up with it, as can be seem in the pedagogical injuctions, prescriptions, or "cultural fictions" present in the various discourses on hysteria, and particularly in that of the *médecine morale*. But neither does one grow out of it: the process of engendering leaves an irremovable trace in every one of us, as a difference within that is more substantial, more permanent perhaps, than a deconstructive approach of difference has commonly lead us to think.

I did not then undertake to visit the hysteric's secret alcove for the *frisson historique* that might be found there. Nor in order to be able to display proudly, as in the glass cases of an old-fashioned museum of anthropology, the specimens of a collection of oddities and long lost objects or customs. This book represents a genealogical inquiry into nineteenth-century representations of hysteria, an inquiry that acknowledges the traces, in the present, of the nineteenth-century hysteric. As an act of cultural and personal memory, it speaks of my own awareness, as a woman and a literary critic, of an internalized and eventually internal difference made by gender, which hysteria renders perceptible. But in my desire to account for hysteria within a literary tradition, as part of the experience of writing and reading and as an element of intellectual history, I am of course not alone.

For Roland Barthes, hysteria is associated with reading and with the possibility of subverting a structure—"Reading . . . leav[es] intact . . . the movement of the subject and of history: reading is the site where structure is made hysterical," he concludes in his essay "From Science to Literature: On Reading" (*Rustle of Language*, 43). For Jean Starobinski, hysteria is a form of writing: in his study of Flaubert's style in *Madame Bovary*, the critic singles out the hysteric's troubled body as the ultimate site of "a human expression that would not be contaminated by clichés and ineptitudes" ("L'échelle," 182), and he speaks of its language as "rekindl[ing] an inner perception of the self bound to . . . the production of an *imaginaire*" (179). As a psychoanalyst and philosopher, Monique David-Ménard gauges carefully, throughout her study, the value of hysteria as a way of retrieving, in a body that thinks, an experience of *jouissance*. But she is aware as well of the cost exacted by the denial that the hysteric embodies—symptoms cancel out knowledge, and the hysteric struggles so violently with the symbolic that discourse is arrested. Sarah Kofman ends her text on Diderot's *La religieuse* hoping for a time when women and literature are no longer bound to hysteria (*Séductions*, 37–38). These few names and quotations summarize my own progress.

This book on the representations of hysteria ends with my recognition that in these readings of desire and knowledge, knowledge ultimately wants the upper hand, and that like Sarah Kofman, I must have been longing for a way of writing, for a mode of representation, that would abolish hysteria. I have wished that the scene of passion, that the hysteric's scene of "passionate denial," would become one of knowledge and of a reason that knows itself—I ended up playing the analyst as if to cure hysteria of its unreason. I have long known, as Michel Foucault put it, that "the soul is a prison to the body" (*Discipline and Punish*, 30), but my work on hysteria revealed gradually that the reverse can be true as well, that the body can be a prison to the soul. As a consequence it is now the mind, with its particular drives or pleasures tied to a femininity that is also a mental condition, that pays the price.[14] As an intellectual and "theorist" who resists the more immediate seductions of the body, I end up walking in the traces of the infamous Fanny Price (surely another example of a hysteric), who withdraws to her secret chamber only too happy to escape from the "grievous imprisonment of body and mind" that besets her when she is put in the presence of the "irresponsible" pleasures that only the body knows.[15]

Let me speak one last time for the life of the mind and the "most hidden recesses of the soul," but knowing that in the shadow of that mind, a body is being forgotten, overlooked, denied. Hysteria speaks of a knowledge that does not know itself, of a consciousness that is absent but comes into its own, belatedly, in the act of reading, where it is endowed with the knowledge of hindsight, the consciousness of gender that was its secret. So it is only in the act of reading and interpretation that the hysteric's body begins to speak; it speaks of the history of a consciousness branded by its gender. Confronted with the fictions of hysteria, the readers become analysts and transform her chamber into

14. This is also the question the philosopher Denise Riley raises very concretely under the heading "Bodies, Identities, Feminisms." She asks: "Are there moments when some, as it were, non-ideological kind of woman-ness irrupts, such that you are for that moment a woman unironically and without compromise? Someone might well retort, against my dark examples, that the experiences of sexual happiness or of childbearing might furnish resonantly optimistic ways of taking up 'being a woman now'" (*Am I That Name?* 97).

15. The quotations are from Jane Austen's *Mansfield Park* (341). These words, expressing the heroine's resistance to seduction, conclude one of Fanny's grievous interviews with Henry Crawford. "She was at liberty," the text significantly continues.

an amphitheater; they, like the hysteric, make of sexual difference the central enigma. But as analysts they also believe in tearing away the secret that she treasures in her symptoms, although they cannot hope to bring about a cure. All they do then is reflect on the consequences of the differences that were made in the name of sexual difference. There they would like to endorse the philosopher's simple statement, which speaks beyond gender: "only man is capable of speaking, because he can *not* show what he could show." But as the readers of the fictions of hysteria they find themselves rehearsing, silently maybe, another formulation, with a different emphasis: "men *and* women are capable of speaking, because they only can *not* show what they *could* show." The question then becomes one of representation, of representing oneself as a subject at a time or in a history when no outside force can convince or coerce a woman to unlearn what she has known or, as a hysteric, to ignore those things that all the while she knew. A desire is then born for new space without divisions, nets and posts to draw the line between the sexes, a time that is the Mallarmean condition of *un vierge et vivace aujourd'hui,* and a page that in its whiteness holds a play of all possibilities.

Bibliography

American Psychiatric Association. *Diagnostic and Statistical Manual of Mental Disorders.* 3d ed. Washington, D.C.: APA, 1984.

Anderson, Quentin. *The American Henry James.* London: John Calder, 1958.

Armstrong, Nancy. *Desire and Domestic Fiction: A Political History of the Novel.* New York: Oxford University Press, 1987.

Austen, Jane. *Mansfield Park.* Harmondsworth: Penguin, 1966.

Barbéris, Pierre. "Preface." In Honoré de Balzac, *La femme de trente ans.* Paris: Gallimard, 1977.

Barthes, Roland. *Le plaisir du texte.* Paris: Seuil, 1973.

——. "Question de tempo." In Lucette Finas, *Le bruit d'Iris.* Paris: Flammarion, 1978.

——. *The Rustle of Language.* Trans. Richard Howard. Berkeley: University of California Press, 1989.

Basuk, Ellen. "The Rest Cure: Repetition or Resolution of Victorian Women's Conflicts?" In *The Female Body in Western Culture,* ed. Susan R. Suleiman. Cambridge: Harvard University Press, 1986.

Baudelaire, Charles. *Curiosités esthétiques et L'art romantique.* Paris: Garnier, 1962.

Beauvoir, Simone de. *Le deuxième sexe.* Paris: Gallimard, 1976.

Beer, Gillian. *George Eliot.* Brighton: Harvester Press, 1986.

Beizer, Janet. *Ventriloquized Bodies: The Narrative Uses of Hysteria in France, 1850–1900.* Ithaca: Cornell University Press, 1995.

Benjamin, Jessica. *Bonds of Love: Psychoanalysis, Feminism and the Problem of Domination.* New York: Pantheon, 1988.

——. "A Desire of One's Own." In *Feminist Studies/Critical Studies,* ed. Teresa de Lauretis. Bloomington: Indiana University Press, 1986.

Bernheimer, Charles, and Claire Kahane, eds. *In Dora's Case: Freud, Hysteria, Feminism.* New York: Columbia University Press, 1985.

Bersani, Leo. *A Future for Astyanax: Character and Desire in Literature.* London: Marion Boyars, 1981.

Bertier, Philippe. "Corambé: Interprétation d'un mythe." In *Colloque de Cerisy: George Sand,* ed. Simone Vierne. Paris: SEDES, 1983.

Blanchot, Maurice. *L'écriture du désastre.* Paris: Gallimard, 1980.

Bonaparte, Felicia. *Will and Destiny: Morality and Tragedy in George Eliot's Novels.* New York: New York University Press, 1975.

Bossis, Mireille. "La maladie comme ressort dramatique dans les romans de George Sand." *Revue d'Histoire Littéraire de France* 76 (1976).

Brachet, Jean-Louis. *Traité complet de l'hypochondrie.* Paris: Baillière, 1844.

——. *Traité de l'hystérie.* Paris: Baillière, 1847.

Brady, Kristin. *George Eliot.* New York: St. Martin's Press, 1992.

Briquet, Pierre. *Traité clinique et thérapeutique de l'hystérie.* Paris: Baillière, 1859.

Brodhead, Richard H. *The School of Hawthorne.* New York: Oxford University Press, 1986.

Brodski, Bella, and Celeste Schenck, eds. *Life/Lines: Theorizing Women's Autobiography.* Ithaca: Cornell University Press, 1988.

Brooks, Peter. *Body Work: Objects of Desire in Modern Narrative.* Cambridge: Harvard University Press, 1993.

——. "Introduction." In Henry James, *The Wings of the Dove.* Oxford: Oxford University Press, 1984.

——. *The Melodramatic Imagination: Balzac, Henry James and the Mode of Excess.* New York: Columbia University Press, 1985.

——. *Reading for the Plot: Design and Intention in Narrative.* New York: Vintage, 1984.

Budick, Sanford, and Wolfgang Iser, eds. *Languages of the Unsayable: The Play of Negativity in Literature and Literary Theory.* New York: Columbia University Press, 1989.

Burgin, Victor, James Donald, and Cora Kaplan, eds. *Formations of Fantasy.* London: Methuen, 1986.

Butler, Judith. *Gender Trouble: Feminism and the Subversion of Identity.* New York: Routledge, 1990.

Cameron, Sharon. *Thinking in Henry James.* Chicago: University of Chicago Press, 1989.

Cargill, Oscar. *The Novels of Henry James.* New York: Macmillan, 1961.

——. "*The Turn of the Screw* and Alice James." *PMLA* 78 (1963).

Carpenter, Mary Wilson. " 'A Bit of Her Flesh': Circumcision and 'The Signification of the Phallus' in *Daniel Deronda*." *Genders* 1 (1988).

Castle, Terry. "The Female Thermometer." *Representations* 17 (1987).

Cavell, Stanley. "Naughty Orators: Negation of Voice in *Gaslight*." In *Languages of the Unsayable: The Play of Negativity in Literature and Literary Theory,* ed. Sanford Budick and Wolfgang Iser. New York: Columbia University Press, 1989.

Chase, Cynthia. "The Decomposition of the Elephants: Double-Reading *Daniel Deronda*." *PMLA* 93 (1978).

Clément, Catherine, and Hélène Cixous. *La jeune née*. Paris: Union Générale d'Éditions, 1975.

Collister, Peter. "Taking Care of Yourself: Henry James and the Life of George Sand." *Modern Language Review* 83 (1988).

Cominos, Peter T. "Innocent Femina Sensualis in Unconscious Conflict." In *Suffer and Be Still*, ed. Martha Vicinus. London: Methuen, 1972.

Cooper, Michael A. "Discipl(in)ing the Master." In *Engendering Men: The Question of Male Feminist Criticism*, ed. Joseph A. Boone and Michael Cadden. London: Routledge, 1990.

Cott, Nancy F. "Passionlessness: An Interpretation of Victorian Sexual Ideology, 1790–1850." *Signs: Journal of Women in Culture and Society* 4, no. 2 (1978).

Cox, James M. "The Memoirs of Henry James: Self-Interest as Autobiography." In *Studies in Autobiography*, ed. James Olney. New York: Oxford University Press, 1988.

Crecelius, Kathryn J. *Family Romance: George Sand's Early Novels*. Bloomington: Indiana University Press, 1987.

Cross, John W. *George Eliot's Life as Related in Her Letters and Journal*, ed. by her husband. 3 vols. London: Blackwood, 1885.

Datlof, Nathalie, ed. *The George Sand Papers: Conference Proceedings*. New York: AMS Press, 1976.

——. *The George Sand Papers: Conference Proceedings*. New York: AMS Press, 1978.

Daugherty, Sarah B. "Henry James, George Sand, and *The Bostonians*: Another Curious Chapter in the Literary History of Feminism." *Henry James Review* 10, no. 1 (1989).

David-Ménard, Monique. *Hysteria from Freud to Lacan: Body and Language in Psychoanalysis*. Trans. Catherine Porter. Ithaca: Cornell University Press, 1989.

de Bolla, Peter. *The Discourse of the Sublime: History, Aesthetics and the Subject*. Oxford: Basil Blackwell, 1989.

de Lauretis, Teresa. *Alice Doesn't: Feminism, Semiotics, Cinema*. Bloomington: Indiana University Press, 1984.

Deleuze, Gilles. "The Schizophrenic and Language: Surface and Depth in Lewis Carroll and Antonin Artaud." In *Textual Strategies*, ed. Josué Harari. Ithaca: Cornell University Press, 1979.

Derrida, Jacques. "How to Avoid Speaking: Denials." In *Languages of the Unsayable: The Play of Negativity in Literature and Literary Theory*, ed. Sanford Budick and Wolfgang Iser. New York: Columbia University Press, 1989.

——. "Me-Psychoanalysis: An Introduction to the Translation of 'The Shell and the Kernel' by Nicolas Abraham." *Diacritics* 9 (1979).

——. *Spurs: Nietzsche's Styles*. Trans. Barbara Harlow. Chicago: University of Chicago Press, 1981.

Didier, Béatrice. "Femme—identité—écriture, A propos de l'*Histoire de ma vie de George Sand.*" *Revue des Sciences Humaines* 168 (1977).

Didier, Béatrice, and Jacques Neefs, eds. *George Sand: Ecritures du romantisme II.* Paris: Presses Universitaires de Vincennes, 1990.

Doane, Mary Ann. "Veiling over Desire: Close-ups of the Woman." In *Feminism and Psychoanalysis*, ed. Richard Feldstein and Judith Roof. Ithaca: Cornell University Press, 1989.

During, Simon. "The Strange Case of Monomania: Patriarchy in Literature, Murder in *Middlemarch*, Drowning in *Daniel Deronda.*" *Representations* 23 (1988).

Edel, Leon. *The Life of Henry James.* 2 vols. Harmondsworth: Penguin, 1977.

Edwards, Michael. "George Eliot and Negative Form." *Critical Quarterly* 17, no. 2 (1975).

Eliot, George. *Daniel Deronda.* Ed. Graham H. Handley. Oxford: Clarendon Press, 1984.

——. *The George Eliot Letters.* Ed. Gordon S. Haight. 9 vols. New Haven: Yale University Press, 1954–1978.

——. *Middlemarch.* Harmondsworth: Penguin, 1976.

——. *The Mill on the Floss.* Oxford: Oxford University Press, 1986.

Ermarth, Elizabeth Deeds. *George Eliot.* Princeton: Princeton University Press, 1985.

Evans, Martha Noel. *Fits and Starts: A Genealogy of Hysteria in Modern France.* Ithaca: Cornell University Press, 1991.

Faderman, Lillian. *Surpassing the Love of Men: Romantic Friendship and Love between Women from the Renaissance to the Present.* New York: William Morrow, 1981.

Feldstein, Richard, and Judith Roof, eds. *Feminism and Psychoanalysis.* Ithaca: Cornell University Press, 1989.

Felman, Shoshana. *Jacques Lacan and the Adventure of Insight: Psychoanalysis in Contemporary Culture.* Cambridge: Harvard University Press, 1987.

——. "Rereading Femininity." *Yale French Studies* 62 (1981).

——. *What Does a Woman Want? Reading and Sexual Difference.* Baltimore: Johns Hopkins University Press, 1993.

——. "Women and Madness: The Critical Phallacy." *Diacritics* 5 (1975).

——. *Writing and Madness: Literature/Philosophy/Psychoanalysis.* Trans. Martha Noel Evans. Ithaca: Cornell University Press, 1987.

Feuerbach, Ludwig. *The Essence of Christianity.* Trans. George Eliot. 2d ed. London: Trübner, 1881.

——. *Das Wesen des Christenthums* (The essence of Christianity). Munich: Frommann Verlag, 1960.

Fish, Stanley. "Withholding the Missing Portion: Power, Meaning, and Persuasion in Freud's *The Wolf-Man.*" In *The Linguistics of Writing: Arguments between Language and Literature*, ed. Nigel Fabb. Manchester: Manchester University Press, 1987.

Flaubert, Gustave. *The Letters of Gustave Flaubert, 1830–1857.* Ed. and trans. Francis Steegmuller. Cambridge: Harvard University Press, 1980.

——. *Madame Bovary.* Trans. Alan Russell. Harmondsworth: Penguin, 1987.

——. *Oeuvres.* Vol. I. Ed. A. Thibaudet and R. Dumesnil. Pléiade ed. Paris: Gallimard, 1966.

——. *Oeuvres complètes de Gustave Flaubert: Correspondance.* Paris: Connard, 1927.

Flaubert, Gustave, and George Sand. *Correspondance,* Ed. Alphonse Jacobs. Paris: Flammarion, 1981.

Flieger, Jerry Aline. "Entertaining the Ménage à Trois: Psychoanalysis, Feminism, and Literature." In *Feminism and Psychoanalysis,* ed. Richard Feldstein and Judith Root. Ithaca: Cornell University Press, 1989.

Foucault, Michel. *Discipline and Punish: The Birth of the Prison.* Trans. A. Sheridan. New York: Vintage, 1979.

——. *Histoire de la folie à l'âge classique.* Paris: Gallimard, 1972.

——. *La volonté de savoir: Histoire de la sexualité I.* Paris: Gallimard, 1976.

Freadman, Richard. *Eliot, James and the Fictional Self: A Study in Character and Narration.* London: Macmillan, 1986.

Freud, Sigmund. *Analysis Terminable and Interminable. SE XXIII.*

——. *An Autobiographical Study. SE XX.*

——. *Briefe, 1873–89.* Ed. Ernst Freud and Lucie Freud. Frankfurt: Fischer, 1978.

——. *'Civilized' Sexual Morality and Modern Nervous Illness. SE IX.*

——. *Creative Writers and Day-Dreaming. SE IX.*

——. *Fragment of a Case of Hysteria* (Dora). *SE VII.*

——. *From the History of an Infantile Neurosis* (Wolf-Man). *SE XVII.*

——. *Gesammelte Werke.* Vol. VII. Ed. Anna Freud et al. London: Imago, 1940.

——. *Hysterical Phantasies and Their Relation to Bisexuality. SE IX.*

——. *The Interpretation of Dreams. SE IV–V.*

——. *Introductory Lectures on Psycho-Analysis. SE XV–XVI.*

——. *The Letters of Sigmund Freud.* Selected and ed. Ernest L. Freud, trans. Tania Stern and James Stern. New York: Basic Books, 1975.

——. *New Introductory Lectures on Psycho-Analysis. SE XXII.*

——. *On Narcissism: An Introduction. SE XIV.*

——. *On the History of the Psycho-Analytic Movement. SE XIV.*

——. *The Origins of Psychoanalysis: Letters to Wilhelm Fliess, Drafts, and Notes.* Ed. Marie Bonaparte. Trans. James Strachey. New York: Basic Boosk, 1954.

——. *Psycho-Analysis and the Establishment of the Facts in Legal Proceedings. SE IX.*

——. *Some General Remarks on Hysterical Attacks. SE IX.*

——. *The Standard Edition of the Complete Psychological Works of Sigmund Freud.* Trans. under the direction of James Strachey. 24 vols. London: Hogarth Press, 1959–72. Cited throughout as *SE.*

——. *Studies on Hysteria. SE II.*

——. *Three Essays on the Theory of Sexuality. SE VII.*

Gardiner, Muriel, ed. *The Wolf-Man and Sigmund Freud.* London: Hogarth Press, 1973.

Gay, Peter. *Freud: A Life for Our Time.* New York: Doubleday, 1989.

Gelley, Alexander. *Narrative Crossings: Theory and Pragmatics of Prose Fiction.* Baltimore: Johns Hopkins University Press, 1987.

Gilbert, Sandra, and Susan Gubar, eds. *The Norton Anthology of Literature by Women.* New York: Norton, 1985.

Girard, René. *Desire, Deceit, and the Novel.* Trans. Yvonne Freccero. Baltimore: Johns Hopkins University Press, 1965.

Glasgow, Janis. *George Sand: Collected Essays on George Sand.* Troy, N.Y.: Whitsun Publishing, 1985.

Goldstein, Jan. *Console and Classify: The French Psychiatric Profession in the Nineteenth Century.* London: Cambridge University Press, 1986.

La grande encyclopédie: Inventaire raisonné des sciences, des lettres, des arts. Paris: Lamirault, 1886–1902.

Green, André. *Le complexe de castration.* Paris: Presses Universitaires de France, 1990.

Habegger, Alfred. *Henry James and the "Woman Business."* Cambridge: Cambridge University Press, 1989.

Haight, Gordon. *George Eliot, a Biography.* Oxford: Oxford University Press, 1968.

Hellerstein, Erna O., et al., eds. *Victorian Women: A Documentary Account of Women's Lives in Nineteenth-Century England, France, and the United States.* Brighton: Harvester Press, 1981.

Hertz, Neil. "Dora's Secrets, Freud's Techniques." In *In Dora's Case: Freud, Hysteria, Feminism,* ed. Charles Bernheimer and Claire Kahane. New York: Columbia University Press, 1985.

——. *The End of the Line.* New York: Oxford University Press, 1985.

——. "Some Words in George Eliot: Nullify, Neutral, Numb, Number." In *Languages of the Unsayable,* ed. Sanford Budick and Wolfgang Iser. New York: Columbia University Press, 1989.

Hirsch, Michèle. "Questions à *Indiana.*" *Revue des Sciences Humaines* 165 (1977).

Horowitz, Mardi J. *Hysterical Personality.* New York: Jason Aronson, 1977.

Hyppolite, Jean. "A Spoken Commentary on Freud's *Verneinung.*" In *The Seminar of Jacques Lacan, Book I,* trans. John Forrester. New York: Norton, 1988.

Irigaray, Luce. *Speculum de l'autre femme.* Paris: Minuit, 1974.

Jackson, John. *Passions du sujet.* Paris: Mercure de France, 1990.

Jacobus, Mary. "The Question of Language: Men of Maxims and *The Mill on the Floss.*" In *Writing and Sexual Difference,* ed. Elizabeth Abel. Brighton: Harvester Press, 1982.

——. *Reading Woman: Essays in Feminist Criticism.* London: Methuen, 1986.

James, Alice. *The Diary of Alice James.* Harmondsworth: Penguin, 1964.

James, Henry. *The Ambassadors.* Harmondsworth: Penguin, 1978.

——. *Autobiography.* Princeton: Princeton University Press, 1983.

——. *The Bostonians.* Oxford: Oxford University Press, 1984.

——. *The Complete Notebooks of Henry James.* Ed. Leon Edel and Lyall H. Powers. Oxford: Oxford University Press, 1987.

——. "*Daniel Deronda:* A Conversation." In *Essays on Literature, American*

Writers, English Writers. Ed. Leon Edel. New York: Library of America, 1984.

——. *The Golden Bowl.* Harmondsworth: Penguin, 1978.

——. *Letters.* Vol. III (1883–95). Ed. Leon Edel. Cambridge: Harvard University Press, 1980.

——. *Letters.* Vol. IV (1895–1916). Ed. Leon Edel. Cambridge: Harvard University Press, 1984.

——. *Literary Criticism: French Writers, Other European Writers, the Prefaces to the New York Edition.* Ed. Leon Edel. Cambridge: Library of America, 1984.

——. *Selected Letters.* Ed. Leon Edel. Cambridge: Harvard University Press, 1987.

—. *The Wings of the Dove.* Oxford: Oxford University Press, 1984.

James, Henry, and Edith Wharton. *Letters, 1900–1915.* Ed. Lyall L. Powers. New York: Charles Scribner's Sons, 1990.

Jenny, Laurent. "Il n'y a pas de récit cathartique." *Poétique* 41 (1981).

Johnson, Barbara. "Is Female to Male as Ground Is to Figure?" In *Feminism and Psychoanalysis*, ed. Richard Feldstein and Judith Roof. Ithaca: Cornell University Press, 1989.

——. *A World of Difference.* Baltimore: Johns Hopkins University Press, 1987.

Jordanova, Ludmilla. *Sexual Visions: Images of Gender in Science and Medicine between the Eighteenth and Twentieth Centuries.* New York: Harvester, 1989.

Kahane, Claire. "Hysteria, Feminism, and the Case of *The Bostonians*." In *Feminism and Psychoanalysis*, ed. Richard Feldstein and Judith Roof. Ithaca: Cornell University Press, 1989.

Kahn, Alan. *Hysteria: The Elusive Neurosis.* Psychological Issues 12, nos. 1–2. New York: International University Press, 1978.

Keller, Evelyn Fox. "Making Gender Visible in the Pursuit of Nature's Secrets." In *American Feminist Thought at Century's End: A Reader*, ed. Linda S. Kauffman. Cambridge, Mass.: Blackwell, 1993.

Kofman, Sarah. *Aberrations: Le devenir-femme d'Auguste Comte.* Paris: Aubier-Flammarion, 1978.

——. *The Enigma of Woman: Woman in Freud's Writings.* Trans. Catherine Porter. Ithaca: Cornell University Press, 1989.

——. "The Narcissistic Woman: Freud and Girard." In *French Feminist Thought: A Reader*, ed. Toril Moi. London: Blackwell, 1987.

——. *Séductions.* Paris: Galilée, 1990.

Kristeva, Julia. "La femme, ce n'est jamais ça." In *Polylogue.* Paris: Seuil, 1977.

——. *Histoires d'amour.* Paris: Denoël, 1983.

——. *La révolution du langage poétique: L'avant-garde à la fin du XIXe siècle—Lautréamont et Mallarmé.* Paris: Seuil, 1974.

Kruks, Sonia. "Genre et subjectivité: Simone de Beauvoir et le féminisme contemporain." *Nouvelles Questions Féministes* 14 (1993).

Kuhn, Annette. *The Power of the Image.* London: Routledge and Kegan Paul, 1985.

Lacan, Jacques. "Intervention on Transference." In *In Dora's Case: Freud, Hys-*

teria, Feminism, ed. Charles Bernheimer and Claire Kahane. New York: Columbia University Press, 1985.

——. *Le séminaire VII: L'éthique de la psychanalyse*. Paris: Seuil, 1986.

——. "Le séminaire sur *La lettre volée*." Paris: Seuil, 1966.

Laplanche, Jean, and Jean-Bernard Pontalis. *Fantasme originaire, fantasme des origines, origines du fantasme*. Paris: Hachette, 1985.

——. "Fantasy and the Origins of Sexuality." In *Formations of Fantasy*, ed. Victor Burgin, James Donald, and Cora Kaplan. London: Methuen, 1986.

——. *Vocabulaire de la psychanalyse*. Paris: Presses Universitaires de France, 1981.

Laqueur, Thomas. *Making Sex: Body and Gender from the Greeks to Freud*. Cambridge: Harvard University Press, 1990.

Larousse, Pierre, ed. *Grand dictionnaire universel du XIXème siècle*. Paris: Larousse, 1865–76.

Leavis, F. R. *The Great Tradition*. London: Chatto and Windus, 1955.

Lecointre, Simone. "Le discours amoureux." In *Colloque de Cerisy: George Sand*, ed. Simone Vierne. Paris: SEDES, 1983.

Le Doeuff, Michèle. "Les chiasmes de Pierre Roussel (du savoir imaginaire à l'imaginaire savant)." In *L'imaginaire philosophique*. Paris: Payot, 1980.

——. *L'étude et le rouet: Des femmes, de la philosophie, etc.* Paris: Seuil, 1989.

Leeming, David. "Henry James and George Sand." *Revue de Littérature Comparée* 43 (1969).

Lewis, R. W. B. *The Jameses: A Family Narrative*. New York: Farrar, Straus, and Giroux, 1991.

Lukacher, Ned. *Primal Scenes: Literature, Philosophy, Psychoanalysis*. Ithaca: Cornell University Press, 1986.

Mann, Karen B. *The Language That Makes George Eliot's Fiction*. Baltimore: Johns Hopkins University Press, 1983.

Mannoni, Octave. *Clefs pour l'Imaginaire ou l'Autre Scène*. Paris: Seuil, 1969.

Marcus, Steven. *The Other Victorians: A Study of Sexuality and Pornography in Nineteenth-Century England*. New York: Basic Books, 1974.

Marin, Louis. *La voix excommuniée: Essais de mémoire*. Paris: Galilée, 1981.

Martin, Biddy. *Women and Modernity: The (Life)Styles of Lou Andréas-Salomé*. Ithaca: Cornell University Press, 1991.

Martin, Jean. *Oeuvre de Jean-Baptiste Greuze: Catalogue raisonné suivi de la liste des gravures exécutées d'après ses ouvrages*. Paris: G. Rapilly, 1908.

Matthiessen, F. O. *The James Family*. New York: Knopf, 1948.

Mauclair, Camille. *Greuze et son temps*. Paris: Albin Michel, 1926.

McLaren, Angus. "Doctor in the House: Medicine and Private Morality in France, 1800–1850." *Feminist Studies* 2 (1975).

Mengrédien, Georges. *La vie littéraire au XVIIème siècle*. Paris: Tallandier, 1947.

Mérimée, Prosper. *Romans et nouvelles*. Paris: Gallimard, 1945.

Merleau-Ponty, Maurice. *Phénoménologie de la perception*. Paris: Gallimard, 1945.

Miller, D. A. "*Cage aux Folles*: Sensation and Gender in Wilkie Collins's *The Woman in White*." In *Speaking of Gender*, ed. Elaine Showalter. New York: Routledge, 1989.

Miller, Nancy K. *Subject to Change: Reading Feminist Writing*. New York: Columbia University Press, 1988.
———. "Writing Fictions: Women's Autobiography in France." In *Life/Lines: Theorizing Women's Autobiography*, ed. Bella Brodzki and Celeste Schenck. Ithaca: Cornell University Press, 1988.
Mitchell, Juliet. *Psychoanalysis and Feminism: A Radical Reassessment of Freudian Psychoanalysis*. Harmondsworth: Penguin, 1974.
———. *Women: The Longest Revolution*. New York: Pantheon Books, 1984.
Moers, Ellen. *Literary Women*. London: Woman's Press, 1986.
Myers, William. *The Teaching of George Eliot*. Leicester: Leicester University Press, 1984.
Naginski, Isabelle. "Les deux *Lélia*: Une reécriture exemplaire." *Revue des Sciences Humaines* 226 (1992).
Nietzsche, Friedrich. *Die fröhliche Wissenschaft* (The gay science). Munich: DTV, 1980.
Normand, Charles. *Jean-Baptiste Greuze*. Paris: Allison et Cie, 1892.
Ozick, Cynthia. "The Lesson of the Master." In *In Praise of What Persists*. New York: Harper and Row, 1983.
Person, Leland S., Jr. "Henry James, George Sand, and the Suspense of Masculinity." *PMLA* 106 (1991).
Planté, Christine. *La petite soeur de Balzac*. Paris: Seuil, 1989.
Plato. *Theaetetus*. Trans. Benjamin Jowett. Oxford: Clarendon Press, 1973.
Poe, Edgar Allan. "The Philosophy of Composition." In *Essays and Reviews*, ed. G. R. Thompson. New York: Library of America, 1984.
Poovey, Mary. *Uneven Developments: The Ideological Work of Gender in Mid-Victorian England*. Chicago: University of Chicago Press, 1988.
Poulet, Georges. "The Phenomenology of Reading." Trans. Richard Macksey. In *Issues of Contemporary Literary Criticism*, ed. Gregory T. Polletta. Boston: Little Brown, 1973.
Raymond, Marcel. "George Sand, la rêverie et la vision transformante." In *Romantisme et rêverie*. Paris: Corti, 1948.
Richards, Carol. V. "Structural Motifs and the Limits of Feminism in *Indiana*." In *The George Sand Papers: Conference Proceedings*, ed. Nathalie Datlof. New York: A.M.S. Press, 1978.
Rigoli, Juan. "Lectures aliénistes, lectures aliénées (le déchiffrement de la folie dans la psychiatrie française de la première moitié du XIXème siècle)." *Equinoxe: Revue Romande des Sciences Humaines* 8 (1992).
Riley, Denise. *"Am I That Name?": Feminism and the Category of "Women" in History*. Minneapolis: University of Minnesota Press, 1988.
Rose, Jacqueline. *Sexuality and the Field of Vision*. London: Verso, 1986.
Rousseau, Jean-Jacques. *Julie ou la nouvelle Héloïse*. Paris: Garnier, 1960.
———. *Lettre à d'Alembert sur les spectacles*. Paris: Garnier-Flammarion, 1967.
Roustang, François. *Un destin si funeste*. Paris: Minuit, 1976.
Royle, Nicholas. *Telepathy and Literature: Essays on the Reading Mind*. Oxford: Basil Blackwell, 1991.
Sadoff, Dianne F. *Monsters of Affection: Dickens, Eliot, and Brontë on Fatherhood*. Baltimore: Johns Hopkins University Press, 1982.

Sand, George. *Correspondance.* Vol. III. Ed. Georges Lubin. Paris: Garnier, 1967.

——. *Correspondance.* Vol. IV. Ed. Georges Lubin. Paris: Garnier, 1968.

——. *The George Sand–Gustave Flaubert Letters.* Trans. Aimée Mackenzie. Chicago: Academy Press, 1977. First ed. 1929.

——. *Histoire de ma vie.* 2 vols. Paris: Gallimard, 1970–71.

——. *Indiana.* Paris: Calmann-Lévy, n.d.

——. *Lélia.* Ed. Pierre Reboul. Paris: Garnier, 1960.

——. *Lélia.* Trans. Maria Espinosa. Bloomington: Indiana University Press, 1978.

——. *Story of My Life: The Autobiography of George Sand.* Group translation ed. Thelma Jurgrau. New York: State University of New York Press, 1991.

——. *Valentine.* Geneva: Slatkine Reprints, 1980. Reprint of the Editions de Paris, 1863–1926.

——. *Valentine.* Trans. George Burnham Ives. Chicago: Academy Press, 1978.

Schor, Naomi. "Female Fetishism: The Case of George Sand." In *The Female Body in Western Culture: Contemporary Perspectives*, ed. Susan Suleiman. Cambridge: Harvard University Press, 1986.

——. *George Sand and Idealism.* New York: Columbia University Press, 1993.

——. "Idealism." In *A New History of French Literature*, ed. Denis Hollier. Cambridge: Harvard University Press, 1989.

——. "The Portrait of a Gentleman: Representing Men in (French) Women's Writing." *Representations* 20 (1987).

——. *Reading in Detail: Aesthetics and the Feminine.* New York: Methuen, 1987.

Sedgwick, Eve Kosofsky. "The Beast in the Closet: James and the Writing of Homosexual Panic." In *Sex, Politics, and Science in the Nineteenth-Century Novel*, selected papers from the English Institute, 1983–84, ed. Ruth Bernard Yeazell. Baltimore: Johns Hopkins University Press, 1986.

——. *Between Men: English Literature and Male Homosocial Desire.* New York: Columbia University Press, 1985.

——. *The Epistemology of the Closet.* Berkeley: University of California Press, 1990.

Showalter, Elaine. *The Female Malady: Women, Madness, and English Culture, 1830–1980.* New York: Pantheon, 1985.

——. "The Other Bostonians: Gender and Literary Study." *Yale Journal of Criticism* 1 (1989).

——, ed. *Speaking of Gender.* New York: Routledge, 1989.

Shuttleworth, Sally. *George Eliot and Nineteenth-Century Science: The Make-Believe of a Beginning.* London: Cambridge University Press, 1984.

Silverman, Kaja. *The Acoustic Mirror: The Female Voice in Psychoanalysis and Cinema.* Indianapolis: Indiana University Press, 1988.

——. "Too Early/Too Late: Subjectivity and the Primal Scene in Henry James." In *Why the Novel Matters: A Postmodern Perplex*, ed. Mark Spilka and Caroline McCracken-Flesher. Bloomington: Indiana University Press, 1990.

Smith-Rosenberg, Carroll. *Disorderly Conduct: Visions of Gender in Victorian America.* New York: Oxford University Press, 1985.

Solomon-Godeau, Abigail. *Photography at the Dock: Essays on Photographic*

History, Institutions, and Practices. Minneapolis: University of Minnesota Press, 1991.

Sontag, Susan. *Illness as Metaphor*. New York: Farrar, Straus, and Giroux, 1978.

Starobinski, Jean. "Acheronta Movebo." *Critical Inquiry* 13 (1987).

———. "L'échelle des températures." In *Le temps de la réflexion*. Paris: Gallimard, 1980.

———. *Le remède dans le mal: Critique et légitimation de l'artifice à l'Âge des Lumières*. Paris: Gallimard, 1989.

Steiner, George. "Eros and Idiom." *On Difficulty and Other Essays*. Oxford: Oxford University Press, 1978.

Stewart, Garrett. *Reading Voices: Literature and the Phonotext*. Berkeley: University of California Press, 1990.

Sudrann, Jean. "*Daniel Deronda* and the Landscape of Exile." *English Literary History* 37 (1970).

Suleiman, Susan R., ed. *The Female Body in Western Culture*. Cambridge: Harvard University Press, 1986.

Swann, Brian. "Eyes in the Mirror: Imagery and Symbolism in *Daniel Deronda*." *Nineteenth-Century Fiction* 23 (1969).

Tanner, Tony. *Adultery in the Novel: Contract and Transgression*. Baltimore: Johns Hopkins University Press, 1979.

———. "*The Bostonians* and the Human Voice." In *Scenes of Nature, Signs of Men*. Cambridge: Cambridge University Press, 1987.

———. *Venice Desired*. Oxford: Blackwell, 1991.

Temoshok, Lydia, and Clifford Attkisson. "Epidemiology of Hysterical Phenomenon: Evidence for Psychosocial Theory." In Mardi J. Horowitz, *Hysterical Personality*. New York: Jason Aronson, 1977.

Thibaudet, Albert. *Gustave Flaubert*. Paris: Gallimard, 1982.

Thompson, Patricia. *George Sand and the Victorians: Her Influence and Reputation in Nineteenth-Century England*. New York: Columbia University Press, 1975.

———. "The Three Georges." *Nineteenth-Century Fiction* 18 (1963).

Trilling, Lionel. *The Opposing Self*. New York: Viking Press, 1955.

van Boheemen, Christine. *The Novel as Family Romance: Language, Gender, and Authority from Fielding to Joyce*. Ithaca: Cornell University Press, 1987.

Vareille, Jean-Claude. "Fantasmes de la fiction—fantasmes de l'écriture." In *Colloque de Cerisy: George Sand*, ed. Simone Vierne. Paris: SEDES, 1983.

Veeder, William, and Susan Griffin, eds. *The Art of Criticism: Henry James and the Theory and Practice of Fiction*. Chicago: University of Chicago Press, 1986.

Veith, Ilza. *Hysteria: The History of a Disease*. Chicago: University of Chicago Press, 1965.

Verjat, Alain. "Formes et fonctions du discours autobiographique." In *Colloque de Cerisy: George Sand*, ed. Simone Vierne. Paris: SEDES, 1983.

Vicinus, Martha, ed. *Suffer and Be Still: Women in the Victorian Age*. London: Methuen, 1982.

Vierne, Simone, ed. *Colloque de Cerisy: George Sand*. Paris: SEDES, 1983.

Virey, Jean-Jacques. *De la femme sous ses rapports physiologique, moral et littéraire.* 3d ed. Brussels: Louis Hauman, 1834.

———. *Histoire naturelle du genre humain.* Paris: Crochard, 1824.

Voisin, François. *Des causes morales et physiques des maladies mentales et de quelques autres affections nerveuses telles que l'hystérie, la nymphomanie et le satyriasis.* Paris: Baillière, 1826.

Watt, Ian. *The Rise of the Novel: Studies in Defoe, Richardson, and Fielding.* London: Chatto and Windus, 1957.

Weeks, Jeffrey. *Sex, Politics and Sexuality: The Revolution of Sex since 1800.* London: Longman, 1981.

Weinstein, Philip M. *The Semantics of Desire: Changing Models of Identity from Dickens to Joyce.* Princeton: Princeton University Press, 1984.

Wilt, Judith. " 'He would come back': The Fathers of Daughters in *Daniel Deronda.*" *Nineteenth-Century Literature* 41 (1987).

Woolf, Virginia. "Professions for Women." In *The Norton Anthology of Literature by Women*, ed. Sandra Gilbert and Susan Gubar. New York: Norton, 1985.

———. *To the Lighthouse.* London: Granada, 1977.

Yeazell, Ruth Bernard. *Fictions of Modesty: Women and Courtship in the English Novel.* Chicago: University of Chicago Press, 1991.

Zwinger, Lynda. *Daughters, Fathers, and the Novel: The Sentimental Romance of Heterosexuality.* Madison: University of Wisconsin Press, 1991.

Index

Activity versus passivity, in women, 51–52, 158–59, 169, 214, 238–39, 269, 280

Aesthetics: and knowledge, 85–87, 174–75; and morality 69, 81–82, 85–87, 113–16, 174–75, 191–96; naturalist, 85–87, 116, 121; romantic, 75–76, 85, 148; as truth versus information, 86–88, 115–16

Affects, affective domain, 10, 197–99, 201, 214, 267, 242–43, 247–48, 250–52; and hysteria, 36–38, 42, 49–50; knowledge and, 171, 176–186, 239–42, 250–52

Alcove, 69–71, 75n, 86, 88, 184–85, 208–12, 216–17, 261–63, 265–67, 273–74, 276–77, 279

Allegory, 61–63, 145; in Eliot, 233; in Freud, 158–59, 164–66, 212–13; in James, 90–92, 139–42, 153–55; of modesty, 53–54, 212–13; in Sand, 177–183

Analyst, 16, 62, 206, 283; Daniel Deronda as, 239–41; Freud as, 13, 108–9, 156–69, 173–75, 275–80; James as, 84–85, 108

Aporia, 61–62, 94–95, 212, 236–38

Autobiography: in Eliot, 231–32, 260–61, 266–67; in Freud, 130–32, 164–66; in James, 9–11, 107, 121–26; in Sand, 216–19, 223–28

Balzac, Honoré de, 33, 106, 195, 209–10

Barthes, Roland, 136n, 256, 260, 266, 273n, 285

Baudelaire, Charles, 4n, 11–12, 136–37

Beizer, Janet, 77n

Belief. See Gender: and belief; Knowledge: and belief

Benjamin, Jessica, 146

Bildungsroman, 72, 191–92, 223–27, 234

Blindness: in Eliot, 236, 267–68; in Freud, 13, 160–62, 173–74, 277–79; in Sand, 221–27

Body: in Freud, 159, 162–66, 212–13, 280; of the hysteric, 159, 239–40, 243, 257–59, 270–72, 284; and soul, 112n, 136–38, 151–52, 155, 286–87; of woman, 30–36, 68–70, 135–37, 155–56, 162, 177–81, 187–89. See also Body and mind

Body and mind, 4, 284–87; in Eliot, 237–40, 243; in hysteria, 14, 33–36, 155–69; in Sand, 178–84, 196–201, 205

Brachet, Jean-Louis, 31–49 passim, 57–65, 70–71, 227, 281–82

Briquet, Pierre, 30–49 passim, 197–205

Brooks, Peter, 7, 155n, 242n, 263, 268, 280n

Butler, Judith, 21n, 32, 33, 38, 43, 53n, 62, 93n, 99, 104, 117, 120, 183

Castration, 275–80; women and, 61–64, 215–17, 241
Cavell, Stanley, 21, 156, 160, 167–69, 235, 236n, 271, 273n
Censorship, 15–16; in Eliot, 267–71; in Freud, 86; in James, 67, 75, 80, 84–87; and literature, 68–71, 84–87, 183–84; in Sand, 189, 214–15, 221–25, 226–27. *See also* Veils, veiling
Civilization, 15, 60; for James, 84–88, 103–4
Clément, Catherine, 206, 232, 260
Condensation, 124–26, 162–63, 216–18, 263–65
Conscience, 14–15, 50, 114, 190–91, 194, 203, 232–33, 246–53. *See also* Consciousness: vs. conscience
Consciousness, 16–17, 44–45n, 165n, 241–46, 256–59; vs. conscience, 2–16, 50, 84–85, 191–92, 203, 232, 241–44, 253, 268–69; in Eliot, 241–53, 267, 269–71, 283–84; in the feminine, 6, 18–20, 23, 166–69, 284–87; and gender, 19–21, 61, 65, 161–62, 171, 177–81, 211–14, 241–46, 271–72, 284–87; history of, 23, 282–83; in James, 7, 84–86, 140–45, 151; and negativity, 14, 16–18, 250, 267, 269–71, 283–84; in Sand, 181–83, 197, 200, 203–4, 211–12, 214–16; and secret, 16–19, 283–88
Conversation: Eliot and, 239–46; Freud and, 156–60, 169; James and, 97–98
Courbet, Gustave, 184
Creusa, 185, 264–65

David-Ménard, Monique, 29n, 166–68, 198n, 199n, 203n, 213n, 220n, 223, 239, 273n, 285
de Beauvoir, Simone, 65, 181, 248
de Bolla, Peter, 208–9n
de Lauretis, Teresa, 92, 162n
Deleuze, Gilles, 260n
Derrida, Jacques, 17–19, 30n, 55n, 236n
Desire, 281–83, 286–87; in Eliot, 231–35, 239–40, 255–61, 266–68; in Freud, 12–14, 162–66, 279–81; in James, 8–11, 67, 72, 83, 124–26, 143; and knowledge, 206–7, 275–81; in Sand, 187–89, 195–96, 206–11, 214, 217
Dissociation, 4, 197–205, 257–59
Doane, Mary Ann, 30n, 55–56, 235n, 236, 237
Dramaturgy: of gender, 3; of hysteria,

22, 199–204, 207, 211–24, 240–41, 270–71; of subjectivity, 254, 257–59. *See also* Scene

Edel, Leon, 107, 121, 123–25n
Eliot, George: autobiography of, 231–32, 260–61, 266–67; and blindness, 236, 267–68; and consciousness, 241–53, 267, 269–271, 283–84; *Daniel Deronda*, 68n, 184–85, 232–72; and desire, 231–35, 239–40, 255–61, 266–68; and eros, 261–62; and Feuerbach, 241–46; and Freud, 240, 262–63, 266, 270; and humanism, 241–46, 248–53; and life, 247–48, 267; *Middlemarch*, 109; *Mill on the Floss*, 170; and power, 238–40, 244–46; and Sand 73, 233–34, 247
Epistemology, 108–9, 177–86, 235–39; in Freud, 108–9, 156–66, 274–81; and gender, 9, 177–78, 185–86, 241–46, 274, 282–83

Felman, Shoshana, 3n, 20n, 39n, 57n, 94–95n, 133n, 145, 241, 252, 254, 271
Femininity: as enigma, 39–40, 82, 138–39, 145–46, 156–62; and hysteria, 43–50; as hysteria, 35–38, 46–47, 284; inscribed in woman's body, 31–32; in James, 77–79, 82–84, 94–95, 101–2, 127–29, 139–44; versus masculinity, 29–30, 132–33, 162–69, 209–14, 217–18, 283–84
Feminism: in *The Bostonians*, 110–11; in Eliot, 244; in James, 101–4; in Sand, 192, 199–200
Fetishism, 63–65
Feuerbach, Ludwig, 241–46, 248
Flaubert, Gustave, 1–5; *Madame Bovary*, 4–5, 68–71, 135–42, 146–148; and gender, 2, 27–29; and hysteria, 25–27, 69–70; and medical knowledge, 26; as a romantic, 148; and Sand, 25–29
Foucault, Michel, 188n, 271, 286
Freud, Sigmund: as an analyst, 13, 108–9, 156–69, 173–75, 275–80; and autobiography, 130–32, 164–66; blindness of, 13, 160–62, 173–4, 277–79; on censorship, 86; and desire, 12–14, 162–66, 279–81; and Dora (*Fragment of a Case of Hysteria*), 12–14, 45n, 125, 155–69, 171–77, 230–32, 262–64, 266; and Eliot, 240, 262–63, 266; and epistemology, 108–9, 156–66, 274–81; and femininity, 39n, 130–31, 161, 163–66, 170–71, 251–

Freud, Sigmund (*cont.*)
52; and gender, 156–61, 163–66,
277–81; *Hysterical Phantasies and
Their Relation to Bisexuality* and
*Some General Remarks on Hysterical
Attacks*, 54, 206–13; and James, 86,
108–9, 125–26, 129–33, 169–70;
knowledge and desire in, 12–14, 63,
161–69, 220–21, 227, 279–81; and
realism, 108–9, 174–75, 276; and
Sand, 206–12; and symbolism, 125n,
156–60, 163–66, 264; *Studies on
Hysteria*, 42, 203–5, 210n; and Wolf-
Man (*From the History of an Infantile
Neurosis*), 274–81, 283–84
Freadman, Richard, 236n, 241n

Gaze: as feminine, 167–69, 180–81,
232, 238–39; and gender, 234–39; as
masculine, 108–9, 172; medical, 9,
44–45, 235; and pudor, 55, 58. *See
also* Vision
Gender, 2, 27, 55–56, 279n; and belief,
45, 60, 63–65, 277–78; and
consciousness, 19–21, 61, 65, 161–62,
171, 177–81, 211–14, 241–46, 271–
72, 284–87; Freud and, 156–61, 163–
66, 277–81; and the gaze, 234–39;
and language, 64n, 152, 163, 279n,
284n; and power, 14–16, 22, 60–61,
156–60, 234, 238–39; and
representation, 88–95, 109, 111, 126–
33, 196, 209–12; as sense of
differences, 9, 76–79, 104, 116–17,
178–85; and sexual difference, 64–65,
277–83, 284n; and violence, 7n, 117–
19, 120–21, 133, 159–62, 166; and
writing, 71, 76–77, 222–28. *See also*
Gender fables
Gender fables, 3; in Brachet, 56–65, 70–
71, 281–82; in Freud, 156–61, 274–
81; in James, 82–92, 94; in Sand, 171,
177–86
Genre, 88, 191–96, 223, 234, 237, 239–
40, 256n
Grammar, of the sexes, 50–101, 155,
162–66, 266, 282. *See also* Law of
gender
Green, André, 61n
Greuze, Jean-Baptiste, 54–55
Gynaecophilia, 172–74, 177–86

Habegger, Alfred, 105–6n, 113, 118,
121, 132
Hertz, Neil, 7, 91n, 163–64, 173, 240,
252n, 266
History: in *The Bostonians*, 105, 121–
26; in the case of George Sand, 99–

104, 218; of consciousness, 23, 282–
83; and gender, 246–53, 271–72; of
gender, 72, 95, 101–4, 129–33, 156–
69; of male sexuality, 123–38, 148–50
Humanism. *See Mensch, Menschheit*
Hypochondria, 36
Hysteria: and admiration, 167–69, 231–
32; contemporary theories of, 30n;
160, 201n; definitions of, 4, 7–9, 14,
124n, 262; and dissociation, 4, 197–
205, 257–59; and history, 31n, 121–
23; and language, 17–19, 40–42, 125–
26, 198, 203–6, 269; and literature,
33, 135–38, 254–55, 269–72; and
masquerade, 60–63, 210–12; in men,
37–38, 88–92, 121–26 ; and morality,
13–16, 34, 42, 192–93, 196–206; and
nineteenth-century anatomy and
physiology, 31–36; and power, 22,
60–61, 156–60, 234, 238–39; and
pudor, 50–52, 54, 62–63, 167, 196–
99, 205–6; and reading, 30, 48–50,
90–92, 156–62, 207, 237–38, 255–59,
268, 278, 283–87; in recent history,
19, 21, 285; and rhetoric, 254–55,
259–65; and secrets, 156–61, 238,
255–56, 268, 281; and sexual
difference, 27–29, 31–38, 162–69,
274–82; and silence, 9, 18, 169, 151–
56; and simulation, 62, 122, 159–60;
style, 30–33, 40–41; and symbolization, 19, 124–26, 156–58, 162–65,
262–65, 271 ; and theory, 93–94,
223–25, 274–83; treatment of, 43–45,
48–49; and violence, 40–41, 264–65.
See also Symptoms; Textual hysteria
Hysterika (the hysterical woman), 5,
155n; Emma Bovary as, 4–5, 135–37;
Dora as, 12–14; 155–62, 262, 266;
Eliot as, 231–32; in Freud, 54, 155n,
212–13; Gwendolen Harleth as, 239–
41, 253–71; Lélia as, 182–83; in
nineteenth-century descriptions, 40–
42; Sand as, 223–24; and her soul, 4,
156, 161, 165–66; Milly Theale as, 7–
10; Valentine as, 196–211

Imagination, 4, 10, 23, 143–44, 273–74;
and representation, 69–70, 136–38,
143, 146–50
Interiority, 2, 22; in Freud, 161–62; for
James, 115–16, 139–40, 144–46; in
Sand's writing, 74–75, 199; women
and, 47–48, 146, 208–9. *See also*
Interiorization
Interiorization, 3, 284; in the case of
women, 47–48, 281, 284; of gender
norms, 21, 57–61, 284; as inward

Interiorization (*cont.*)
  drama 199, 206, 254; as inward turn,
  20, 236–37, 242n, 249–50, 268–72,
  274
Irigaray, Luce, 18, 30n, 39, 56, 120,
  138–39, 141n, 145, 161, 167, 169n,
  221

James, Henry: *The Ambassadors*, 79n,
  96; and Jane Austen, 73n; and
  autobiography, 9–11, 107, 121–26;
  The Bostonians, 150–55, 171–77,
  230–31; and censorship, 86–88, 91; as
  a critic, 6, 71–79, 99–104, 138–45,
  147–50; and consciousness, 84–86,
  140–45; and *Daniel Deronda*, 6, 10,
  218n; desire in, 8–11, 67, 72, 83,
  124–26, 143; and Eliot, 73, 142–44,
  230–31, 252; and feminism, 101–104,
  129, 154; and femininity, 77–79, 82–
  84, 94–95, 101–2, 127–29, 139–44;
  on Flaubert, 147–50; and Freud, 86,
  129–33, 108–9, 125–26, 129–33; and
  hysteria, 80–81, 88–93, 107, 117–25;
  and identification, 6, 80, 82, 90–93,
  110, 139–44, 147–50; and
  intelligence, 11, 142, 151–52; and
  Alice James, 172–73; and William
  James, 9, 106, 113–15, 117, 127; and
  Madame Bovary, 139–45, 147–48;
  and privacy, 59–60, 116, 120, 129;
  and *The Portrait of a Lady*, 10, 109–
  10, 140n, 142–45, 148–49; and
  realism, 104, 106–10; and
  representation, 74–75, 80–81, 84–88,
  94–96, 104–10, 113–17; on Sand,
  150–52, 190–93, 229–30; and sexism,
  77–80; as a theorist, 80–92, 104–10,
  113–17, 138–45; and Minny Temple,
  9–11; *Wings of the Dove*, 7–9; and
  writing, 89–92, 95–98. *See also* Scenic
  method; Veils, veiling; Wharton,
  Edith; Woolson, Constance Fenimore
James, William. *See* James, Henry
Johnson, Barbara, 138, 177–79

Kahane, Claire, 105–6n, 113, 119, 233–
  34n
Knowledge: and aesthetics, 85–87, 174–
  75; and affects, 171, 176–186, 239–
  42, 250–52; and belief, 45, 60, 63–65,
  275, 277–78; and gender, 39, 47–50,
  156–69, 177–85, 263–65; and guilt,
  14–16; as *méconnaissance*, 10, 263,
  271; and representation, 106–9, 141–
  46; and sexual difference, 61–63, 68,

92–94, 167–69, 181–82, 217–18,
  221–23, 237–38; transmission of,
  170–71, 175–86, 265–66
Kofman, Sarah, 111n, 129n, 245n, 286
Kristeva, Julia, 127, 165n, 227–28

Lacan, Jacques, 17n, 19n, 239, 269,
  279n
Lafayette, Madame de, 191, 195
Laplanche, Jean, 14, 89, 92–93, 276,
  278
Law: and gender, 68–71; of gender, 8–9,
  68, 94, 127–32, 211–12, 281–85. *See
  also* Grammar of the sexes
Le Doeuff, Michèle, 32n, 51n
Life, living: Eliot on, 247–48, 267; at
  first hand, 78–79, 83, 171; James on,
  78–79, 141; and literature, 3, 115;
  vicarious, 78–79, 149–50; and
  writing, 76–79, 82–84

Madonna. *See* Virgin
Male writer, 71–81, 137–38, 146–50,
  174–75
Mannoni, Octave, 63, 64n, 163, 279n,
  284n
Masculinity: in Eliot, 244–45; in Freud,
  161–66, 212–13, 280–82; in James,
  9–11, 120; of James, 81–93, 123–36;
  in Sand, 180, 211–12, 215–16; of
  Sand, 75n, 77–79, 82, 100–102. *See
  also* Femininity: vs. masculinity
Masquerade, 60–63, 120–21, 127–28,
  150, 210–12. *See also* Style
Medea, 185, 264–65
Médecine morale, 34, 39–41, 197–206
Medusa, 91–92, 238, 245, 265–66
Men: and insight, 39, 56–60, 108–9,
  172; and knowledge, 108–9, 155–66;
  as readers, 179–85; in women's texts,
  217–18, 221–22
Mensch, Menschheit (as universal man)
  130–31, 161, 241–49
Mérimée, Prosper, 70, 82, 90, 188
Merleau-Ponty, Maurice, 14, 61, 282n
Metaphor, woman as, 9, 135–36, 141–
  46. *See also* Condensation
Miller, D.A., 256n
Modesty. *See* Pudor
Morality: aesthetics and, 69, 81–82, 85–
  87, 113–16, 174–75, 191–96; in Eliot,
  246–52; hysteria and, 13–16, 34, 42,
  192–93, 196–206; in James, 75–79,
  81–82, 113–16; in Sand, 192–94,
  200–206
Musset, Alfred de, 76, 83, 90

Narcissism, 180–81, 217, 220–21, 245, 247
Nietzsche, Friedrich, 56–59, 167, 236

Oppression: in the case of hysteria, 56–57; of women, 65, 118–19, 287

Pain. *See* Suffering
Passion, 79–88; and denial, 277, 279, 284; experienced in literature, 15–16, 149–50; perceptual, 237–38, 275; representation of, 73–75, 187–89, 196–204, 218–20; in women, 69, 82–84, 175–76, 187–89
Pathos, 6–12, 151, 243, 247–48, 267. *See also* Suffering
Patriarchy: in Eliot, 234; in Freud, 13–14; in Sand, 191, 194–95
Pedagogy: in Eliot, 242–46; and gender, 6–7, 177–83; and James and Sand, 72–75; and maïeutics, 59–60; in Rousseau, 15–16; in Sand, 219–28; applied to women, 43–44, 47–50; between women, 170–71, 175–86, 219–20. *See also* Knowledge: transmission of
Phantasmatic, 90–92, 265–68, 277
Phenomenon, 12, 20, 116, 168n; vs. theory, 43–44, 50, 163, 277–81
Phenomenology, 3n, 61, 181, 282n; of hysteria, 209, 213–14, 257, 261–63, 265
Philosophy: and gender, 16–20, 240–46; and hysteria 248–53, 271, 283, 287; Sand and, 28–29, 227–28
Pontalis, Jean-Bernard, 14, 89, 92–93, 276, 278
Pornography, 88–92, 93n, 94, 261
Primal scene: in Freud, 276–81; in James, 83; in Sand, 171, 196, 216–17
Psychology, 22, 33–34, 52–53, 155n; and aesthetics, 72, 75–59; in *The Bostonians*, 106–7; in James, 111–21, 139–40; and literature, 73–74
Pudicité, 53–54, 58, 62, 128, 168, 230n
Pudor, 50–56, 59, 62–63; in Freud, 54–55; and hysteria, 51, 55, 167; in James, 67–68, 75; in Sand, 196–203, 205–6. *See also* Veils, veiling

Reading: and desire, 4, 23, 283–87; and hysteria 30, 48–50, 90–92, 156–62, 207, 237–38, 255–59, 268, 278; and sympathy, 247–48
Reboul, Pierre, 7, 179–184

Representation: fictional and medical 26, 31–32, 41–43, 198–99; and hysteria, 14, 195–203, 210–12, 254, 266–72; and imagination, 69–70, 136–38, 143, 146–50; impossibility of, 68n, 236–37, 253, 271, 284; James on, 74–75, 80–81, 84–88, 94–96, 104–10, 113–17; and knowledge, 106–9, 141–46; of passion, 73–75, 187–89, 196–204, 218–20; as representativity, 102, 139–45; and sexual difference, 137–46, 239; of subjectivity, 141–46, 270–71, 287; theory of, 80–81, 84–88
Repression, 18–20, 145, 269, 281–82; Freud and, 207–8, 211–21; in James, 95–96; and pudor, 51–52, 59, 61–62; in Sand, 207–212. *See also* Censorship
Riley, Denise, 23, 27n, 31n, 181, 286n
Rose, Jacqueline, 237, 254n
Rousseau, Jean-Jacques, 15, 34, 38, 194, 209

Sand, George: blindness in, 221–27; and Michel de Bourges, 187–89; and Briquet, 197–205; and consciousness, 181–83, 197, 200, 203–4, 211–12, 214–16; and desire, 187–89, 195–96, 206–11, 214, 217; and Flaubert, 25–29; and Freud, 206–12; and gender, 27–29, 181–83, 196–206, 208–16; *Histoire de ma vie*, 216–19, 223–28; in history, 99–104; and hysteria, 27–29, 182–83, 196–211, 223–24; *Lélia*, 177–86; letters of, 25–29, 82–83, 187–89; and mothers, grandmothers, and daughters, 190–91, 219–20, 223–28; and Mérimée, 70, 82, 90, 188; and Musset, 76, 83, 90; and passion, 73–77, 187–89; as a realist, 73–77; as a romantic 75–76, 85, 148; and sensuality, 177, 180–81, 187–89, 221–23; and style, 75–77, 80, 187–89, 214–15, 223–24; *Valentine*, 190–97, 199–205, 208–11, 213–15, 217–18; on women, 226–27
Scene, 3, 21; in the alcove, 69–71, 75n, 184–85, 208–12, 216–17, 261–63, 279; of hysteria, 88–95, 171–91, 196–99, 208–16, 237, 240–41, 250–51, 253–54, 275–76; of passion, 73n, 80–88, 135–36, 141; of seduction, 54, 148–49, 159–60, 208–211, 213–34; between women, 175, 177–86, 265–66. *See also* Dramaturgy; Scenic method
Scenic method, 71n, 96, 104–13, 115

Schor, Naomi, 27–29, 139n, 171, 177n–78n, 181, 193, 215, 227n

Screens, 68–70, 96–98, 148, 156, 173, 207, 216, 222–23. *See also* Censorship; Veils, veiling

Sedgwick, Eve Kosofsky, 111n, 191n

Sensuality: in Eliot, 261–62; in Sand, 177, 180–81, 187–89, 221–23

Sexism, in James, 77–80

Sexual difference, 21, 57, 62–64; in Freud, 274–81; gender and, 64–65, 277–83, 284n; hysteria and, 27–29, 31–38, 162–69, 274–82; and knowledge, 61–63, 68, 92–94, 167–69, 181–82, 217–18, 221–23, 237–38; and representation, 137–46, 239

Sexual ideology, 30–50 passim, 105, 119, 127–33

Sexuality, as an emerging concept, 27n, 43, 131–32; and knowledge, 162–69, 184–85; and textuality, 72–98, 162–66, 187–89. *See also* Alcove

Showalter, Elaine, 123, 153

Sign, 238–39, 244, 253, 255–56; hysteria as a, 265–68; vs. signifier, 239

Silence, 7–9, 18, 155–62, 237, 240–41, 249, 268; and women, 137–38, 151–56, 170–77

Silverman, Kaja, 83n, 92, 163, 166n, 267, 272, 275n

Solomon-Godeau, Abigail, 33, 93n, 94

Soul, 4, 22, 112n, 136–38, 151–52, 155–56, 161–62, 248–49, 274, 286–87

Starobinski, Jean, 136, 164–65, 285

Steiner, George, 7, 259

Stewart, Garrett, 96n, 259n

Style: of Flaubert, 136; of the flesh, 30–38, 40–41; of James, 88–92, 96–98, 153–54; of Sand, 75–77, 80, 187–89, 214–15, 223–24. *See also* Masquerade; Textual hysteria; Writing

Sublime: in Eliot, 68n, 236–38, 253; in James, 8–10

Suffering, 4, 151, 183–84, 233, 240–46, 268 ; in hysteria 45–47, 202, 205–6, 210–11. *See also* Pathos

Symbolization, 19, 124–26, 156–58, 162–65, 262–65, 271

Symptoms (of hysteria), 25–26, 121–25, 137, 157–61, 255; vs. affects 210–12; and the signifier, 259–61; as signs, 239

Tanner, Tony, 7, 78n, 90n, 105–6n, 113, 194

Textual hysteria, 67, 72; in Eliot, 253–71; in James, 80, 88–94, 110, 119; in Sand, 206, 215–18, 223–24

Theory: and gender, 162–66, 178–83; and hysteria, 93–94, 223–25, 274–83; James and, 80–92, 104–10, 113–17, 138–45; and literary performance, 4; and myths, 29, 33; vs. phenomena, 43–44, 50, 163, 277–81; and representation, 80–81, 84–88

Transference: as in analysis, 146, 157–161, 239, 250; in reading, 252–53; in writing, 136, 142

Trilling, Lionel, 7, 107, 129, 132

Veils, veiling, 57n, 180, 276; in Eliot, 269–70; and gender, 55–56, 80, 212–13; in James, 67, 75, 80, 86–87, 92–94; of modesty, 15, 54–56, 60–61, 68–69, 86–87; in Sand, 213–25. *See also* Censorship; Pudor; Screens

Virey, Jean-Jacques, 30–49 passim, 52–53; and Freud, 42–43

Virgin, 167–69, 193–94, 204, 231–32

Vision: in Eliot, 236–39, 246–49, 258–59; in Freud, 167–69, 275–81; in James, 108–9; in Sand, 179–81, 221–23. *See also* Gaze

Voice, 135–38, 235, 237, 283; feminine, 150–53; in James, 110; in Sand, 187–89, 195, 203–4, 208, 224; signifier and, 259–61

Voisin, François, 31–49 passim

Wharton, Edith, 83, 90n, 96–98, 229–30

Woman writer, 16, 68, 82–84, 92–94, 100, 153–54, 189

Women: and affections, 10, 42, 46, 251–53; and castration, 61–64, 215–17, 241; and (day)-dreaming, 167–69, 208–9, 221–23; as enigma, 39–40, 82–92, 94–96, 138–39, 145–46, 156–62, 170–77, 237–38, 253; as excluded from knowledge, 13–14, 20, 161–67, 203–6, 211–12, 214; and friendship, 111–13, 160–61, 172–76, 226, 263–65; as hysterical, *see* Hysterika; as impressionable, 34–37, 40, 46–49, 52; and intelligence, 10, 12–24, 62–63; and knowledge, 170–71, 177–86, 223–28; and language, 150, 152–55; and manners, 60–61; as metaphors or mirrors, 9, 120, 135–36, 141–46, 156; morality, 243–44, 247; and passion, 69, 82–84, 175–76, 187–89; and pathos, 7–10, 114, 151, 233, 243; and pudor, 57–65; and purity 12–16, 40–43, 223–24; and reading, 13, 15–16,

Women: and affections (*cont.*)
48–50, 229–30; and secrets, 17–21,
39–41, 156–59, 162, 165–66, 170–71;
and seduction, 158–61; and sexual
desire, 42–43, 202, 208–11; and
sexual ignorance, 10–16, 59–61, 219–
20, 223–27; and silence 137–38, 151–
56, 176; as spectacle, 32–33, 93–94,
223–39; and suffering, 4, 45–47, 151,
202, 205–6; and truth, 76–78, 150; as
vessels, 141–46; and women, 137–38,
151–156, 170–77. *See also* Activity vs.
passivity
Woolf, Virginia, 23, 120, 224, 283
Woolson, Constance Fenimore, 112–13

Writing, 224n, 260, 266–67, 283; and
gender, 71, 76–77, 222–28; and
hysteria, 254–272; and illusion
(*Wahndichtung*), 207–11; James and,
89–92, 95–98; and "life" 76–79, 82–
84; and phonemics 96n, 153–54,
259n; Sand and, 74–75, 187–189,
199; and sexual difference, 218–24;
and silence 237–40; and transference,
136, 142; and the unconscious, 266,
269–70. *See also* Style; Textual
hysteria

Zola, Emile, 85, 90, 106, 239
Zwinger, Lynda, 17, 195n, 215n